# 2nd Workshop on Multi-lingual Representation Learning (MRL 2022)

AA001560

Abu Dhabi, United Arab Emirates
8 December 2022

ISBN: 978-1-7138-9118-5

**Printed from e-media with permission by:**

Curran Associates, Inc.
57 Morehouse Lane
Red Hook, NY 12571

**Some format issues inherent in the e-media version may also appear in this print version.**

Copyright© (2022) by the Association for Computational Linguistics
All rights reserved.

Printed with permission by Curran Associates, Inc. (2024)

For permission requests, please contact the Association for Computational Linguistics at the address below.

Association for Computational Linguistics
209 N. Eighth Street
Stroudsburg, Pennsylvania 18360

Phone: 1-570-476-8006
Fax: 1-570-476-0860

acl@aclweb.org

**Additional copies of this publication are available from:**

Curran Associates, Inc.
57 Morehouse Lane
Red Hook, NY 12571 USA
Phone: 845-758-0400
Fax: 845-758-2633
Email: curran@proceedings.com
Web: www.proceedings.com

MRL 2022

# The 2nd Workshop on Multi-lingual Representation Learning

## Proceedings of the Workshop

December 8, 2022

# Organizing Committee

**Organizers**

Duygu Ataman, New York University
Hila Gonen, Meta, University of Washington
Sebastian Ruder, Google
Orhan Firat, Google
Gözde Gül Sahin, Koc University
Jamshidbek Mirzakhalov, Salesforce

# Program Committee

**Reviewers**

Arya McCarthy, Johns Hopkins University
Jannis Vamvas, University of Zurich
Ankur Bapna, Google
Clara Vania, Amazon
Ivan Vulić, University of Cambridge
Biao Zhang, Google
Tilek Chubakov, Koc University
Hila Gonen, Meta, University of Washington
Phillip Rust, University of Copenhagen
Emre Can Acikgoz, Koc University
Sneha Kudugunta, Google
Duygu Ataman, New York University
Orhan Firat, Google
Omer Goldman, Bar-Ilan University
Jamshidbek Mirzakhalov, Salesforce
Shauli Ravfogel, Bar-Ilan University

# Keynote Talk: Ev Fedorenko

**Ev Fedorenko**
Massachusetts Institute of Technology

**Bio:** Ev Fedorenko seeks to understand the cognitive and neural mechanisms that underpin language. This quintessentially human ability allows us to both gain knowledge of the world and to share it with others. Building on Wernicke and Broca's seminal work, Fedorenko has implicated specific brain regions, together comprising the language network, in linguistic processing. She uses a range of approaches, including behavioral analysis, brain imaging (fMRI, ERP, and MEG), genotyping, intracranial recording in patients, and study of neurodevelopmental disorders. Through these methods, Fedorenko is building a picture of the computations and representations that underlie language processing in the human brain. Fedorenko joined the McGovern Institute and MIT in July 2019, having established her lab at Massachusetts General Hospital/ Harvard Medical School in 2014. She earned her PhD in Cognitive Sciences at MIT in 2007, where she also conducted her postdoctoral research.

# Keynote Talk: Kyunghyun Cho

**Kyunghyun Cho**
New York University

**Bio:** Kyunghyun Cho is an associate professor of computer science and data science at New York University and CIFAR Fellow of Learning in Machines & Brains. He is also a senior director of frontier research at the Prescient Design team within Genentech Research & Early Development (gRED). He was a research scientist at Facebook AI Research from June 2017 to May 2020 and a postdoctoral fellow at University of Montreal until Summer 2015 under the supervision of Prof. Yoshua Bengio, after receiving PhD and MSc degrees from Aalto University April 2011 and April 2014, respectively, under the supervision of Prof. Juha Karhunen, Dr. Tapani Raiko and Dr. Alexander Ilin. He received an honour of being a recipient of the Samsung Ho-Am Prize in Engineering in 2021. He tries his best to find a balance among machine learning, natural language processing, and life, but almost always fails to do so.

# Keynote Talk: Razvan Pascanu

**Razvan Pascanu**
Deepmind

**Bio:** Razvan Pascanu is a research scientist at DeepMind with research interests including optimization and learning with multiple tasks, graph neural networks, generative models and theory for deep representation and learning networks. He holds a MSc from Jacobs University, Bremen in 2009 and a PhD from University of Montreal (2014), with the supervision of prof. Yoshua Bengio. He was involved in developing Theano and published several papers on topics surrounding the topics of deep learning and deep reinforcement learning.

# Table of Contents

# Program

**Thursday, December 8, 2022**

| | |
|---|---|
| 09:00 - 09:15 | *Opening Remarks* |
| 09:15 - 10:00 | *Oral Session 1* |
| 10:00 - 10:30 | *Shared task session* |
| 10:30 - 11:00 | *Coffee Break* |
| 11:00 - 12:30 | *Poster Session* |
| 12:30 - 14:00 | *Lunch Break* |
| 14:00 - 14:45 | *Invited Talk by Razvan Pascanu, Deepmind* |
| 14:45 - 15:30 | *Oral Session 2* |
| 15:30 - 16:00 | *Coffee Break* |
| 16:00 - 16:45 | *Invited Talk by Kyunghyun Cho, NYU* |
| 16:45 - 17:00 | *Mini Break* |
| 17:00 - 17:45 | *Invited Talk by Ev Fedorenko, MIT* |
| 17:45 - 18:00 | *Closing Remarks* |

# Entity Retrieval from Multilingual Knowledge Graphs

**Saher Esmeir**
Bloomberg
London, United Kingdom
sesmeir2@bloomberg.net

**Arthur Câmara***
Delft University of Technology
Delft, The Netherlands
A.BarbosaCamara@tudelft.nl

**Edgar Meij**
Bloomberg
London, United Kingdom
emeij@bloomberg.net

## Abstract

Knowledge Graphs (KGs) are structured databases that capture real-world entities and their relationships. The task of entity retrieval from a KG aims at retrieving a ranked list of entities relevant to a given user query. While English-only entity retrieval has attracted considerable attention, user queries, as well as the information contained in the KG, may be represented in multiple—and possibly distinct—languages. Furthermore, KG content may vary between languages due to different information sources and points of view. Recent advances in language representation have enabled natural ways of bridging gaps between languages. In this paper, we, therefore, propose to utilise language models (LMs) and diverse entity representations to enable truly *multilingual entity retrieval*. We propose two approaches: (i) an array of monolingual retrievers and (ii) a single multilingual retriever trained using queries and documents in multiple languages. We show that while our approach is on par with the significantly more complex state-of-the-art method for the English task, it can be successfully applied to virtually any language with an LM. Furthermore, it allows languages to benefit from one another, yielding significantly better performance, both for low- and high-resource languages.

## 1 Introduction

Knowledge graphs (**KGs**) are key for many search applications. Consider, for example, the user query "chess world champions". Modern search engines often present users with a list of world chess champions along with additional facts encoded as relations in a KG. The queries themselves, as well as the information contained in a KG, may be represented in multiple—and possibly distinct—languages. This poses a challenge to traditional entity retrieval methods usually optimised for a single language. In this work, we aim to tackle the task of *multilingual entity retrieval*: given a query in any language, and a KG holding data in multiple languages, retrieve a ranked list of relevant entities.

The task of entity retrieval, when both the query and KG are in English, is well-studied. Recent years have seen remarkable progress, resulting in over 20% improvement on DBpedia-Entity v2 (**DE-v2**), the standard test collection for the task (Hasibi et al., 2017). Works like ESim (Gerritse et al., 2020) and KEWER (Nikolaev and Kotov, 2020) utilised word embedding techniques to represent entities and user queries in the same latent space. Meanwhile, EM-BERT (Gerritse et al., 2022) combines a powerful entity extractor that enhances user queries with a pre-trained language model (LM), fine-tuned on another ranking task, to establish a new state-of-the-art. These methods, however, operated on a single language at a time and were not studied in a multilingual setting.

While DE-v2 is an English-only collection, Wikipedia and DBpedia (Auer et al., 2007) provide a unique opportunity: because the contributors to each language edition come from different backgrounds and have different views, we often see rich and diverse entity representations that go well beyond word-for-word translation. Moreover, many entities are available only in some chapters but not in others (see Appendix G for examples). Thanks to its graph-based nature, DBpedia facilitates mapping between languages and different entities representing the same subject. This, in turn, allows us to build rich, multilingual representations.

Expanding DE-v2 to multiple languages, however, carries several risks. The collection was developed based on English DBpedia; therefore, its pooling stage uses keyword-based retrievers optimised for English. Moreover, annotators were only presented with English content. In this paper, we discuss these challenges through example queries

*Research conducted when the author was doing an internship at Bloomberg.



*Proceedings of the The 2nd Workshop on Multi-lingual Representation Learning (MRL)*, pages 1 - 15
December 8, 2022 ©2022 Association for Computational Linguistics

and stress the importance of building a truly multilingual collection end-to-end.

To address the task of multilingual entity retrieval, we introduce BERTE, a multi- and crosslingual entity ranking framework. Despite its simple design and its flexibility to use any LM out of the box, it is comparable to the state-of-the-art on `DE-v2` in its original English form and thrives in a variety of languages, including Spanish, Arabic, and Hebrew. Furthermore, our experiments show that BERTE can benefit greatly from combining information from multiple languages to boost its performance, establishing a new state-of-the-art for a large subset of the queries.

The main contributions of our work are threefold: (i) A novel and simple yet effective entity retriever for the monolingual setup; (ii) A system for multilingual entity retrieval; and (iii) A systematic way to extend `DE-v2` to multiple languages accompanied with a set of strong baseline results.

## 2 Background and Related Work

**Entity Retrieval** While earlier works on retrieving entities from a KG relied heavily on the graph's structure (Ciglan et al., 2012; Neumayer et al., 2012; Nikolaev et al., 2016), recent works have shown a tendency towards using graph *embeddings* instead (Gerritse et al., 2020; Nikolaev and Kotov, 2020; Komamizu, 2020; Jameel et al., 2017; Liu et al., 2019; Naseri et al., 2018). These methods generally implement a keyword-based first-stage ranker, such as BM25 (Robertson et al., 1995) and then a learned reranker. Meanwhile, the current state-of-the-art on `DE-v2`, EM-BERT, relies on a state-of-the-art entity extractor (van Hulst et al., 2020) to add textual representations of entities to user queries, combined with a pretrained LM, which already entails part of the domain knowledge (Petroni et al., 2019). To do so, they apply a linear transformation with aligned entity and word piece vectors, similar to E-BERT (Poerner et al., 2020). EM-BERT also uses a two-stage fine-tuning procedure: First, on MS MARCO (Campos et al., 2016), a large passage ranking dataset. Then, the model is further fine-tuned on the actual query-entity pairs from the training set of `DE-v2`. While powerful, this approach is restricted due to its requirements. On the other hand, our work achieves similar performance in English without relying on an entity extractor, pre-calculated entity embeddings, or additional large-scale fine-tuning. It is, therefore, much easier to extend to other languages

**Entity Linking** Entity linking aims at identifying and assigning entity mentions in a piece of text (FitzGerald et al., 2021; van Hulst et al., 2020; Shen et al., 2021). GENRE (De Cao et al., 2020), for instance, uses BART (Lewis et al., 2019) and Beam Search to generate names of entities. On the other hand, BLINK (Wu et al., 2020) uses a two-stage zero-shot linking algorithm, where a very short textual description represents each entity. While methods could be shared between both tasks, here we focus purely on a retrieval task, where user queries are formed by a specific information need.

**Neural Information Retrieval** Neural methods have been shown to improve significantly keyword-based retrievers in a wide range of tasks (Mitra and Craswell, 2018), including ad-hoc retrieval (Nogueira et al., 2019; Dai and Callan, 2020; Yu et al., 2021; Nogueira and Cho, 2019; Akkalyoncu Yilmaz et al., 2019; MacAvaney et al., 2019; Câmara and Hauff, 2020), question answering (Yu et al., 2021), semantic reasoning (Xu et al., 2020), and link prediction (Daza et al., 2021). Several *Retrievers* that ditch the initial keyword-based ranking in favour of an end-to-end approach have recently been proposed (Khattab and Zaharia, 2020; Karpukhin et al., 2020; Xiong et al., 2020; Formal et al., 2021). While we do not tackle this problem in this paper, we acknowledge that it is a natural direction for future work on entity retrieval.

**Knowledge Graph Embeddings** Graph embeddings have evolved greatly. With the introduction of Graph Neural Networks (Wu et al., 2021), methods like TransH (Wang et al., 2014), HINGE (Rosso et al., 2020) and StarE (Galkin et al., 2020) rose quickly in popularity. With the inclusion of LMs, even more powerful methods appeared (Poerner et al., 2020; Broscheit, 2019; Liu et al., 2020a). These methods are usually focused on general-purpose embeddings and then utilised by entity retrieval systems, such as EM-BERT.

**Multilingual and Crosslingual Retrieval** A system is considered *multilingual* when information can be retrieved in two or more languages. Meanwhile, *crosslingual* systems enable queries to benefit from information sources in different languages, even if not explicitly trained in these (Peters et al., 2012; Conneau and Lample, 2019). For example, Nair et al. (2020) use neural methods to translate queries in context, while Litschko et al. (2018) employ an unsupervised approach with multilingual embeddings. Recently, van der Heijden et al. (2021) studied how meta-learning can help with multilingual and crosslingual text classifications using a version of XLM. (Conneau and Lample, 2019). These multilingual models, even before the fine-tuning stage, Even before the fine-tuning stage, these multilingual models already have crosslingual capabilities thanks to the multilingual sources presented during pretraining (Muller et al., 2021). Winata et al. (2021) studied the applicability of few-shot learning in a multilingual setting on natural language understanding tasks. They demonstrated that given a few examples in English, the model could perform better than random in other unseen languages. Zhang et al. (2021) presented Mr. TYDI, a multilingual collection for mono-lingual retrieval in multiple languages, designed to evaluate ranking with learned representations and zero-shot results.

**Multilingual Entity Retrieval** The task of multilingual entity retrieval is somewhat unexplored, given the lack of a truly multilingual benchmark. De Cao et al. (2021) presented mGENRE for multilingual entity linking. It matches its input against generated entity names from multiple languages, which allows for exploiting language connections and the richness of Wikipedia. Similarly, Botha et al. (2020) provided a method for linking entities in 100 languages using BERT encoders. Tsai and Roth (2016) addressed the related task of crosslingual Wikification, where the goal is to find the English title given a foreign mention.

## 3 Multilingual Entity Retrieval

To tackle the entity retrieval task, we follow a standard two-staged approach: we first use a keyword-based method to retrieve a set of entities and then rerank them. Both steps rely exclusively on textual information extracted from the KG. Similar to the guidelines in `DE-v2`, each entity representation is composed by concatenating its direct literal attributes.[1] For an entity $e$, with $n_a$ textual attributes, its representation $e_d$ is defined as $[a_t, a_{la}, a_1, \ldots, a_{n_a}]$, where $a_t$ is the title, $a_{la}$ is the long abstract and $a_i$ is the $i^{th}$ attribute. Appendix A provides an overview of our proposed system.

For the first-stage retrieval, we use the well-established and language-agnostic BM25. It scores documents in relation to a query based on term frequency, document frequency, document length and term saturation. Where possible, and to allow a fair comparison with earlier works, we use officially available run files[2] of BM25 or BM25F$_{ca}$.[3]

### 3.1 Neural Reranker

BERT-based rankers are generally classified as cross or bi-encoders. The former concatenate queries and documents to form a single input to the base LM (Nogueira and Cho, 2019; MacAvaney et al., 2019), while the latter computes query and entity embeddings separately and uses the similarity between their embeddings to estimate relevance (Hofstätter et al., 2020; Karpukhin et al., 2020). Here we opt for bi-encoders, given their ability to compute document embeddings offline.

In practical terms, given a query $q$ (up to $n_q = 32$ tokens) and an entity textual representation $e$ (up to $n_e = 200$ tokens), we score the pair using the dot product of their embeddings $E_q \cdot E_e$, where:

$$E_q = W^T \cdot \text{BERT}(\text{“}[Q] q_0 q_1, \ldots q_{n_q}\text{”}), \quad (1)$$

$$E_e = W^T \cdot \text{BERT}(\text{“}[D] e_0 e_1, \ldots e_{n_e}\text{”}). \quad (2)$$

While the score from the dot product is sufficient to rerank, we follow the common practice in Entity Retrieval (Gerritse et al., 2020; Nikolaev and Kotov, 2020) of mixing the LM-based score with the normalised scores of the first-stage retriever:

$$BERT\text{E}(q,e) = \beta \cdot BM25(q,e) + (1-\beta) \cdot (E_q \cdot E_e)$$

### 3.2 Monolingual Entity Reranking

The wide adoption of LMs in English NLP led to the introduction of many language-specific models, such as ArBERT (Abdul-Mageed et al., 2021) for Arabic, AlephBERT (Seker et al., 2021) for Hebrew, and Berto (Cañete et al., 2020) for Spanish. Recall that our first-stage retriever uses the language agnostic BM25. In the monolingual setup, with queries and documents in the same language $l$, we first retrieve entities covered in the $l$ subgraph of the KG and then rerank using a BERT model pretrained on $l$ and fine-tuned on triples $\langle q, e^+, e^- \rangle$ built from that subgraph. We refer to this version as BERTE$_l$. While including the structural components of the KG can be useful, we hypothesise that fine-tuning BERT using queries and textual data of entities is sufficient. Beyond that, it has been shown that a pretrained BERT model already has implicit domain knowledge (Bouraoui et al., 2020; Wang et al., 2020; Petroni et al., 2019).

[1] Unlike `DE-v2`, we use flat, unfielded documents.

[2] The run file provides, for each query, a scored list of 1000 entities retrieved by a keyword-based model.

[3] A fine-tuned version that uses fielded documents.

### 3.3 Entity Retrieval by Query Translation

Given a multilingual KG and a query in a non-English language $l$, a system could Machine Translation (MT) to obtain an English version of the query and then feed it to the English $\text{BERTE}_{en}$. It then utilises the graph to map the ranked entities back to $l$, if they exist.[4] We refer to this query translation method in our experiments as $\text{qtBERTE}_{en}$.

Due to its simplicity, $\text{qtBERTE}_{en}$ suffers from several shortcomings when used on a multilingual KG, such as DBpedia. Mainly, it is restricted to content in English, even if the graph holds information in multiple languages, and entities without English representation or entities with additional essential information in other languages will be missed. *This forces the English point of view on all users and ignores other, potentially more diverse, viewpoints.* Another issue with $\text{qtBERTE}_{en}$ is its reliance on MT. Despite the impressive progress, MT still needs improvement, especially for low-resource languages, with named entities presenting a significant challenge (Li et al., 2021). Moreover, in gender-marking languages, like Arabic, Hebrew and Spanish, gender hints will be lost.

### 3.4 Multilingual Entity Retrieval System

$\text{BERTE}_l$, by design, supports a single language. To handle queries and entities in multiple languages, an array of $\text{BERTE}_l$ models is needed, each of which uses a different LM. However, training an LM for a new language requires large amounts of data and significant computing power, limiting advances in NLP to a small subset of languages (Joshi et al., 2020). Moreover, fine-tuning and storing a model for each language is prohibitively expensive when the task involves more than a handful of languages. To overcome these challenges, multilingual LMs such as mBERT (Devlin et al., 2019) and mLUKE (Ri et al., 2021) were proposed, with the idea of training a single model for many languages.

multiBERTE, our proposed multilingual ranker, can handle any language supported by its base multilingual LM. We explore two approaches for multiBERTE: $\text{multi}_{\text{en}}\text{BERTE}$, which fine-tunes the multilingual BERT model using English data only, and a *few-shot* approach, $\text{multi}_{\text{few}}\text{BERTE}$, where training data from a few languages is concatenated. In the latter, the model has no explicit knowledge of what language it will use and only has a few training samples in each (Longpre et al., 2021).

[4] Section 4 shows how the DBpedia entity mapping works.

Given training data in a language $l$, we can extend it to another language $l^{\times}$ by: (i) machine-translating the queries; and (ii) using the entity documents generated from the subgraph of $l^{\times}$.

Figure 1 compares the workflows of $\text{BERTE}_l$ and multiBERTE. The former only sees data in one language, both when pretrained and fine-tuned. Therefore, an array of $\text{BERTE}_l$ models is needed in a multilingual setup. multiBERTE, on the other hand, is pretrained with over 100 languages and can handle pairs in any of these languages, even if fine-tuned only on a subset of them.

### 3.5 Mixture of Language Rankers

Given a query written in a language $l$, $\text{qtBERTE}_{en}$ searches the English subgraph only, and its results are limited to entities that can be mapped to $l$. $\text{BERTE}_l$, on the other hand, considers only entities represented in $l$ and uses the textual representation available in $l$ in both stages. Consequently, information in other languages is not utilised. $\text{multi}_{\text{few}}\text{BERTE}$ can take advantage of content from multiple sources during the fine-tuning stage but uses only $l$ for retrieval.

We believe that, by mixing multiple models during retrieval, we can further benefit from the unique traits of individual subgraphs while diminishing biases that may have been encoded due to reliance on a single source. One option is to concatenate the different textual representations into a single multilingual document and use the combined document for fine-tuning and scoring. This approach will only work with multiBERTE. Even then, the limited document size most LMs can handle presents a barrier. An alternative is to translate the query to multiple languages and retrieve a scored list of entities for each language. We denote this approach of using multiple retrievers by adding the superscript $L_{\text{mix}}$ to the model name. Formally, let $l$ be the target language and $L_{\text{mix}}$ be the set of additional languages we want to blend in, the mixed score is:

$$\text{BERTE}_l^{L_{\text{mix}}}(q,e) = \sum_{l^{\oplus} \in \{l\} \cup L_{\text{mix}}} \mu_{l^{\oplus}} \cdot \text{BERTE}_{l^{\oplus}}(q,e). \quad (3)$$

Note that $\text{BERTE}_{l^{\oplus}}$ could be a different $\text{BERTE}_l$ model for each language or a single multiBERTE model shared between all languages. $\mu_{l^{\oplus}}$, the weight each language gets in the final score can be learned based on factors including geographical location, language similarity, or user preference. In this work, we assign a fixed weight of $\mu_l = 0.75$ to

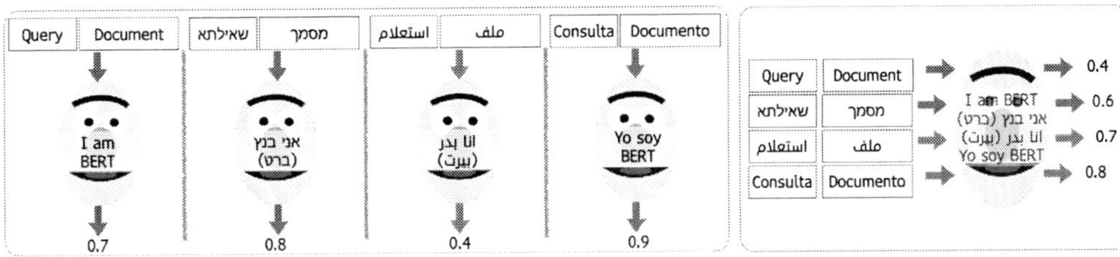


Figure 1: We consider two architectures for a multilingual retrieval system: $\text{BERTE}_l$, a collection of monolingual retrievers (left) and a single multilingual model, multiBERTE, trained using query-document pairs from multiple languages (right).

the target language ranker and split the remaining weight equally between the rest. For example, if the target language is Arabic, $\text{BERTE}_{ar}^{\{en\}}$ will be a mixture of $\text{BERTE}_{ar}$ and $\text{BERTE}_{en}$. The Arabic and English versions of the queries are used. The weight of the $\text{BERTE}_{ar}$ score will be $\mu = 0.75$ and the weight of $\text{BERTE}_{en}$ will be 0.25.

Appendix B compares the various configurations in our multilingual retrieval system.

## 4 Empirical Evaluation

We conducted a series of experiments on `DE-v2` to analyse our proposed approaches. We also used `DE-v2`'s 5-fold train-test split to allow comparison with previous works. $\beta$, the weight given to the first-stage retriever, is fine-tuned using a validation set (one training fold). We found $\beta = 0.75$ to work best for English and used it across all experiments.

In each language $l$, we adopt the same procedure when training the respective $\text{BERTE}_l$ model. For every training query $q$ and relevant entity $e^+$, we generate 10 triplets of the form $\langle q, e^+, e^- \rangle$, where $e^-$ is a randomly drawn judged non-relevant entity for $q$. We use a pairwise softmax cross-entropy loss, AdamW optimiser, with a learning rate of $1e^{-6}$, and train for 20,000 steps, with a batch size of 32. The embedding vectors are of size 128.

We first evaluate BERTE on the original English collection and the Arabic subset of `DE-v2`, the only publicly available non-English resource for the task. We then discuss how to extend `DE-v2` to other languages systematically and evaluate $\text{BERTE}_l$ (monolingual LMs) and multiBERTE (multilingual LMs) on the complete set of queries, machine-translated to Spanish, Arabic, and Hebrew. Finally, we demonstrate how English can benefit from other languages. Note that we optimise for English only and fix $\beta = 0.75$ for all experiments and languages. Optimising $\beta$ per language will likely further improve results.

Table 1: Reranking results. Statistically significant improvements (paired t-test with $\alpha = 0.05$) over ESim and KEWER are indicated by ($\star$) and ($\dagger$) respectively.

| Model | $\text{nDCG}_{10}$ | $\text{nDCG}_{100}$ | MAP |
|---|---|---|---|
| $\text{BM25F}_{ca}$ | 0.461 | 0.551 | 0.380 |
| KEWER | 0.483 | 0.560 | 0.396 |
| ESim | 0.487 | 0.572 | 0.403 |
| EM-BERT | $0.541^{\star\dagger}$ | $0.604^{\star\dagger}$ | - |
| $\text{BERTE}_{en}$ | $0.525^{\star\dagger}$ | $0.602^{\star\dagger}$ | $0.433^{\star\dagger}$ |

### 4.1 Evaluating BERTE on English

`DE-v2` comes with a set of baseline results. The official metrics are nDCG (Normalized Discounted Cumulative Gain) at 10 and 100. Similar to other works, we also report MAP (Mean Average Precision) at 1,000. We utilise the recently introduced embedding-based techniques KEWER and ESim, as well as EM-BERT, which uses LMs, as baselines.[5] We reproduced the baselines reported results using their published runs, if available. Table 1 shows the overall results. [6] Our proposed $\text{BERTE}_{en}$ and the current state-of-the-art EM-BERT significantly outperform the other methods (paired t-test with $\alpha = 0.05$). Between them, the differences in nDCG are statistically insignificant. We believe, however, that $\text{BERTE}_{en}$ is preferred, even in a monolingual setting, for the following reasons: (i) it uses a smaller LM (BERT-base vs BERT-large); (ii) it does not require additional annotated data and instead has a single fine-tuning step; (iii) it does not depend on the availability of entity embeddings and entity extractors; (iv) it re-ranks directly from BM25 instead of ESim.

Our main focus in this work, nevertheless, is the multilingual setting. We, therefore, use Appendix

[5]We use the model with the best reported overall result for each: $\text{BM25F}_{ca}$+KEWER, $\text{BM25F}_{ca}$+$\text{ESim}_{CG}$, and EM-BERT with GEEER and dual fine-tuning.

[6]Note that KEWER used a custom 5-fold split for cross-validation. MAP at 1000 could not be reported for EM-BERT because the run files are limited to 100 results.

C to dive deeper into the differences between the different methods in the English setup and show that an even better result can be achieved by combining them. In Appendix D, we also present insights from sample query analysis.

### 4.2 Evaluating BERTE on Arabic

Esmeir (2021) has recently used human-translators to extend DE-v2 to Arabic. Only 139 queries with sufficient relevant entities in Arabic were included. Along the translations, two baseline results were reported: BM25 and SERAG, an adaption of KEWER to Arabic.

Table 2: Reranking results on the Arabic collection. Significant improvements over SERAG and BM25 are indicated by ($\star$) and ($\dagger$) respectively.

| Model | nDCG$_{10}$ | nDCG$_{100}$ | MAP |
|---|---|---|---|
| SERAG | 0.226 | 0.303 | 0.183 |
| BM25 | 0.273$^\star$ | 0.3482$^\star$ | 0.223$^\star$ |
| BERTE$_{ar}$ | **0.308**$^{\star\dagger}$ | **0.382**$^{\star\dagger}$ | **0.247**$^{\star\dagger}$ |

As shown in Table 2, our BM25 first stage is already enough to outperform SERAG. We believe that this is due to better document generation. BERTE$_{ar}$ model provides a further statistically significant improvement.

### 4.3 Extending DE-v2

DBpedia can be viewed as a large-scale multilingual KG (Lehmann et al., 2015). Each chapter holds structured content extracted from the corresponding Wikipedia edition. Inter-language entity-mapping files allow us to link entity URIs from one language to another. Given an entity in the graph, we can extract its multilingual counterparts using the `owl#sameAs` property. Figure 2 illustrates how this linking works for the entity representing "Ibn Khaldun". Appendix E provides coverage statistics of the DBpedia 2015 chapters we use.

While there is at most one Wikipedia article per topic per language, the content of the articles may vary across languages. Moreover, editors and administrators from different editions may have different points of view. They may also have access to different sources, only available in that specific language. Finally, different languages may encode different biases into the LM (Bartl et al., 2020). Consider, for example, the topic *"Mujaddara"*, a popular dish in several parts of the world. Examining the info-boxes in different languages, we found over ten different answers to where they originated (as of early 2022). A good retriever, therefore, will attempt to benefit from the *richness of DBpedia by considering information from multiple languages.*

In DE-v2, retrieving an entity that does not exist in English may hurt the results. First, only entities with English content were judged by the annotators. Other entities, even if relevant to the query, will not have a judgement and will default to non-relevancy. Second, placing a relevant but unjudged entity in a high-ranking position may push other judged relevant entities outside the top $k$ and hurt the measured performance. We restrict the first-stage retrieval to entities available in English DBpedia to solve the latter. This step, however, should not be applied in the general case, where judgements are truly multilingual.

To translate the queries, we opted for MT. While human translation provides major benefits, MT allows it to scale to over 100 languages.[7]

### 4.4 Monolingual Language Models

We next study Spanish, Arabic, and Hebrew versions of DE-v2, using the set of machine-translated queries. Table 3 shows the results. We first consider models that use a single-language subgraph (top three lines), where the language-agnostic BM25 is provided as a baseline. Similar to the English results, a BERTE$_l$ model fine-tuned in the same language significantly outperforms BM25. Interestingly, qtBERTE$_{en}$, which uses English queries to search the English chapter of DE-v2 and maps the results back to the target language, outperforms BERTE$_l$.

While the "English-first" approach seems to perform better than searching specifically on a given language, we must treat this result with caution due to the "English nature" of DE-v2: (i) English is the largest chapter with the most coverage, (ii) entities were pooled using methods optimised for English, and (iii) the annotators had English Wikipedia in mind when judging the entities. In addition, recall that we have the original queries in English so BERTE$_{en}$ operated on optimal translations. We view this result as a strong baseline but not one that can generalise for the wealth of retrieval tasks in a truly multilingual universe.

Next, we investigate what happens if we *mix* the scores of BERTE$_l$ on a language $l$ with those of

[7]We used `http://translate.google.com` and asked native speakers to verify that the output was generally in line with the input. We did not have to make any changes.

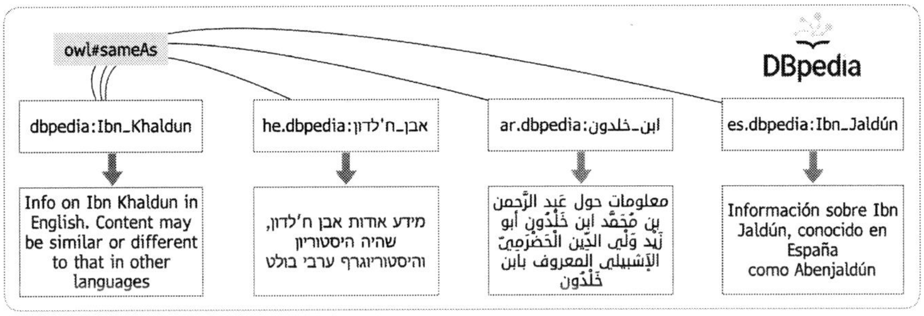


Figure 2: Entity mapping between entities in DBpedia chapters. In this example, the English entity for "Ibn Khaldun" is mapped to the respective entities in Arabic, Hebrew and Spanish. The graph and content in each language may differ (the texts in the example are for illustration only).

Table 3: Reranking results in the multilingual setup. BERTE$_l$ is trained solely on $l$. qtBERTE$_{en}$ uses query translation from $l$ to English, searches the English KG and maps the results to entities in the $l$ graph. multi$_{en}$BERTE and multi$_{few}$BERTE are multilingual models, fine-tuned in English or few languages, respectively. multi$_{en}$BERTE$^{\{en\}}$ and multi$_{few}$BERTE$^{\{en\}}$ mix in the scores from qtBERTE$_{en}$. Best result in each column in **bold**. ↑ denotes significant improvements over the preceding line.

| | English | | Spanish | | Arabic | | Hebrew | |
|---|---|---|---|---|---|---|---|---|
| **Model** | **nDCG$_{10}$** | **nDCG$_{100}$** | **nDCG$_{10}$** | **nDCG$_{100}$** | **nDCG$_{10}$** | **nDCG$_{100}$** | **nDCG$_{10}$** | **nDCG$_{100}$** |
| BM25 (BM25F$_{ca}$ for English) | 0.461 | 0.551 | 0.271 | 0.320 | 0.216 | 0.265 | 0.216 | 0.266 |
| BERTE$_l$ | 0.525 ↑ | 0.602 ↑ | 0.299 ↑ | 0.353 ↑ | 0.242 ↑ | 0.293 ↑ | 0.238 ↑ | 0.290 ↑ |
| qtBERTE$_{en}$ | - | - | 0.345 ↑ | 0.446 ↑ | 0.271 ↑ | 0.349 ↑ | 0.263 ↑ | 0.345 ↑ |
| BERTE$_l^{\{en\}}$ | - | - | 0.472 ↑ | 0.497 ↑ | 0.421 ↑ | 0.452 ↑ | 0.415 ↑ | 0.439 ↑ |
| multi$_{en}$BERTE | **0.530** | **0.608** | 0.311 | 0.363 | 0.236 | 0.287 | 0.244 | 0.293 |
| multi$_{en}$BERTE$^{\{en\}}$ | - | - | **0.473** ↑ | **0.498** ↑ | 0.420 ↑ | 0.452 ↑ | 0.414 ↑ | 0.437 ↑ |
| multi$_{few}$BERTE | 0.529 | 0.607 | 0.317 | 0.371 | 0.238 | 0.289 | 0.249 | 0.299 |
| multi$_{few}$BERTE$^{\{en\}}$ | - | - | **0.473** ↑ | 0.497 ↑ | **0.422** ↑ | **0.453** ↑ | **0.417** ↑ | **0.440** ↑ |

qtBERTE$_{en}$. The results in the fourth row of Table 3 shows that *mixing languages is highly beneficial.*

To illustrate that, consider the Hebrew version of the query "Chefs with a show on the Food Network". "Julia Child" is the highest-scored entity from DBpedia Hebrew. While BM25 includes it in the first stage, BERTE$_l$ ranks it outside the top 100. "the Food Network" was translated literally into *RESHET HAMAZON*, failing to identify the named entity. By mixing in the English score, "Julia Child" breaks into the top 10. In some cases, however, mixing scores is not strictly beneficial: The Spanish BERTE$_l$, for example, does better on the query "Madrid" without mixing English, perhaps unsurprisingly.

In our experiments, while models could leverage information from multiple languages, they return only entities covered in the language of the query. In some scenarios, however, it is useful to see entities that exist only in other languages. In Appendix G, we provide further insights into this setup and explain how BERTE can be adapted to handle it using score mixing.

## 4.5 Multilingual LMs

The results for the multiBERTE variants are presented in the last four rows of Table 3. Both multi$_{en}$BERTE (a multilingual model fine-tuned on English queries) and multi$_{few}$BERTE (a multilingual model fine-tuned with queries in multiple languages) exhibit comparable performance to the respective monolingual models, especially when mixing in the scores from English (rows 6 and 8), indicating that score blending offers an orthogonal advantage. While not reflected in the numbers, we believe that multi$_{few}$BERTE is the better choice, given its ability to incorporate knowledge from multiple languages and the fact that it can adapt quickly to a new language. We expect it to shine when using information from multiple languages is essential. We hope to collaborate with the community to build such truly multilingual collections.

Another advantage of multiBERTE variants is that they can be used for over 100 languages without having to fine-tune the models on these, thanks to the cross lingual capabilities of multilingual LMs,

Table 4: Results on queries with good coverage across languages. Sig. improvements are denoted by ($\star$).

| Model | nDCG$_{10}$ | nDCG$_{100}$ | MAP |
|---|---|---|---|
| BERTE$_{en}$ | 0.515 | 0.616 | 0.434 |
| BERTE$_{en}^{\{es,ar,he\}}$ | **0.540**$^\star$ | **0.634**$^\star$ | **0.452**$^\star$ |

leading to a strong baseline for many languages on the task. In Appendix F we provide results for six additional languages obtained following the same methodology as our main result. multi$_{\text{few}}$BERTE$^{\{en\}}$ was consistently the best performer, and its advantage over BM25 and multi$_{\text{few}}$BERTE was statistically significant.

While the multiBERTE variants offer apparent advantages, there are cases where BERTE$_l$ is necessary: (i) there are hundreds of languages that are not supported by existing multilingual LMs but have their own monolingual LM, and (ii) domain specific LMs, such as FinBERT (Liu et al., 2020b), were shown to be superior in many tasks.

### 4.6 English Benefits from Collaboration

Above, we demonstrated that mixing in the scores from BERTE$_{en}$ helps other languages. We next ask if English, the largest and richest chapter, can also benefit from the diverse coverage in other languages. To answer this, we mix Spanish, Arabic, and Hebrew scores to rerank English entities. We refer to this model as BERTE$_{en}^{\{es,ar,he\}}$.

When tested on the entire dataset, this approach did not yield any improvement. Error analysis, however, indicated that for queries where the Spanish, Arabic, and Hebrew runs of BM25 obtained a sufficient number of relevant entities, and the performance of BERTE$_{en}^{\{es,ar,he\}}$ on English improved. When entities do not exist in another language, or when their representation does not match the query textually, BM25 fails to retrieve them, negatively impacting the corresponding BERTE$_l$ and subsequently BERTE$_{en}^{\{es,ar,he\}}$. We, therefore, focus on a subset of the queries with good performance of BM25 in the other three languages. More formally, we calculate the optimal nDCG$_{100}$ of the first-stage retrieval, which provides an upper bound on reranking performance. Queries with a score of 0.3 or more in all languages are kept, resulting in a subset of 113 queries. Table 4 lists the results for this subset showing that the performance of BERTE$_{en}^{\{es,ar,he\}}$ is significantly better than BERTE$_{en}$. Consider, for example, the query "Chess world champions". The query is about a global topic with coverage in many languages. BERTE$_{en}$ listed 4 relevant names in its top 10 results. With the help of other languages, this number increased to 6. This demonstrates that *even high resource languages can benefit from multilingual retrieval.* Instead of pre-selecting a subset of queries, in the future, we plan to apply a meta-learner to decide which languages a query should use automatically.

## 5 Conclusion

In this paper, we introduced BERTE, a highly effective multilingual entity retrieval system. We showed that in a monolingual environment, it is on par with current state-of-the-art methods on DE-v2 despite being simpler and requiring less data. We then explored the multilingual setup, where both the graph and the queries may be presented in multiple languages. We proposed a systematic way to extend DE-v2 beyond English and discussed the risks of such approach. We believe it is vital for the community to curate truly multilingual collections that come from different sources and involve native speakers. To address the multilingual retrieval task, we considered both a collection of monolingual models and a single multilingual one. We showed that combining the scores from different languages significantly boosts the performance of low and high-resourced languages.

Our work can enable many downstream tasks. Consider, for example, a virtual assistant answering questions in Arabic about a topic covered mainly in the English edition of Wikipedia or an English speaker analyst covering a multi-national company interested in taking diverse points of view coming from content in different languages. In both cases, BERTE allows handling queries and KGs in multiple languages.

We hope that this work opens interesting avenues of research. As discussed in Appendix C, the improvements brought by BERTE are orthogonal to those by the other state-of-the-art method, EMBERT. Therefore, we hope that combining each method's contributions will establish a new state-of-the-art for the English task. On the multilingual front, works that adapt the retrieval task to user preference, such as language, region, or past actions, may benefit from the flexibility of BERTE in combining different sources.

## References


Muhammad Abdul-Mageed, AbdelRahim Elmadany, and El Moatez Billah Nagoudi. 2021. ARBERT & MARBERT: Deep bidirectional transformers for Arabic. In *Proceedings of the 59th Annual Meeting of the Association for Computational Linguistics and the 11th International Joint Conference on Natural Language Processing (Volume 1: Long Papers)*, pages 7088–7105, Online. Association for Computational Linguistics.

Zeynep Akkalyoncu Yilmaz, Shengjin Wang, Wei Yang, Haotian Zhang, and Jimmy Lin. 2019. Applying BERT to document retrieval with birch. In *Proceedings of the 2019 Conference on Empirical Methods in Natural Language Processing and the 9th International Joint Conference on Natural Language Processing (EMNLP-IJCNLP): System Demonstrations*, pages 19–24, Hong Kong, China. Association for Computational Linguistics.

S. Auer, Christian Bizer, Georgi Kobilarov, Jens Lehmann, Richard Cyganiak, and Zachary G. Ives. 2007. Dbpedia: A nucleus for a web of open data. In *ISWC/ASWC*.

Marion Bartl, Malvina Nissim, and Albert Gatt. 2020. Unmasking contextual stereotypes: Measuring and mitigating BERT's gender bias. In *Proceedings of the Second Workshop on Gender Bias in Natural Language Processing*, pages 1–16, Barcelona, Spain (Online). Association for Computational Linguistics.

Jan A. Botha, Zifei Shan, and Daniel Gillick. 2020. Entity Linking in 100 Languages. In *Proceedings of the 2020 Conference on Empirical Methods in Natural Language Processing (EMNLP)*, pages 7833–7845, Online. Association for Computational Linguistics.

Zied Bouraoui, Jose Camacho-Collados, and Steven Schockaert. 2020. Inducing relational knowledge from bert. *Proceedings of the AAAI Conference on Artificial Intelligence*, 34(05):7456–7463.

Samuel Broscheit. 2019. Investigating entity knowledge in BERT with simple neural end-to-end entity linking. In *Proceedings of the 23rd Conference on Computational Natural Language Learning (CoNLL)*, pages 677–685, Hong Kong, China. Association for Computational Linguistics.

Arthur Câmara and Claudia Hauff. 2020. Diagnosing bert with retrieval heuristics. In *Advances in Information Retrieval*, pages 605–618, Cham. Springer International Publishing.

Daniel Fernando Campos, Tri Nguyen, Mir Rosenberg, Xia Song, Jianfeng Gao, Saurabh Tiwary, Rangan Majumder, Li Deng, and Bhaskar Mitra. 2016. Ms marco: A human generated machine reading comprehension dataset. *ArXiv*, abs/1611.09268.

José Cañete, Gabriel Chaperon, Rodrigo Fuentes, Jou-Hui Ho, Hojin Kang, and Jorge Pérez. 2020. Spanish pre-trained bert model and evaluation data. In *PML4DC at ICLR 2020*.

Marek Ciglan, Kjetil Nørvåg, and Ladislav Hluchý. 2012. The SemSets model for ad-hoc semantic list search. In *Proceedings of the 21st international conference on World Wide Web*, WWW '12, pages 131–140, New York, NY, USA. Association for Computing Machinery.

Alexis Conneau and Guillaume Lample. 2019. Cross-lingual language model pretraining. In *Proceedings of NeurIPS*.

Zhuyun Dai and Jamie Callan. 2020. Context-aware document term weighting for ad-hoc search. In *Proceedings of The Web Conference 2020*, WWW '20, page 1897–1907, New York, NY, USA. Association for Computing Machinery.

Daniel Daza, Michael Cochez, and Paul Groth. 2021. Inductive entity representations from text via link prediction. In *Proceedings of the Web Conference 2021*, WWW '21, page 798–808, New York, NY, USA. Association for Computing Machinery.

Nicola De Cao, Gautier Izacard, Sebastian Riedel, and Fabio Petroni. 2020. Autoregressive entity retrieval. *arXiv preprint arXiv:2010.00904*.

Nicola De Cao, Ledell Wu, Kashyap Popat, Mikel Artetxe, Naman Goyal, Mikhail Plekhanov, Luke Zettlemoyer, Nicola Cancedda, Sebastian Riedel, and Fabio Petroni. 2021. Multilingual autoregressive entity linking. *arXiv preprint arXiv:2103.12528*.

Jacob Devlin, Ming-Wei Chang, Kenton Lee, and Kristina Toutanova. 2019. BERT: Pre-training of deep bidirectional transformers for language understanding. In *Proceedings of the 2019 Conference of the North American Chapter of the Association for Computational Linguistics: Human Language Technologies, Volume 1 (Long and Short Papers)*, pages 4171–4186, Minneapolis, Minnesota. Association for Computational Linguistics.

Saher Esmeir. 2021. SERAG: Semantic entity retrieval from Arabic knowledge graphs. In *Proceedings of the Sixth Arabic Natural Language Processing Workshop*, pages 219–225, Kyiv, Ukraine (Virtual). Association for Computational Linguistics.

Nicholas FitzGerald, Dan Bikel, Jan Botha, Daniel Gillick, Tom Kwiatkowski, and Andrew McCallum. 2021. MOLEMAN: Mention-only linking of entities with a mention annotation network. In *Proceedings of the 59th Annual Meeting of the Association for Computational Linguistics and the 11th International Joint Conference on Natural Language Processing (Volume 2: Short Papers)*, pages 278–285, Online. Association for Computational Linguistics.

Thibault Formal, Benjamin Piwowarski, and Stéphane Clinchant. 2021. Splade: Sparse lexical and expansion model for first stage ranking. *Proceedings of the 44th International ACM SIGIR Conference on Research and Development in Information Retrieval.*

Mikhail Galkin, Priyansh Trivedi, Gaurav Maheshwari, Ricardo Usbeck, and Jens Lehmann. 2020. Message passing for Hyper-Relational knowledge graphs. In *Proceedings of the 2020 Conference on Empirical Methods in Natural Language Processing (EMNLP)*, pages 7346–7359. Association for Computational Linguistics.

Emma Gerritse, Faegheh Hasibi, and Arjen De Vries. 2022. Entity-aware Transformers for Entity Search. In *Proc. of the 45th International ACM SIGIR Conference on Research and Development in Information Retrieval*, SIGIR '22.

Emma J. Gerritse, Faegheh Hasibi, and Arjen P. de Vries. 2020. Graph-embedding empowered entity retrieval. *Advances in Information Retrieval*, pages 97–110.

Faegheh Hasibi, Fedor Nikolaev, Chenyan Xiong, Krisztian Balog, Svein Erik Bratsberg, Alexander Kotov, and Jamie Callan. 2017. Dbpedia-entity v2: A test collection for entity search. In *Proceedings of the 40th International ACM SIGIR Conference on Research and Development in Information Retrieval*, SIGIR '17, pages 1265–1268. ACM.

Sebastian Hofstätter, Sophia Althammer, Michael Schröder, Mete Sertkan, and Allan Hanbury. 2020. Improving efficient neural ranking models with cross-architecture knowledge distillation. *arXiv preprint arXiv:2010.02666.*

Shoaib Jameel, Zied Bouraoui, and Steven Schockaert. 2017. MEmbER: Max-Margin based embeddings for entity retrieval. In *Proceedings of the 40th International ACM SIGIR Conference on Research and Development in Information Retrieval*, SIGIR '17, pages 783–792, New York, NY, USA. Association for Computing Machinery.

Pratik Joshi, Sebastin Santy, Amar Budhiraja, Kalika Bali, and Monojit Choudhury. 2020. The state and fate of linguistic diversity and inclusion in the NLP world. In *Proceedings of the 58th Annual Meeting of the Association for Computational Linguistics*, pages 6282–6293, Online. Association for Computational Linguistics.

Vladimir Karpukhin, Barlas Oğuz, Sewon Min, Patrick Lewis, Ledell Wu, Sergey Edunov, Danqi Chen, and Wen-tau Yih. 2020. Dense passage retrieval for open-domain question answering. *arXiv preprint arXiv:2004.04906.*

Omar Khattab and Matei Zaharia. 2020. Colbert: Efficient and effective passage search via contextualized late interaction over bert. In *Proceedings of the 43rd International ACM SIGIR Conference on Research and Development in Information Retrieval*, SIGIR '20, page 39–48, New York, NY, USA. Association for Computing Machinery.

Takahiro Komamizu. 2020. Random walk-based entity representation learning and re-ranking for entity search. *Knowledge and Information Systems*, 62:2989–3013.

Jens Lehmann, Robert Isele, Max Jakob, Anja Jentzsch, Dimitris Kontokostas, Pablo N. Mendes, Sebastian Hellmann, Mohamed Morsey, Patrick van Kleef, Sören Auer, and Christian Bizer. 2015. Dbpedia - a large-scale, multilingual knowledge base extracted from wikipedia. *Semantic Web*, 6:167–195.

Mike Lewis, Yinhan Liu, Naman Goyal, Marjan Ghazvininejad, Abdelrahman Mohamed, Omer Levy, Ves Stoyanov, and Luke Zettlemoyer. 2019. Bart: Denoising sequence-to-sequence pre-training for natural language generation, translation, and comprehension. *arXiv preprint arXiv:1910.13461.*

Panpan Li, Mengxiang Wang, and Jian Wang. 2021. Named entity translation method based on machine translation lexicon. *Neural Computing and Applications*, 33:1–9.

Robert Litschko, Goran Glavaš, Simone Paolo Ponzetto, and Ivan Vulić. 2018. Unsupervised cross-lingual information retrieval using monolingual data only. In *The 41st International ACM SIGIR Conference on Research & Development in Information Retrieval*, pages 1253–1256.

Liyuan Liu, Jingbo Shang, and Jiawei Han. 2019. Arabic named entity recognition: What works and what's next. In *Proceedings of the Fourth Arabic Natural Language Processing Workshop*, pages 60–67, Florence, Italy. Association for Computational Linguistics.

Weijie Liu, Peng Zhou, Zhe Zhao, Zhiruo Wang, Qi Ju, Haotang Deng, and Ping Wang. 2020a. K-BERT: Enabling language representation with knowledge graph. *AAAI*, 34(03):2901–2908.

Zhuang Liu, Degen Huang, Kaiyu Huang, Zhuang Li, and Jun Zhao. 2020b. Finbert: A pre-trained financial language representation model for financial text mining. In *Proceedings of the Twenty-Ninth International Joint Conference on Artificial Intelligence, IJCAI-20*, pages 4513–4519. International Joint Conferences on Artificial Intelligence Organization. Special Track on AI in FinTech.

Shayne Longpre, Yi Lu, and Joachim Daiber. 2021. Mkqa: A linguistically diverse benchmark for multilingual open domain question answering. *Transactions of the Association for Computational Linguistics*, 9:1389–1406.

Sean MacAvaney, Andrew Yates, Arman Cohan, and Nazli Goharian. 2019. CEDR: Contextualized embeddings for document ranking. In *Proceedings of the 42nd International ACM SIGIR Conference on*

*Research and Development in Information Retrieval*, SIGIR'19, pages 1101–1104, New York, NY, USA. Association for Computing Machinery.

Bhaskar Mitra and Nick Craswell. 2018. An introduction to neural information retrieval. *Foundations and Trends® in Information Retrieval*, 13(1):1–126.

Benjamin Muller, Yanai Elazar, Benoît Sagot, and Djamé Seddah. 2021. First align, then predict: Understanding the cross-lingual ability of multilingual BERT. In *Proceedings of the 16th Conference of the European Chapter of the Association for Computational Linguistics: Main Volume*, pages 2214–2231, Online. Association for Computational Linguistics.

Suraj Nair, Petra Galuscakova, and Douglas W Oard. 2020. Combining contextualized and non-contextualized query translations to improve clir. In *Proceedings of the 43rd International ACM SIGIR Conference on Research and Development in Information Retrieval*, pages 1581–1584.

Shahrzad Naseri, John Foley, J. Allan, and Brendan T. O'Connor. 2018. Exploring summary-expanded entity embeddings for entity retrieval. In *CIKM Workshops*.

Robert Neumayer, Krisztian Balog, and Kjetil Nørvåg. 2012. On the modeling of entities for Ad-Hoc entity search in the web of data. In *Advances in Information Retrieval*, pages 133–145. Springer Berlin Heidelberg.

Fedor Nikolaev and Alexander Kotov. 2020. Joint word and entity embeddings for entity retrieval from a knowledge graph. In *Advances in Information Retrieval*, pages 141–155, Cham. Springer International Publishing.

Fedor Nikolaev, Alexander Kotov, and Nikita Zhiltsov. 2016. Parameterized fielded term dependence models for ad-hoc entity retrieval from knowledge graph. In *Proceedings of the 39th International ACM SIGIR Conference on Research and Development in Information Retrieval*, SIGIR '16, pages 435–444, New York, NY, USA. Association for Computing Machinery.

Rodrigo Nogueira and Kyunghyun Cho. 2019. Passage re-ranking with BERT. *CoRR*, abs/1901.04085.

Rodrigo Nogueira, Wei Yang, Jimmy Lin, and Kyunghyun Cho. 2019. Document expansion by query prediction. *CoRR*, abs/1904.08375.

Carol Peters, Martin Braschler, and Paul Clough. 2012. *Multilingual information retrieval: From research to practice*. Springer Science & Business Media.

Fabio Petroni, Tim Rocktäschel, Patrick Lewis, Anton Bakhtin, Yuxiang Wu, Alexander H. Miller, and Sebastian Riedel. 2019. Language models as knowledge bases? In *EMNLP*.

Nina Poerner, Ulli Waltinger, and Hinrich Schütze. 2020. E-BERT: Efficient-Yet-Effective entity embeddings for BERT. In *Findings of the Association for Computational Linguistics: EMNLP 2020*, pages 803–818, Online. Association for Computational Linguistics.

Miriam Redi, Martin Gerlach, Isaac Johnson, Jonathan Morgan, and Leila Zia. 2021. A taxonomy of knowledge gaps for wikimedia projects (second draft). *ArXiv*.

Ryokan Ri, Ikuya Yamada, and Yoshimasa Tsuruoka. 2021. mluke: The power of entity representations in multilingual pretrained language models. *CoRR*, abs/2110.08151.

Stephen E. Robertson, Steve Walker, and Micheline Hancock-Beaulieu. 1995. Large test collection experiments on an operational, interactive system: Okapi at TREC. *Inf. Process. Manag.*, 31(3):345–360.

Paolo Rosso, Dingqi Yang, and Philippe Cudré-Mauroux. 2020. Beyond triplets: Hyper-relational knowledge graph embedding for link prediction. In *Proceedings of The Web Conference 2020*, WWW '20, page 1885–1896, New York, NY, USA. Association for Computing Machinery.

Amit Seker, Elron Bandel, Dan Bareket, Idan Brusilovsky, Refael Shaked Greenfeld, and Reut Tsarfaty. 2021. Alephbert:a hebrew large pre-trained language model to start-off your hebrew nlp application with.

Wei Shen, Yuhan Li, Yinan Liu, Jiawei Han, Jianyong Wang, and Xiaojie Yuan. 2021. Entity linking meets deep learning: Techniques and solutions. *IEEE Transactions on Knowledge and Data Engineering*.

Chen-Tse Tsai and Dan Roth. 2016. Cross-lingual wikification using multilingual embeddings. In *Proceedings of the 2016 Conference of the North American Chapter of the Association for Computational Linguistics: Human Language Technologies*, pages 589–598, San Diego, California. Association for Computational Linguistics.

Niels van der Heijden, Helen Yannakoudakis, Pushkar Mishra, and Ekaterina Shutova. 2021. Multilingual and cross-lingual document classification: A meta-learning approach. In *Proceedings of the 16th Conference of the European Chapter of the Association for Computational Linguistics: Main Volume*, pages 1966–1976.

Johannes M. van Hulst, Faegheh Hasibi, Koen Dercksen, Krisztian Balog, and Arjen P. de Vries. 2020. Rel: An entity linker standing on the shoulders of giants. In *Proceedings of the 43rd International ACM SIGIR Conference on Research and Development in Information Retrieval*, SIGIR '20. ACM.

Chenguang Wang, Xiao Liu, and Dawn Song. 2020. Language models are open knowledge graphs. *CoRR*, abs/2010.11967.

Zhen Wang, Jianwen Zhang, Jianlin Feng, and Zheng Chen. 2014. Knowledge graph embedding by translating on hyperplanes. In *Proceedings of the Twenty-Eighth AAAI Conference on Artificial Intelligence*, AAAI'14, page 1112–1119. AAAI Press.

Genta Indra Winata, Andrea Madotto, Zhaojiang Lin, Rosanne Liu, Jason Yosinski, and Pascale Fung. 2021. Language models are few-shot multilingual learners. In *Proceedings of the 1st Workshop on Multilingual Representation Learning*, pages 1–15, Punta Cana, Dominican Republic. Association for Computational Linguistics.

Ledell Wu, Fabio Petroni, Martin Josifoski, Sebastian Riedel, and Luke Zettlemoyer. 2020. Scalable zero-shot entity linking with dense entity retrieval. In *Proceedings of the 2020 Conference on Empirical Methods in Natural Language Processing (EMNLP)*, pages 6397–6407, Online. Association for Computational Linguistics.

Zonghan Wu, Shirui Pan, Fengwen Chen, Guodong Long, Chengqi Zhang, and Philip S Yu. 2021. A comprehensive survey on graph neural networks. *IEEE Trans Neural Netw Learn Syst*, 32(1):4–24.

Lee Xiong, Chenyan Xiong, Ye Li, Kwok-Fung Tang, Jialin Liu, Paul Bennett, Junaid Ahmed, and Arnold Overwijk. 2020. Approximate nearest neighbor negative contrastive learning for dense text retrieval. *arXiv preprint arXiv:2007.00808*.

Weidi Xu, Xingyi Cheng, Kunlong Chen, and Taifeng Wang. 2020. Symmetric regularization based BERT for pair-wise semantic reasoning. In *SIGIR*, pages 1901–1904. ACM.

Puxuan Yu, Hongliang Fei, and Ping Li. 2021. Cross-lingual language model pretraining for retrieval. In *Proceedings of the Web Conference 2021*, WWW '21, page 1029–1039, New York, NY, USA. Association for Computing Machinery.

Xinyu Zhang, Xueguang Ma, Peng Shi, and Jimmy Lin. 2021. Mr. TyDi: A multi-lingual benchmark for dense retrieval. In *Proceedings of the 1st Workshop on Multilingual Representation Learning*, pages 127–137, Punta Cana, Dominican Republic. Association for Computational Linguistics.

## A Entity Retrieval Illustration

An overview of the task setup and our proposed system can be seen in Figure 3.

## B Characteristics of the Various Models

In Section 3 we presented various configurations of BERTE and Table 5 compares them when used on a set of languages $L$. For each configuration, the table lists the number of pretrained LMs used, the languages involved in each retrieval stage, the direction of query translation (if any), and whether the system can handle languages unseen during fine-tuning.

qtBERTE$_{en}$ needs a single LM and uses only English sources in all stages, with non-English content being ignored. Because of that, queries in other languages should be translated into English. Hence, the system may be sensitive to translation errors. Recall that, in this work, we had the English version of all queries, with no need for translation.

Each BERTE$_l$ model can support a single language. Therefore, to support all languages in $L$, we need an array of $|L|$ BERTE$_l$ models, each of which is initialised with a different pretrained LM. For each language $l \in L$, the retriever only considers entities covered in $l$.

For multiBERTE variants, on the other hand, a single multilingual LM is sufficient to support all languages in $L$ and beyond. Multilingual LMs can then be tuned only on the English dataset or on a subset of languages ($L_{\text{few}}$). In all cases, scores from the target language can be mixed with scores from other languages to improve the ranking, in which case query translation from $l$ is needed. One main difference between multi$_{\text{en}}$BERTE and multi$_{\text{few}}$BERTE is in what language the training tuples are used when fine-tuning. While multi$_{\text{en}}$BERTE uses only English tuples, multi$_{\text{few}}$BERTE uses triples in several languages.

## C English Results Deep Dive

To test whether the improvements from BERTE and EM-BERT are orthogonal, we linearly combine their scores (with equal weights). This hybrid retriever outperforms each of its components significantly, achieving an nDCG$_{10}$ score of 0.571, nDCG$_{100}$ of 0.634, and MAP of 0.467. While such a retriever is cumbersome and has many dependencies, it indicates that each model is complementary to each other, and combining them further increases their performance.

Another consideration to be made is about the type of queries each method excels in. Recall that DE-v2 consists of a set of heterogeneous entity-bearing queries assembled from various benchmarking efforts. Queries are therefore categorised into four groups based on their source. Table 6 breaks down the English results of BERTE$_{en}$ by category. For three out of the four categories, BERTE$_{en}$ and EM-BERT were significantly better than the other methods. Specifically for SemSearch, which consisted of named entities, such as "Brooklyn Bridge", all methods were comparable and achieved relatively high scores. We hypothesise that this is due to the simpler nature of these queries. The simpler queries, usually only consisting of the target's name, make keyword-based retrieval methods, such as BM25, effective for most queries. Another noteworthy fact is that, like KEWER and ESim, a mixture model that combines BM25F$_{ca}$ and a neural ranker was better than its components, indicating that, despite the deep representation of entities in BERTE$_{en}$, term matching based techniques were still extremely valuable in many scenarios. Between BERTE$_{en}$ and EM-BERT, BERTE$_{en}$ had better performance for INEX-LD (IR style queries), while EM-BERT was better at QALD-2 (natural language questions).

## D BERTE$_{en}$ Query Analysis

We analyse several queries to study the effectiveness of BERTE$_{en}$. For the query "What is the capital of Canada?", BERTE$_{en}$ ranks the entity for "Ottawa" in the $6^{th}$ position, while KEWER and ESim leave it outside the top 10. Meanwhile, for the query "Ellis college", there is only one relevant judged entity, "Ellis University". While other methods focused on people named Ellis or on institutes with "college" in their name, BERTE$_{en}$ ranked "Ellis University" in the top 10. It shows how BERTE$_{en}$ properly leveraged the contextual similarity of "college" and "university". to rank the correct entity. In their work, Nikolaev and Kotov (2020) specifically mentioned the query "goodwill of michigan" as one where KEWER struggled with disambiguation ("Goodwill Games" vs "Goodwill Industries"). BERTE$_{en}$, however, had no problems with this query, with most top 10 results being correctly related to "Goodwill Industries".

One of the queries where BERTE$_{en}$ underper-

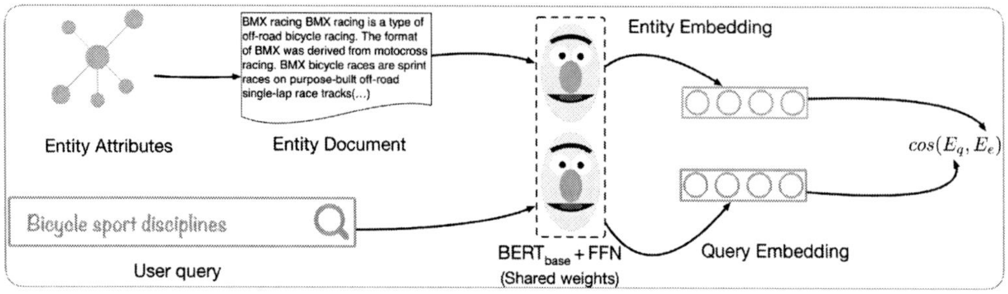


Figure 3: Entity documents are generated by concatenating their literal attributes. BERTE starts with a set of candidate entities. Queries and entity documents are fed separately through the same BERT model and a fully connected layer, resulting in two vector embeddings. Final relevance estimation is computed using cosine similarity.

Table 5: Let $l$ be the target language, $L$ be the set of languages available to the system, and $L_{\text{mix}}$ and $L_{\text{few}}$ be subsets of $L$ used for fine-tuning and mixing respectively. Here we summarise the different characteristics of the models we explore.

| Model | No. of LMs | First Stage | Fine-tuning | Reranking | Query translate | Handle unseen |
|---|---|---|---|---|---|---|
| qtBERTE$_{en}$ | 1 | en | en | en | $l \rightarrow$ en | ✓ |
| $\{$BERTE$_{l^\oplus} \mid l^\oplus \in L\}$ | $\|L\|$ | $l$ | $l$ | $l$ | – | × |
| multi$_{\text{en}}$BERTE | 1 | $l$ | en | $l$ | – | ✓ |
| multi$_{\text{few}}$BERTE | 1 | $l$ | $L_{\text{few}}$ | $l$ | – | ✓ |
| BERTE$_l{}^{L_{\text{mix}}}$ | $\|L\|$ | $\{l\} \cup L_{\text{mix}}$ | $\{l\} \cup L_{\text{mix}}$ | $\{l\} \cup L_{\text{mix}}$ | $l \rightarrow L_{\text{mix}}$ | × |
| multi$_{\text{en}}$BERTE$^{L_{\text{mix}}}$ | 1 | $\{l\} \cup L_{\text{mix}}$ | en | $\{l\} \cup L_{\text{mix}}$ | $l \rightarrow L_{\text{mix}}$ | ✓ |
| multi$_{\text{few}}$BERTE$^{L_{\text{mix}}}$ | 1 | $\{l\} \cup L_{\text{mix}}$ | $L_{\text{few}}$ | $\{l\} \cup L_{\text{mix}}$ | $l \rightarrow L_{\text{mix}}$ | ✓ |

Table 6: Results by query category. The following symbols indicate statistically significant improvement over: ESim ($\star$), KEWER ($\dagger$), EM-BERT ($\diamond$) , and BERTE$_{en}$ ($\circ$). Best result in each column is in boldface.

| | SemSearch | | | INEX-LD | | | QALD-2 | | | ListSearch | | |
|---|---|---|---|---|---|---|---|---|---|---|---|---|
| **Model** | **nDCG$_{10}$** | **nDCG$_{100}$** | **MAP** | **nDCG$_{10}$** | **nDCG$_{100}$** | **MAP** | **nDCG$_{10}$** | **nDCG$_{100}$** | **MAP** | **nDCG$_{10}$** | **nDCG$_{100}$** | **MAP** |
| BM25F$_{ca}$ | 0.628 | 0.72 | 0.529 | 0.439 | 0.5296 | 0.341 | 0.3689 | 0.461 | 0.305 | 0.425 | 0.511 | 0.359 |
| KEWER | 0.661 | 0.733 | **0.563** | 0.467 | 0.53 | 0.342 | 0.467 | 0.53 | 0.315 | 0.44 | 0.521 | 0.375 |
| ESim | 0.660 | 0.736 | 0.55 | 0.466 | 0.552$^{\dagger}$ | 0.364$^{\dagger}$ | 0.39 | 0.483 | 0.326 | 0.452 | 0.535 | 0.386 |
| EM-BERT | 0.664 | **0.744** | - | 0.479 | 0.561$^{\dagger}$ | - | **0.483**$^{\star\dagger\circ}$ | **0.543**$^{\star\dagger}$ | - | **0.544**$^{\star\dagger\circ}$ | 0.579$^{\star\dagger}$ | - |
| BERTE$_{en}$ | **0.669** | 0.734 | 0.557 | **0.509**$^{\star\dagger\diamond}$ | **0.585**$^{\star\dagger\diamond}$ | **0.392**$^{\star\dagger}$ | 0.441$^{\star\dagger}$ | 0.521$^{\star\dagger}$ | **0.361**$^{\star\dagger}$ | 0.499$^{\star\dagger}$ | **0.58**$^{\star\dagger}$ | **0.434**$^{\star\dagger}$ |

Table 7: Reranking results using multi$_{\text{few}}$BERTE and multi$_{\text{few}}$BERTE$^{\{\text{en}\}}$ for a range of additional languages. The best result for each language and metric pair is in boldface.

| | BM25 | | | multi$_{\text{few}}$BERTE | | | multi$_{\text{few}}$BERTE$^{\{\text{en}\}}$ | | |
|---|---|---|---|---|---|---|---|---|---|
| **Model** | **nDCG$_{10}$** | **nDCG$_{100}$** | **MAP** | **nDCG$_{10}$** | **nDCG$_{100}$** | **MAP** | **nDCG$_{10}$** | **nDCG$_{100}$** | **MAP** |
| Dutch | 0.223 | 0.265 | 0.184 | 0.26 | 0.305 | 0.215 | **0.317** | **0.411** | **0.262** |
| German | 0.208 | 0.25 | 0.171 | 0.254 | 0.296 | 0.208 | **0.361** | **0.459** | **0.297** |
| Turkish | 0.155 | 0.184 | 0.129 | 0.181 | 0.214 | 0.15 | **0.254** | **0.332** | **0.212** |
| Portuguese | 0.202 | 0.243 | 0.158 | 0.24 | 0.288 | 0.191 | **0.336** | **0.431** | **0.279** |
| Farsi | 0.218 | 0.276 | 0.185 | 0.249 | 0.31 | 0.209 | **0.285** | **0.374** | **0.232** |
| Russian | 0.177 | 0.214 | 0.138 | 0.205 | 0.246 | 0.16 | **0.345** | **0.441** | **0.286** |

Table 8: Statistics of the studied chapters with respect to DE-v2. The last two rows differ due to entities relevant to more than one query.

| | English | Spanish | Hebrew | Arabic |
|---|---|---|---|---|
| Has abstract | 4,641,784 | 1,100,382 | 161,769 | 368,330 |
| No English | - | 383,963 | 36,710 | 135,527 |
| DE-v2 Judged | 45,685 | 17,028 | 6,749 | 7,924 |
| DE-v2 Relevant | 16,700 | 7,082 | 2,629 | 3,025 |

formed, however, is "Madrid". Examining the results, however, shows that the poor performance can be attributed in part to the annotation step. Without context, this query is open-ended and ambiguous. However, in its top 10, BERTE$_{en}$ included 7 Madrid-based sports teams, of which only 3 were judged as relevant. For example, the entity "Real Madrid C.F.", an arguably highly relevant entity that was included in the top-10 by BERTE$_{en}$, was not judged by the annotators. On the other hand, the top 10 lists of ESim and KEWER were more diverse and better matched the annotators.

## E DBpedia Language Chapters

DE-v2 consists of 467 queries, with entities drawn from the 2015-10 dump from DBPedia. Additionally, relevance assessments are provided for 49,280 query-entity pairs using a 0–2 scale, with 0 being not relevant and 2 highly relevant.

The size of Wikipedia, and thus DBpedia, varies significantly across languages. Table 8 provides statistics of DBpedia 2015 for the languages we studied. English has the largest number of entities, while Arabic and Hebrew are significantly smaller, with Spanish somewhere in the middle. In the context of DE-v2, the lower coverage results in a smaller number of judged entities. Thanks to the Wikimedia foundation's efforts (Redi et al., 2021), the gap between languages is narrowing, but many languages remain low-resourced, covering 10,000 entities or less, with tens of languages, as of 2022, with chapters even smaller than Arabic or Hebrew in 2015.

## F Additional Languages

Recall that multi$_{en}$BERTE and multi$_{few}$BERTE can be used for over 100 languages without fine-tuning the models on these. This allows multi$_{en}$BERTE to be a strong baseline for many languages on the task, thanks to the domain knowledge obtained in the pretraining stage and to the cross lingual capabilities of multilingual LMs. Table 7 lists the results for six additional languages, obtained following the same methodology as our main results. multi$_{few}$BERTE$^{\{en\}}$ was consistently the best performer and its advantage over BM25 and multi$_{few}$BERTE was statistically significant.

## G Missing Entities

In this work, we assumed that while information from different languages may be utilised to rank entities, only entities with coverage in the target language should be returned. There are scenarios, however, where the user would like to retrieve relevant entities even if they are covered only in other languages. Consider, for example, the query "chess world champions". Of the 93 relevant entities covered in the English chapter of DBpedia 2015, only 31 had an Arabic entity. While a user who submits this query in Arabic would typically prefer to see entities in Arabic, they may also be interested in English (or some other language) if relevant entities are unavailable in Arabic.

While the English version of DBPedia is by far the largest, Spanish, Arabic, and Hebrew still offer many entities do not have an English counterpart. For instance, the entities "Roman Ornament" and "Mais el Reem" are only present in the Arabic version. The former, arguably relevant to the query "Roman architecture" (part of DE-v2), was ranked by BERTE in the top 10 for that query. The latter, a play starring Fairuz, a famous Arab singer, demonstrates that, in some cases, entities may only be of interest to speakers of the respective language.

While we hope to explore this setup in future work, initial experiments indicate that, at least in the case of Arabic queries, allowing English entities without Arabic coverage to be returned in the first stage and blending in the English scores like in multi$_{few}$BERTE$^{\{en\}}$, can improve performance by over 30%. We would stress, however, that the way to judge non-Arabic entities is not trivial and may depend on the task.

This brings the question: Are all languages equal in terms of their relevance, or do users prefer some languages over others? We hope that truly multilingual collections will be made available to allow evaluation of this scenario.

# Few-Shot Cross-Lingual Learning for Event Detection

**Luis F. Guzman-Nateras[1], Viet Dac Lai[1],**
**Franck Dernoncourt[2], and Thien Huu Nguyen[1]**
[1] Department of Computer Science, University of Oregon, Eugene, OR, USA
[2] Adobe Research, Seattle, WA, USA
{lfguzman,vietl,thien}@cs.uoregon.edu,
franck.dernoncourt@adobe.com

## Abstract

Cross-Lingual Event Detection (CLED) models are capable of performing the Event Detection (ED) task in multiple languages. Such models are trained using data from a *source* language and then evaluated on data from a distinct *target* language. Training is usually performed in the standard supervised setting with labeled data available in the source language. The Few-Shot Learning (FSL) paradigm is yet to be explored for CLED despite its inherent advantage of allowing models to better generalize to unseen event types. As such, in this work we study the CLED task under an FSL setting. Our contribution is threefold: first, we introduce a novel FSL classification method based on Optimal Transport (OT); second, we present a novel regularization term to incorporate the global distance between the support and query sets; and third, we adapt our approach to the cross-lingual setting by exploiting the alignment between source and target data. Our experiments on three, syntactically-different, target languages show the applicability of our approach and its effectiveness at improving the cross-lingual performance of few-shot models for event detection.

## 1 Introduction

Event Detection (ED) is a significant sub-task within the larger task of Information Extraction (IE) in Natural Language Processing (NLP). Its core purpose is to identify the words, or phrases, that most clearly express the occurrence of an event, known as event *triggers*, and to correctly categorize them into a discrete set of classes. For instance, in the sentence:

*Frank* ***purchased*** *his dream house yesterday.*

the word "**purchased**" should be identified by an ED system as the trigger of a `Transaction:Transfer-Ownership` event type[1]. Event detection is a highly active research area which has been lately dominated by deep-learning-based approaches (Sha et al., 2018; Wadden et al., 2019; Zhang et al., 2019a; Yang et al., 2019a; Nguyen and Nguyen, 2019; Zhang et al., 2020; Liu et al., 2020; Lu et al., 2021). Most of these works use the standard supervised learning paradigm in which lots of labeled data is required during training. However, a significant limitation of models trained in this manner is their inability to properly generalize to new event types that were unobserved during training (Lai et al., 2020b).

**Few-Shot Learning**: In contrast to the supervised approach, Few-Shot Learning (FSL) proposes a training setting in which a model must quickly learn new concepts from just a few examples, similar to how humans can learn to detect and identify new objects after having observed only a couple of instances. During an FSL training iteration, a model is given a *support* set and a *query* set, each of which contains only a handful of examples for a set of classes. Then, the model is trained to predict the classes for the query samples based on the labeled support samples. Under these constrained training settings, supervised training easily results in model overfitting due to the limited availability of training data. Furthermore, in FSL, a model is evaluated on its ability to generalize to new, unobserved types. To achieve this, during testing an FSL model is provided with new support and query sets whose samples belong to entirely new classes never observed during training.

Typical FSL approaches consist of obtaining a vector representation for each sample and then performing classification based on the distance between such vectors, e.g., Matching Networks (Vinyals et al., 2016), Relation Networks (Sung et al., 2018), and Prototypical Networks (Snell et al., 2017). The key differences between these approaches often come down to the way the sample representations are generated, and how the distance between such representations is

[1]Event type example taken from ACE05 dataset.



*Proceedings of the The 2nd Workshop on Multi-lingual Representation Learning (MRL)*, pages 16 - 27
December 8, 2022 ©2022 Association for Computational Linguistics

determined.

FSL training allows a model to easily extend to new classes as it only needs to see a few labeled examples in order to successfully classify them. FSL has been applied successfully for many tasks. Recently, there have been several efforts that explore event detection under a few-shot learning setting (FSLED) (Lai et al., 2020a,b; Deng et al., 2020; Lai et al., 2021a,b; Cong et al., 2021; Shen et al., 2021; Chen et al., 2021).

**Cross-Lingual Event Detection**: Cross-Lingual Learning (CLL) is a paradigm that aims at transferring the knowledge from one language to another (Pikuliak et al., 2021). CLL can help overcome the lack of data availability that plagues many languages and allow for the creation of NLP-based tools that can benefit their communities.

As such, Cross-lingual Event Detection (CLED) aims at detecting and classifying event triggers with the added complexity of operating on two separate languages. These two languages are referred to as *source* and *target*, respectively. In standard *zero-shot* training, a CLED model is trained using labeled data belonging to the source language exclusively. Then, at testing time, data from the target language is used to evaluate the model's performance (M'hamdi et al., 2019; Majewska et al., 2021; Nguyen et al., 2021; Guzman-Nateras et al., 2022).

**Contributions**: A proper effort on CLED under FSL conditions has yet to be explored despite the potential advantages it could contribute to cross-lingual models. Hence, we recognize this opportunity and propose the novel Few-Shot Cross-Lingual Event Detection (FSCLED) task to integrate these two settings. We consider the following as our main contributions:

- To the best of our knowledge, this is the first effort at integrating the few-shot and cross-lingual settings for the event detection task. To provide foundation for future research, we first evaluate the performance of representative FSL methods (Vinyals et al., 2016; Snell et al., 2017; Sung et al., 2018) in this task.
- We propose a novel optimal-transport-based method for FSL classification that leverages the optimal alignment between the support and query samples.
- We address a limitation of traditional FSL methods by incorporating a novel regularization term that considers the global distance between the support and query sets.
- To adapt our approach to the cross-lingual setting, we promote language-invariant representation learning by integrating the distance between source and target data into our model.
- Our experiments on three diverse target languages (Arabic, Chinese, and Spanish) show that our approach improves the best-performing FSL methods in the new FSCLED setting and that our proposed training signals can be seamlessly incorporated with other FSL models to improve their performance on the challenging FSCLED task.

The rest of the paper is organized as follows: Section 2 provides a formal definition for FSCLED task, Section 3 describes the details our proposed approach, Section 4 presents the results of our experiments, and finally, we present our conclusions in Section 6.

## 2 Problem Definition

### 2.1 Few-shot Event Detection

We follow the same problem formulation as in prior work for few-shot ED (Lai et al., 2020b; Deng et al., 2020; Lai et al., 2021a). In particular, we cast event detection as a token classification task in which a model must learn to correctly classify the trigger tokens. In a standard FSL setting, an iteration involves a support set $\mathcal{S}$ and a query set $\mathcal{Q}$ that cover sample sentences for $N$ distinct classes; each class is represented by $K \in [1, 10]$ examples. Additionally, for event detection, $\mathcal{S}$ and $\mathcal{Q}$ are extended with an additional negative, or non-event, type *NULL* (also with $K$ examples) (Lai et al., 2021a). In this manner, given an input sentence along with an trigger candidate, an FSL model for ED should be able to predict whether the candidate is an event trigger as well as which event type is evoked by the trigger (if any).

Hence, the formal definition of the FSL task is as follows. The $\mathcal{S}$ and $\mathcal{Q}$ sets are defined by:

$$\mathcal{S} = \{(s_i^{j(S)}, t_i^{j(S)}, y_i^{j(S)})\}$$
$$\mathcal{Q} = \{(s_i^{j(\mathcal{Q})}, t_i^{j(\mathcal{Q})}, y_i^{j(\mathcal{Q})})\}$$

where $i \in [1, K]^2$, $j \in [0, N]$ ($j = 0$ is used for the non-event type), and a single sample

[2] We use the same number of samples for each class in both the support and query sets.

$(s_i^{j(\cdot)}, t_i^{j(\cdot)}, y_i^{j(\cdot)})$ contains a sentence $s_i^{j(\cdot)}$, a trigger candidate word $t_i^{j(\cdot)}$ in $s_i^{j(\cdot)}$, and an event label type $y_i^{j(\cdot)}$. As per FSL requirements, the label set used when training the model must be disjoint from those used when evaluating the model to properly assess the model's ability to generalize to unobserved classes.

### 2.2 Few-shot Cross-lingual Event Detection

Cross-Lingual Learning (CLL) methods (Pikuliak et al., 2021) emerged from the need to create NLP models for low-resource *target* languages that lack the required labeled data to perform supervised learning. The core idea is to train models using available labeled data from a high-resource *source* language with techniques that allow them to learn task-specific language-invariant features. The models are then evaluated on the desired target language without access to target-language labeled data during training. This setting is known as *zero-shot* cross-lingual transfer learning[3].

As such in the zero-shot cross-lingual ED task, the labeled samples used during training $\mathcal{D}_{train}$ and development $\mathcal{D}_{dev}$ belong to the source language while the ones used for testing $\mathcal{D}_{test}$ correspond to the target languages (M'hamdi et al., 2019; Majewska et al., 2021).

In this work, we combine the aforementioned *zero-shot* approach to cross-lingual evaluation with the added intricacy of the standard few-shot setting. During training, the models are presented with a support set $\mathcal{S}^{src}$ and a query set $\mathcal{Q}^{src}$ that belong to the source language. Then, at testing time, the support set $\mathcal{S}^{tgt}$ and query set $\mathcal{Q}^{tgt}$ are taken from the target language for evaluation. Furthermore, given the FSL setting, the label set used during training is disjoint from the label set for development and testing. We designate this novel task as Few-Shot Cross-Lingual Event Detection (FSCLED).

## 3 Model

As done in prior FSL models for ED (Lai et al., 2021a), our model for FSCLED involves two main components: an encoder $E$ and a classifier $C$.

### 3.1 Encoder

The encoder's purpose is to obtain a representation vector $v_i^{j(\cdot)}$ for each sample in the support $\mathcal{S}$ and query $\mathcal{Q}$ sets:

$$v_i^{j(\cdot)} = E(s_i^{j(\cdot)}, t_i^{j(\cdot)}) \in \mathbb{R}^d$$

where $d$ is the vector size, and $\cdot$ can be either $\mathcal{S}$ or $\mathcal{Q}$.

Following recent work on CLED, we leverage the pretrained multilingual language model (mLM) mBERT (Devlin et al., 2019) for our encoder to take advantage of its ability to induce language-invariant representations (Majewska et al., 2021). Additionally, we stack a Multi-Layer Perceptron (MLP) layer on top of the transformer outputs to create our multilingual encoder, called BERTMLP (Yang et al., 2019b). Then, we employ the vector representation for $t_i^{j(\cdot)}$ generated by BERTMLP to serve as the representation $v_i^{j(\cdot)}$.

### 3.2 Classifier

For convenience, let $v^s$ and $v^q$ be the representation vectors for the sample $s \in \mathcal{S}$ and $q \in \mathcal{Q}$, and $V^{(\mathcal{S})}$ and $V^{(\mathcal{Q})}$ be the sets of representation vectors for all samples in the support and query sets, respectively.

The classifier $C$ aims to predict a label $y^q$ for each instance $q$ in the query set based on its representation $v^q$ and the representations of the samples in the support set $V^{(\mathcal{S})}$:

$$y^q = C(v^q, V^{(\mathcal{S})})$$

Given the multilingual representations $v_i^{j(\cdot)}$, a feasible approach is to employ existing FSL models (e.g., Matching, Relation, or Prototypical networks) to perform classification in FSCLED. The models can then be trained using the standard cross-entropy loss.

#### 3.2.1 Optimal Transport

We recognize, nonetheless, a potential issue with traditional FSL models in that they only consider local distances between individual pairs of samples in the support and query sets. In the case of Prototypical Networks (Snell et al., 2017), for example, the distance is between a query sample and a class prototype. Hence, if the overall global distance between the support and query sets is large, a small difference between the distances of two individual samples becomes less reliable to determine the label assignments. In turn, we argue that the global distances between $\mathcal{S}$ and $\mathcal{Q}$ should be minimized to improve the reliability of the distances between individual pairs for accurate FSCLED.

[3]Not to be confused with standard zero-shot learning where zero data for a new class is used by models to perform prediction.

To this end, we propose utilizing Optimal Transport (OT) (Villani, 2008) to estimate the distance between the support $\mathcal{S}$ and query $\mathcal{Q}$ sets for FSCLED. In broad terms, OT aims to find the most cost-effective transformation between two discrete probability distributions. Optimal transport employs a cost function to compute the cost of transforming data points from one distribution to the other. If a distance function (Euclidean, Cosine, etc.) is used as such cost function, the obtained minimum cost is known as the Wasserstein distance. Formally, OT solves the following optimization problem:

$$\pi^*(x,z) = \min_{\pi \in \prod(x,z)} \sum_{x \in \mathcal{X}} \sum_{z \in \mathcal{Z}} \pi(x,z)\ D(x,z)$$
$$\textbf{s.t. } x \sim P(x) \text{ and } z \sim P(z)$$

where $P(x)$ and $P(z)$ are probability distributions for the $\mathcal{X}$ and $\mathcal{Z}$ domains, and $D$ is a distance-based cost function for mapping $\mathcal{X}$ to $\mathcal{Z}$, $D(x,z) : \mathcal{X} \times \mathcal{Z} \longrightarrow \mathbb{R}_+$. Finally, $\pi^*(x,z)$ is the optimal joint distribution over the set of all joint distributions $\prod(x,z)$ (i.e., the optimal transformation between $\mathcal{Z}$ and $\mathcal{X}$). The described OT optimization problem is, however, intractable as it requires optimizing over the infinite set $\prod(x,z)$. In practice, we instead solve an entropy-based relaxation of the discrete OT problem using the Sinkhorn algorithm (Cuturi, 2013).

#### 3.2.2 Few-Shot Classification via OT

To adapt FSL classification into an OT formulation we consider the support $\mathcal{S}$ and query $\mathcal{Q}$ sets as the two domains to be transformed. Each sample in $\mathcal{S}$ and $\mathcal{Q}$ represents a data point in the corresponding distribution. The probability distributions $P(\mathcal{S})$ and $P(\mathcal{Q})$ are estimated using an *event-presence* module $F$. In our work, $F$ is a feed-forward neural network (FFNN) with a single output and sigmoid activation that scores the likelihood that a trigger candidate word is actually an event trigger. $F$ receives as input the vector representation of a trigger $v^{(\cdot)}$ from either $\mathcal{S}$ or $\mathcal{Q}$, and outputs a scalar in the range [0-1]. Then, the probability distributions for $\mathcal{S}$ and $\mathcal{Q}$ are obtained by computing the Softmax over $F$'s outputs for the samples in each set:

$$P(\mathcal{S}) = \mathit{Softmax}(F(V^{(\mathcal{S})}))$$
$$P(\mathcal{Q}) = \mathit{Softmax}(F(V^{(\mathcal{Q})}))$$

To supervise the event-presence module $F$, we include the cross-entropy loss for event identification into the overall loss function:

$$\mathcal{L}_{ident} = \sum_{s \in \mathcal{S}} i^s \cdot \sigma(F(v^s)) + (1 - i^s) \cdot \sigma(1 - F(v^s))$$

where $i^s$ is the golden binary variable to indicate if $s$ corresponds to an event trigger or not, and $\sigma$ is the sigmoid function.

In our model, the distance $D(q,s)$ between a sample in $q \in \mathcal{Q}$ and a sample $s \in \mathcal{S}$ is based on the Euclidean distance between their representation vectors $v^s$ and $v^q$:

$$D(q,s) = \sqrt{\sum_{i \in d} (v_i^q - v_i^s)^2}$$

Once the OT algorithm converges, or the maximum number of iterations is reached, the obtained optimal alignment matrix $\pi^*$ is a squared matrix with dimensions $((N+1)*K) \times ((N+1)*K)$ where each entry $\pi^*_{r,c}$ represents the alignment score between the $r$-th query sample and $c$-th support sample.

The conversion from matrix index ($r$, $c$) to event type ($j$) and sample number ($i$) can be computed in a straightforward manner as all samples from the same class (event type) are contiguous: $j = r//K, i = r \ \% \ K$ where // and % are the integer division and modulo operators.

To perform sample classification and train our FSCLED model, we first use the optimal alignment matrix $\pi^*$ to compute a likelihood vector $\alpha$ for each query sample (i.e., the $r$-th) by performing class-based pooling with respect to the $N+1$ classes:

$$\alpha_r^j = \sum_{i \in [0, K-1]} \pi^*_{r,(j*K)+i}$$

where $j \in [0, N]$. As such, the resulting $\alpha_r$ vectors have $N+1$ dimensions. And the complete $\alpha$ matrix has a $((N+1)*K) \times (N+1)$ size. We then apply a Softmax operation over $\alpha_r$ to obtain a class distribution $P_r$ for the $r$-th query sample: $P_r = \mathit{Softmax}(\alpha_r)$. $P_r$ will then be used for training and inference in our model. In particular, we use the negative log-likelihood loss as the main term of our overall training loss:

$$\mathcal{L}_{class} = -\sum_r P_r(y_r)$$

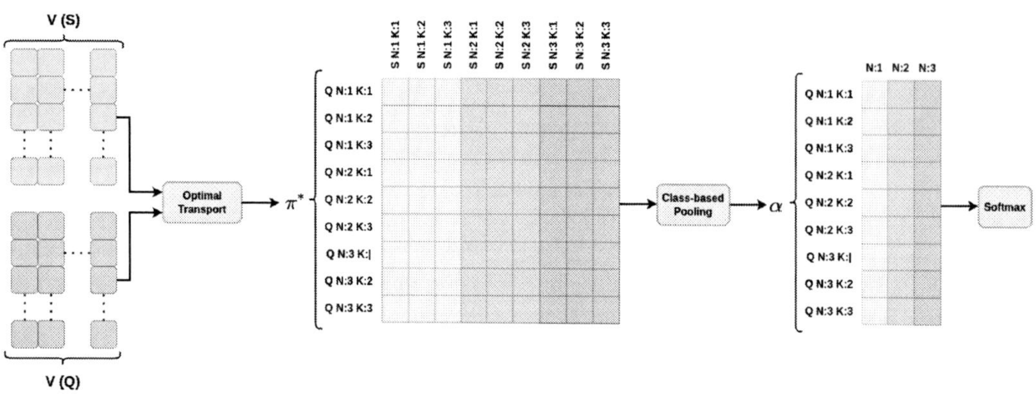


Figure 1: OT-based classification procedure example for a 3-way, 3-shot setting.

where $y_r$ is the golden class for the $r$-th query example. Figure 1 shows a visualization of the described procedure for a 3-way, 3-shot setting. As such, a key distinction is that the class distribution $P_r$ in our FSL method is obtained from the support-query alignment scores $\pi^*$ in optimal transport. This is in contrast to previous FSL models where the class distributions tend to be computed directly from sample representations.

### 3.3 Support-Query Distance

In addition to our optimal-transport-based FSL classifier, we propose computing the Wasserstein distance between $\mathcal{S}$ and $\mathcal{Q}$ and including it into the loss function as a regularization term to minimize the overall distance between the support and query sets for reliable predictions. We obtain the aforementioned Wasserstein distance using the optimal alignment matrix $\pi^*$:

$$\mathcal{L}_{dist} = \sum_{s \in \mathcal{S}} \sum_{q \in \mathcal{Q}} \pi^*_{r,c} \, D(q, s)$$

where $r$ and $c$ are the matrix indexes for $q$ and $s$, respectively.

### 3.4 Cross-Lingual Distance

To adapt our approach to the cross-lingual setting, we aim to encourage language-invariant representation learning by regularizing our model so the representation vectors of samples in the source and target languages are closer to each other in the embedding space.

Following the work by Guzman-Nateras et al. (2022), which leveraged OT to successfully align samples taken the source and target languages to improve adversarial language adaptation, we propose to further use OT to estimate the distance between samples in the source and target languages so that it can be included in the overall loss function as an additional regularization term for minimization.

To this end, given the unavailability of labeled data in the target language, we make use of unlabeled data – often readily available for most languages – instead. For convenience, let $\mathcal{R}$ and $\mathcal{T}$ represent the source-language and target-language data set respectively. In any given FSL training iteration, the support $\mathcal{S}$ and the query $\mathcal{Q}$ sets comprise the $\mathcal{R}$ set for the source language. To constitute the set representing the target language $\mathcal{T}$, we collect enough unlabeled samples to match the size of $\mathcal{R}$.

Thus, similarly to the OT formulation described in section 3.2.2 that computes the optimal alignment between two domains $\mathcal{S}$ and $\mathcal{Q}$, in this context we consider the source- and target-language data set $\mathcal{R}$ and $\mathcal{T}$ as the domains to be transformed. Subsequently, we employ our BERTMLP multilingual encoder to obtain representation vectors for the samples in both $\mathcal{R}$ and $\mathcal{T}$ that will serve as the inputs for the OT algorithm.

It is important to note that, due to the unavailability of the class information for the target-language samples $\mathcal{T}$ for training, it is less reliable to estimate the probability distribution $P(\mathcal{T})$ for the target language using the event-presence prediction module $F$ as performed for $P(\mathcal{S})$ and $P(\mathcal{Q})$. Hence, we initialize $P(\mathcal{R})$ and $P(\mathcal{T})$ as uniform distributions for the OT computation in this case.

Under this setting, we solve the OT equation to obtain the optimal alignment matrix $\rho^*$ between $\mathcal{R}$ and $\mathcal{T}$. The Wasserstein distance $\mathcal{L}_{cross}$ is then computed and integrated into the overall loss function for regularization:

$$\mathcal{L}_{cross} = \sum_{r \in \mathcal{R}} \sum_{t \in \mathcal{T}} \rho^*_{n,m} D(r, t)$$

where $n$ and $m$ are the matrix indexes for $r$ and $t$, respectively.

#### 3.4.1 Full Model

Finally, the overall loss function $\mathcal{L}$ used to train our Optimal-Transport-based Event Detection (OTED) model is: $\mathcal{L} = \mathcal{L}_{class} + \alpha\mathcal{L}_{ident} + \beta\mathcal{L}_{dist} + \gamma\mathcal{L}_{cross}$ where $\alpha$, $\beta$, and $\gamma$ are trade-off hyperparameters.

## 4 Experiments

### 4.1 Datasets

We use the ACE05 (Walker et al., 2006) and ERE05 (Song et al., 2015) datasets, which are frequently used as the standard benchmarks in cross-lingual event detection efforts (M'hamdi et al., 2019; Majewska et al., 2021; Nguyen et al., 2021; Guzman-Nateras et al., 2022), to evaluate our FSCLED models. In particular, we utilize data in three languages (English, Chinese, and Arabic) from ACE05 and two languages (English and Spanish) from ERE05. Both ACE05 and ERE05 organize their event classes in a hierarchical structure of types and subtypes. For example, in the `Transaction:Transfer-Ownership` class, `Transaction` is the main event type and `Transfer-Ownership` is the subtype. The two datasets have distinct label sets as ACE05 includes 33 event subtypes and ACE05-ERE has 38 event subtypes. Each language in the datasets has its own training/development/test split.

| Dataset | # Types | Removed Types |
|---|---|---|
| ACE05-English (train) | 19 | Justice:Extradite<br>Justice:Pardon |
| ACE05-English (dev) | 12 | |
| ACE05-Chinese (test) | 11 | Life:Divorce |
| ACE05-Arabic (test) | 9 | Life:Be-Born<br>Life:Divorce<br>Personnel:Nominate |
| ERE05-English (train) | 22 | Business:Bankrupcy |
| ERE05-English (dev) | 15 | |
| ERE05-Spanish (test) | 14 | Personnel:Nominate |

Table 1: Dataset preparation for FSCLED. The total number of remaining types is shown for each data section alongside the removed subtypes without a sufficient number of samples for episodic training.

#### 4.1.1 FSL Preprocessing

Standard datasets used for supervised learning, such as ACE05 and ERE05, can also be exploited for FSL by simulating a limited-data-availability setting via *episodic training* (Lai et al., 2021a). An *episode* is created by sampling a set of $K$ examples from a small subset of classes $N$ out of the total number of classes in the dataset. This setting is referred to as *N-way, K-shot* and $N$ and $K$ are usually selected in the range of 1 to 10.

Following previous work on FSL for ED (Lai et al., 2020b), we further truncate the training, development, and testing portions of the datasets for each language to satisfy the conditions for FSL: (1) the set of event types in the training data must be disjoint from those for the development and test data; (2) the types in each set must contain at least 5 samples (to facilitate 5+1-way 5-shot learning with the additional +1 class being used for non-triggers); and (3) the training set should have as many samples as possible.

Adapting these criteria to cross-lingual FSL, we separate the samples belonging to the `Business`, `Contact`, `Conflict`, and `Justice` types to be used for training purposes. Meanwhile, we leave the samples belonging to the `Life`, `Movement`, `Personnel`, and `Transaction` event types for development and testing. Furthermore, we remove any subtypes that do not contain enough samples to construct an episode (5 samples minimum). Table 1 shows the total number of remaining classes for each portion of data in different languages for our FSCLED setting. We also list the event subtypes that are removed to meet the criteria in each dataset portion. Note that, while the training label set must be disjoint from the development and testing label sets, there is no requirement for the latter two to be disjoint as done in (Lai et al., 2020b).

As the final step in our data preprocessing, we obtain the samples for the non-event type by selecting words, other than the actual triggers, from annotated sentences similar to the approach taken by Lai et al. (2020b).

### 4.2 Training Details

#### 4.2.1 Episode Composition

In all our experiments, English is considered the sole source language as it is often used as the benchmark source language in cross-lingual efforts. As such, training and development episodes are constructed from English data. However, given the FSL constraints, their samples must come from

| Model Version | Chinese P | Chinese R | Chinese F1 | Arabic P | Arabic R | Arabic F1 | Spanish P | Spanish R | Spanish F1 |
|---|---|---|---|---|---|---|---|---|---|
| Relation | 78.62 | 79.1 | 78.86 | 52.89 | 53.35 | 53.12 | 48.53 | 48.77 | 48.65 |
| Matching | 85.44 | 85.79 | 85.64 | 66.21 | 65.92 | 66.06 | 56.77 | 56.95 | 56.86 |
| Prototypical | 85.81 | 86.12 | 85.96 | 70.02 | 70.44 | 70.23 | 60.87 | 61.17 | 61.02 |
| OTED (ours) | **86.05** | **86.29** | **86.17** | **70.66** | **70.98** | **70.82** | **62.25** | **62.49** | **62.37** |

Table 2: Performance for cross-lingual few-shot event detection. English is the source language used for training. The experiments for Chinese and Arabic are done over ACE05 while ERE05 is used for Spanish.

disjoint label sets. Hence, in any training iteration, the samples used for both the support $\mathcal{S}$ and query $\mathcal{Q}$ sets are in English and belong to the training subtypes of the `Business`, `Contact`, `Conflict`, or `Justice` types. In contrast, during validation, $\mathcal{S}$ and $\mathcal{Q}$ will still be in English but their samples belong to the validation subtypes of the `Life`, `Movement`, `Personnel`, or `Transaction` types.

Furthermore, as cross-lingual models are evaluated on the target language, during testing, episodes are created from target-language data and their samples belong to the same types as the development episodes, i.e., the `Life`, `Movement`, `Personnel`, or `Transaction` types.

#### 4.2.2 Additional Settings

We utilize a fixed 6-way (5 event types plus the non-event), 5-shot setting for all the experiments. We initialize our encoder $E$ with the pretrained `bert-base-multilingual-cased` transformer model (Devlin et al., 2019) and add a single linear layer followed by a hyperbolic tangent non-linearity on top. Our final encoder representations have 512 dimensions. All hyperparameters were tuned on the development data of the source language, and all reported values are the average obtained from five runs with different random seeds. Our fine-tuning process suggests the following values:

- AdamW (Loshchilov and Hutter, 2017) as the optimizer.
- Using 5 warm up epochs.
- Learning rate is set to $3e^{-4}$.
- The $\alpha, \beta$ and $\gamma$ hyper-parameters are set to $0.1, 0.01$, and $0.01$ respectively.
- The batch size is set to 16.
- 512 for the dimensionality of the layers in the feed-forward networks.
- A dropout of 10% for added regularization during training.

### 4.3 Results

We compare our Optimal-Transport-based Event Detection (OTED) model, against three typical FSL models adapted to FSCLED as the baselines: Matching networks (Vinyals et al., 2016), Prototypical networks (Snell et al., 2017), and Relation networks (Sung et al., 2018). All models utilize the same mBERT-based encoder for a fair comparison. We use English as the source language during training as it is recurrently utilized the source-language benchmark (M'hamdi et al., 2019; Majewska et al., 2021) due to its high-resource availability.

Our main experiment results are presented in Table 2 which shows that our OTED model consistently outperforms the best-performing baselines in every target language: Chinese (+0.21%), Arabic (+0.59%), and Spanish (+1.35%). We believe these results validate OTED as a suitable and effective alternative for FSCLED.

Furthermore, an additional benefit of OTED's training signals (i.e., the loss terms $\mathcal{L}_{ident}$, $\mathcal{L}_{dist}$, and $\mathcal{L}_{cross}$) is that they can be directly integrated into any existing FSL methods. Thus, we conduct a supplementary set of experiments where we integrate the loss function terms from OTED into Relation, Matching, and Prototypical networks (i.e., combining our training signals in OTED with the standard cross-entropy losses of such FSL baselines). The performance for these integrated models are presented in Table 3. Comparing the corresponding performance in Tables 2 and 3, it is evident that integrating OTED with traditional FSL methods leads to overall performance improvement across different target languages and FSL models, further demonstrating the benefits and applicability of OTED for FSCLED.

| Model Version | Target Language | | |
|---|---|---|---|
| | **Chinese** | **Arabic** | **Spanish** |
| Relation + OTED | 79.36 | 53.41 | 48.89 |
| Matching + OTED | 85.88 | 66.21 | 56.97 |
| Prototypical + OTED | **86.42** | **71.11** | **62.43** |

Table 3: Model performance for integrating OTED into traditional FSL methods. F1 scores are reported.

| Model | Target Language | | |
|---|---|---|---|
| | Chinese | Arabic | Spanish |
| OTED (full) | 86.17 | 70.82 | 62.37 |
| -$\mathcal{L}_{dist}$ | 85.63 | 70.57 | 61.85 |
| -$\mathcal{L}_{cross}$ | 85.45 | 70.22 | 61.78 |
| -$\mathcal{L}_{dist}$ -$\mathcal{L}_{cross}$ | 85.25 | 69.44 | 61.19 |
| -$\mathcal{L}_{ident}$ - $\mathcal{L}_{dist}$ - $\mathcal{L}_{cross}$ | 84.67 | 68.21 | 60.65 |

Table 4: Ablation results over the test data.

### 4.4 Ablation study

To evaluate the contribution of different proposed components (i.e., $\mathcal{L}_{ident}$, $\mathcal{L}_{dist}$, and $\mathcal{L}_{cross}$), we perform an ablation study whose outcomes are presented in Table 4. The left-most column indicates the components being removed from the overall loss $\mathcal{L}$. The first two rows show the performance when either the Wasserstein-distance loss term, i.e., $\mathcal{L}_{dist}$ or $\mathcal{L}_{cross}$ is removed. As expected, removing any of them hurts the performance of OTED across different target languages. This demonstrates the importance of considering the global distances between query and support sets, and the necessity of adapting to the cross-lingual setting by leveraging unlabeled target-language data. Furthermore, the performance of OTED suffers even more when both $\mathcal{L}_{dist}$ and $\mathcal{L}_{cross}$ are excluded.

Similarly, when $\mathcal{L}_{ident}$ is removed in the last row, the performance is also further reduced, dropping significantly by more than 1.5% for Chinese and Arabic compared to the full model. Note that removing $\mathcal{L}_{ident}$ has deeper implications as, in such case, the event-presence module $F$ is not trained. In turn, the $P(\mathcal{S})$ and $P(\mathcal{Q})$ distributions for the support and query sets cannot be estimated reliably and are instead initialized using uniform distributions in the OT computation. These results thus confirm the usefulness of the event identification loss to support the OT computation in our model.

## 5 Related Work

Event detection has been thoroughly studied over the years. Early ED efforts were based on handcrafted features (Ahn, 2006; Ji and Grishman, 2008; Patwardhan and Riloff, 2009; Liao and Grishman, 2010a,b; Hong et al., 2011; McClosky et al., 2011; Li et al., 2013; Miwa et al., 2014; Yang and Mitchell, 2016). More recently, deep learning techniques such as recurrent neural networks (Nguyen et al., 2016a; Sha et al., 2018; Nguyen and Nguyen, 2019), convolutional neural networks (Nguyen and Grishman, 2015; Chen et al., 2015; Nguyen et al., 2016b), graph convolutional networks (Nguyen and Grishman, 2018a; Yan et al., 2019), adversarial networks (Hong et al., 2018)(Zhang et al., 2019b), pre-trained language models (Wadden et al., 2019; Zhang et al., 2019a; Yang et al., 2019a; Zhang et al., 2020; Liu et al., 2020), and generative models (Lu et al., 2021) have been prevalent. Nevertheless, these works study ED under a supervised or semi-supervised setting.

Alternatively, ED was recently formulated as a few-shot task (Lai et al., 2021a). In a short time, several methods have been proposed using a variety of techniques such as meta-learning(Deng et al., 2020, Shen et al., 2021), cross task prototyping (Lai et al., 2021a), dependency graphs (Lai et al., 2021b), causal modeling (Cong et al., 2021), and label dependency via conditional random fields (Chen et al., 2021).

Previous works on cross-lingual ED generally make use of cross-lingual resources such as bilingual dictionaries or parallel corpora (Muis et al., 2018; Liu et al., 2019) to address the differences between languages. More recent approaches exploit the language-invariant characteristics of pre-trained multilingual language models (Hambardzumyan et al., 2020) along with complementary features such as label dependency (M'hamdi et al., 2019), verb-class knowledge (Majewska et al., 2021), and class-aware cross-lingual alignment (Nguyen et al., 2021).

Optimal transport has also been recently used in cross-lingual settings for information extraction tasks such as event co-reference resolution (Phung et al., 2021) and event detection (Guzman-Nateras et al., 2022). However, the amalgamation of the few-shot and cross-lingual settings creates unique challenges that have not been tackled by any related work. Consequently, our proposed use of OT differs from related works as it addresses the global alignment between the support and query sets for few-shot learning and between source and target languages for the cross-lingual setting.

## 6 Conclusion

We explore a novel few-shot cross-lingual setting for event detection that combines the limited training-data conditions of FSL with zero-shot cross-lingual transfer learning. We provide the performance of typical FSL models as the foundations for future research. More importantly, we introduce a novel method for FSCLED that leverages the optimal alignment between query and support sets obtained via OT to perform FSL classification. Our method is complemented by two additional regularization terms that aim at integrating the global distance between support and query sets and fostering language-invariant representations by leveraging unlabeled data in the target language. Our experiments on three target languages demonstrate the advantages of our approach and its general applicability to traditional FSL models. As future work, we intend to extend our method to other related tasks in IE such as relation extraction.

## 7 Limitations

As is the case for any research effort, the scale of our work is restricted by time and resource limitations. Supplementary experiments with diverse source/target language pairs could provide a more comprehensive overview of our method's performance and additional insight into its strengths and weaknesses. Episode composition also plays an key role during few-shot training which can introduce some variance in the results. Furthermore, the cross-lingual setting and casting the problem as a token classification task places some important restrictions as prior knowledge of event triggers is required even for target-language data (only the trigger is required, not its label) which could limit the applicability of our method for some low-resource languages. Finally, considerable GPU resources are required to be able to train our model, particularly in order to fit the multilingual transformer encoder.

## Acknowledgement

This research has been supported by the Army Research Office (ARO) grant W911NF-21-1-0112 and the NSF grant CNS-1747798 to the IUCRC Center for Big Learning. This research is also based upon work supported by the Office of the Director of National Intelligence (ODNI), Intelligence Advanced Research Projects Activity (IARPA), via IARPA Contract No. 2019-19051600006 under the Better Extraction from Text Towards Enhanced Retrieval (BETTER) Program. The views and conclusions contained herein are those of the authors and should not be interpreted as necessarily representing the official policies, either expressed or implied, of ARO, ODNI, IARPA, the Department of Defense, or the U.S. Government. The U.S. Government is authorized to reproduce and distribute reprints for governmental purposes notwithstanding any copyright annotation therein. This document does not contain technology or technical data controlled under either the U.S. International Traffic in Arms Regulations or the U.S. Export Administration Regulations.

## References

David Ahn. 2006. The stages of event extraction. In *Proceedings of the Workshop on Annotating and Reasoning about Time and Events*.

Jiawei Chen, Hongyu Lin, Xianpei Han, and Le Sun. 2021. Honey or poison? solving the trigger curse in few-shot event detection via causal intervention. In *Proceedings of the 2021 Conference on Empirical Methods in Natural Language Processing*, pages 8078–8088, Online and Punta Cana, Dominican Republic. Association for Computational Linguistics.

Yubo Chen, Liheng Xu, Kang Liu, Daojian Zeng, and Jun Zhao. 2015. Event extraction via dynamic multi-pooling convolutional neural networks. In *Proceedings of the Annual Meeting of the Association for Computational Linguistics (ACL)*.

Xin Cong, Shiyao Cui, Bowen Yu, Tingwen Liu, Wang Yubin, and Bin Wang. 2021. Few-Shot Event Detection with Prototypical Amortized Conditional Random Field. In *Findings of the Association for Computational Linguistics: ACL-IJCNLP 2021*, pages 28–40, Online. Association for Computational Linguistics.

Marco Cuturi. 2013. Sinkhorn distances: Lightspeed computation of optimal transport. In *Proceedings of the 26th International Conference on Neural Information Processing Systems - Volume 2*.

Shumin Deng, Ningyu Zhang, Jiaojian Kang, Yichi Zhang, Wei Zhang, and Huajun Chen. 2020. *Meta-Learning with Dynamic-Memory-Based Prototypical Network for Few-Shot Event Detection*.

Jacob Devlin, Ming-Wei Chang, Kenton Lee, and Kristina Toutanova. 2019. Bert: Pre-training of deep bidirectional transformers for language understanding. In *NAACL-HLT*.

Luis Guzman-Nateras, Minh Van Nguyen, and Thien Nguyen. 2022. Cross-lingual event detection via optimized adversarial training. In *Proceedings of the 2022 Conference of the North American Chapter of the Association for Computational Linguistics: Human Language Technologies*, pages 5588–5599, Seattle, United States. Association for Computational Linguistics.

Karen Hambardzumyan, Hrant Khachatrian, and Jonathan May. 2020. The role of alignment of multilingual contextualized embeddings in zero-shot cross-lingual transfer for event extraction. In *Collaborative Technologies and Data Science in Artificial Intelligence Applications*.

Yu Hong, Jianfeng Zhang, Bin Ma, Jianmin Yao, Guodong Zhou, and Qiaoming Zhu. 2011. Using cross-entity inference to improve event extraction. In *Proceedings of the Annual Meeting of the Association for Computational Linguistics (ACL)*.

Yu Hong, Wenxuan Zhou, Jingli Zhang, Guodong Zhou, and Qiaoming Zhu. 2018. Self-regulation: Employing a generative adversarial network to improve event detection. In *Proceedings of the 56th Annual Meeting of the Association for Computational Linguistics (Volume 1: Long Papers)*, pages 515–526, Melbourne, Australia. Association for Computational Linguistics.

Heng Ji and Ralph Grishman. 2008. Refining event extraction through cross-document inference. In *Proceedings of the Annual Meeting of the Association for Computational Linguistics (ACL)*.

Viet Lai, Franck Dernoncourt, and Thien Huu Nguyen. 2021a. Learning prototype representations across few-shot tasks for event detection. In *Proceedings of the 2021 Conference on Empirical Methods in Natural Language Processing*, pages 5270–5277, Online and Punta Cana, Dominican Republic. Association for Computational Linguistics.

Viet Dac Lai, Franck Dernoncourt, and Thien Huu Nguyen. 2020a. Exploiting the matching information in the support set for few shot event classification. In *Advances in Knowledge Discovery and Data Mining*.

Viet Dac Lai, Minh Van Nguyen, Thien Huu Nguyen, and Franck Dernoncourt. 2021b. *Graph Learning Regularization and Transfer Learning for Few-Shot Event Detection*.

Viet Dac Lai, Thien Huu Nguyen, and Franck Dernoncourt. 2020b. Extensively matching for few-shot learning event detection. In *Proceedings of the First Joint Workshop on Narrative Understanding, Storylines, and Events*, pages 38–45, Online. Association for Computational Linguistics.

Qi Li, Heng Ji, and Liang Huang. 2013. Joint event extraction via structured prediction with global features. In *Proceedings of the Annual Meeting of the Association for Computational Linguistics (ACL)*.

Shasha Liao and Ralph Grishman. 2010a. Filtered ranking for bootstrapping in event extraction. In *Proceedings of the International Conference on Computational Linguistics (COLING)*.

Shasha Liao and Ralph Grishman. 2010b. Using document level cross-event inference to improve event extraction. In *Proceedings of the Annual Meeting of the Association for Computational Linguistics (ACL)*.

Jian Liu, Yubo Chen, Kang Liu, Wei Bi, and Xiaojiang Liu. 2020. Event extraction as machine reading comprehension. In *Proceedings of the 2020 Conference on Empirical Methods in Natural Language Processing (EMNLP)*.

Jian Liu, Yubo Chen, Kang Liu, and Jun Zhao. 2019. Neural cross-lingual event detection with minimal parallel resources. In *Proceedings of the 2019 Conference on Empirical Methods in Natural Language Processing and the 9th International Joint Conference on Natural Language Processing (EMNLP-IJCNLP)*, pages 738–748, Hong Kong, China. Association for Computational Linguistics.

Ilya Loshchilov and Frank Hutter. 2017. Fixing weight decay regularization in adam.

Yaojie Lu, Hongyu Lin, Jin Xu, Xianpei Han, Jialong Tang, Annan Li, Le Sun, Meng Liao, and Shaoyi Chen. 2021. Text2Event: Controllable sequence-to-structure generation for end-to-end event extraction. In *Proceedings of the 59th Annual Meeting of the Association for Computational Linguistics and the 11th International Joint Conference on Natural Language Processing (Volume 1: Long Papers)*, pages 2795–2806, Online. Association for Computational Linguistics.

Olga Majewska, Ivan Vulić, Goran Glavaš, Edoardo Maria Ponti, and Anna Korhonen. 2021. Verb knowledge injection for multilingual event processing. In *Proceedings of the 59th Annual Meeting of the Association for Computational Linguistics and the 11th International Joint Conference on Natural Language Processing*.

David McClosky, Mihai Surdeanu, and Christopher Manning. 2011. Event extraction as dependency parsing. In *BioNLP Shared Task Workshop*.

Meryem M'hamdi, Marjorie Freedman, and Jonathan May. 2019. Contextualized cross-lingual event trigger extraction with minimal resources. In *Proceedings of the 23rd Conference on Computational Natural Language Learning (CoNLL)*.

Makoto Miwa, Paul Thompson, Ioannis Korkontzelos, and Sophia Ananiadou. 2014. Comparable study of event extraction in newswire and biomedical domains. In *Proceedings of the International Conference on Computational Linguistics (COLING)*.

Aldrian Obaja Muis, Naoki Otani, Nidhi Vyas, Ruochen Xu, Yiming Yang, Teruko Mitamura, and Eduard Hovy. 2018. Low-resource cross-lingual event type detection via distant supervision with minimal effort. In *Proceedings of the 27th International Conference on Computational Linguistics*.

Minh Van Nguyen, Tuan Ngo Nguyen, Bonan Min, and Thien Huu Nguyen. 2021. Crosslingual transfer learning for relation and event extraction via word category and class alignments. In *Proceedings of the 2021 Conference on Empirical Methods in Natural Language Processing*, pages 5414–5426, Online and Punta Cana, Dominican Republic. Association for Computational Linguistics.

Thien Huu Nguyen, Kyunghyun Cho, and Ralph Grishman. 2016a. Joint event extraction via recurrent neural networks. In *Proceedings of the Conference of the North American Chapter of the Association for Computational Linguistics: Human Language Technologies (NAACL-HLT)*.

Thien Huu Nguyen, Lisheng Fu, Kyunghyun Cho, and Ralph Grishman. 2016b. A two-stage approach for extending event detection to new types via neural networks. In *Proceedings of the 1st ACL Workshop on Representation Learning for NLP (RepL4NLP)*.

Thien Huu Nguyen and Ralph Grishman. 2015. Event detection and domain adaptation with convolutional neural networks. In *Proceedings of the Annual Meeting of the Association for Computational Linguistics (ACL)*.

Thien Huu Nguyen and Ralph Grishman. 2018a. Graph convolutional networks with argument-aware pooling for event detection. In *AAAI*.

Trung Minh Nguyen and Thien Huu Nguyen. 2019. One for all: Neural joint modeling of entities and events. In *Association for the Advancement of Artificial Inteligence(AAAI)*.

Siddharth Patwardhan and Ellen Riloff. 2009. A unified model of phrasal and sentential evidence for information extraction. In *Proceedings of the Conference on Empirical Methods in Natural Language Processing (EMNLP)*.

Duy Phung, Hieu Minh Tran, Minh Van Nguyen, and Thien Huu Nguyen. 2021. Learning cross-lingual representations for event coreference resolution with multi-view alignment and optimal transport. In *Proceedings of the 1st Workshop on Multilingual Representation Learning*, pages 62–73, Punta Cana, Dominican Republic. Association for Computational Linguistics.

Matúš Pikuliak, Marián Šimko, and Mária Bieliková. 2021. Cross-lingual learning for text processing: A survey. In *Expert Systems with Applications*.

Lei Sha, Feng Qian, Baobao Chang, and Zhifang Sui. 2018. Jointly extracting event triggers and arguments by dependency-bridge rnn and tensor-based argument interaction. In *Proceedings of the Association for the Advancement of Artificial Intelligence (AAAI)*.

Shirong Shen, Tongtong Wu, Guilin Qi, Yuan-Fang Li, Gholamreza Haffari, and Sheng Bi. 2021. Adaptive knowledge-enhanced Bayesian meta-learning for few-shot event detection. In *Findings of the Association for Computational Linguistics: ACL-IJCNLP 2021*, pages 2417–2429, Online. Association for Computational Linguistics.

Jake Snell, Kevin Swersky, and Richard Zemel. 2017. Prototypical networks for few-shot learning. In *Advances in Neural Information Processing Systems*.

Zhiyi Song, Ann Bies, Stephanie Strassel, Tom Riese, Justin Mott, Joe Ellis, Jonathan Wright, Seth Kulick, Neville Ryant, and Xiaoyi Ma. 2015. From light to rich ERE: Annotation of entities, relations, and events. In *Proceedings of the The 3rd Workshop on EVENTS: Definition, Detection, Coreference, and Representation*, pages 89–98, Denver, Colorado. Association for Computational Linguistics.

Flood Sung, Yongxin Yang, Li Zhang, Tao Xiang, Philip H. S. Torr, and Timothy M. Hospedales. 2018. Learning to compare: Relation network for few-shot learning.

C. Villani. 2008. *Optimal Transport: Old and New*. Grundlehren der mathematischen Wissenschaften. Springer Berlin Heidelberg.

Oriol Vinyals, Charles Blundell, Timothy Lillicrap, koray kavukcuoglu, and Daan Wierstra. 2016. Matching networks for one shot learning. In *Advances in Neural Information Processing Systems*.

David Wadden, Ulme Wennberg, Yi Luan, and Hannaneh Hajishirzi. 2019. Entity, relation, and event extraction with contextualized span representations. In *Proceedings of the 2019 Conference on Empirical Methods in Natural Language Processing and the 9th International Joint Conference on Natural Language Processing (EMNLP-IJCNLP)*.

Christopher Walker, Stephanie Strassel, Julie Medero, and Kazuaki Maeda. 2006. Ace 2005 multilingual training corpus. In *Technical report, Linguistic Data Consortium*.

Haoran Yan, Xiaolong Jin, Xiangbin Meng, Jiafeng Guo, and Xueqi Cheng. 2019. Event detection with multi-order graph convolution and aggregated attention. In *Proceedings of the 2019 Conference on Empirical Methods in Natural Language Processing and the 9th International Joint Conference on Natural Language Processing (EMNLP-IJCNLP)*, pages 5766–5770, Hong Kong, China. Association for Computational Linguistics.

Bishan Yang and Tom M. Mitchell. 2016. Joint extraction of events and entities within a document context. In *Proceedings of the Conference of the North American Chapter of the Association for Computational Linguistics: Human Language Technologies (NAACL-HLT)*.

Sen Yang, Dawei Feng, Linbo Qiao, Zhigang Kan, and Dongsheng Li. 2019a. Exploring pre-trained language models for event extraction and generation. In *Proceedings of the Annual Meeting of the Association for Computational Linguistics (ACL)*.

Sen Yang, Dawei Feng, Linbo Qiao, Zhigang Kan, and Dongsheng Li. 2019b. Exploring pre-trained language models for event extraction and generation. In *Proceedings of the 57th Annual Meeting of the Association for Computational Linguistics*, pages 5284–5294, Florence, Italy. Association for Computational Linguistics.

Junchi Zhang, Yanxia Qin, Yue Zhang, Mengchi Liu, and Donghong Ji. 2019a. Extracting entities and events as a single task using a transition-based neural model. In *IJCAI*.

Tongtao Zhang, Heng Ji, and Avirup Sil. 2019b. Joint Entity and Event Extraction with Generative Adversarial Imitation Learning. *Data Intelligence*, 1(2):99–120.

Yunyan Zhang, Guangluan Xu, Yang Wang, Daoyu Lin, Feng Li, Chenglong Wu, Jingyuan Zhang, and Tinglei Huang. 2020. A question answering-based framework for one-step event argument extraction. In *IEEE Access, vol 8, 65420-65431*.

# Zero-shot Cross-Lingual Counterfactual Detection via Automatic Extraction and Prediction of Clue Phrases

**Asahi Ushio**[1]
[1]Cardiff University
UshioA@cardiff.ac.uk

**Danushka Bollegala** [2,3]
[2]Amazon, [3]University of Liverpool
danubol@amazon.com

## Abstract

Counterfactual statements describe events that did not or cannot take place unless some conditions are satisfied. Existing counterfactual detection (CFD) methods assume the availability of manually labelled statements for each language they consider, limiting the broad applicability of CFD. In this paper, we consider the problem of zero-shot cross-lingual transfer learning for CFD. Specifically, we propose a novel loss function based on the clue phrase prediction for generalising a CFD model trained on a source language to multiple target languages, without requiring *any* human-labelled data. We obtain clue phrases that express various language-specific lexical indicators of counterfactuality in the target language in an unsupervised manner using a neural alignment model. We evaluate our method on the Amazon Multilingual Counterfactual Dataset (AMCD) for English, German, and Japanese languages in the zero-shot cross-lingual transfer setup where no manual annotations are used for the target language during training. The best CFD model fine-tuned on XLM-R improves the macro F1 score by 25% for German and 20% for Japanese target languages compared to a model that is trained only using English source language data.

## 1 Introduction

A counterfactual statement describes an event that may not, did not, or cannot take place, and the subsequent consequence(s) or alternative(s) did not take place (Milmed, 1957). Counterfactual statements can take the form – *If p was true, then q would be true* (i.e. assertions whose antecedent ($p$) and consequent ($q$) are known or assumed to be false). Counterfactual detection (CFD) is an important task in NLP, which has found broad applications such as customer review analysis in e-commerce (O'Neill et al., 2021), social media analysis (Son et al., 2017) and automatic psychological assessment (Janocko et al., 2016). To further explain the CFD task, consider the following counterfactual statement extracted from a product review: *I wish the trouser had ruching so that it could fit me well.* This is considered a counterfactual statement because it has the subjunctive mood *wished* and the author of the review wishes that the trouser had ruching, whereas it does not have in reality. In this particular example, *trouser had ruching* is the antecedent and *it could fit me well* is the consequent. Ideally, for a user who is searching for *trousers with ruching* we should *not* display this particular trouser because it does not have rouching. By accurately detecting counterfactual statements, we can prevent such irrelevant search results.

Almost all prior work on CFD has been limited to the English language (Yang et al., 2020; Son et al., 2017; Ding et al., 2020; Fajcik et al., 2020; Lu et al., 2020; Ojha et al., 2020; Yabloko, 2020) with the notable exception of O'Neill et al. (2021), who looked at German and Japanese counterfactuals in addition to English. However, *all* existing work on CFD require manually labelled language-specific counterfactual statements for the target language of choice. Extending CFD to different target languages has been hindered so far by two main challenges. First, manual annotation of counterfactuality is a time consuming and a costly task, which requires professional linguists as shown by O'Neill et al. (2021). Moreover, such expert annotators might not be available for all languages we would like to perform CFD. Second, counterfactual clues such as *wished, would have* (in English) or *fehlt, wenn es* (in German) etc. are highly language-specific, which makes it difficult to transfer a model trained on a source language to a different target language without neither labelled counterfactual examples nor clue phrase lists.

To address the above-mentioned challenges, we propose a zero-shot cross-lingual transfer learning method for CFD that learns a CFD model for a tar-



*Proceedings of the The 2nd Workshop on Multi-lingual Representation Learning (MRL)*, pages 28 - 37
December 8, 2022 ©2022 Association for Computational Linguistics

get language without using any labelled data for that target language. Our proposed method consists of two steps: (a) **automatic clue phrase extraction** for the target language and (b) learning a CFD classifier for the target language by **predicting the clue phrases in the text**. We use a neural alignment model (Dou and Neubig, 2021) to align machine-translated source language counterfactual sentences to find clue phrases for the target language. We then use those automatically extracted target language clue phrases to induce sequential labels for the sentences in the target language to train a CFD model. For this purpose, we propose a novel training objective that consists of a main task (i.e. predicting whether a given sentence contains a counterfactual statement or not) and an auxiliary task (i.e. predicting whether a given token in a sentence is a clue phrase or not). To the best of our knowledge, we are the first to propose a transfer learning method for cross-lingual CFD, let alone in a zero-shot setting that does not require neither counterfactual clues nor labelled training instances for the target language.

Using the Amazon Multilingual Counterfactual Detection dataset (AMCD) (O'Neill et al., 2021), we evaluate the proposed method for its ability to perform cross-lingual zero-shot transfer. Specifically, we use token-embeddings obtained from XLM-R (Conneau et al., 2019) and mBERT[1] to train CFD models for German and Japanese target languages using counterfact labelled sentences for English source language and automatically extracted clue phrases for each target language. In particular, no human counterfact annotations for the target language are used during training. Our proposed method establishes a new state-of-the-art for zero-shot cross-lingual transfer with an improvement of 25% in macro-averaged F1 score for German and that of 20% for Japanese. The Source code implementation for the proposed method will be publicly released upon paper acceptance.

## 2 Related Work

For training and evaluating CFD methods, a dataset was annotated in the SemEval-2020 Task 5 (Yang et al., 2020) covering two subtasks. The first subtask is to classify a given sentence as to whether it expresses a counterfactual statement or not, whereas in the second subtask the participating teams must extract the antecedent and consequent from a given counterfactual statement. Our goal in this paper is close to the first subtask, which can be modelled as a sentence-level binary classification problem. Most of the high performing methods (Ding et al., 2020; Fajcik et al., 2020; Lu et al., 2020; Ojha et al., 2020; Yabloko, 2020) submitted to SemEval-2020 Task 5 use state-of-the-art pretrained language models (Devlin et al., 2019; Liu et al., 2019; Lan et al., 2019; Yang et al., 2019) to represent sentences. Traditional machine learning methods, such as support vector machines and random forests were also used but with less success (Ojha et al., 2020). However, none of these previously proposed methods consider cross-lingual nor zero-shot CFD settings. To achieve the best prediction quality, ensemble strategies are employed. The top performing systems use an ensemble of transformers (Ding et al., 2020; Fajcik et al., 2020; Lu et al., 2020), while others include Convolutional Neural Networks (CNNs) with Global Vectors (Pennington et al., 2014) embeddings (Ojha et al., 2020). Various structures are used on top of transformers. For example, Lu et al. (2020); Ojha et al. (2020) use a CNN as the top layer, while Bai and Zhou (2020) use a Bi-GRUs and Bi-LSTMs. Some other proposed methods use additional modules, such as constituency and dependency parsers in the lower layers of the architectures (Yabloko, 2020).

O'Neill et al. (2021) created the AMCD counterfactual dataset by annotating sentences selected from Amazon product reviews. Unlike the SemEval dataset, which covers only English counterfactuals, AMCD covers Japanese and German counterfactuals in addition to English. AMCD is the only publicly available multilingual CFD dataset. Therefore, we use AMCD to evaluate the cross-lingual zero-shot CFD models we propose in this paper. O'Neill et al. (2021) trained CFD models using different approaches such as bag-of-words representations of sentences as well as by fine-tuning pre-trained masked language models for each language separately. They also considered a cross-lingual zero-shot setting where they first machine translated the source (English) dataset into each of the target languages (German and Japanese), and train CFD models for those target languages using the translated training instances. However, the performance of this approach was significantly worse than that of the in-

[1] https://github.com/google-research/bert/blob/master/multilingual.md

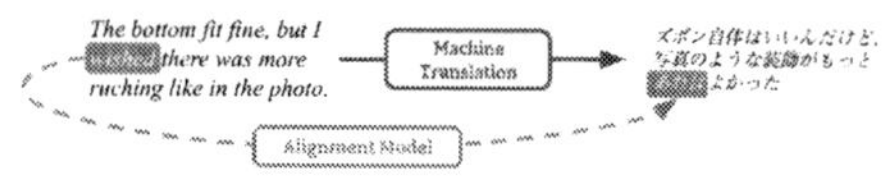


(a) Alignment-based clue phrase extraction.

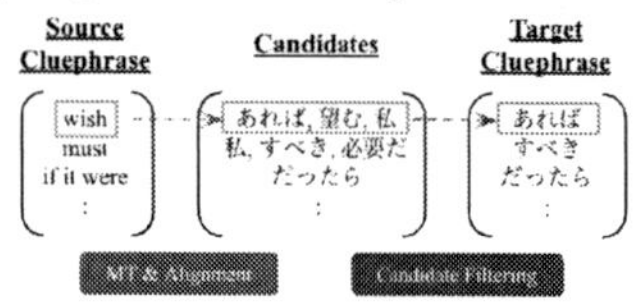


(b) End-to-end pipeline for extracting clue phrases.

Figure 1: An example of extracting clue phrase candidates for Japanese target language from a pair of sentences obtained by machine translating an English source language sentence to Japanese. The alignment model aligns the English clue phrase *wished* with the Japanese term あれば(*areba*), which is then extracted as a candidate Japanese clue phrase.

language baselines, which lead to their conclusion "*simply applying MT on test data is not an alternative to annotating counterfactual datasets from scratch for a novel target language.*" This highlights the difficulty of the cross-lingual zero-shot transfer problem setting for CFD, which we consider in this paper.

One approach to learn accurate multilingual representations with less supervision in downstream tasks is the few-shot or zero-shot cross-lingual transfer learning. Here, the goal is to transfer a model trained in the source language into the target language with minimal loss in performance. Few-shot transfer learning assumes the availability of a small number of labelled instances in the target language, while the zero-shot setting assumes none. Recently, Pfeiffer et al. (2020) proposed MAD-X, a zero-shot and few-shot language model transfer framework based on the adaptor framework (Houlsby et al., 2019). Moreover, XTREME (Hu et al., 2020), a multilingual benchmark containing many tasks, reported the translate-train performance, where a model is trained on a machine-translated version of the source language dataset into the target languages as a baseline for zero-shot transfer learning. However, to the best of our knowledge, ours is the first-ever model proposed for cross-lingual zero-shot transfer for CFD.

## 3 Cross-lingual Zero-shot CFD

Let us denote a sentence $x = w_1, w_2, \ldots, w_{|x|}$ consisting of a sequence of $|x|$ tokens $w_j$. CFD is considered as a binary classification task in this paper, where the goal is to predict whether a sentence $x$ contains a counterfactual statement ($y(x) = 1$) or otherwise ($y(x) = 0$), indicated by the binary label $y(x)$. In the cross-lingual zero-shot CFD setting, we consider the problem of transferring a CFD model trained on a source language $s$ to a different target language $t$. For this purpose we assume the availability of a counterfactual-labelled dataset, $\mathcal{D}_s = \{(x_{s,i}, y(x_{s,i}))\}_{i=1}^{|\mathcal{D}_s|}$ for the source language and an unlabelled dataset, $\mathcal{D}_t = \{x_{t,i}\}_{i=1}^{|\mathcal{D}_t|}$, for the target language. Here, we use the notation $x_{s,i}$ to indicate the $i$-th sentence in the source (for the target $x_{t,i}$) language dataset and its associated counterfactual label $y(x_{s,i})$. The source language is assumed to be a language for which it is relatively easier to create a large annotated dataset because it is easier to recruit annotators than for the target language. Following prior work on cross-lingual transfer (Hu et al., 2020; O'Neill et al., 2021), we use a machine translation (MT) system to translate the sentences in $\mathcal{D}_s$ into the target language with the labels unchanged to create a machine-translated version of $\mathcal{D}_s$, denoted by $\mathcal{D}_{mt}$.

Counterfactual statements are rare in natural language sentences and Son et al. (2017) report that only 1-2% of sentences contain counterfactual statements in a random collection of sentences. Therefore, randomly selecting sentences for annotation purposes results in a waste of annotation resources such as annotator time and cost, and will only result in an imbalanced and low-coverage datasets. To address this issue, prior work (Son et al., 2017; O'Neill et al., 2021; Yang et al., 2020) creating annotated datasets for counterfactuality has used language-specific *clue phrases* that indicate various expressions frequently used to indicate the presence of a counterfactual to filter candidate sentences for annotation. We use such counterfactual clue phrases as auxiliary training data for cross-lingual transfer. Specifically, we require that a CDF model can not only (a) predict whether a given sentence $x$ is a counterfactual or not (*main task*), but also be able to (b) predict whether a token $w$ in $x$ is a clue phrase or not (*auxiliary task*). Unlike obtaining annotations for counterfactual statements in the target language, it is relatively easier to obtain a list of counterfactual clue phrases for the target language. More importantly, as we show later in § 3.1, it is possible to automatically extract an accurate set of target language clue phrases, $\mathcal{V}_t$, using $\mathcal{D}_s$, $\mathcal{D}_{mt}$ and a set of clue phrases for the source language, $\mathcal{V}_s$.

The auxiliary task is motivated by prior work in semi-supervised learning (Ando and Zhang, 2005) and masked language modelling (Devlin et al., 2019), where it has been shown that by predicting tokens that are highly related (i.e. clue phrases) to the downstream task (i.e. sentence-level counterfactual detection) we can learn task-specific correlations between tokens. In contrast to the main task, which is modelled as a sentence-level binary classification task, we model the auxiliary task as a token-level sequence labelling task. However, unlike for the main task, where we have at least counterfactual labelled sentences from the source language (i.e. $\mathcal{D}_s$), we do not have any manually annotated training data neither for the source nor for the target languages for the auxiliary task. For this reason, we automatically label training data for the auxiliary task as follows. For the source language, we assign a binary-valued token label $y(w_j)$ for each token $w_j$ in each sentence $x_i$ in $\mathcal{D}_s$, where $y(w_j) = 1$, if $w_j \in \mathcal{V}_s$ and $y(w_j) = 0$ otherwise. For example, given a sentence "*The bottom fits fine, but I wished there was more ruching like in the photo.*" we label "*wished*", corresponding to a clue phrase in English as 1 and other tokens as 0. To generate training data for the target language we can use either sentences in $\mathcal{D}_t$ or $\mathcal{D}_{mt}$. We empirically compare the different combinations of training data later in §5.1.

Next, we describe the training objectives associated with the main and auxiliary tasks. Let us consider a multilingual masked language model (MLM), $h$, with pretrained parameters $\boldsymbol{\theta}$ that assigns a vector $h(w, x; \theta)$ to a word $w$ in a sentence $x$. We train a feed forward neural network $f$ with parameters $\boldsymbol{\phi}$ and a sigmoid output unit such that given the embedding $\boldsymbol{x}$ of a sentence $x$ it predicts whether $x$ is counterfactual (i.e. $f(\boldsymbol{x}; \boldsymbol{\phi}) = 1$) or otherwise (i.e. $f(\boldsymbol{x}; \boldsymbol{\phi}) = 0$). Different methods can be used to create sentence embeddings from MLMs such as mean or max pooling, attention-based weighting or by simply considering the embedding for the classification (i.e. [CLS]) token (Devlin et al., 2019). In our preliminary investigations we found that considering the [CLS] token embedding as a sentence representation to produce the best cross-lingual CFD performance despite its simplicity. However, we note that our proposed method is independent of the choice of the sentence encoder and can be combined with more complex sentence encoder architectures. In the subsequent discussion we denote $\boldsymbol{x} = h([\text{CLS}], x; \boldsymbol{\theta})$. Given that our main task of CFD is modelled as a binary classification task, the negative log-likelihood (NLL) loss for this prediction task can be written as in (1).

$$L_{\text{cfd}}(\mathcal{D}) = -\sum_{x \in \mathcal{D}} [(1 - y(x))(\log(f(\boldsymbol{x})) - 1) + y(x) \log(f(\boldsymbol{x}))] \quad (1)$$

For the auxiliary task, we train a feed forward neural network, $g(h(w, x); \boldsymbol{\psi})$, that takes in the contextualised embedding $h(w, x)$ of token $w$ in sentence $x$ and returns 1, if $w$ is a clue phrase or 0 otherwise. We compute the NLL loss for the clue phrase prediction task as in (2).

$$L_{\text{cp}}(\mathcal{D}) = -\sum_{x \in \mathcal{D}} \sum_{j=1}^{|x|} [(1 - y(w_j))(1 - \log(z)) + y(w_j) \log(z)] \quad (2)$$
$$z = g(h(w_j, x); \boldsymbol{\psi})$$

Finally we add the losses for the main and auxiliary tasks to compute the total loss. Our zero-shot transfer model uses $\mathcal{D}_{mt}$ on the main task (1) and either of $\mathcal{D}_{mt}$ or $\mathcal{D}_t$ on the auxiliary task (2), i.e. $L_{\text{cfd}}(\mathcal{D}_{mt}) + L_{\text{cp}}(\mathcal{D}_t)$ or $L_{\text{cfd}}(\mathcal{D}_{mt}) + L_{\text{cp}}(\mathcal{D}_{mt})$ where we have dropped the model parameters for notational convenience. Further details on model training are provided in §4.

### 3.1 Automatic Clue Phrase Extraction

In some target languages such as low-resource languages, it might be even challenging to obtain a sufficiently large list of clue phrases covering various constructions used to express counterfactuality because of the difficulties in recruiting annotators. Moreover, in a true zero-shot spirit it is desirable not to assume any human supervision for the target language – neither for the main nor auxiliary tasks. Therefore, in this section, we propose a method to automatically extract clue phrases for the target language using the list of clue phrases for the source language, $\mathcal{V}_s$, counterfactual labelled dataset for the source language, $\mathcal{D}_s$, and its machine translated version, $\mathcal{D}_{mt}$. First, we use Awesome Aligner (Dou and Neubig, 2021), an off-the-shelf neural alignment model, and compute the alignment between each sentence $x_{s,i}$ in $\mathcal{D}_s$ and its translation $x_{mt,i}$. Next, for a token $w_s$ in $x_{s,i}$, which is a clue phrase in the source language (i.e. $w_s \in \mathcal{V}_s$), we find the list of target language tokens, $\mathcal{A}_t(w_s)$. aligned with $w_s$ in all sentence pairs, $\forall_{i=1}^{|\mathcal{D}_s|}(x_{s,i}, x_{mt,i})$. The candidate clue phrases in $\mathcal{A}_t(w_s)$ are further filtered following three criteria as described below. The end-to-end pipeline for target language clue phrase extraction is illustrated in Figure 1b between English (source) and Japanese (target) languages. To differentiate from the human annotated clue phrases (referred to as *gold* clue phrases here onwards), we call the clue phrases extracted via this alignment process as *auto-generated* clue phrases.

**Criterion 1: Non-counterfactual Sentence Exclusion:** Note that clue phrases can be ambiguous with regard to whether they express counterfactuality or not. For example, the clue phrase *wish* indicates a counterfactual statement in the sentence *I **wish** this shirt was available in red*, whereas it does not in *My **wish** came true*. Such ambiguous occurrences of counterfactual clues are likely to be aligned with non-counterfactual expressions in the target language. To reduce the noise due to this ambiguity in the unsupervised alignment process, we exclude non-counterfactual sentences from $\mathcal{D}_s$ and $\mathcal{D}_{mt}$ during the alignment process. In other words, we consider alignment between only sentence pairs $(x_{s,i}, x_{mt,i})$ such that $y(x_{s,i}) = 1$.

**Criterion 2: Shared Term Exclusion:** If a particular term $w_t$ appears in candidate sets $\mathcal{A}_t(w_s)$ extracted for many distinct source language clue phrases $w_s$, it is likely that $w_t$ is not a clue phrase but a high frequent functional word or a stop word. Therefore, we remove candidates appearing in more than one candidate set $\mathcal{A}_t(w_s)$ from target language clue phrase set.

**Criterion 3: Majority Filtering:** If a target language token $w_t$ is aligned with the same source language clue phrase $w_s$ in multiple sentence pairs, $(x_{s,i}, x_{mt,i})$, it increases the reliability of $w_t$ as a clue phrase in the target language. We use this intuition to filter candidates, where for each source language clue phrase we select only the most frequently aligned target language token as a clue phrase. We refer to this filtering criterion as the *majority filtering*. In cases where there are multiple target language tokens with the same highest frequency of alignment with a specific source language clue phrase, we select all such tokens as target language clue phrases according to the majority filtering criterion.

| | EN | DE | JA |
|---|---|---|---|
| Train | 807 / 7,193 | 3865 / 1735 | 525 / 5,075 |
| Dev | 73 / 593 | 325 / 141 | 46 / 420 |
| Test | 150 / 1,184 | 650 / 284 | 96 / 838 |

Table 1: The number of sentences in AMCD with positive/negative label are shown respectively.

## 4 Experimental Settings

**Dataset:** We use the AMCD dataset, which contains counterfactual statements annotated from Amazon product reviews for three languages: English (EN), German (DE), and Japanese (JA). We use the original published training/development/test splits[2] in our experiments, for which the number of sentences are shown in Table 1. Throughout the experiments, we regard EN as the source language and DE and JA as the target languages. To create machine translated versions (i.e. $\mathcal{D}_{mt}$) of the EN dataset into the target languages, we use Amazon MT.[3]

**Clue Phrase:** The human annotated clue phrases provided by AMCD are considered as the gold clue phrases for each language. For the automatic clue phrase extraction described in § 3.1, we use Awesome Aligner (Dou and Neubig, 2021) as the neural alignment model.

To evaluate the level of cross-lingual counterfactual detection (XCFD) performance that can be obtained by directly translating the source language clue phrases to the target language, we create a **Clue Phrase Translation** (CP Translation) baseline. This baseline uses Google Translate [4] to translate individual clue phrases in the source language to the target language without using any contexts for those clue phrases.

**Models and Hyperparameters:** To obtain token embeddings, we use two multilingual language models in our experiments:

[2] https://github.com/amazon-research/amazon-multilingual-counterfactual-dataset

[3] https://aws.amazon.com/translate/

[4] https://translate.google.com

| Model | $L_{\text{cfd}}$ | $L_{\text{cp}}$ | DE | | JA | |
|---|---|---|---|---|---|---|
| | $\mathcal{D}_t$ | | *90.3* | [88.1, 92.2] | *83.7* | [79.7, 87.3] |
| | $\mathcal{D}_s$ | | 28.4 | [26.0, 30.9] | 47.3 | [46.7, 47.8] |
| mBERT | $\mathcal{D}_{mt}$ | | 70.9 | [67.9, 73.8] | 67.3 | [62.7, 71.7] |
| | $\mathcal{D}_{mt}$ | $\mathcal{D}_t$ | **65.7** | [62.6, 68.7] | **68.6** | [64.6, 72.4] |
| | $\mathcal{D}_{mt}$ | $\mathcal{D}_{mt}$ | **73.0** | [70.1, 75.9] | **68.3** | [64.0, 72.4] |
| | $\mathcal{D}_t$ | | *89.3* | [87.1, 91.4] | *86.2* | [82.4, 89.8] |
| | $\mathcal{D}_s$ | | 45.1 | [41.8, 48.3] | 59.2 | [53.8, 64.6] |
| XLM-R | $\mathcal{D}_{mt}$ | | 64.7 | [61.7, 67.7] | 81.1 | [76.8, 84.9] |
| | $\mathcal{D}_{mt}$ | $\mathcal{D}_t$ | **68.0** | [65.1, 71.0] | **82.9** | [79.0, 86.6] |
| | $\mathcal{D}_{mt}$ | $\mathcal{D}_{mt}$ | **70.3** | [67.4, 73.3] | **81.9** | [77.6, 85.8] |

Table 2: F1 scores on the test set of each target language with 95% confidence intervals in the brackets. The columns $L_{\text{cfd}}$ and $L_{\text{cp}}$ represent the dataset used respectively for the main (1) and auxiliary tasks (2). Models with blank $L_{\text{cp}}$ are trained without the auxiliary task. The results of in-domain performance where labelled data from the target language is used to train a CDF model are shown in italics, the results with the auxiliary task are in shown bold face, and the best zero-shot result in each language is underlined.

mBERT (Devlin et al., 2019) and XLM-R (large model) (Conneau et al., 2019). Both of those models are transformer-based (Vaswani et al., 2017), but mBERT has been pretrained Wikipedia articles covering the 104 languages with the largest Wikipedias. On the other hand, XLM-R has been trained on 2.5TB of filtered CommonCrawl data containing 100 languages. The initial weights are taken from the `bert-base-multilingual-cased` and `xlm-roberta-large` model checkpoints, made available at the Huggingface transformers model hub (Wolf et al., 2020). We use the Adam optimizer (Kingma and Ba, 2014) with a batch size of 128, an initial learning rate of 0.00001 and train our CFD models for 5 epochs. As the evaluation metric, we report the macro-averaged F1 scores with 95% bootstrap estimated confidence intervals (Efron and Tibshirani, 1994).[5]

## 5 Results

### 5.1 Zero-shot Transfer with Auxiliary Task

Table 2 shows our main results of zero-shot cross-lingual transfer with the auxiliary task $L_{\text{cp}}$ (2) together with the main task $L_{\text{cfd}}$ (1). As an upper bound on performance, we train a CFD model using labelled data for the target language $L_{\text{cfd}}(\mathcal{D}_t)$

[5]https://docs.scipy.org/doc/scipy/reference/generated/scipy.stats.bootstrap.html

| $L_{\text{cp}}$ | Clue Phrase Type | DE | | JA | |
|---|---|---|---|---|---|
| | Human | 66.9 | [64.0, 69.9] | 79.0 | [76.0, 83.7] |
| | CP Translation | 67.4 | [64.4, 70.3] | 79.0 | [74.9, 82.7] |
| | Alignment | 64.9 | [61.8, 68.0] | 80.1 | [75.9, 83.9] |
| | Alignment$^{1}$ | 66.0 | [63.0, 69.0] | **82.9** | [79.0, 86.6] |
| | Alignment$^{2}$ | 62.9 | [59.9, 66.0] | 77.5 | [73.4, 81.4] |
| $\mathcal{D}_t$ | Alignment$^{3}$ | **68.0** | [65.1, 71.0] | 79.5 | [75.4, 83.3] |
| | Alignment$^{1,2}$ | 58.5 | [55.4, 61.7] | 79.1 | [74.6, 83.2] |
| | Alignment$^{2,3}$ | 65.5 | [62.5, 68.5] | 80.0 | [75.7, 83.9] |
| | Alignment$^{1,2,3}$ | 63.4 | [60.3, 66.5] | 78.9 | [74.7, 82.7] |
| | Alignment$^{1,3}$ | 65.8 | [62.7, 68.9] | 80.4 | [76.3, 84.1] |
| | Human | **70.3** | [67.4, 73.3] | 81.6 | [77.4, 85.6] |
| | CP Translation | 64.2 | [61.1, 67.2] | 81.3 | [77.1, 85.3] |
| | Alignment | 65.8 | [62.9, 68.8] | 81.6 | [77.4, 85.5] |
| | Alignment$^{1}$ | 68.0 | [65.0, 70.9] | 79.5 | [75.5, 83.4] |
| | Alignment$^{2}$ | 67.4 | [64.4, 70.3] | 81.7 | [77.4, 85.6] |
| $\mathcal{D}_{mt}$ | Alignment$^{3}$ | 66.8 | [63.7, 69.7] | **81.9** | [77.6, 85.8] |
| | Alignment$^{1,2}$ | 64.2 | [61.1, 67.2] | 78.2 | [73.8, 82.2] |
| | Alignment$^{2,3}$ | 65.3 | [62.3, 68.3] | 75.7 | [70.5, 80.5] |
| | Alignment$^{1,2,3}$ | 63.2 | [60.1, 66.3] | 78.4 | [73.8, 82.4] |
| | Alignment$^{1,3}$ | 65.3 | [62.3, 68.3] | 79.6 | [75.6, 83.3] |

Table 3: F1 scores of XLM-R trained along different clue phrase types. All the scores are evaluated on the test set of each target language with 95% confidence intervals shown in the brackets. The filtering criteria used in each alignment approach is noted in its superscript. The best results in each language and $L_{\text{cp}}$ are in bold face.

with mBERT and XLM-R separately. Recall that in the zero-shot setting we consider in this paper, we will not have access to such counterfactual labelled sentences for the target language. As a comparison, we report baselines, which are models trained on the main task with the source $L_{\text{cfd}}(\mathcal{D}_s)$ or the translation $L_{\text{cfd}}(\mathcal{D}_{mt})$ without the auxiliary task. We see that the best zero-shot cross-lingual transfer results are obtained using our proposed method for mBERT as well as XLM-R for both DE and JA. Specifically, F-score for DE improves from 70.9 to 73.0 in mBERT and for JA it improves from 81.1 to 82.9 in XLM-R by adding the auxiliary task to the main task on $\mathcal{D}_{mt}$. This supports our proposal to use clue phrase prediction in the target language as an auxiliary task for cross-lingual CFD.

From Table 2 we see that among the models trained with the auxiliary tasks, XLM-R-based models ($L_{cp} \in \{\mathcal{D}_{mt}, \mathcal{D}_t\}$) perform better for JA than those obtained with mBERT, while the best model for DE ($L_{cp} = \mathcal{D}_{mt}$) is obtained using mBERT. In particular the best performance for JA is obtained with XLM-R (82.9), which is significantly better than the best performance for

| $L_{cp}$ | Clue Phrase Type | DE | JA |
|---|---|---|---|
| $\mathcal{D}_t$ | Human | 63.7 [60.6, 66.8] | 65.3 [61.6, 69.2] |
| | CP Translation | 61.9 [58.7, 65.0] | 66.4 [62.4, 70.2] |
| | Alignment | 63.6 [60.5, 66.7] | 64.7 [61.0, 68.6] |
| | Alignment[1] | 63.7 [60.5, 66.7] | 61.9 [58.3, 65.5] |
| | Alignment[2] | 63.7 [60.6, 66.7] | **68.6** [64.6, 72.4] |
| | Alignment[3] | 64.4 [61.3, 67.4] | 66.4 [62.4, 70.3] |
| | Alignment[1,2] | 62.6 [59.5, 65.7] | **68.6** [64.6, 72.4] |
| | Alignment[2,3] | 64.3 [61.2, 67.3] | 66.1 [62.2, 69.9] |
| | Alignment[1,2,3] | 65.2 [62.1, 68.3] | 65.4 [61.6, 69.3] |
| | Alignment[1,3] | **65.7** [62.6, 68.7] | 67.6 [63.5, 71.5] |
| $\mathcal{D}_{mt}$ | Human | 70.7 [67.8, 73.7] | **68.3** [64.0, 72.4] |
| | CP Translation | 71.6 [68.7, 74.5] | **68.3** [63.9, 72.4] |
| | Alignment | 70.8 [67.9, 73.8] | 65.8 [61.1, 70.2] |
| | Alignment[1] | 70.8 [67.8, 73.7] | 67.0 [62.3, 71.5] |
| | Alignment[2] | 70.0 [67.0, 73.0] | 64.9 [60.1, 69.5] |
| | Alignment[3] | 72.7 [69.8, 75.6] | 66.4 [61.9, 70.7] |
| | Alignment[1,2] | 71.7 [68.7, 74.6] | 66.2 [61.6, 70.4] |
| | Alignment[2,3] | 72.5 [69.6, 75.4] | 66.7 [62.1, 70.9] |
| | Alignment[1,2,3] | **73.0** [70.1, 75.9] | 65.1 [60.4, 69.5] |
| | Alignment[1,3] | 72.4 [69.5, 75.3] | 64.5 [59.8, 69.0] |

Table 4: F1 scores of mBERT trained along different clue phrase types. All the scores are evaluated on the test set of each target language with 95% confidence intervals shown in brackets. The filtering criteria used in each alignment approach is noted in its superscript. The best results in each language and $L_{\text{cp}}$ are in bold face.

JA obtained with mBERT (68.6). Although the best performance for DE obtained with mBERT (73.0) is better than that with XLM-R (70.3), the performance difference between these two results are *not* statistically significant as evident from the overlapping confidence intervals. Note that compared to mBERT, which is trained on Wikipedias for different languages, XLM-R is trained on a much larger CommonCrawl corpus. Moreover, JA Wikipedia (530M tokens) is significantly smaller than that of DE (10297M tokens). Because mBERT tokenises CJK languages into individual characters and uses a 110K shared WordPiece vocabulary, the coverage of Japanese (which has lower overlap of subtokens with other languages) is less in mBERT. Therefore, XLM-R is capable of learning better representations for Japanese than mBERT, leading to better XCFD performance for JA.

In terms of the datasets used for the auxiliary task, the best model in DE uses the translation $\mathcal{D}_{mt}$, while that in JA uses the target corpus $\mathcal{D}_t$ for both mBERT and XLM-R. In general, the translation from EN to JA is harder than that from EN to DE as reported in Aiken (2019). Therefore, it

| Model | $L_{\text{cfd}}$ | $L_{\text{cp}}$ | DE | JA |
|---|---|---|---|---|
| mBERT | $\mathcal{D}_{mt}$ | $\mathcal{D}_t$ | 63.9 [60.7, 66.9] | 68.1 [64.1, 72.0] |
| | | $\mathcal{D}_{mt}$ | 73.1 [70.2, 76.0] | 67.3 [63.0, 71.4] |
| XLM-R | $\mathcal{D}_{mt}$ | $\mathcal{D}_t$ | 63.5 [60.5, 66.6] | 79.7 [75.5, 83.4] |
| | | $\mathcal{D}_{mt}$ | 68.8 [65.8, 71.6] | 77.5 [73.5, 81.2] |

Table 5: F1 scores of models trained on both of the human annotated and the automatically extracted clue phrase (the best clue phrase type shown in Table 2 is used). All the scores are evaluated on the test set of each target language with 95% confidence intervals shown in brackets.

is better to use $\mathcal{D}_t$ for the auxiliary task instead of $\mathcal{D}_{mt}$ when the translation quality for the target language is low such as from English to Japanese. Considering that $\mathcal{D}_{mt}$ is already used for the main task, by using $\mathcal{D}_t$ for the auxiliary task, which provides additional information not available by simply machine translating the sentences from the source language, we can provide extra supervision to the model.

### 5.2 Effect of Clue Phrase Choices

Table 3 and Table 4 show the results when using respectively XLM-R and mBERT as the text encoders with different clue phrase types including the human annotation, clue phrase translation, and our proposed alignment-based method (see § 4 for detailed setting). The alignment-based method optionally has the three criteria described in § 3.1 for filtering clue phrase candidates in the target language: **1** (*non-counterfactual sentence exclusion*), **2** (*shared term exclusion*), and **3** (*majority filtering*). We evaluate all possible combinations of filtering methods with the **Alignment** method, indicated by superscripts in Table 3. Alignment without any superscripts correspond to applying none of the candidate filtering criteria. Note that the results of XLM-R with the auxiliary task in Table 2 are the best results within each target language in Table 3.

From Table 3, we see that our alignment-based clue phrases can outperform manual clue phrases in both of $L_{\text{cp}}(\mathcal{D}_t)$ and $L_{\text{cp}}(\mathcal{D}_{mt})$ in JA, and $L_{\text{cp}}(\mathcal{D}_t)$ in DE with the best configuration. Furthermore, the best alignment-based clue phrases are better than clue phrase translation, which is still competitive compared to the human annotated clue phrases. This shows that high quality clue phrases can be automatically extracted using the method described in § 3.1. We reemphasize that

| clue | context |
|---|---|
| **wäre** (would be) | dieses Produkt wäre toll, wenn... (This product would be great if ...) |
| **wünschte** (wished) | ich wünschte dieses Produkt wäre ...(I wish this product was ...) |
| **hätte** (would have) | hätte dieses Produkt ... (would this product ...) |
| **könnte** (could) | dieses Produkt könnte besser sein, wenn es ... (this product could be better if it ...) |
| と思っていた (thought it was) | Mサイズだと思っていた (thought it was M-size) |
| 希望 (hope) | プラスチック製の物を希望していた (hope it was made from plastic) |
| かもしれない(could) | もう少し小さければ良かったかもしれない (could be better if it was smaller ) |
| があれば(if it had) | 蓋があれば良かった (if it had a lid) |

Table 6: Automatically extracted clue phrases and their contexts for German (top) and Japanese (bottom) target languages. English translations are shown in brackets.

it is beneficial to be able to automatically extract clue phrases in zero-shot adaptation, because we might not always be able to recruit human annotators to manually compile clue phrase lists for all the target languages we would like to adapt to.

Table 4 shows the level of performance the proposed method would obtain if mBERT was used as the text encoding model. We see that the best performance for DE (73.0) is obtained by applying all filtering criteria, whereas with XLM-R the best performance for DE (70.3) was obtained with human-written clue phrases. However, as explained previously in § 5.1, the differences between these two results are not statistically significant. On the other hand, for JA we see that mBERT results are consistently lower than the corresponding XLM-R results across all filtering settings considered in Table 4 and Table 3. This comparison shows that the multilingual MLM used to encode text is an important choice for the performance of XCFD. However, this choice has been largely overlooked in prior work. For example, O'Neill et al. (2021) used only a single multilingual MLM (i.e mBERT only) in their cross-lingual evaluations. Although their reported best XCFD results with mBERT for JA and DE is better than those with our mBERT results, these results cannot be directly compared because unlike our zero-shot approach that does *not* use any labelled data for the target language, O'Neill et al. (2021) proposed a fully-supervised method where they use *all* of the available labelled data for the target language.

### 5.3 Combining Automatic Clue Phrase with Human Annotated Clue Phrase

We study the effect of incorporating both types of clue phrases (human annotated and automatically extracted) in the training process for the auxiliary task in Table 5. Compared to the best performances reported in Table 2 and Table 3 using the automatically extracted clue phrases, we see no further gains (in some cases even a drop) in performances for the target languages when using human annotated clue phrases in addition to the automatically extracted clue phrases in the auxiliary task. This shows that automatically extracted clue phrases are of a higher quality than the human-written clue phrases, and already capture the counterfactual clues contained in the human-written gold clue phrases. Some example clue phrases automatically extracted by the method described in § 3.1 are shown in Table 6 for German and Japanese target languages. We see that informative clue phrases are extracted by the proposed method for both of those target languages.

## 6 Conclusion

We studied zero-shot cross-lingual transfer learning for CFD and proposed a novel training objective that combines (a) token-level clue phrase prediction in target language sentences and (b) sentence-level counterfactuality prediction for source language (and translated to target language) sentences. Moreover, we proposed a method to automatically extract clue phrase for a given target language, which obviates the need for manually compiled clue phrases. Predicting clue phrases as an auxiliary task improves cross-lingual transfer from English source to German and Japanese target languages, obtaining state-of-the-art performances on AMCD.

## 7 Ethical Considerations

In this section, we discuss the ethical considerations related to these contributions. With regard to the dataset, we use the AMCD where the sentences were selected from a publicly available Amazon product review dataset. We do not collect or release any additional product reviews not included in the original AMCD as part of this paper. Although the dataset is manually verified that the sentences in the dataset do not contain any customer sensitive information, product reviews can contain socially biased opinions. However, we do not apply any bias mitigation methods in this paper, thus it is possible that the dataset biases present (if any) in AMCD are also encoded in the models we train in this paper. We use two pretrained multilingual language models, mBERT and XLM-RoBERTa, to obtain cross-lingual zero-shot CFD models. Those pretrained language models are known to be biased due to the curated pretraining corpus from web (Bommasani et al., 2020). Likewise for the dataset, we do not filter such social biases in the the language models. Therefore, we recommend that further evaluations to be performed before deploying the CFD models we train in this paper in real-world NLP systems.

## References


Milam Aiken. 2019. An updated evaluation of google translate accuracy. *Studies in linguistics and literature*, 3(3):253–260.

Rie Kubota Ando and Tong Zhang. 2005. A framework for learning predictive structures from multiple tasks and unlabeled data. *Journal of Machine Learning Research*, 6:1817–1853.

Yang Bai and Xiaobing Zhou. 2020. Byteam at semeval-2020 task 5: Detecting counterfactual statements with bert and ensembles. In *Proceedings of the Fourteenth Workshop on Semantic Evaluation*, pages 640–644.

Rishi Bommasani, Kelly Davis, and Claire Cardie. 2020. Interpreting Pretrained Contextualized Representations via Reductions to Static Embeddings. In *Proceedings of the 58th Annual Meeting of the Association for Computational Linguistics*, pages 4758–4781, Online. Association for Computational Linguistics.

Alexis Conneau, Kartikay Khandelwal, Naman Goyal, Vishrav Chaudhary, Guillaume Wenzek, Francisco Guzmán, Edouard Grave, Myle Ott, Luke Zettlemoyer, and Veselin Stoyanov. 2019. Unsupervised Cross-lingual Representation Learning at Scale. *arXiv preprint arXiv:1911.02116*.

Jacob Devlin, Ming-Wei Chang, Kenton Lee, and Kristina Toutanova. 2019. BERT: Pre-training of deep bidirectional transformers for language understanding. In *Proceedings of the 2019 Conference of the North American Chapter of the Association for Computational Linguistics: Human Language Technologies, Volume 1 (Long and Short Papers)*, pages 4171–4186, Minneapolis, Minnesota. Association for Computational Linguistics.

Xiao Ding, Dingkui Hao, Yuewei Zhang, Kuo Liao, Zhongyang Li, Bing Qin, and Ting Liu. 2020. Hitscir at semeval-2020 task 5: Training pre-trained language model with pseudo-labeling data for counterfactuals detection. In *Proceedings of the Fourteenth Workshop on Semantic Evaluation*, pages 354–360.

Zi-Yi Dou and Graham Neubig. 2021. Word alignment by fine-tuning embeddings on parallel corpora. In *Proceedings of the 16th Conference of the European Chapter of the Association for Computational Linguistics: Main Volume*, pages 2112–2128, Online. Association for Computational Linguistics.

Bradley Efron and Robert J Tibshirani. 1994. *An introduction to the bootstrap*. CRC press.

Martin Fajcik, Josef Jon, Martin Docekal, and Pavel Smrz. 2020. BUT-FIT at SemEval-2020 task 5: Automatic detection of counterfactual statements with deep pre-trained language representation models. In *Proceedings of the Fourteenth Workshop on Semantic Evaluation*, pages 437–444, Barcelona (online). International Committee for Computational Linguistics.

Neil Houlsby, Andrei Giurgiu, Stanislaw Jastrzebski, Bruna Morrone, Quentin De Laroussilhe, Andrea Gesmundo, Mona Attariyan, and Sylvain Gelly. 2019. Parameter-efficient transfer learning for NLP. In *Proceedings of the 36th International Conference on Machine Learning*, volume 97 of *Proceedings of Machine Learning Research*, pages 2790–2799. PMLR.

Junjie Hu, Sebastian Ruder, Aditya Siddhant, Graham Neubig, Orhan Firat, and Melvin Johnson. 2020. XTREME: A Massively Multilingual Multi-task Benchmark for Evaluating Cross-lingual Generalisation. In *International Conference on Machine Learning*, pages 4411–4421. PMLR.

Anthony Janocko, Allegra Larche, Joseph Raso, and Kevin Zembroski. 2016. Counterfactuals in the language of social media: A natural language processing project in conjunction with the world well being project. Technical report, University of Pennsylvania.

Diederik P Kingma and Jimmy Ba. 2014. Adam: A Method for Stochastic Optimization. *arXiv preprint arXiv:1412.6980*.

Zhenzhong Lan, Mingda Chen, Sebastian Goodman, Kevin Gimpel, Piyush Sharma, and Radu Soricut. 2019. ALBERT: A lite BERT for self-supervised learning of language representations. In *International Conference on Learning Representations*.

Yinhan Liu, Myle Ott, Naman Goyal, Jingfei Du, Mandar Joshi, Danqi Chen, Omer Levy, Mike Lewis, Luke Zettlemoyer, and Veselin Stoyanov. 2019. RoBERTa: A robustly optimized BERT pretraining approach. *CoRR*, abs/1907.11692.

Yaojie Lu, Annan Li, Hongyu Lin, Xianpei Han, and Le Sun. 2020. Iscas at semeval-2020 task 5: Pre-trained transformers for counterfactual statement modeling. In *Proceedings of the Fourteenth Workshop on Semantic Evaluation*, pages 658–663.

Bella K Milmed. 1957. Counterfactual statements and logical modality. *Mind*, 66(264):453–470.

Anirudh Anil Ojha, Rohin Garg, Shashank Gupta, and Ashutosh Modi. 2020. Iitk-rsa at semeval-2020 task 5: Detecting counterfactuals. In *Proceedings of the Fourteenth Workshop on Semantic Evaluation*, pages 458–467.

James O'Neill, Polina Rozenshtein, Ryuichi Kiryo, Motoko Kubota, and Danushka Bollegala. 2021. I wish i would have loved this one, but i didn't–a multilingual dataset for counterfactual detection in product reviews. In *Proceedings of the 2021 Conference on Empirical Methods in Natural Language Processing*. Association for Computational Linguistics.

Jeffrey Pennington, Richard Socher, and Christopher Manning. 2014. GloVe: Global vectors for word representation. In *Proceedings of the 2014 Conference on Empirical Methods in Natural Language Processing*, pages 1532–1543, Doha, Qatar. Association for Computational Linguistics.

Jonas Pfeiffer, Ivan Vulić, Iryna Gurevych, and Sebastian Ruder. 2020. MAD-X: An Adapter-Based Framework for Multi-Task Cross-Lingual Transfer. In *Proceedings of the 2020 Conference on Empirical Methods in Natural Language Processing*, pages 7654–7673, Online. Association for Computational Linguistics.

Youngseo Son, Anneke Buffone, Joe Raso, Allegra Larche, Anthony Janocko, Kevin Zembroski, H Andrew Schwartz, and Lyle Ungar. 2017. Recognizing counterfactual thinking in social media texts. In *Proceedings of the 55th Annual Meeting of the Association for Computational Linguistics (Volume 2: Short Papers)*, pages 654–658, Vancouver, Canada. Association for Computational Linguistics.

Ashish Vaswani, Noam Shazeer, Niki Parmar, Jakob Uszkoreit, Llion Jones, Aidan N Gomez, Łukasz Kaiser, and Illia Polosukhin. 2017. Attention is all you need. In *Advances in neural information processing systems*, pages 5998–6008.

Thomas Wolf, Lysandre Debut, Victor Sanh, Julien Chaumond, Clement Delangue, Anthony Moi, Pierric Cistac, Tim Rault, Remi Louf, Morgan Funtowicz, Joe Davison, Sam Shleifer, Patrick von Platen, Clara Ma, Yacine Jernite, Julien Plu, Canwen Xu, Teven Le Scao, Sylvain Gugger, Mariama Drame, Quentin Lhoest, and Alexander Rush. 2020. Transformers: State-of-the-art natural language processing. In *Proceedings of the 2020 Conference on Empirical Methods in Natural Language Processing: System Demonstrations*, pages 38–45, Online. Association for Computational Linguistics.

Len Yabloko. 2020. Ethan at semeval-2020 task 5: Modelling causal reasoning in language using neuro-symbolic cloud computing. In *Proceedings of the Fourteenth Workshop on Semantic Evaluation*, pages 645–652.

Xiaoyu Yang, Stephen Obadinma, Huasha Zhao, Qiong Zhang, Stan Matwin, and Xiaodan Zhu. 2020. SemEval-2020 task 5: Counterfactual recognition. In *Proceedings of the Fourteenth Workshop on Semantic Evaluation*, pages 322–335, Barcelona (online). International Committee for Computational Linguistics.

Zhilin Yang, Zihang Dai, Yiming Yang, Jaime G. Carbonell, Ruslan Salakhutdinov, and Quoc V. Le. 2019. XLNet: Generalized autoregressive pretraining for language understanding. *CoRR*, abs/1906.08237.

# Zero-shot Cross-Language Transfer of Monolingual Entity Linking Models

**Elliot Schumacher** **James Mayfield** **Mark Dredze**
Johns Hopkins University
eschuma7@jhu.edu mayfield@jhu.edu mdredze@cs.jhu.edu

## Abstract

Most entity linking systems, whether mono or multilingual, link mentions to a single English knowledge base. Few have considered linking non-English text to a non-English KB, and therefore, transferring an English entity linking model to both a new document and KB language. We consider the task of zero-shot cross-language transfer of entity linking systems to a new language and KB. We find that a system trained with multilingual representations does reasonably well, and propose improvements to system training that lead to improved recall in most datasets, often matching the in-language performance. We further conduct a detailed evaluation to elucidate the challenges of this setting.

## 1 Introduction

Entity linking – the process of matching mentions of people, places or organizations with a relevant knowledge base (KB) entry – has often focused on linking English text. Cross-language linking often uses English KBs for matching to non-English text. While transferring a system to a new document language presents challenges, it does not consider issues that arise when transferring to a new KB language. KBs in different languages consider different topics, and matching text within the same language presents different challenges from building cross-language representations. People build KBs in many different languages, and we should explore how to link documents to these KBs.

This paper considers zero-shot cross-language adaptation of a trained entity linking system to a new monolingual setting: the same new language for both the query document and KB. We consider adaptation so as to utilize the extensive annotated data resources for English, improving entity linking on languages that have little to no training data. Consider the example in Figure 1, which links the Spanish language mention *Senado* (*Senate*) to the KB entry *Senado de la República* (*Senate of the Republic of Mexico*). An entity linker uses the mention text and surrounding sentence paired with the KB entry (including information such as the name, description) to score the likelihood of a match. Many approaches to entity linking learn these linkages by training on a set of hand-annotated links in the desired language. If there are no or few language-specific annotations, how can we train a model on an annotation-rich language to perform well on other languages?

Similar to the architecture used in a cross-language setting (Schumacher et al., 2021), we take a neural approach to entity linking and use a multilingual pretrained transformer model, XLM-Roberta (XLM-R) (Conneau et al., 2019), to build representations of the available text for a mention and candidate entity pair. We feed each of these representations through a feed forward neural model to produce a likelihood score. XLM-R is a multilingual model that yields robust representations of text in a wide variety of languages. However, we find that even with the cross-language ability of XLM-R, in-language annotation data is key to an accurate linker. We thus propose ways to improve zero-shot cross-language transfer of a trained linker from one language to another.

We adapt a method from Chen and Cardie (2018) to add an adversarial objective to linker training which uses an intermediate layer in the linker to transform language-specific embeddings to language-agnostic via a language classification module. Similar approaches (Chen et al., 2019) have been used in other multilingual NLP tasks, but have yet to be explored in EL. To train this language-agnostic layer, we force the language classifier alone to predict the incorrect language label for unannotated portions of the source (*e.g.,* English) and target (*e.g.,* Spanish) text. We jointly train the ranker and the language classifier using the correct source (*e.g.,* English) language labels.



*Proceedings of the The 2nd Workshop on Multi-lingual Representation Learning (MRL)*, pages 38 - 51
December 8, 2022 ©2022 Association for Computational Linguistics

...lo acompañan el presidente del ***Senado*** ...

| | |
|---|---|
| name | *Senado de la República* |
| desc. | *El Senado de los Estados Unidos ...* |

Figure 1: Example Spanish mention *Senado*, which is a link to the Spanish KB entity *Senado de la República* (the Senate of Mexico)

which encourages the name and mention representation to be language-independent.

Second, we augment the entity linker with information from the target language KB to capture popularity of each entity, better handling entities that are common in the target language but rare in the source. We find that both model adjustments improve zero-shot performance on several language pairs, and that the adversarial model specifically produces consistent improvement in recall. Overall, we demonstrate that entity linking models can be effectively adapted to a new language for both the query document and KB.

## 2 Entity Linking Model

Figure 1 shows an example mention in Spanish (*Senado*) linked to a Spanish-language KB entry – *Senado de la República* for the Spanish mention. A linker will compare the text of the mention to the name of the entity, and consider information available in the context of the mention (the surrounding sentences). the entity description, and the mention and entity types.

One approach to handling linking in multiple langages is to train separate models. While this works well for languages with a large amount of *annotated* data (English), others have far less (Spanish). Additionally, training a new model for each language does not scale well to many languages. Instead, we pursue building a model that can be trained on entity linking annotations in a single language and transferred to another without additional annotations: cross-language entity linking.

### 2.1 Architecture

We use a standard neural ranking architecture to focus on the mechanisms of transfer that has been applied successfully in cross-language entity linking (Schumacher et al., 2021). To score a mention $m$ and and candidate entity $e$, we leverage a pointwise neural ranker inspired by the architecture of Dehghani et al. (2017). This produces a score for each mention-entity pair, creating a ranking of entities specific to each mention. Additionally, this pointwise approach allows scoring of previously unseen entities. We select a subset of entities to score using a triage system (§5.)

Our ranker captures two common sources of information about the entity – the mention string and entity name, and the context of the mention and the entity description. These sources are not KB specific (*e.g.*, type information) and thus transfer to different KBs. We create separate multilingual representations for the mention string and entity name ($m_s$ and $e_s$), and the mention and entity context ($m_c$ and $e_c$). The string and context pairs are fed into separate multilayer perceptrons (MLP), outputting an embedding that models the relationship between the entity and the mention. For example, we input $m_s$ and $e_s$ into a text-specific hidden layer $h_s$ which outputs a combined representation $r_s$, and we input $m_c$ and $e_c$ into a context-specific hidden layer $h_c$ which outputs a representation $r_c$. These representations $r_s$ and $r_c$ are then fed into a final MLP, which produces a score between $-1$ and 1.

To train our model parameters $\theta$, we score a mention $m$ and a correct entity link $e_+$, and separately score the same mention paired with $n$ randomly sampled negative entities $e_-$. We apply hinge loss between the positive pair and the best performing negative pair;

$$L(\theta) = \mathbf{max}\{0, \epsilon - (S(\{m, e_+\}; \theta) - \mathbf{max}\{S(\{m, e_{0-}\}; \theta) \ldots S(\{m, e_{n-}\}; \theta)\}\}$$

We use the resulting loss to backpropagate through the entire network. We use random combinations of parameters to select the best model configuration. For parameter values see Appendix Table 3.

### 2.2 Multilingual Representations

To create representations of the name and context for a mention-entity pair, we use XLM-Roberta (XLM-R) (Conneau et al., 2019), a multilingual transformer representation model. XLM-R outperforms other transformer models (such as mBERT (Devlin et al., 2019)) on multilingual tasks, and we confirmed this behavior in our initial experiments. Consider the Spanish example in Figure 1. We create a representation of the mention text $m_s$, *Senado*, by feeding the entire sentence through XLM-R, and form a single representation using max pooling on only the subwords of the mention. We create a representation of the entity name $e_s$, *Senado de la República* in the same way, except without any surrounding context.

To create $m_c$, we select the sentences surrounding the mention up to XLM-R's sub-word limit. We use max pooling over XLM-R to create a single representation, following Schumacher et al. (2021). The same process is used to encode the entity context $e_c$, but uses the definition in the KB, using the first 512 subword tokens from that description.

## 3 Multilingual Transfer

The use of XLM-R makes our model inherently multilingual, allowing a single model to build representations in several languages. While this allows our models to do fairly well on previously unseen languages, we consider ways to further improve models during transfer: adaptation of the name matching model, and adaptation to the new knowledge base.

### 3.1 Language Adaptation

One source of error may arise from a linker learning language-specific patterns which do not generalize to other languages. Consider the example in Figure 1: would the model recognize that Spanish mention *Senado* is not linked to the *United States Senate*? While XLM-R provides a multilingual representation, the entity linking model has not been trained to learn this nuance in Spanish.

We add an adversarial objective to ensure that the model focuses on language-agnostic representations of the text, which will better transfer to other languages. The advantage of this approach is that it does not require annotated training data, but uses unannotated data to encourage desired model behavior. Chen and Cardie (2018) train a text classification system with an adversarial objective that forces the network to learn domain-invariant features. In addition to a standard text classifier that uses features from a shared and domain specific feature extractor, they add a domain discriminator which uses the shared feature extractor as input. They run two training passes: 1) a training pass for the entire network that uses the correct classification and domain labels; 2) an adversarially trained domain discriminator and only the shared feature extractor, which uses the inverse of domain labels as the target. Prediction only uses the standard classification output. This objective improves performance when classifying text from previously unseen domains. We use this approach to learn language-invariant representations for our linking task, so they can be transferred to a new languages using only source-language linking annotations.

Our proposed adversarial approach is described in Algorithm 1 and illustrated in Figure 2. For each epoch, we first adversarially train the language classifier. Using pairs of unannotated English $\mathbb{A}$ and L2 $\mathbb{B}$ text, we create representations in the same method as for $m_s$ as described §2.2. Initially, we use randomly selected names from the ontology for $\mathbb{A}$ and $\mathbb{B}$ (see §6.3 for other approaches). Each of the two representations are fed into the shared invariant layer $h_{s0}$, the language classifier $h_{adv}$, and softmaxed to produce separate language likelihood scores for the English $p_A$ and L2 $p_B$ text. Importantly, we calculate the mean squared error (MSE) using the inverted language labels – for the English input, we calculate the error as if it was labelled as L2, and for the L2 input, we treat it as English. If we train with multiple L2 languages at the same time; all incorrect labels are applied with equal probability. We stop training the adversarial step after 50 epochs for one dataset (Wiki) based on development data performance.

We also run a standard entity linking training pass, in which we jointly train the linker and the language classifier using our set of training mentions $\mathbb{M}$ and corresponding entity labels $\mathbb{E}$. The entity linking loss is unchanged from §2.1, except that the $m_s$ and $e_s$ are first fed separately through the shared invariant layer $h_{s0}$. All $h$ hidden layers in the model are randomly initialized weight vectors and learned in the training process. The loss for the language classifier is unchanged from the first step except that the correct labels are used. The effect of the language classifier loss is controlled by the parameter $\lambda$, which we set to be either 0.25 or 0.01 depending on the dataset. Models including this are referred to as **+A**. Further implementation details are available in §6.3. We experimented with adding the additional layers $h_s0$ and not applying the adversarial objective, and feeding both the language-invariant (*e.g.*, $m$) and language-specific representations (*e.g.*, $r_m$)) into the linker, but both performed worse in development experiments.

## 4 Algorithms

### 4.1 KB Adaptation

A second source of error comes from a change in the coverage of the KB, not necessarily due to the

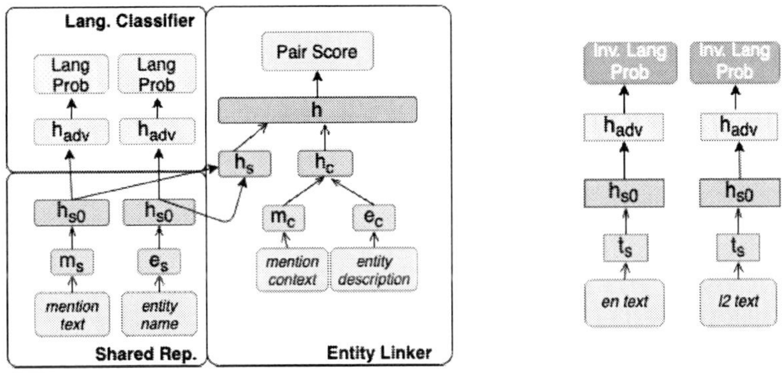


Figure 2: Our adversarial training approach consists of two steps – standard entity linking paired with training a language classifier (center), and adversarially training the language classifier (right). The hidden layer $h_{s0}$ is shared.

**Algorithm 1** Pseudo-code of adversarial model training. In each epoch, a random set of text ($y = 5$) is used to adversarially train the language classifier. Then, the entity linker and the language classifier with the correct labels are jointly trained.

**Require:** Mentions $\mathbb{M}$, entity labels $\mathbb{E}$; English Text $\mathbb{A}$; L2 Text $\mathbb{B}$; Hyperparameter $\lambda > 0$, $y$, $z \in N$, $num\_epochs$

**for** $ep = 0$ to $num\_epochs$ **do**
  $l_{adv}, l = 0$
  **for** $i = 0$ to $y$ **do** ▷ Adversarial Step
    $t_A$ = representation of $\mathbb{A}_i$
    $t_B$ = representation of $\mathbb{B}_i$
    $p_A = \mathcal{H}_{adv}(\mathcal{H}_{s0}(t_A))$
    $p_B = \mathcal{H}_{adv}(\mathcal{H}_{s0}(t_B))$ ▷ Calculate Lang scores
    $l_{adv}$ += MSE($p_A$, **L2**) + MSE($p_B$, **ENG**) ▷ Calculate Loss using reversed labels
  Update $\mathcal{H}_{adv}$ using $l_{adv}$
  **for** $i = 0$ to $z$ **do** ▷ Main Step
    $m$ = representation of $\mathbb{M}_i$
    $r_m = \mathcal{H}_{s0}(m)$
    $e$ = representation of $\mathbb{E}_i$
    $r_e = \mathcal{H}_{s0}(e)$
    $l$ = EL Loss (Eq. 1) with $r_m$ and $r_e$
    $p_M = \mathcal{H}_{adv}(r_m)$
    $p_E = \mathcal{H}_{adv}(r_e)$
    ▷ Calculate Lang scores
    $l$ += $\lambda$ (MSE($p_M$, **ENG**) + MSE($p_E$, **ENG**)) ▷ Calculate Loss using correct labels
  Update all parameters except $\mathcal{H}_{adv}$ using $l$

change in language. Trained entity linkers tend to do well on popular, or previously seen entities. New entities, which are common when a linker changes to a new KB, do worse. Consider the example in Figure 1: a linker trained on English will favor the KB entry for the U.S. Senate, more common in English language documents, as opposed to the Mexican Senate, which is more common in Spanish documents. This is especially important since we consider models transferred from TAC to our Wiki data (§5), which cover different topics.

We adapt the model to a KB in a new language by supplying the entity linker with popularity measures drawn from the new KB. This information could normally be derived from some annotated entity linking data, but in the zero-shot cross-language transfer setting we instead leverage the cross-links among entities in the KB, a good indicator of entity popularity. For example, the entity *Senado de la República* might have a link to the lower legislature of Mexico, *Cámara de Diputados*, and the President of Senate, *Presidente de la Cámara de Senadores*. Others, such as *Senado de Arizona*, are likely to have fewer. We count unique cross-links between entities, divide by the median number of links, and feed the result into the final feed forward neural network $h$ (indicated as **+P**).

## 5 Datasets

We consider entity linking datasets in multiple languages from two sources. We treat each language as having a distinct KB, although entities may overlap in different languages. We predict NILs (mentions with no matching entity) as those where all candidate entities are below a given threshold ($-1$

unless otherwise noted). We evaluate using the script from Ji et al. (2015): Precision, Recall, $F_1$, and Micro-averaged precision. See Appendix Section A for implementation details.

**TAC.** The 2015 TAC KBP Entity Discovery and Linking dataset (Ji et al., 2015) consists of newswire and discussion posts in English, Spanish, and Mandarin Chinese. A mention is linked to NIL if there is no relevant entity in the KB. The KB is based on BaseKB. KB entities without non-English names are omitted.

**Wiki.** We created a multi-language entity linking dataset from Wikipedia links (Pan et al., 2017a) for Farsi and Russian. A preprocessed version of Wikipedia[1] is annotated with links to in-language pages, which we treat as entities. We consider this to be silver-standard data because–unlike TAC – the annotations are automatically derived. Thus the resulting distribution of mentions is different. Comparing the number of exact matches between the mention text and the entity name in Wikipedia (*e.g.*,, in Farsi 54.5%) to TAC (*e.g.*,, in Spanish 21.2%) underscores that TAC is a more illustrative dataset, thus we caution against treating Wikipedia as a replacement for a human-annotated entity linking dataset.

**Triage.** We use the triage system of Upadhyay et al. (2018), which retrieves a reduced set of entities for a mention for us to score. For a given gold mention $m$, a triage system will provide a set of $k$ candidate entities $e_1 \dots e_k$. The system uses Wikipedia cross-links to generate a prior probability $\mathtt{P_{prior}}(e_i|m)$ by estimating counts from those mentions. Originally, this system was designed to produce links for non-English mentions to English titles. We tweak this approach by applying the same pipeline, but for in-language titles, which did not require any major algorithmic adaptations.

## 6 Model Evaluation

We begin with a zero-shot evaluation: how well does a model trained on English (TAC) transfer to a new language without in-language training data? This baseline, which uses the same architecture as Schumacher et al. (2021), leverages only the crosslingual ability of XLM-R to apply English language annotations to the new languages. We evaluate the English trained model on Spanish (es) and Chinese (zh) for TAC, and Russian (ru) and Farsi (fa) for Wiki. We also train a separate model for each of these languages to establish an in-language performance baseline. We illustrate the difference in performance of an English-only model as compared to an in-language trained one in Figure 3; the dashed line above each metric shows the increase in performance. To control for the effect of training set size we ensure that the training sets are of equivalent size for each language by randomly downsizing the larger training dataset (*e.g.*, English) to match the smaller (*e.g.*, Spanish). For comparison, we include a simple nearest neighbor baseline (noted as **nn**), which selects the highest scoring mention-entity pair using cosine similarity between the mention name $m_s$ and the entity representation $e_s$.

We then apply our language (noted as **+A**) and KB (noted as **+AP**) adaptation strategies for each language, and measure the performance on both the target and English language. In all cases, reported metrics are averaged over three runs. We report results for each language in the form of micro-averaged precision (micro), recall (r), and $F_1$. See Appendix Table 4 for full results and additional metrics, and Tables 5 and 6 for development results.

### 6.1 Transfer Performance

Figure 3 shows that zero-shot cross-language transfer from English gives worse performance compared to in-language models. Absolute values are included in Appendix Table 4. For TAC languages (es and zh) there is a large decrease in micro-avg and $F_1$, and the same for Wiki languages (fa and ru), except that $F_1$ decreases more significantly than recall, illustrating a drop in precision. The overall drop in performance is not large - the largest drop in $F_1$ is only .1 less compared to the in-language baseline. This illustrates that the linker is able to transfer across language and knowledge bases effectively. Compared to the baseline nearest neighbor model, which one has the higher performance improvement depends on the language. For example, while Spanish $F_1$ is nearly the same, Chinese $F_1$ is slightly higher with the **nn**, but in Farsi the English-trained model is an improvement for $F_1$.

We also evaluate other languages as sources of transfer. Appendix Table 4 shows results on training models on Chinese using the **+A** approach and testing on Spanish, demonstrating that our results are not specific to English. Note that the same

[1]We thank the authors of Pan et al. (2017a) for providing us with a preprocessed Wikipedia. We will work with the authors to release the dataset.

pattern appears when transferring from a Chinese trained model to a Spanish model. While the Spanish performance is understandably worse when transferring from Chinese instead of English, the reduction of $F_1$ performance is only $-.086$.

### 6.2 Language and KB adaptation

We train the TAC and Wiki datasets with different configurations based on development results (see §6.3): TAC: $\lambda = 0.25$ and the adversarial step covers all of training; Wiki: $\lambda = 0.01$ and stop the adversarial step after 50 epochs.

Applying the adversarial objective to English-trained models usually increases recall compared to the baseline English-trained models, and often even compared to the in-language trained models. For example, the English-trained, Chinese-tested model sees a large drop in recall which is almost completely eliminated when applying the adversarial objective. This increase in recall leads to nearly-equivalent $F_1$ performance in Spanish and Chinese in-language models and English trained models with the adversarial objective. In short, adversarial training greatly improves the models ability to locate the right KB entry, suggesting better name matching. This recall-focused improvement is useful for settings where high-recall is desired, such as in search. The exception to this is Farsi – this is likely because the high recall 0.934 of the zero-shot model established a high starting point. Compared to the nearest neighbor baseline, the **+A** outperforms the baseline in all languages for $F_1$, nn $F_1$, micro-avg., and recall. The same pattern appears when transferring a Chinese model instead of English. The $F_1$ performance is only $-.017$ below the in-language trained model despite not sharing a writing system.

We also explored transferring a multilingual model: training on English with **+A** and testing on all target languages at once (see Appendix Table 4). In almost all cases, the multilingual adversarial approach performs worse than a single-language one, but only slightly; it may be preferable when targeting multiple languages. KB popularity (**+AP**) has the largest effect on micro-average precision by doing much better on rarer entities, specifically in the TAC dataset. While in Chinese the improvement in micro-average is larger in the **+AP** models than in **+A**, in all other cases the micro-average is close to the **+A** model.

We explored model behavior on different types of entities using the TAC evaluation dataset and provided mention types (see Appendix Table A). For *Person* mentions, we see consistent performance between in-language, English, and English+**A** trained models. While this is not unexpected in Spanish (which has similar names to English), it is also true in Chinese, which uses a different orthography than English. The largest performance change occurred in *Geo-Political Entities*. For Chinese, $F_1$ drops 0.15 for an English trained model compared to an in-language trained model, but the deficit is erased in the English+**A** model. A similar pattern occurs in Spanish, suggesting that the adversarial model is able to improve the more challenging entity types.

### 6.3 Design of Adversarial objective

How does the configuration of the **+A** model change its behavior? We vary three factors and measure results on TAC evaluation (full results shown in Table 1): 1) the size of the coefficient $\lambda$; 2) whether to train using the entity linking objective only for an additional 50 epochs instead of for all epochs (for lower $\lambda$ and additional entity linking training, we found that both worked better on Wiki development data, while a higher $\lambda$ and full training worked better for TAC); and 3) training **+A** using randomly selected names from English and the target language plausibly learns a better name model than it does language-invariant representations, so we instead train with the first 512 subwords of randomly selected descriptions.

Comparing to a Chinese trained model, we considered versions with all non-baseline models trained on the joint entity linking and adversarial objective for 50 epochs, and the +EL models trained on EL data for an additional 50. Our reported setting for TAC, $\lambda = 0.25$ with name data, performs best on recall, $F_1$, and non-NIL $F_1$. However, when using the description data and $\lambda = 0.01$ with or without additional EL training, a better micro-averaged precision is achieved. Generally, the models using name data perform slightly better than those using descriptions, but the overall difference is slight (*e.g.*, $+.009$ $F_1$ for $\lambda = 0.25$ with name, $-.015$ $F_1$ with description), suggesting that the model is learning better multilingual representations. Finally, recall generally performs best with a higher $\lambda$ and full adversarial training, and improves less with a lower $\lambda$ and EL only training.

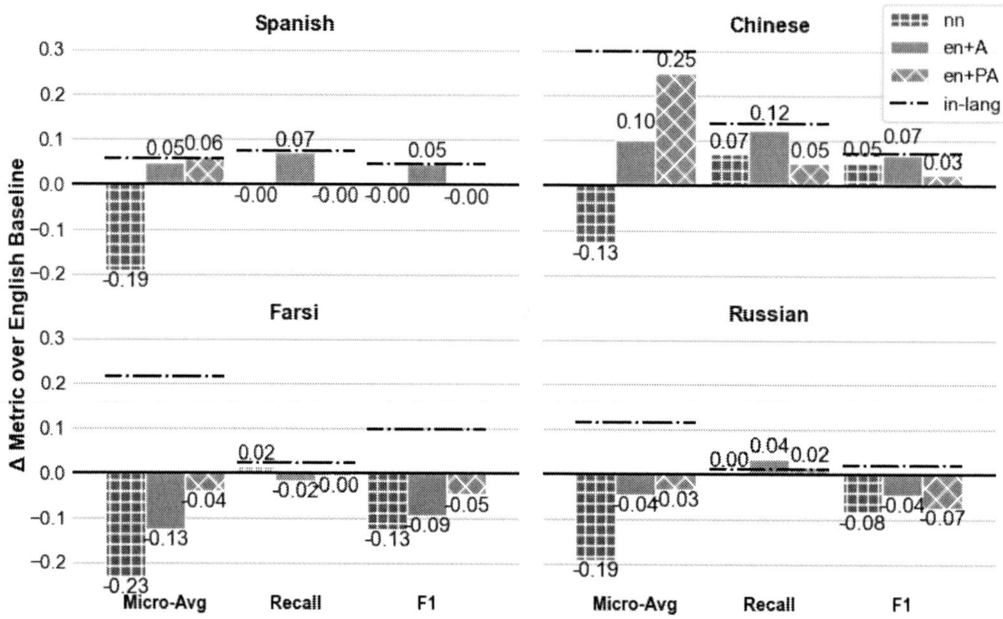


Figure 3: Compared to an English-only baseline (0.0 on y-axis), how do models with the adversarial objective (**+A**), the adversarial objective with popularity (**+PA**), and a nearest neighbor baseline (**nn**) perform? While in most cases, the performance of all models is below that of an in-language trained model (dashed line), **+A** most closely matches the recall in most cases. Additionally, **+PA** is best able to improve micro-average, especially compared to the poor performance of **nn**. All results and additional metrics are provided in Appendix Table 4.

### 6.4 Effect on English performance

What effect does forcing an English-trained model to better orient to a target language have on English-language performance? Table 2 shows TAC English evaluation results in three settings: 1) a baseline linker with English training data matched to the size of the target language's training data; 2) the added **+A** objective; 3) the added **+AP** objective. These are the same models as in Table 2, except tested on English.

Interestingly, the performance change is very small: a small increase for micro-average and a small decrease in $F_1$ and non-NIL $F_1$. The largest drop in performance is less than 0.05. This illustrates the capacity of the model: it can adapt to a new language while maintaining its performance on the source language.

| | Test | micro | r | $F_1$ | nn $F_1$ |
|---|---|---|---|---|---|
| | zh | 0.674 | 0.789 | 0.824 | 0.846 |
| | en base | −.341 | −.123 | −.060 | −.071 |
| +A name | .25 | −.190 | −.001 | +.009 | −.003 |
| +A name | .01 | −.202 | −.078 | −.033 | −.036 |
| +A name | .25+ | −.205 | −.123 | −.062 | −.073 |
| +A name | .01+ | −.230 | −.137 | −.072 | −.087 |
| +A desc | .25 | −.317 | −.048 | −.015 | −.012 |
| +A desc | .01 | −.169 | −.088 | −.041 | −.046 |
| +A desc | .25+ | −.287 | −.188 | −.108 | −.133 |
| +A desc | .01+ | −.145 | −.150 | −.080 | −.097 |

Table 1: How do adversarial settings affect performance? We consider the coefficient $\lambda$, type of text (names or descriptions), and entity-only training for 50 more epochs (*i.e.,* we stop updating the language classifier, indicated by +). Comparing an in-language to an English trained model using TAC Chinese evaluation, we find that $\lambda = .25$ with name data performs best in terms of recall, $F_1$, and nn $F_1$.

### 6.5 Analysis

While our training methods are effective, they are inconsistent across our experiments. **+A** improves performance more on TAC data (Spanish and Chinese) than Wiki data (Farsi and Russian).

We postulate several explanations for this trend.

First, the distribution of mentions is different between the two datasets. The lexical similarity between mentions and entity names – one measure of how easy the mentions are to link – is much higher in Wiki. For Farsi development mentions, 54.5% were exact matches and also had an overall Jaro-Winkler (Winkler, 1990) lexical similarity of 94.1%. Compared to Spanish TAC (21.1% exact, 71.4% similarity) and Chinese (28% exact, 66.1% similarity), the Farsi data is relatively easy to link. While many entity linking studies rely on Wikipedia data due to its availability, it is not representative of other data types; we should build more human-annotated entity linking resources in non-English languages.

When comparing the drop in performance from an in-language trained model to an English trained model, recall drops in the TAC data, while precision drops in the Wiki data. The drop in precision may be due to the fact that we use English TAC data to train the zero-shot Wiki models, and that recall is fairly easy given the high mention-entity similarity. Another factor is the possibility that Wikipedia text is less suited as adversarial training data, compared to that from TAC. Thus, while see an increase in recall in the Wiki models, but this does not cancel out the reduction in precision.

## 7 Related Work

Many studies on entity linking (Dredze et al., 2010; Durrett and Klein, 2014; Gupta et al., 2017; Lample et al., 2016; Francis-Landau et al., 2016; Cao et al., 2018; Mueller and Durrett, 2018; Wang et al., 2015; Witten and Milne, 2008; Piccinno and Ferragina, 2014; Orr et al., 2020) have served as the basis for developing cross-language systems, as has increasing research in monolingual model transfer in other information extraction tasks (Johnson et al., 2019; Rahimi et al., 2019).

One multilingual model is Raiman and Raiman (2018), which transfers an English-trained system to French-language Wikipedia. They formulate a type system as a mixed integer problem, which they use to learn a type system from knowledge graph relations. Their training approach uses broad amounts of annotated data with type information (*e.g.,* all of English Wikipedia). Since we do not train English Wikipedia models, and also do not use that magnitude of training data, we were not able to produce numbers using their system that are comparable to ours despite our best efforts to do so.

| Target | micro | $F_1$ | nn $F_1$ |
|---|---|---|---|
| en | 0.484 | 0.672 | 0.797 |
| zh+A | +.009 | +.014 | +.015 |
| zh+P | +.030 | −.025 | −.031 |
| en | 0.472 | 0.678 | 0.802 |
| es+A | +.004 | −.014 | −.017 |
| es+P | +.011 | −.036 | −.043 |

Table 2: Compared to a baseline English TAC model (with training set size reduced to the noted language's training set size), we find that English performance is largely unchanged for both **+A** and **+P**.

Other recent work (Botha et al., 2020) uses a neural approach to link mentions in multiple languages, but differs from us by targeting language-agnostic KBs that include text in multiple languages. Work using unsupervised graph methods, such as Wang et al. (2015), are applied in non-English language pairs, such as Chinese, but are not transferred from a secondary language.

The related task of cross-language entity linking motivates approaches like transliteration (McNamee et al., 2011; Pan et al., 2017b), or monolingual entity linking paired with translation (Ji et al., 2015). Some (Tsai and Roth, 2016; Upadhyay et al., 2018) use the cross-language structure of Wikipedia to build entity linkers, or Rijhwani et al. (2019) study cross-language entity linking on low-resource languages.

## 8 Conclusion

We explored how to build a monolingually-trained entity linker that can be transferred to new languages that do not have annotated training data. With a neural ranker model using XLM R, we see that while in-language trained models perform better than English-trained models applied to second languages, the performance decrease is not large.

We have validated several ways to improve these zero-shot models and find that an adversarial language classifier improves recall and $F_1$ on many datasets. Furthermore, by adjusting the adversarial parameters, different performance objectives can be achieved, such as maximizing recall. We also present an analysis of our models, demonstrating which settings have the highest expectation of success. Overall, we find that training the model to learn language-invariant representations is effective in improving performance when transferring to both text and a KB in a new language.

## References


Jan A. Botha, Zifei Shan, and Daniel Gillick. 2020. Entity Linking in 100 Languages. In *Proceedings of the 2020 Conference on Empirical Methods in Natural Language Processing (EMNLP)*, pages 7833–7845, Online. Association for Computational Linguistics.

Yixin Cao, Lei Hou, Juanzi Li, and Zhiyuan Liu. 2018. Neural collective entity linking. In *Proceedings of the 27th International Conference on Computational Linguistics*, pages 675–686, Santa Fe, New Mexico, USA. Association for Computational Linguistics.

Xilun Chen, Ahmed Hassan Awadallah, Hany Hassan, Wei Wang, and Claire Cardie. 2019. Multi-source cross-lingual model transfer: Learning what to share. In *Proceedings of the 57th Annual Meeting of the Association for Computational Linguistics*, pages 3098–3112, Florence, Italy. Association for Computational Linguistics.

Xilun Chen and Claire Cardie. 2018. Multinomial adversarial networks for multi-domain text classification. In *Proceedings of the 2018 Conference of the North American Chapter of the Association for Computational Linguistics: Human Language Technologies, Volume 1 (Long Papers)*, pages 1226–1240, New Orleans, Louisiana. Association for Computational Linguistics.

Alexis Conneau, Kartikay Khandelwal, Naman Goyal, Vishrav Chaudhary, Guillaume Wenzek, Francisco Guzmán, Edouard Grave, Myle Ott, Luke Zettlemoyer, and Veselin Stoyanov. 2019. Unsupervised cross-lingual representation learning at scale. *arXiv preprint arXiv:1911.02116*.

Mostafa Dehghani, Hamed Zamani, Aliaksei Severyn, Jaap Kamps, and W Bruce Croft. 2017. Neural ranking models with weak supervision. In *Proceedings of the 40th International ACM SIGIR Conference on Research and Development in Information Retrieval*, pages 65–74. ACM.

Jacob Devlin, Ming-Wei Chang, Kenton Lee, and Kristina Toutanova. 2019. BERT: Pre-training of deep bidirectional transformers for language understanding. In *Proceedings of the 2019 Conference of the North American Chapter of the Association for Computational Linguistics: Human Language Technologies, Volume 1 (Long and Short Papers)*, pages 4171–4186, Minneapolis, Minnesota. Association for Computational Linguistics.

Mark Dredze, Paul McNamee, Delip Rao, Adam Gerber, and Tim Finin. 2010. Entity disambiguation for knowledge base population. In *Conference on Computational Linguistics (COLING)*, pages 277–285. Association for Computational Linguistics.

Greg Durrett and Dan Klein. 2014. A joint model for entity analysis: Coreference, typing, and linking. *Transactions of the Association for Computational Linguistics*, 2:477–490.

Matthew Francis-Landau, Greg Durrett, and Dan Klein. 2016. Capturing semantic similarity for entity linking with convolutional neural networks. In *Proceedings of the 2016 Conference of the North American Chapter of the Association for Computational Linguistics: Human Language Technologies*, pages 1256–1261, San Diego, California. Association for Computational Linguistics.

Nitish Gupta, Sameer Singh, and Dan Roth. 2017. Entity linking via joint encoding of types, descriptions, and context. In *Proceedings of the 2017 Conference on Empirical Methods in Natural Language Processing*, pages 2681–2690, Copenhagen, Denmark. Association for Computational Linguistics.

Heng Ji, Joel Nothman, Ben Hachey, and Radu Florian. 2015. Overview of TAC-KBP2015 Tri-lingual Entity Discovery and Linking. *TAC*.

Andrew Johnson, Penny Karanasou, Judith Gaspers, and Dietrich Klakow. 2019. Cross-lingual transfer learning for Japanese named entity recognition. In *Proceedings of the 2019 Conference of the North American Chapter of the Association for Computational Linguistics: Human Language Technologies, Volume 2 (Industry Papers)*, pages 182–189, Minneapolis, Minnesota. Association for Computational Linguistics.

Guillaume Lample, Miguel Ballesteros, Sandeep Subramanian, Kazuya Kawakami, and Chris Dyer. 2016. Neural architectures for named entity recognition. In *Proceedings of the 2016 Conference of the North American Chapter of the Association for Computational Linguistics: Human Language Technologies*, pages 260–270, San Diego, California. Association for Computational Linguistics.

Paul McNamee, James Mayfield, Dawn Lawrie, Douglas Oard, and David Doermann. 2011. Cross-language entity linking. In *Proceedings of 5th International Joint Conference on Natural Language Processing*, pages 255–263, Chiang Mai, Thailand. Asian Federation of Natural Language Processing.

David Mueller and Greg Durrett. 2018. Effective use of context in noisy entity linking. In *Proceedings of the 2018 Conference on Empirical Methods in Natural Language Processing*, pages 1024–1029, Brussels, Belgium. Association for Computational Linguistics.

Laurel Orr, Megan Leszczynski, Simran Arora, Sen Wu, Neel Guha, Xiao Ling, and Christopher Re. 2020. Bootleg: Chasing the tail with self-supervised named entity disambiguation.

Xiaoman Pan, Boliang Zhang, Jonathan May, Joel Nothman, Kevin Knight, and Heng Ji. 2017a. Cross-lingual name tagging and linking for 282 languages. In *Proceedings of the 55th Annual Meeting of the Association for Computational Linguistics (Volume 1: Long Papers)*, volume 1, pages 1946–1958.

Xiaoman Pan, Boliang Zhang, Jonathan May, Joel Nothman, Kevin Knight, and Heng Ji. 2017b. Cross-lingual name tagging and linking for 282 languages. In *Proceedings of the 55th Annual Meeting of the Association for Computational Linguistics (Volume 1: Long Papers)*, pages 1946–1958, Vancouver, Canada. Association for Computational Linguistics.

Francesco Piccinno and P. Ferragina. 2014. From tagme to wat: a new entity annotator. In *ERD '14*.

Afshin Rahimi, Yuan Li, and Trevor Cohn. 2019. Massively multilingual transfer for NER. In *Proceedings of the 57th Annual Meeting of the Association for Computational Linguistics*, pages 151–164, Florence, Italy. Association for Computational Linguistics.

Jonathan Raphael Raiman and Olivier Michel Raiman. 2018. Deeptype: multilingual entity linking by neural type system evolution. In *Thirty-Second AAAI Conference on Artificial Intelligence*.

Shruti Rijhwani, Jiateng Xie, Graham Neubig, and Jaime Carbonell. 2019. Zero-shot neural transfer for cross-lingual entity linking. In *Proceedings of the AAAI Conference on Artificial Intelligence*, volume 33, pages 6924–6931.

Elliot Schumacher, James Mayfield, and Mark Dredze. 2021. Cross-lingual transfer in zero-shot cross-language entity linking. In *Findings of the Association for Computational Linguistics: ACL-IJCNLP 2021*, pages 583–595, Online. Association for Computational Linguistics.

Chen-Tse Tsai and Dan Roth. 2016. Cross-lingual Wikification Using Multilingual Embeddings. In *Proceedings of the 2016 Conference of the North American Chapter of the Association for Computational Linguistics: Human Language Technologies*, pages 589–598, Stroudsburg, PA, USA. Association for Computational Linguistics.

Shyam Upadhyay, Nitish Gupta, and Dan Roth. 2018. Joint multilingual supervision for cross-lingual entity linking. In *Proceedings of the 2018 Conference on Empirical Methods in Natural Language Processing*, pages 2486–2495, Brussels, Belgium. Association for Computational Linguistics.

Han Wang, Jin Guang Zheng, Xiaogang Ma, Peter Fox, and Heng Ji. 2015. Language and domain independent entity linking with quantified collective validation. In *Proceedings of the 2015 Conference on Empirical Methods in Natural Language Processing*, pages 695–704, Lisbon, Portugal. Association for Computational Linguistics.

William E Winkler. 1990. String comparator metrics and enhanced decision rules in the fellegi-sunter model of record linkage. *ERIC*.

Ian H Witten and David N Milne. 2008. An effective, low-cost measure of semantic relatedness obtained from wikipedia links.

## A Dataset

**TAC** The training set consists of mentions across 447 documents, and the evaluation set consists of mention annotations across 502 documents. This leaves us $14,793$ development mentions, of which $11,344$ are non-NIL.

**Wiki** Some BaseKB entities used in the TAC dataset have Wikipedia links provided; we used those links as seed entities for retrieving mentions, retrieving a sample mention of those and adding the remaining links in the page. We mark 20% of the mentions as NIL.

**Triage** We use the system discussed in for both the **TAC** and **Wiki** datasets. However, while the triage system provides candidates in the same KB as the **Wiki** data, not all entities in the **TAC** KB have Wikipedia page titles. Therefore, the **TAC** triage step requires an intermediate step - using the Wikipedia titles generated by triage ($k = 10$), we query a Lucene database of BaseKB for relevant entities. For each title, we query BaseKB proportional to the prior provided by the triage system, meaning that we retrieve more BaseKB entities for titles that have a higher triage score, resulting in $l = 200$ entities. First, entities with Wikipedia titles are queried, followed by the entity name itself. If none are found, we query the mention string - this provides a small increase in triage recall.

| **Parameter** | **Values** |
|---|---|
| Context Layer(s) | [768], **[512]**, [256], [512,256] |
| Mention Layer(s) | [768], **[512]**, [256], [512,256] |
| Final Layer(s) | **[512,256]**, [256,128], [128,64], [1024,512], [512], [256] |
| Dropout probability | 0.1, **0.2**, 0.5 |
| Learning rate | 1e-5, 5e-4, **1e-4**, 5e-3, 1e-3 |

Table 3: To select parameters for the ranker, we tried 10 random combinations of the above parameters and selected the configuration that performed best on the TAC development set. The selected parameter is in bold.

| | Spanish (es) evaluation | | | | | Chinese (zh) evaluation | | | | |
|---|---|---|---|---|---|---|---|---|---|---|
| Training | micro | p | r | $F_1$ | nn $F_1$ | micro | p | r | $F_1$ | nn $F_1$ |
| same | 0.623 | 0.910 | 0.711 | 0.798 | 0.870 | 0.670 | 0.862 | 0.787 | 0.822 | 0.844 |
| nn | 0.375 | 0.924 | 0.633 | 0.751 | 0.809 | 0.244 | 0.910 | 0.719 | 0.803 | 0.826 |
| en | 0.565 | 0.925 | 0.635 | 0.753 | 0.810 | 0.371 | 0.893 | 0.647 | 0.750 | 0.757 |
| en+A | 0.615 | 0.923 | 0.706 | 0.800 | 0.876 | 0.472 | 0.877 | 0.770 | 0.820 | 0.839 |
| en+P | 0.632 | 0.919 | 0.616 | 0.738 | 0.790 | 0.462 | 0.869 | 0.636 | 0.734 | 0.734 |
| en+PA | 0.628 | 0.921 | 0.633 | 0.750 | 0.808 | 0.622 | 0.871 | 0.698 | 0.775 | 0.790 |
| en+A (all) | 0.562 | 0.917 | 0.694 | 0.790 | 0.862 | 0.466 | 0.882 | 0.722 | 0.794 | 0.813 |
| zh | 0.492 | 0.924 | 0.579 | 0.712 | 0.755 | — | — | — | — | — |
| zh+A | 0.523 | 0.901 | 0.690 | 0.781 | 0.852 | — | — | — | — | — |
| | Farsi (fa) evaluation | | | | | Russian (ru) evaluation | | | | |
| Training | micro | p | r | $F_1$ | nn $F_1$ | micro | p | r | $F_1$ | nn $F_1$ |
| same | 0.838 | 0.902 | 0.958 | 0.929 | 0.908 | 0.526 | 0.729 | 0.827 | 0.775 | 0.721 |
| nn | 0.392 | 0.560 | 0.950 | 0.705 | 0.585 | 0.362 | 0.654 | 0.868 | 0.746 | 0.680 |
| en | 0.623 | 0.748 | 0.934 | 0.830 | 0.774 | 0.552 | 0.798 | 0.863 | 0.829 | 0.791 |
| en+A | 0.498 | 0.616 | 0.918 | 0.737 | 0.639 | 0.508 | 0.697 | 0.899 | 0.785 | 0.729 |
| en+A (all) | 0.525 | 0.631 | 0.955 | 0.759 | 0.668 | 0.516 | 0.758 | 0.852 | 0.802 | 0.755 |
| en+P | 0.627 | 0.700 | 0.958 | 0.809 | 0.741 | 0.565 | 0.700 | 0.889 | 0.783 | 0.728 |
| en+PA | 0.584 | 0.679 | 0.930 | 0.785 | 0.709 | 0.519 | 0.661 | 0.881 | 0.755 | 0.691 |

Table 4: Compared to an in-language trained model and a nearest-neighbor baseline (**nn**), how does a zero-shot model trained only on English transfer? We find that while there is usually a performance improvement, it is often not large. Can we recover some of that lost performance by using an adversarial objective (**+A**) or adding knowledge base information (**+P**), or both (**+PA**)? We find that when applying an adversarial objective specifically, recall is increased leading to higher $F_1$ scores. For each setting, we report Micro-avg., precision, recall, $F_1$, and non-NIL $F_1$ on TAC and Wiki datasets.

| Train / Test | Model | All micro | All p | All r | All f1 | Non-NIL micro | Non-NIL p | Non-NIL r | Non-NIL f1 | Epoch |
|---|---|---|---|---|---|---|---|---|---|---|
| zh/zh | Baseline | 0.795 | 0.890 | 0.830 | 0.859 | 0.801 | 0.884 | 0.884 | 0.884 | 50 |
| en/zh | Baseline | 0.202 | 0.905 | 0.697 | 0.788 | 0.077 | 0.899 | 0.721 | 0.800 | 100 |
| en/zh | +A | 0.439 | 0.897 | 0.732 | 0.806 | 0.367 | 0.892 | 0.764 | 0.823 | 50 |
| en/zh | +A | 0.381 | 0.911 | 0.756 | 0.827 | 0.296 | 0.907 | 0.794 | 0.847 | 50 |
| en/zh | +PA | 0.635 | 0.889 | 0.753 | 0.815 | 0.606 | 0.881 | 0.789 | 0.833 | 100 |
| en/zh | +A (Desc) | 0.266 | 0.908 | 0.718 | 0.802 | 0.156 | 0.903 | 0.747 | 0.818 | |
| en/zh | +PA (Desc) | 0.645 | 0.885 | 0.774 | 0.826 | 0.618 | 0.877 | 0.815 | 0.845 | |
| en/zh | +P | 0.544 | 0.894 | 0.685 | 0.776 | 0.494 | 0.888 | 0.707 | 0.787 | 200 |
| es/es | Baseline | 0.714 | 0.933 | 0.777 | 0.848 | 0.739 | 0.930 | 0.891 | 0.910 | 50 |
| en/es | Baseline | 0.488 | 0.942 | 0.643 | 0.764 | 0.444 | 0.944 | 0.716 | 0.815 | 100 |
| en/es | +A | 0.469 | 0.938 | 0.693 | 0.797 | 0.420 | 0.939 | 0.782 | 0.853 | 150 |
| en/es | +A (multi) | 0.548 | 0.952 | 0.753 | 0.841 | 0.523 | 0.956 | 0.860 | 0.906 | 50 |
| en/es | +PA | 0.654 | 0.931 | 0.695 | 0.796 | 0.660 | 0.931 | 0.784 | 0.851 | 100 |
| en/es | +A (Desc) | 0.496 | 0.943 | 0.737 | 0.828 | 0.455 | 0.949 | 0.839 | 0.891 | |
| en/es | +PA (Desc) | 0.650 | 0.937 | 0.692 | 0.796 | 0.656 | 0.939 | 0.780 | 0.852 | |
| en/es | +P | 0.664 | 0.928 | 0.698 | 0.797 | 0.674 | 0.930 | 0.788 | 0.853 | 150 |
| zh/es | Baseline | 0.378 | 0.942 | 0.661 | 0.777 | 0.301 | 0.943 | 0.739 | 0.829 | 550 |
| zh/es | +A | 0.514 | 0.939 | 0.785 | 0.855 | 0.479 | 0.945 | 0.902 | 0.923 | 49 |

Table 5: Single runs of Development TAC results for our reported models, and the training epoch we report for that configuration in the evaluation results table. Note that while we report results with the training sets equalized (zh and en training are set to be of equal size) for evaluation, the full development results do not have equalized training set sizes.

| Train/Test | Model | micro | p | r | f1 | Eval Epoch |
|---|---|---|---|---|---|---|
| ru/ru | Baseline | 0.650 | 0.823 | 0.888 | 0.854 | 800 |
| en/ru | Baseline | 0.484 | 0.762 | 0.855 | 0.806 | 550 |
| en/ru | +A | 0.451 | 0.712 | 0.893 | 0.792 | 50 |
| en/ru | +A (multi) | 0.4188 | 0.6517 | 0.8652 | 0.7434 | 200 |
| en/ru | +P | 0.473 | 0.685 | 0.860 | 0.762 | 50 |
| fa/fa | Baseline | 0.832 | 0.881 | 0.966 | 0.922 | 800 |
| en/fa | Baseline | 0.603 | 0.720 | 0.928 | 0.811 | 150 |
| en/fa | +A | 0.447 | 0.555 | 0.948 | 0.700 | 200 |
| en/fa | +A (multi) | 0.448 | 0.538 | 0.966 | 0.691 | 50 |

Table 6: Single runs of Development Wiki results for select reported models, and the training epoch we report for that configuration in the evaluation results table. Note that while we report results with the training sets equalized (ru and en training are set to be of equal size) for evaluation, the full development results do not have equalized training set sizes. For the +AP model, we report at Epoch 150 for Russian and 200 for Farsi, and for +P Farsi we report Epoch 50 (same as in Russian). Note that with the Farsi +A (multi) model, since the best performing epoch was at 50, in effect to EL-only training was performed.

| | | | In-Language | | | En | | | En+A | | |
|---|---|---|---|---|---|---|---|---|---|---|---|
| type | lang | count | micro | r | f1 | micro | r | f1 | micro | r | f1 |
| CMN | FAC | 59 | 0.169 | 0.631 | 0.756 | 0.119 | 0.515 | 0.670 | 0.169 | 0.632 | 0.768 |
| CMN | GPE | 3933 | 0.856 | 0.906 | 0.912 | 0.108 | 0.685 | 0.796 | 0.510 | 0.887 | 0.916 |
| CMN | LOC | 461 | 0.729 | 0.947 | 0.886 | 0.488 | 0.810 | 0.840 | 0.547 | 0.933 | 0.892 |
| CMN | ORG | 1441 | 0.160 | 0.726 | 0.774 | 0.299 | 0.629 | 0.722 | 0.127 | 0.799 | 0.821 |
| CMN | PER | 3116 | 0.708 | 0.682 | 0.797 | 0.612 | 0.676 | 0.792 | 0.610 | 0.676 | 0.792 |
| SPA | FAC | 59 | 0.051 | 0.294 | 0.454 | 0.068 | 0.285 | 0.444 | 0.102 | 0.289 | 0.448 |
| SPA | GPE | 1570 | 0.664 | 0.891 | 0.927 | 0.338 | 0.674 | 0.791 | 0.532 | 0.830 | 0.888 |
| SPA | LOC | 174 | 0.144 | 0.824 | 0.874 | 0.672 | 0.717 | 0.810 | 0.787 | 0.863 | 0.892 |
| SPA | ORG | 799 | 0.451 | 0.681 | 0.782 | 0.444 | 0.678 | 0.779 | 0.444 | 0.691 | 0.788 |
| SPA | PER | 2022 | 0.715 | 0.624 | 0.755 | 0.693 | 0.602 | 0.741 | 0.723 | 0.624 | 0.755 |

Table 7: How do the results of in-language training compare to English-only trained models and models trained with the adversarial objective? We find that some types perform consistently, such as PER (or Persons) even in languages that do not share scripts. Others, such as GPE (Geo-Political Entities) and ORG (Organizations) see a substantial drop in performance when applying a English-only model, but see more of that regained when using an adversarial objective. These results are taken from a single run of the TAC evaluation data.

# Rule-Based Clause-Level Morphology for Multiple Languages

**Tillmann Dönicke**
Göttingen Centre for Digital Humanities
University of Göttingen
tillmann.doenicke@uni-goettingen.de

## Abstract

This paper describes an approach for the morphosyntactic analysis of clauses, including the analysis of composite verb forms and both overt and covert pronouns. The approach uses grammatical rules for verb inflection and clause-internal word agreement to compute a clause's morphosyntactic features from the morphological features of the individual words. The approach is tested for eight typologically diverse languages in the 1st Shared Task on Multilingual Clause-Level Morphology, where it achieves F1 scores between 79% and 99% (94% in average).

## 1 Introduction

Until recently the prediction of clause-level morphological / morphosyntactic features has been approached for a few individual languages only (see Žáčková et al. (2000) for Czech, Choudhary et al. (2014) for Hindi, Faro and Pavone (2015) for Italian, Ramm et al. (2017) for English, French and German, Myers and Palmer (2019) for English revisited, and Dönicke (2020) for German revisited). Most of the approaches are rule-based, first of all because annotated training data barely exists. On the other hand, it seems intuitive to approach this task in a rule-based manner, since morphosyntax follows strict grammatical rules (as opposed to heuristics) that can be implemented by a linguist. The first work to our knowledge which considers multiple and typologically diverse languages at a time is that of Dönicke (2021), who presents a cross-linguistic algorithm for composite-verb analysis and implements it for 11 languages, but refrains from evaluating the approach due to the lack of annotated gold data. The 1st Shared Task on Multilingual Clause-Level Morphology tackles this lack of data and provides data sets for eight typologically diverse languages. We re-implement and extend Dönicke (2021)'s algorithm for the shared task (Section 3), evaluate it (Section 4) and discuss its advantages and shortcomings (Section 5).

## 2 Shared Task and Data

The 1st Shared Task on Multilingual Clause-Level Morphology (Task 3 Analysis) provides data sets for eight languages. Training sets (10,000 samples each) and development sets (2,000 samples each) for six languages were released first, and test sets (1,000 samples each) as well as all sets for two surprise languages (Spanish and Swahili) were released two weeks before the system submission deadline. Each sample consists of a short sentence and a gold analysis. The sentence consists of a single clause and contains one verb form that can be simple (e.g. *he* <u>*looks*</u>) or composite (e.g. *he* <u>*had not been looking*</u>) as well as pronouns, adpositions and a sentence-final punctuation mark. The gold analysis consists of the main verb's lemma, the analysis of the verb form and the analyses of all pronouns, both overtly expressed pronouns (as in <u>*he*</u> *looks*) and covertly expressed ones (as in <u>*∅*</u> *look!*). The analyses are represented with UniMorph features (Sylak-Glassman, 2016). The task was to predict an analysis for an input sentence. Since the test sets were provided without gold analyses, the submission and evaluation of systems was performed via CodaLab.[1]

## 3 Method

### 3.0 Motivation

Computing the morphosyntactic analysis of a clause can be modeled as a mapping from word-level morphological features to clause-level morphological features. This process follows grammatical rules, in particular (language-specific) rules for verb inflection and (language-independent) rules of agreement between words in a clause. Figure 1

[1]https://codalab.lisn.upsaclay.fr/competitions/6830?secret_key=44e813c2-96c8-4889-b0fc-24dbe83ad2c6



*Proceedings of the The 2nd Workshop on Multi-lingual Representation Learning (MRL)*, pages 52 - 63
December 8, 2022 ©2022 Association for Computational Linguistics

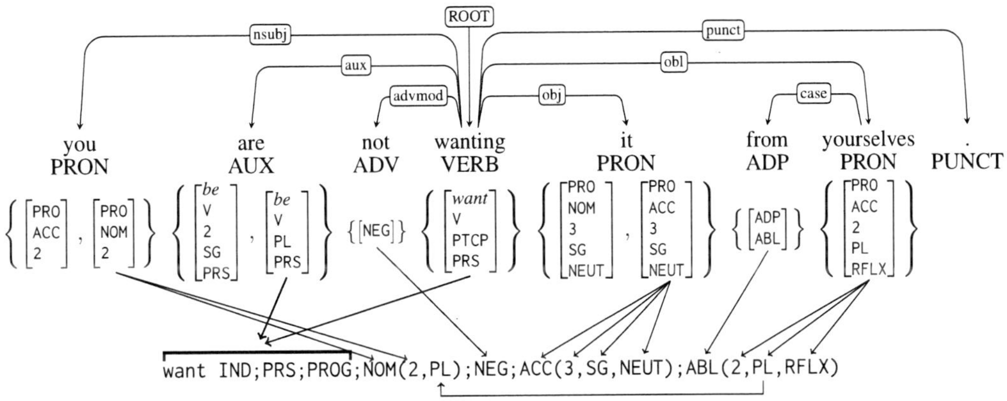


Figure 1: Mapping from word-level features to clause-level features for an English clause.

illustrates this for an English example sentence with a dependency tree on top and morphological analyses below each word. Some of the words are morphologically ambiguous and thus have more than one morphological analysis. The inflectional paradigm of English tells us that a finite present-tense (PRS) form of *be* and the present (PRS) participle (PTCP) of another verb expresses the indicative (IND) present (PRS) progressive (PROG) form of the latter verb, here *want*. To find the subject, it is to find a pronoun with nominative case (NOM), which could either be *you* or *it*. Since the subject has to agree with the finite verb *are* in person and number, the subject can only be *you*. In the consequence, *it* must be an object and cannot have nominative case, hence it receives the accusative (ACC) analysis. The third pronoun, *yourselves*, is reflexive (RFLX) and must therefore agree in person and number with another pronoun in the clause, where the only candidate is *you*. Because of the agreement of *you* and *yourselves*, *you* (which has no morphological number feature) has to be analyzed as plural (PL) and copies this features from *yourselves*. The adposition *from*, which is syntactically governed by *yourselves*, overrides the morphological case of the pronoun.

Our entirely rule-based approach analyzes a clause in a very similar manner as in the example. The following subsections give an overview of the processing steps that an input sentence goes through to compute the output analysis. There are also two examples for French input sentences in the appendix. Further details can also be found in the documented source code.[2]

[2]https://gitlab.gwdg.de/tillmann.doenicke/mrl2022-tmvm

### 3.1 Preprocessing

All languages are preprocessed with spaCy.[3] We use the pretrained models for French, Russian and Spanish, and trained new models on the Universal Dependencies (UD) treebanks (Zeman et al., 2022) for German (HDT), English (GUM), Hebrew (IAHLTwiki) and Turkish (Kenet). To improve the tokenization of spaCy, the raw text is preprocessed for some languages. For English, contractions are converted to full forms (e.g. *won't* ↦ *will not*) using the Python package `contractions`[4] and some additional conversions using regular expressions. Similarly, hyphenated contractions are converted to full forms for French by replacing - and *-t-* with a space (e.g. *regarde-t-il* ↦ *regarde il*, *m'avaient-elles* ↦ *m'avaient elles*). Since we could only train a spaCy model for unvocalized Hebrew, vocalized Hebrew is converted to unvocalized Hebrew using `unikud`[5] before processing it with spaCy and afterwards replaced back with the original tokens.

Unfortunately, even for sentences as simple as in the shared task's data, spaCy makes errors in all processing steps: part-of-speech (POS) tagging, lemmatization and parsing. We fix the most errors with a mix of language-independent and language-specific rules. First, we look up the word-level analysis for every token in UniMorph (see Section 3.2 below) and overwrite the POS tag and/or lemma assigned by spaCy with that from UniMorph if it is unambiguous. Then, we apply some fixes to the parse tree according to the POS tags.

As there is no UD treebank for Swahili, it is

[3]https://spacy.io/

[4]https://pypi.org/project/contractions/

[5]https://pypi.org/project/unikud/

also not possible to train a spaCy model for the language. Here, we directly set the POS tags and lemmas according to the word-level analysis. As far at is concerns the shared task, parsing is not necessary for Swahili since we only need parses to connect adpositions or verbal particles with their heads, and Swahili has no such multi-word constructions.

### 3.2 Word-Level Analysis

We use UniMorph for word-level morphological analysis. UniMorph provides large word lists with POS and morphological analysis,[6] however, only for verbs, nouns and adjectives. We therefore added analyses for pronouns, adpositions and in some languages also for auxiliary verbs (e.g. forms of *be* in English) if they are missing in the UniMorph files. Table 1 shows the number of word form analyses in the files from UniMorph and our extensions. Since UniMorph does not provide resources for Swahili,[7] we only added analyses for the six personal pronouns and assume that every other input word is a verb, which we then analyze with the regular expression[8]

$$(\textit{Prefix})?(\textit{Subject})?(\textit{Tense})?(\textit{Object})?(\textit{Stem})(\textit{Vowel}),$$

where *Prefix*, *Subject*, *Tense* and *Object* can be any morpheme from an according predefined dictionary, e.g. $\textit{Subject} \in \left\{\texttt{ni}: \left\{\begin{bmatrix}\texttt{1}\\ \texttt{SG}\end{bmatrix}\right\}, \texttt{u}: \left\{\begin{bmatrix}\texttt{2}\\ \texttt{SG}\end{bmatrix}, \begin{bmatrix}\texttt{3}\\ \texttt{SG}\\ \texttt{M\_MI}\end{bmatrix}, \begin{bmatrix}\texttt{3}\\ \texttt{SG}\\ \texttt{U}\end{bmatrix}\right\}, \dots\right\}$, *Stem* = `.+?[aeiou]+[^aeiou]+` and *Vowel* = `([aeiou]?[aeiou])|(([aeiou]l)?(ia|ea))`.

The word-level analyses are filtered and post-corrected in some cases depending on the context and using language-specific rules. For example, if the Spanish (usually reflexive) pronoun *se* precedes *la*, *las*, *lo* or *los*, it could also be a replacement for *le* or *les*, so the analyses of *le* and *les* are added.

### 3.3 Clause-Level Analysis

Composite verb forms are analyzed with the algorithm from Dönicke (2020, 2021), which maps the word-level features of the involved verbs to clause-level features. The algorithm itself is mostly language-independent and its application to different languages is possible by setting language-specific parameters, including the language's basic word order (OV vs. VO) and a look-up table with the complete inflectional paradigm (i.e. all simple and composite forms, such as $\left\{\begin{bmatrix}\textit{be}\\ \texttt{PRS}\end{bmatrix}, \begin{bmatrix}\texttt{PTCP}\\ \texttt{PRS}\end{bmatrix}\right\} \mapsto \begin{bmatrix}\texttt{IND}\\ \texttt{PRS}\\ \texttt{PROG}\end{bmatrix}$, for English). Table 1 shows the number of verb forms that are included in the look-up table for every language. Since every word may have several morphological analyses, there might also be several clause-level analyses, all of which we let return by the algorithm. The algorithm further identifies the finite verb in each composite analysis, which we return as well. This gives us tuples of the form $(a, v)$, where $a$ is the analysis of the (possibly composite) verb form and $v$ is the analysis of the finite verb in that form.

| Language | UM | UM+ | VF |
|---|---:|---:|---:|
| English | 652,482 | 43 | 25 |
| French | 367,732 | 123 | 10 |
| German | 519,143 | 93 | 15 |
| Hebrew | 33,177 | 190 | 6 |
| Russian | 473,481 | 109 | 6 |
| Spanish | 1,196,245 | 65 | 19 |
| Swahili | – | 6 | 24 |
| Turkish | 570,420 | 193 | 60 |

Table 1: Number of analyses in UniMorph (UM) and in our extension (UM+), and number of verb forms in the look-up table (VF).

In a subsequent step, we determine all possible morphological analyses for every pronoun in the input clause. If a pronoun has an adposition, we override the case of the pronoun with the case assigned by the adposition.[9] Then, we construct all valid combinations of analyses $(a, v, s, N)$, where $s$ is the analysis of the subject pronoun and $N \not\ni s$ are the analyses of the other pronouns. A combination is valid iff $s$ features nominative case and $s$ agrees with $v$ in all nominal features, i.e. number, person, formality and gender. If no valid combination is found, a covert subject pronoun with nominative case and the nominal features of $v$ is introduced for $s$ (this largely affects pro-drop languages like He-

[6] https://github.com/unimorph/

[7] UniMorph provides resources for Congo Swahili, another Swahili variant than that in the shared task's data.

[8] The regular expression is mainly based on the *Swahili Cheat Sheet* which can be found at https://www.swahilicheatsheet.com/.

[9] In some languages, the case assigned by an adposition can depend on the inherent case of the pronoun. For example, the German adposition *in* assigns IN+ALL to a dative pronoun and IN+ESS to an accusative pronoun. In these cases, we created case-specific entries for adpositions in our UniMorph extension and our algorithm selects the case for an adposition based on the case of the pronoun.

brew but also imperatives in some other languages). Covert object pronouns are also added to $N$ if the verb form encodes these (this only affects Swahili).

In a last step, we search the clause for question marks and words of negation and add the corresponding features if applicable, yielding combinations of the form $(a, v, s, N, c)$ with $c \sqsubseteq \begin{bmatrix}\text{NEG}\\ \text{Q}\end{bmatrix}$.

### 3.4 Filtering and Pooling

The number of analyses can be quite high but some analyses are more plausible than others. We therefore filter the analyses successively by the following steps:

1. If the clause contains an exclamation mark, only keep imperative analyses.
   Motivation: In the shared task's data, all clauses with an exclamation mark contain an imperative verb and vice versa.
2. For German only: If the clause contains a question mark and the clause is in V2 word order (i.e. it is not syntactically a question), remove the Q feature and only keep quotative analyses.[10]
   Motivation: In the shared task's data, all clauses with a question mark contain the Q feature and vice versa, except for German.
3. Only keep analyses where the subject pronoun features nominative case.
   Motivation: In the shared task's data, the subject always features nominative case. Generally, the nominative case marks the subject of a clause in many languages, although there are languages that also have non-nominative subjects (e.g. Bejar, 2002, p. 313).[11]
4. Only keep analyses where a minimal number of non-subject pronouns features nominative case.
   Motivation: In the shared task's data, non-subject pronouns never feature nominative case. Generally, nominative non-subjects only occur in specific linguistic constructions (e.g. to mark the predicate in copula constructions) or together with a non-nominative subject (cf. Bejar, 2002, p. 313).
5. Only keep analyses with a non-reflexive subject pronoun.
   Motivation: In the shared task's data, there are no reflexive subjects. Generally, there do not appear to be any languages with reflexive subjects (Schachter, 1977).[12]
6. Only keep analyses where every reflexive pronoun agrees with a non-reflexive pronoun. In case of agreement, the non-reflexive pronoun copies missing features from the reflexive pronoun.
   Motivation: In the shared task's data, every reflexive pronoun has an antecedent in the same clause. Generally, reflexive pronouns must have an antecedent in the same sentence ("Binding Principle A" of Chomsky (1981)).[13]
7. Only keep analyses where the pronouns feature a maximal number of different cases.
   Motivation: In the shared task's data, every case appears maximally once per clause. Generally, cases encode grammatical (and in a wider sense also semantic) roles and clauses typically contain every role only once (cf. Jaworski and Przepiórkowski, 2014, p. 84).
8. For French only: Only keep analyses where every past participle agrees with the pronoun determined by the non-trivial French participle agreement rules (cf. Past Participle Agreement in French, 2017). In case of agreement, the pronoun copies missing features from the participle.
   Motivation: In French and other Romance languages, past participles do not always agree with the subject (as it is usually the case) but sometimes with an object (cf. Kayne, 1989).
9. Only keep analyses where a maximal number of reflexive pronouns agrees with the subject pronoun. In case of agreement, the reflexive pronoun copies missing features from the subject pronoun.
   Motivation: In the shared task's data, reflexive pronouns in ambiguous sentences are sometimes annotated as having subjects and sometimes annotated as having non-subjects as antecedents. Generally, subjects are preferred over non-subjects as antecedents for reflexive pronouns in ambiguous sentences (cf. White et al., 1997, p. 148).

If one of the steps would filter out all analyses, the step is skipped.

[10]What is labeled as 'quotative' (QUOT) in the German data is usually called present subjunctive or subjunctive I in the literature and, unlike the labeling in the shared task suggests, not only used in quoted speech.

[11]Not forgetting ergative languages, in which the subject's case depends on the (transitivity of the) verb.

[12]English allows statistically rare exceptions (cf. Song (2017), or Kirk and Kallen (2006, p. 104) for the use of reflexive pronouns as subjects with a focus on Irish English).

[13]Again, English allows statistically rare exceptions (cf. Kim et al., 2020, p. 296).

In a pooling step, redundant features are removed from the analyses, which may result in some of the analyses becoming identical and hence collapsing into one. For example, if there are three analyses for a French input that differ in the analysis of the pronoun *leur*, $\begin{bmatrix}\texttt{PRO}\\\texttt{DAT}\\\texttt{3}\\\texttt{PL}\\\texttt{MASC}\end{bmatrix}$ vs. $\begin{bmatrix}\texttt{PRO}\\\texttt{DAT}\\\texttt{3}\\\texttt{PL}\\\texttt{FEM}\end{bmatrix}$ vs. $\begin{bmatrix}\texttt{PRO}\\\texttt{DAT}\\\texttt{3}\\\texttt{PL}\\\texttt{NEUT}\end{bmatrix}$, then $\begin{bmatrix}\texttt{PRO}\\\texttt{DAT}\\\texttt{3}\\\texttt{PL}\end{bmatrix}$ becomes the reduced analysis of *leur* in each of the analyses. If the three analyses are now completely identical, they are combined into one analysis. On the contrary, if there are two analyses for a German input that differ in the analysis of the pronoun *ihm*, $\begin{bmatrix}\texttt{PRO}\\\texttt{DAT}\\\texttt{3}\\\texttt{SG}\\\texttt{MASC}\end{bmatrix}$ vs. $\begin{bmatrix}\texttt{PRO}\\\texttt{DAT}\\\texttt{3}\\\texttt{SG}\\\texttt{NEUT}\end{bmatrix}$, the gender feature is not redundant (since *ihm* cannot be feminine) and can therefore not be removed.

### 3.5 Ranking

The analyses that are not filtered out are assumed to be correct by the program and can all be output. For the shared task, we rank the analyses according to the following sorting procedures and choose the first one as final result:

1. Choose verb analyses in this order: *lemma of non-auxiliary verb* > *lemma of auxiliary verb*.
   Motivation: Analyses with a lemma of an auxiliary verb usually result from errors in the word- or clause-level analysis steps, so we prefer analyses with a lemma of a non-auxiliary verb.
2. Choose pronoun analyses in this order: MASC > FEM > NEUT > no gender.
   Motivation: We did not find a general preference for any grammatical gender of ambiguous pronouns in the shared task's data, but we wanted our system to not arbitrarily choose one and this is the order in which many grammars name the genders.
3. Choose pronoun analyses in this order: no class > any class (this only affects Swahili).
   Motivation: We experimented with both variants on the training and development set for Swahili and matched the gold analysis in more cases by preferring analyses without class feature over analyses with class feature.
4. Choose pronoun analyses in this order: not LGSPEC3 > LGSPEC3 (this only affects Spanish).
   Motivation: We experimented with both variants on the training and development set for Spanish and matched the gold analysis in more cases by preferring analyses without LGSPEC3 feature over analyses with LGSPEC3 feature.
5. Choose pronoun analyses in this order: NOM > ACC > DAT > other case (this effectively prefers analyses where the cases of pronouns appear in this word order).
   Motivation: We observed that sentences with ambiguous pronouns always receive cases in this order in the shared task's gold analyses.
6. Choose pronoun analyses in this order: RFLX > not RFLX (except for Spanish, where the sorting is reversed).
   Motivation: We experimented with both variants on the training and development set for every language and (for all languages but Spanish) matched the gold analysis in more cases by preferring reflexive readings over non-reflexive readings for ambiguous pronouns.[14]

Note that later sorting procedures ignore the previous ones and are therefore more effective.

### 3.6 Postprocessing

Sometimes, UniMorph contains incorrect lemmas with a trailing *e* for English (e.g. *answere* instead of *answer*). We fix this using NLTK's `WordNetLemmatizer`[15] and the Python package `pyspellchecker`.[16]

The result analysis is then converted to a string in the output format of the shared task.

## 4 Evaluation and Results

For the evaluation, the gold analysis and the predicted analysis are decomposed into features. For example, the analysis

`IND;PST;PFV;NOM(3,PL,MASC);ACC(1,PL,MASC);NEG;Q`

is decomposed into the features

$\Phi = \{\texttt{IND}, \texttt{PST}, \texttt{PFV}, \texttt{NOM-3}, \texttt{NOM-PL}, \texttt{NOM-MASC}, \texttt{ACC-1}, \texttt{ACC-PL}, \texttt{ACC-MASC}, \texttt{NEG}, \texttt{Q}\}$.

Given the features for the gold analysis $\Phi_g$ and for the predicted analysis $\Phi_p$, the F1 score for one sample is calculated as follows:

$$P = \frac{|\Phi_p \cap \Phi_g| + s_\ell}{|\Phi_p| + w_\ell} \qquad R = \frac{|\Phi_p \cap \Phi_g| + s_\ell}{|\Phi_g| + w_\ell}$$

[14] An example for an ambiguous pronoun is German *mich*, which can mean 'me' or 'myself' (cf. Hole, 2005, p. 65).

[15] https://www.nltk.org/api/nltk.stem.wordnet.html

[16] https://pypi.org/project/pyspellchecker/

| Language | Train | Dev | Test |
|---|---|---|---|
| English | .994 | .995 | .993 |
| French | .973 | .974 | .977 |
| German | .946 | .952 | .974 |
| Hebrew (unvoc) | .959 | .955 | .965 |
| Hebrew (voc) | .966 | .970 | .955 |
| Russian | .908 | .917 | .931 |
| Spanish | .931 | .920 | .943 |
| Swahili | .730 | .760 | .789 |
| Turkish | .934 | .928 | .929 |
| **Average** | .927 | .930 | .940 |

Table 2: F1 scores for all languages on the respective training, development and test sets.

| Language | Train | Dev | Test |
|---|---|---|---|
| English | .976 (.975) | .977 (.977) | .974 |
| French | .637 (.845) | .676 (.870) | .693 |
| German | .452 (.590) | .465 (.619) | .550 |
| Hebrew (unvoc) | .765 (.765) | .744 (.739) | .827 |
| Hebrew (voc) | .794 (.794) | .807 (.815) | .748 |
| Russian | .459 (.452) | .456 (.472) | .609 |
| Spanish | .492 (.537) | .473 (.553) | .637 |
| Swahili | .041 (.048) | .048 (.066) | .067 |
| Turkish | .841 (.842) | .806 (.808) | .816 |
| **Average** | .606 (.650) | .606 (.658) | .658 |

Table 3: Exact matches for all languages on the respective training, development and test sets.

$$F_1 = \frac{2 \cdot P \cdot R}{P + R}$$

Hereby, $s_\ell = 3$ if the predicted lemma matches the gold lemma and $s_\ell = 0$ otherwise, and $w_\ell = 3$. While the development and training sets always contain only one gold analysis per sample, the test sets contain multiple gold analyses for samples with an ambiguous sentence. In case of such ambiguous sentences, the predicted analysis is compared to each gold analysis and the highest F1 score is chosen. The F1 for a data set (e.g. for the English test set) is the average F1 over all samples in that set.

The results using our method are shown in Table 2. We achieve F1 scores over 92% on the test sets for each language except Swahili (79%), and an average F1 score of 94% (96% without Swahili). Since our approach is not based on machine learning methods, we observe a relatively stable performance on all data splits (training, development, test) and, in particular, no decrease on the test set.

For completeness, we also show the accuracies in terms of exact matches, i.e. the percentage of predicted analyses that exactly match a gold analysis (including ordering of the features), in Table 3, although we consider this metric to be inadequate for the evaluation of the task since the elements of a feature structure are naturally unordered. Since our rule-based approach cannot learn the ordering of the features from examples, we hard-coded the order of the features in the output string so that it roughly complies with the ordering in the shared task's data for most languages. After the final system submission, we noticed a mistake in the ordering of the features `NEG` and `Q`. Therefore, numbers in brackets in Table 3 show exact-match performance after fixing their ordering, while the other numbers are the performances of the system as submitted.[17] The high differences that result from this small change in some languages (e.g. +15% in German) further illustrate the inadequateness of the metric.

## 5 Discussion

The main advantage of the presented method is probably the performance, although there is naturally some room for improvement. The second major advantage of the method is that it does not require any training data. This makes it a promising option for analyzing every language where manually annotated gold data is not available. No training also means that no training bias can be induced by the data, which arguably makes the method's performance more stable across text domains. In terms of languages, the algorithm is relatively universally applicable since the underlying mechanisms of inflection and agreement are the same across natural languages. This is also indicated by the performance that is very similar across languages and language families.[18]

However, the method is not without shortcomings, all of which are clearly visible in the case of

[17] Since gold analyses for the test data have not been released, yet, we cannot re-evaluate our system on the test sets, but we can assume that the performance is nearly the same as on the other splits, or even a bit higher since the test sets can contain more than one gold analysis per sample.

[18] The languages in the shared task belong to the following families: Indo-European (English, French, German, Russian, Spanish), Afro-Asiatic (Hebrew), Niger-Congo (Swahili), Turkic (Turkish). Dönicke (2021) also implements the composite-verb analysis for languages from other families.

Swahili. First of all, the method requires a (word-level) morphological analysis and a parser for the language to analyze. We decided to use UniMorph because the output format in the shared task also uses UniMorph features. Dönicke (2021), on the other hand, does not only use the parser but also the morphological analyzer that can be trained by spaCy on a UD treebank.[19] The current version of the UD treebanks includes treebanks for 130 languages and 61 languages are listed as possible future extensions—Swahili being one of them—, and UniMorph currently provides resources for 167 languages. Nonetheless, the current lack of both a treebank and morphological resources for Swahili forced us to implement a workaround resulting in a much lower performance compared to the other languages. Another drawback of our method is that knowledge about the grammar of the language to analyze is required to set-up the language-specific inflection table, the list of auxiliary verbs, the word-order parameter (OV vs. VO), and in the current implementation also a list of words of negation as well as UniMorph-style entries for pronouns and adpositions. Dönicke (2021) already mentions that the study of composite verb forms in a foreign language can be extensive, but it is also prone to errors. It may be a coincidence that the languages with the best performance (English, French, German) are those languages which the author of this paper has the profoundest knowledge of, but it may also be due to the incomplete knowledge about the other languages acquired in the short term. Although the algorithm is designed to be language-independent (with language-specific operations being controlled through the aforementioned parameters), its performance can be sometimes improved by language-specific special rules (e.g. the rules for participle agreement in French), which again can only be implemented by someone who has the according knowledge of the language. Table 4 shows how many of these rules are hard-coded in our implementation. It should be added, however, that some of these rules are only implemented to meet the output format of the shared task and are not related to the morphosyntactic nature of the language. For example, there is no apparent reason why all gold analyses for Swahili have the feature V (verb) while the analyses for the other languages do not; but for the shared task there had to be a special rule that adds this feature to every output analysis for Swahili. Probably, the requirement of linguistic knowledge is not that much of a disadvantage, since research teams working on a language usually include some speakers of that language.

| Language | P1 | A1 | A2 | F | R | P2 | $\sum$ |
|---|---|---|---|---|---|---|---|
| English | 1 | 2 | 1 | 0 | 0 | 1 | 5 |
| French | 1 | 2 | 1 | 1 | 0 | 0 | 5 |
| German | 0 | 1 | 1 | 1 | 0 | 0 | 3 |
| Hebrew | 2 | 0 | 1 | 1 | 0 | 0 | 4 |
| Russian | 0 | 0 | 1 | 0 | 0 | 0 | 1 |
| Spanish | 0 | 1 | 0 | 0 | 1 | 0 | 2 |
| Swahili | 1 | 1 | 2 | 1 | 0 | 1 | 6 |
| Turkish | 0 | 0 | 1 | 0 | 0 | 1 | 2 |
| $\sum$ | 5 | 7 | 8 | 4 | 1 | 3 | 28 |

Table 4: Number of hard-coded language-specific rules in the code. P1: preprocessing, A1: word-level analysis, A2: clause-level analysis, F: filtering and pooling, R: ranking, P2: postprocessing.

## 6 Conclusion

We presented a method to predict clause-level morphological / morphosyntactic features. The main advantages are its performance (94% F1 on average), that it does not require training data and that it is applicable for multiple languages. The disadvantages are that it requires a preceding word-level morphological analysis, linguistic knowledge about the language to analyze and some time to set-up the method for a new language. While the implementation within the frame of the shared task is not applicable for general use (mainly because of the pre- and postprocessing), interested readers may want to have a look at the implementation from Dönicke (2021).

## Acknowledgements

This work is funded by Volkswagen Foundation.

## References

Susana Bejar. 2002. Movement, morphology and learnability. *Syntactic Effects of Morphological Change*, pages 307–325.

Noam Chomsky. 1981. Lectures on government and binding.

Narayan Choudhary, Pramod Pandey, and Girish Nath Jha. 2014. A rule based method for the identification of TAM features in a PoS tagged corpus. In

[19]McCarthy et al. (2018) compare UD features and UniMorph features and also provide a tool to convert the former into the latter.

*Human Language Technology Challenges for Computer Science and Linguistics*, pages 178–188, Cham. Springer International Publishing.

Tillmann Dönicke. 2020. Clause-level tense, mood, voice and modality tagging for German. In *Proceedings of the 19th International Workshop on Treebanks and Linguistic Theories*, pages 1–17, Düsseldorf, Germany. Association for Computational Linguistics.

Tillmann Dönicke. 2021. Delexicalised multilingual discourse segmentation for DISRPT 2021 and tense, mood, voice and modality tagging for 11 languages. In *Proceedings of the 2nd Shared Task on Discourse Relation Parsing and Treebanking (DISRPT 2021)*, pages 33–45, Punta Cana, Dominican Republic. Association for Computational Linguistics.

Simone Faro and Arianna Pavone. 2015. Refined tagging of complex verbal phrases for the Italian language. In *Proceedings of the Prague Stringology Conference 2015*, pages 132–145, Czech Technical University in Prague, Czech Republic.

Daniel Hole. 2005. Zur Sprachgeschichte einiger deutscher Pronomina. *Sprachwissenschaft*, 430(1):49–75.

Wojciech Jaworski and Adam Przepiórkowski. 2014. Semantic roles in grammar engineering. In *Proceedings of the Third Joint Conference on Lexical and Computational Semantics (*SEM 2014)*, pages 81–86, Dublin, Ireland. Association for Computational Linguistics and Dublin City University.

Richard S. Kayne. 1989. Facets of Romance past participle agreement. In Paola Benincá, editor, *Dialect Variation and the Theory of Grammar*, pages 85–104. De Gruyter Mouton, Berlin, Boston.

Ji-Hye Kim, Soojin An, and Ahreum Jung. 2020. Binding conditions of English reflexives and pronouns in the ICE-USA. *Lanaguage Research*, 56(3):287–307.

John M. Kirk and Jeffrey L. Kallen. 2006. Irish Standard English: How Celticised? How Standardised? *The Celtic Englishes IV*, pages 88–113.

Arya D. McCarthy, Miikka Silfverberg, Ryan Cotterell, Mans Hulden, and David Yarowsky. 2018. Marrying Universal Dependencies and Universal Morphology. In *Proceedings of the Second Workshop on Universal Dependencies (UDW 2018)*, pages 91–101, Brussels, Belgium. Association for Computational Linguistics.

Skatje Myers and Martha Palmer. 2019. ClearTAC: Verb tense, aspect, and form classification using neural nets. In *Proceedings of the First International Workshop on Designing Meaning Representations*, pages 136–140, Florence, Italy. Association for Computational Linguistics.

Past Participle Agreement in French. 2017. Study.com. March 11.

Anita Ramm, Sharid Loáiciga, Annemarie Friedrich, and Alexander Fraser. 2017. Annotating tense, mood and voice for English, French and German. In *Proceedings of ACL 2017, System Demonstrations*, pages 1–6, Vancouver, Canada. Association for Computational Linguistics.

Paul Schachter. 1977. Reference-related and role-related properties of subjects. In Peter Cole and Jerrold M. Sadock, editors, *Grammatical Relations*, Syntax and Semantics, pages 279 – 306. Brill, Leiden, The Netherlands.

Sanghoun Song. 2017. A corpus study of unbound reflexive pronouns in English. 영어학, 17(2):275–305.

John Sylak-Glassman. 2016. The composition and use of the universal morphological feature schema (UniMorph schema). Johns Hopkins University.

Lydia White, Joyce Bruhn-Garavito, Takako Kawasaki, Joe Pater, and Philippe Prévost. 1997. The researcher gave the subject a test about himself: Problems of ambiguity and preference in the investigation of reflexive binding. *Language Learning*, 47(1):145–172.

Eva Žáčková, Luboš Popelínský, and Miloslav Nepil. 2000. Automatic tagging of compound verb groups in Czech corpora. In *Text, Speech and Dialogue*, pages 115–120, Berlin, Heidelberg. Springer Berlin Heidelberg.

Daniel Zeman, Joakim Nivre, Mitchell Abrams, Elia Ackermann, Noëmi Aepli, Hamid Aghaei, Željko Agić, Amir Ahmadi, Lars Ahrenberg, Chika Kennedy Ajede, Gabrielė Aleksandravičiūtė, Ika Alfina, Avner Algom, Erik Andersen, Lene Antonsen, Katya Aplonova, Angelina Aquino, Carolina Aragon, Glyd Aranes, Maria Jesus Aranzabe, Bilge Nas Arıcan, Hórunn Arnardóttir, Gashaw Arutie, Jessica Naraiswari Arwidarasti, Masayuki Asahara, Deniz Baran Aslan, Cengiz Asmazoğlu, Luma Ateyah, Furkan Atmaca, Mohammed Attia, Aitziber Atutxa, Liesbeth Augustinus, Elena Badmaeva, Keerthana Balasubramani, Miguel Ballesteros, Esha Banerjee, Sebastian Bank, Verginica Barbu Mititelu, Starkaður Barkarson, Rodolfo Basile, Victoria Basmov, Colin Batchelor, John Bauer, Seyyit Talha Bedir, Kepa Bengoetxea, Yifat Ben Moshe, Gözde Berk, Yevgeni Berzak, Irshad Ahmad Bhat, Riyaz Ahmad Bhat, Erica Biagetti, Eckhard Bick, Agnė Bielinskienė, Kristín Bjarnadóttir, Rogier Blokland, Victoria Bobicev, Loïc Boizou, Emanuel Borges Völker, Carl Börstell, Cristina Bosco, Gosse Bouma, Sam Bowman, Adriane Boyd, Anouck Braggaar, Kristina Brokaitė, Aljoscha Burchardt, Marie Candito, Bernard Caron, Gauthier Caron, Lauren Cassidy, Tatiana Cavalcanti, Gülşen Cebiroğlu Eryiğit, Flavio Massimiliano Cecchini, Giuseppe G. A. Celano, Slavomír Čéplö, Neslihan Cesur, Savas Cetin, Özlem Çetinoğlu, Fabricio Chalub, Shweta Chauhan, Ethan Chi, Taishi Chika, Yongseok Cho, Jinho Choi, Jayeol Chun, Juyeon Chung, Alessandra T. Cignarella, Silvie Cinková, Aurélie Collomb,

Çağrı Çöltekin, Miriam Connor, Daniela Corbetta, Marine Courtin, Mihaela Cristescu, Philemon Daniel, Elizabeth Davidson, Mathieu Dehouck, Martina de Laurentiis, Marie-Catherine de Marneffe, Valeria de Paiva, Mehmet Oguz Derin, Elvis de Souza, Arantza Diaz de Ilarraza, Carly Dickerson, Arawinda Dinakaramani, Elisa Di Nuovo, Bamba Dione, Peter Dirix, Kaja Dobrovoljc, Timothy Dozat, Kira Droganova, Puneet Dwivedi, Hanne Eckhoff, Sandra Eiche, Marhaba Eli, Ali Elkahky, Binyam Ephrem, Olga Erina, Tomaž Erjavec, Aline Etienne, Wograine Evelyn, Sidney Facundes, Richárd Farkas, Federica Favero, Jannatul Ferdaousi, Marília Fernanda, Hector Fernandez Alcalde, Jennifer Foster, Cláudia Freitas, Kazunori Fujita, Katarína Gajdošová, Daniel Galbraith, Federica Gamba, Marcos Garcia, Moa Gärdenfors, Sebastian Garza, Fabrício Ferraz Gerardi, Kim Gerdes, Filip Ginter, Gustavo Godoy, Iakes Goenaga, Koldo Gojenola, Memduh Gökırmak, Yoav Goldberg, Xavier Gómez Guinovart, Berta González Saavedra, Bernadeta Griciūtė, Matias Grioni, Loïc Grobol, Normunds Grūzītis, Bruno Guillaume, Céline Guillot-Barbance, Tunga Güngör, Nizar Habash, Hinrik Hafsteinsson, Jan Hajič, Jan Hajič jr., Mika Hämäläinen, Linh Hà Mỹ, Na-Rae Han, Muhammad Yudistira Hanifmuti, Takahiro Harada, Sam Hardwick, Kim Harris, Dag Haug, Johannes Heinecke, Oliver Hellwig, Felix Hennig, Barbora Hladká, Jaroslava Hlaváčová, Florinel Hociung, Petter Hohle, Jena Hwang, Takumi Ikeda, Anton Karl Ingason, Radu Ion, Elena Irimia, Ọlájídé Ishola, Kaoru Ito, Siratun Jannat, Tomáš Jelínek, Apoorva Jha, Anders Johannsen, Hildur Jónsdóttir, Fredrik Jørgensen, Markus Juutinen, Sarveswaran K, Hüner Kaşıkara, Andre Kaasen, Nadezhda Kabaeva, Sylvain Kahane, Hiroshi Kanayama, Jenna Kanerva, Neslihan Kara, Ritván Karahóǧa, Boris Katz, Tolga Kayadelen, Jessica Kenney, Václava Kettnerová, Jesse Kirchner, Elena Klementieva, Elena Klyachko, Arne Köhn, Abdullatif Köksal, Kamil Kopacewicz, Timo Korkiakangas, Mehmet Köse, Natalia Kotsyba, Jolanta Kovalevskaitė, Simon Krek, Parameswari Krishnamurthy, Sandra Kübler, Oğuzhan Kuyrukçu, Aslı Kuzgun, Sookyoung Kwak, Veronika Laippala, Lucia Lam, Lorenzo Lambertino, Tatiana Lando, Septina Dian Larasati, Alexei Lavrentiev, John Lee, Phương Lê Hồng, Alessandro Lenci, Saran Lertpradit, Herman Leung, Maria Levina, Cheuk Ying Li, Josie Li, Keying Li, Yuan Li, KyungTae Lim, Bruna Lima Padovani, Krister Lindén, Nikola Ljubešić, Olga Loginova, Stefano Lusito, Andry Luthfi, Mikko Luukko, Olga Lyashevskaya, Teresa Lynn, Vivien Macketanz, Menel Mahamdi, Jean Maillard, Aibek Makazhanov, Michael Mandl, Christopher Manning, Ruli Manurung, Büşra Marşan, Cătălina Mărănduc, David Mareček, Katrin Marheinecke, Stella Markantonatou, Héctor Martínez Alonso, Lorena Martín Rodríguez, André Martins, Jan Mašek, Hiroshi Matsuda, Yuji Matsumoto, Alessandro Mazzei, Ryan McDonald, Sarah McGuinness, Gustavo Mendonça, Tatiana Merzhevich, Niko Miekka, Karina Mischenkova, Margarita Misirpashayeva, Anna Missilä, Cătălin Mititelu, Maria Mitrofan, Yusuke Miyao, AmirHossein Mojiri Foroushani, Judit Molnár, Amirsaeid Moloodi, Simonetta Montemagni, Amir More, Laura Moreno Romero, Giovanni Moretti, Keiko Sophie Mori, Shinsuke Mori, Tomohiko Morioka, Shigeki Moro, Bjartur Mortensen, Bohdan Moskalevskyi, Kadri Muischnek, Robert Munro, Yugo Murawaki, Kaili Müürisep, Pinkey Nainwani, Mariam Nakhlé, Juan Ignacio Navarro Horñiacek, Anna Nedoluzhko, Gunta Nešpore-Bērzkalne, Manuela Nevaci, Lương Nguyễn Thị, Huyền Nguyễn Thị Minh, Yoshihiro Nikaido, Vitaly Nikolaev, Rattima Nitisaroj, Alireza Nourian, Hanna Nurmi, Stina Ojala, Atul Kr. Ojha, Adédayọ Olúòkun, Mai Omura, Emeka Onwuegbuzia, Noam Ordan, Petya Osenova, Robert Östling, Lilja Øvrelid, Şaziye Betül Özateş, Merve Özçelik, Arzucan Özgür, Balkız Öztürk Başaran, Teresa Paccosi, Alessio Palmero Aprosio, Hyunji Hayley Park, Niko Partanen, Elena Pascual, Marco Passarotti, Agnieszka Patejuk, Guilherme Paulino-Passos, Giulia Pedonese, Angelika Peljak-Łapińska, Siyao Peng, Cenel-Augusto Perez, Natalia Perkova, Guy Perrier, Slav Petrov, Daria Petrova, Andrea Peverelli, Jason Phelan, Jussi Piitulainen, Tommi A Pirinen, Emily Pitler, Barbara Plank, Thierry Poibeau, Larisa Ponomareva, Martin Popel, Lauma Pretkalniņa, Sophie Prévost, Prokopis Prokopidis, Adam Przepiórkowski, Tiina Puolakainen, Sampo Pyysalo, Peng Qi, Andriela Rääbis, Alexandre Rademaker, Mizanur Rahoman, Taraka Rama, Loganathan Ramasamy, Carlos Ramisch, Fam Rashel, Mohammad Sadegh Rasooli, Vinit Ravishankar, Livy Real, Petru Rebeja, Siva Reddy, Mathilde Regnault, Georg Rehm, Ivan Riabov, Michael Rießler, Erika Rimkutė, Larissa Rinaldi, Laura Rituma, Putri Rizqiyah, Luisa Rocha, Eiríkur Rögnvaldsson, Mykhailo Romanenko, Rudolf Rosa, Valentin Roșca, Davide Rovati, Ben Rozonoyer, Olga Rudina, Jack Rueter, Kristján Rúnarsson, Shoval Sadde, Pegah Safari, Benoît Sagot, Aleksi Sahala, Shadi Saleh, Alessio Salomoni, Tanja Samardžić, Stephanie Samson, Manuela Sanguinetti, Ezgi Sanıyar, Dage Särg, Baiba Saulīte, Yanin Sawanakunanon, Shefali Saxena, Kevin Scannell, Salvatore Scarlata, Nathan Schneider, Sebastian Schuster, Lane Schwartz, Djamé Seddah, Wolfgang Seeker, Mojgan Seraji, Syeda Shahzadi, Mo Shen, Atsuko Shimada, Hiroyuki Shirasu, Yana Shishkina, Muh Shohibussirri, Dmitry Sichinava, Janine Siewert, Einar Freyr Sigurðsson, Aline Silveira, Natalia Silveira, Maria Simi, Radu Simionescu, Katalin Simkó, Mária Šimková, Kiril Simov, Maria Skachedubova, Aaron Smith, Isabela Soares-Bastos, Shafi Sourov, Carolyn Spadine, Rachele Sprugnoli, Vivian Stamou, Steinhȏr Steingrímsson, Antonio Stella, Milan Straka, Emmett Strickland, Jana Strnadová, Alane Suhr, Yogi Lesmana Sulestio, Umut Sulubacak, Shingo Suzuki, Daniel Swanson, Zsolt Szántó, Chihiro Taguchi, Dima Taji, Yuta Takahashi, Fabio Tamburini, Mary Ann C. Tan, Takaaki Tanaka, Dipta Tanaya, Mirko Tavoni, Samson Tella, Isabelle Tellier, Marinella Testori, Guillaume Thomas, Sara Tonelli, Liisi Torga, Marsida Toska, Trond Trosterud, Anna Trukhina, Reut Tsarfaty, Utku Türk, Francis Tyers, Sumire Uematsu, Roman Untilov, Zdeňka Urešová,

Larraitz Uria, Hans Uszkoreit, Andrius Utka, Elena Vagnoni, Sowmya Vajjala, Rob van der Goot, Martine Vanhove, Daniel van Niekerk, Gertjan van Noord, Viktor Varga, Uliana Vedenina, Eric Villemonte de la Clergerie, Veronika Vincze, Natalia Vlasova, Aya Wakasa, Joel C. Wallenberg, Lars Wallin, Abigail Walsh, Jing Xian Wang, Jonathan North Washington, Maximilan Wendt, Paul Widmer, Shira Wigderson, Sri Hartati Wijono, Seyi Williams, Mats Wirén, Christian Wittern, Tsegay Woldemariam, Tak-sum Wong, Alina Wróblewska, Mary Yako, Kayo Yamashita, Naoki Yamazaki, Chunxiao Yan, Koichi Yasuoka, Marat M. Yavrumyan, Arife Betül Yenice, Olcay Taner Yıldız, Zhuoran Yu, Arlisa Yuliawati, Zdeněk Žabokrtský, Shorouq Zahra, Amir Zeldes, He Zhou, Hanzhi Zhu, Anna Zhuravleva, and Rayan Ziane. 2022. Universal dependencies 2.10. LINDAT/CLARIAH-CZ digital library at the Institute of Formal and Applied Linguistics (ÚFAL), Faculty of Mathematics and Physics, Charles University.

## A French Example 1

**Input:** ne nous avaient-ils pas acceptés?
**Gold Output:** `accepter IND;PST;PFV;NOM(3,PL,MASC);ACC(1,PL,MASC);NEG;Q`

After preprocessing and word-level analysis:

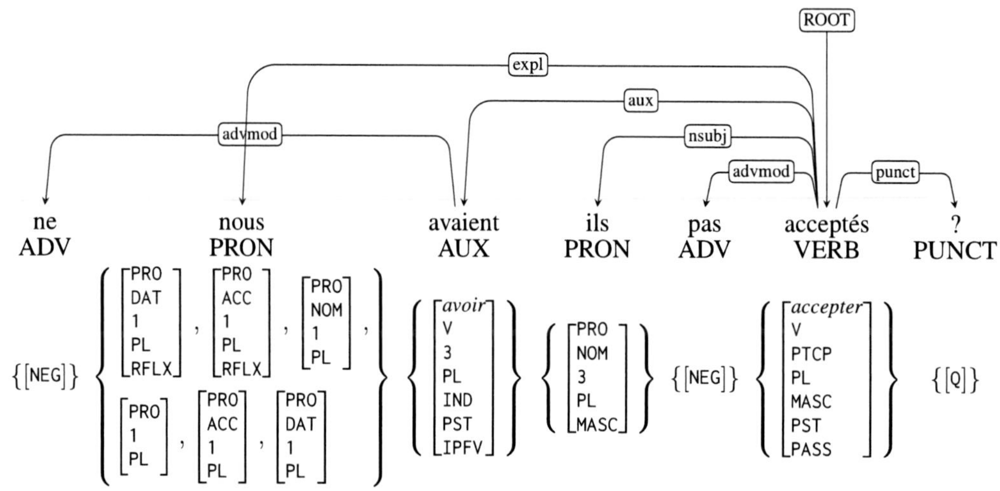


| After ... | $a$ | $v$ | $s$ | $N$ | $c$ |
|---|---|---|---|---|---|
| add $a, v$ | [*accepter* IND PST PFV] | [*avoir* V 3 PL IND PST IPFV] | | | |
| add $s$ | [*accepter* IND PST PFV] | [*avoir* V 3 PL IND PST IPFV] | [PRO NOM 3 PL MASC] | | |
| add $N$ | [*accepter* IND PST PFV] | [*avoir* V 3 PL IND PST IPFV] | [PRO NOM 3 PL MASC] | {[PRO DAT 1 PL RFLX]} | |
| | [*accepter* IND PST PFV] | [*avoir* V 3 PL IND PST IPFV] | [PRO NOM 3 PL MASC] | {[PRO ACC 1 PL RFLX]} | |
| | [*accepter* IND PST PFV] | [*avoir* V 3 PL IND PST IPFV] | [PRO NOM 3 PL MASC] | {[PRO NOM 1 PL]} | |
| | [*accepter* IND PST PFV] | [*avoir* V 3 PL IND PST IPFV] | [PRO NOM 3 PL MASC] | {[PRO 1 PL]} | |
| | [*accepter* IND PST PFV] | [*avoir* V 3 PL IND PST IPFV] | [PRO NOM 3 PL MASC] | {[PRO ACC 1 PL]} | |
| | [*accepter* IND PST PFV] | [*avoir* V 3 PL IND PST IPFV] | [PRO NOM 3 PL MASC] | {[PRO DAT 1 PL]} | |
| add $c$ | [*accepter* IND PST PFV] | [*avoir* V 3 PL IND PST IPFV] | [PRO NOM 3 PL MASC] | {[PRO DAT 1 PL RFLX]} | [NEG Q] |
| | [*accepter* IND PST PFV] | [*avoir* V 3 PL IND PST IPFV] | [PRO NOM 3 PL MASC] | {[PRO ACC 1 PL RFLX]} | [NEG Q] |
| | [*accepter* IND PST PFV] | [*avoir* V 3 PL IND PST IPFV] | [PRO NOM 3 PL MASC] | {[PRO NOM 1 PL]} | [NEG Q] |
| | [*accepter* IND PST PFV] | [*avoir* V 3 PL IND PST IPFV] | [PRO NOM 3 PL MASC] | {[PRO 1 PL]} | [NEG Q] |
| | [*accepter* IND PST PFV] | [*avoir* V 3 PL IND PST IPFV] | [PRO NOM 3 PL MASC] | {[PRO ACC 1 PL]} | [NEG Q] |
| | [*accepter* IND PST PFV] | [*avoir* V 3 PL IND PST IPFV] | [PRO NOM 3 PL MASC] | {[PRO DAT 1 PL]} | [NEG Q] |
| filter 4 | [*accepter* IND PST PFV] | [*avoir* V 3 PL IND PST IPFV] | [PRO NOM 3 PL MASC] | {[PRO DAT 1 PL RFLX]} | [NEG Q] |
| | [*accepter* IND PST PFV] | [*avoir* V 3 PL IND PST IPFV] | [PRO NOM 3 PL MASC] | {[PRO ACC 1 PL RFLX]} | [NEG Q] |
| | [*accepter* IND PST PFV] | [*avoir* V 3 PL IND PST IPFV] | [PRO NOM 3 PL MASC] | {[PRO 1 PL]} | [NEG Q] |
| | [*accepter* IND PST PFV] | [*avoir* V 3 PL IND PST IPFV] | [PRO NOM 3 PL MASC] | {[PRO ACC 1 PL]} | [NEG Q] |
| | [*accepter* IND PST PFV] | [*avoir* V 3 PL IND PST IPFV] | [PRO NOM 3 PL MASC] | {[PRO DAT 1 PL]} | [NEG Q] |
| filter 6 | [*accepter* IND PST PFV] | [*avoir* V 3 PL IND PST IPFV] | [PRO NOM 3 PL MASC] | {[PRO 1 PL]} | [NEG Q] |
| | [*accepter* IND PST PFV] | [*avoir* V 3 PL IND PST IPFV] | [PRO NOM 3 PL MASC] | {[PRO ACC 1 PL]} | [NEG Q] |
| | [*accepter* IND PST PFV] | [*avoir* V 3 PL IND PST IPFV] | [PRO NOM 3 PL MASC] | {[PRO DAT 1 PL]} | [NEG Q] |
| filter 7 | [*accepter* IND PST PFV] | [*avoir* V 3 PL IND PST IPFV] | [PRO NOM 3 PL MASC] | {[PRO ACC 1 PL]} | [NEG Q] |
| | [*accepter* IND PST PFV] | [*avoir* V 3 PL IND PST IPFV] | [PRO NOM 3 PL MASC] | {[PRO DAT 1 PL]} | [NEG Q] |
| ranking | [*accepter* IND PST PFV] | [*avoir* V 3 PL IND PST IPFV] | [PRO NOM 3 PL MASC] | {[PRO ACC 1 PL]} | [NEG Q] |
| | [*accepter* IND PST PFV] | [*avoir* V 3 PL IND PST IPFV] | [PRO NOM 3 PL MASC] | {[PRO DAT 1 PL]} | [NEG Q] |

**Pred. Output:** `accepter IND;PST;PFV;NOM(3,PL,MASC);ACC(1,PL,MASC);NEG;Q`

## B French Example 2

**Input:** ne te prouvez pas à elle par elles!
**Gold Output:** `prouver IMP;PRS;NOM(2,PL);PROL(3,PL,FEM);ACC(2,SG);DAT(3,SG,FEM);NEG`

After preprocessing and word-level analysis:

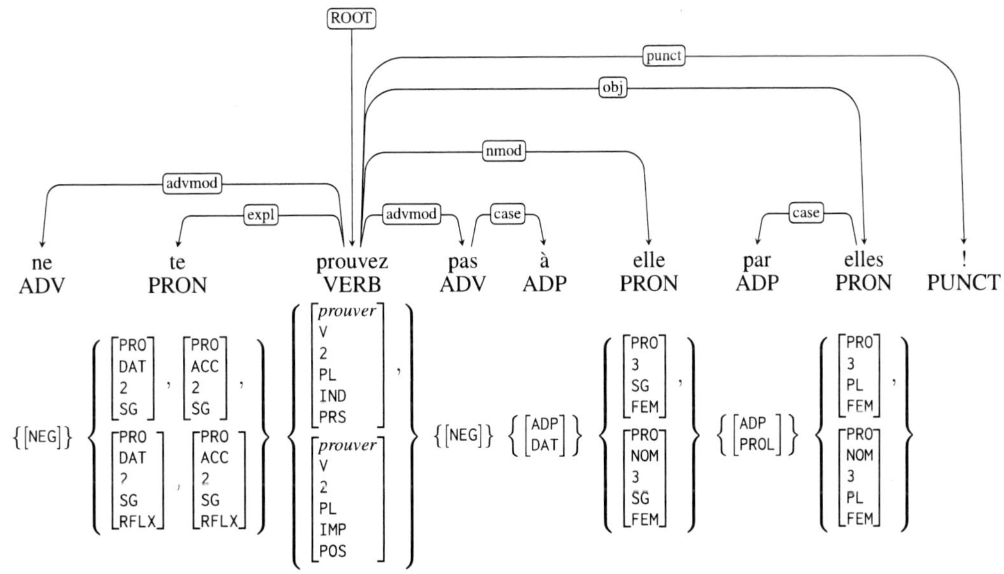


| After ... | $a$ | $v$ | $s$ | $N$ | $c$ |
|---|---|---|---|---|---|
| add $a, v$ | [*prouver* IND PRS] | [*prouver* V 2 PL IND PRS] | | | |
| | [*prouver* IMP PRS] | [*prouver* V 2 PL IMP PRS] | | | |
| add $s$ | [*prouver* IND PRS] | [*prouver* V 2 PL IND PRS] | [NOM 2 PL] | | |
| | [*prouver* IMP PRS] | [*prouver* V 2 PL IMP PRS] | [NOM 2 PL] | | |
| add $N$ | [*prouver* IND PRS] | [*prouver* V 2 PL IND PRS] | [NOM 2 PL] | {[PRO DAT 2 SG], [PRO DAT 3 SG FEM], [PRO PROL 3 PL FEM]} | |
| | [*prouver* IND PRS] | [*prouver* V 2 PL IND PRS] | [NOM 2 PL] | {[PRO ACC 2 SG], [PRO DAT 3 SG FEM], [PRO PROL 3 PL FEM]} | |
| | [*prouver* IND PRS] | [*prouver* V 2 PL IND PRS] | [NOM 2 PL] | {[PRO DAT 2 SG RFLX], [PRO DAT 3 SG FEM], [PRO PROL 3 PL FEM]} | |
| | [*prouver* IND PRS] | [*prouver* V 2 PL IND PRS] | [NOM 2 PL] | {[PRO ACC 2 SG RFLX], [PRO DAT 3 SG FEM], [PRO PROL 3 PL FEM]} | |
| | [*prouver* IMP PRS] | [*prouver* V 2 PL IMP PRS] | [NOM 2 PL] | {[PRO DAT 2 SG], [PRO DAT 3 SG FEM], [PRO PROL 3 PL FEM]} | |
| | [*prouver* IMP PRS] | [*prouver* V 2 PL IMP PRS] | [NOM 2 PL] | {[PRO ACC 2 SG], [PRO DAT 3 SG FEM], [PRO PROL 3 PL FEM]} | |
| | [*prouver* IMP PRS] | [*prouver* V 2 PL IMP PRS] | [NOM 2 PL] | {[PRO DAT 2 SG RFLX], [PRO DAT 3 SG FEM], [PRO PROL 3 PL FEM]} | |
| | [*prouver* IMP PRS] | [*prouver* V 2 PL IMP PRS] | [NOM 2 PL] | {[PRO ACC 2 SG RFLX], [PRO DAT 3 SG FEM], [PRO PROL 3 PL FEM]} | |
| add $c$ | [*prouver* IND PRS] | [*prouver* V 2 PL IND PRS] | [NOM 2 PL] | {[PRO DAT 2 SG], [PRO DAT 3 SG FEM], [PRO PROL 3 PL FEM]} | [NEG] |
| | [*prouver* IND PRS] | [*prouver* V 2 PL IND PRS] | [NOM 2 PL] | {[PRO ACC 2 SG], [PRO DAT 3 SG FEM], [PRO PROL 3 PL FEM]} | [NEG] |
| | [*prouver* IND PRS] | [*prouver* V 2 PL IND PRS] | [NOM 2 PL] | {[PRO DAT 2 SG RFLX], [PRO DAT 3 SG FEM], [PRO PROL 3 PL FEM]} | [NEG] |
| | [*prouver* IND PRS] | [*prouver* V 2 PL IND PRS] | [NOM 2 PL] | {[PRO ACC 2 SG RFLX], [PRO DAT 3 SG FEM], [PRO PROL 3 PL FEM]} | [NEG] |
| | [*prouver* IMP PRS] | [*prouver* V 2 PL IMP PRS] | [NOM 2 PL] | {[PRO DAT 2 SG], [PRO DAT 3 SG FEM], [PRO PROL 3 PL FEM]} | [NEG] |
| | [*prouver* IMP PRS] | [*prouver* V 2 PL IMP PRS] | [NOM 2 PL] | {[PRO ACC 2 SG], [PRO DAT 3 SG FEM], [PRO PROL 3 PL FEM]} | [NEG] |
| | [*prouver* IMP PRS] | [*prouver* V 2 PL IMP PRS] | [NOM 2 PL] | {[PRO DAT 2 SG RFLX], [PRO DAT 3 SG FEM], [PRO PROL 3 PL FEM]} | [NEG] |
| | [*prouver* IMP PRS] | [*prouver* V 2 PL IMP PRS] | [NOM 2 PL] | {[PRO ACC 2 SG RFLX], [PRO DAT 3 SG FEM], [PRO PROL 3 PL FEM]} | [NEG] |
| filter 1 | [*prouver* IMP PRS] | [*prouver* V 2 PL IMP PRS] | [NOM 2 PL] | {[PRO DAT 2 SG], [PRO DAT 3 SG FEM], [PRO PROL 3 PL FEM]} | [NEG] |
| | [*prouver* IMP PRS] | [*prouver* V 2 PL IMP PRS] | [NOM 2 PL] | {[PRO ACC 2 SG], [PRO DAT 3 SG FEM], [PRO PROL 3 PL FEM]} | [NEG] |
| | [*prouver* IMP PRS] | [*prouver* V 2 PL IMP PRS] | [NOM 2 PL] | {[PRO DAT 2 SG RFLX], [PRO DAT 3 SG FEM], [PRO PROL 3 PL FEM]} | [NEG] |
| | [*prouver* IMP PRS] | [*prouver* V 2 PL IMP PRS] | [NOM 2 PL] | {[PRO ACC 2 SG RFLX], [PRO DAT 3 SG FEM], [PRO PROL 3 PL FEM]} | [NEG] |
| filter 6 | [*prouver* IMP PRS] | [*prouver* V 2 PL IMP PRS] | [NOM 2 PL] | {[PRO DAT 2 SG], [PRO DAT 3 SG FEM], [PRO PROL 3 PL FEM]} | [NEG] |
| | [*prouver* IMP PRS] | [*prouver* V 2 PL IMP PRS] | [NOM 2 PL] | {[PRO ACC 2 SG], [PRO DAT 3 SG FEM], [PRO PROL 3 PL FEM]} | [NEG] |
| filter 7 | [*prouver* IMP PRS] | [*prouver* V 2 PL IMP PRS] | [NOM 2 PL] | {[PRO ACC 2 SG], [PRO DAT 3 SG FEM], [PRO PROL 3 PL FEM]} | [NEG] |
| ranking | [*prouver* IMP PRS] | [*prouver* V 2 PL IMP PRS] | [NOM 2 PL] | {[PRO ACC 2 SG], [PRO DAT 3 SG FEM], [PRO PROL 3 PL FEM]} | [NEG] |

**Pred. Output:** `prouver IMP;PRS;NOM(2,PL);PROL(3,PL,FEM);ACC(2,SG);DAT(3,SG,FEM);NEG`

# Comparative Analysis of Cross-lingual Contextualized Word Embeddings

**Hossain Shaikh Saadi**[1], **Viktor Hangya**[2,3], **Tobias Eder**[1] and **Alexander Fraser**[2,3]
[1]Technical University of Munich, Germany
[2]Center for Information and Language Processing, LMU Munich, Germany
[3]Munich Center for Machine Learning
shaikh.saadi@tum.de, tobias.eder@in.tum.de,
{hangyav,fraser}@cis.lmu.de

## Abstract

Contextualized word embeddings have emerged as the most important tool for performing NLP tasks in a large variety of languages. In order to improve the cross-lingual representation and transfer learning quality, contextualized embedding alignment techniques, such as mapping and model fine-tuning, are employed. Existing techniques however are time-, data- and computational resource-intensive. In this paper we analyze these techniques by utilizing three tasks: bilingual lexicon induction (BLI), word retrieval and cross-lingual natural language inference (XNLI) for a high resource (German-English) and a low resource (Bengali-English) language pair. In contrast to previous works which focus only on a few popular models, we compare five multilingual and seven monolingual language models and investigate the effect of various aspects on their performance, such as vocabulary size, number of languages used for training and number of parameters. Additionally, we propose a parameter-, data- and runtime-efficient technique which can be trained with 10% of the data, less than 10% of the time and have less than 5% of the trainable parameters compared to model fine-tuning. We show that our proposed method is competitive with resource heavy models, even outperforming them in some cases, even though it relies on less resources.

## 1 Introduction

Contextualized word representations generated from pre-trained language models have outperformed previously standard static embeddings. Static distributional word representations offer a single representation for a word regardless of its current context (Mikolov et al., 2013a; Bojanowski et al., 2017). Contrarily, a word's contextual representation is influenced by the context in which it is used. Contextualized embeddings have demonstrated ground-breaking performance across several NLP tasks and languages, and accommodate many semantic and syntactic aspects of words (Devlin et al., 2019; Conneau et al., 2020; Brown et al., 2020). From the introduction of ELMo (Peters et al., 2018) and ULMFiT (Howard and Ruder, 2018) to the present, different types of language models have been proposed (Devlin et al., 2019; Lan et al., 2020; Clark et al., 2020; Conneau et al., 2020; Sanh et al., 2019; Radford et al., 2019; Brown et al., 2020) of which the most influential is BERT (Devlin et al., 2019) which initiated an era of Transformer (Vaswani et al., 2017) based language models.

Multilingual Language Models (MLMs) can perform various tasks across different languages. Previous works (Cao et al., 2020; Liu et al., 2019) have showed that the MLM's performance in different transfer learning tasks can further be improved by alignment. The idea of aligning contextualized embeddings is to move the representations of words with similar meaning from different languages closer to each other. There are several ways to perform alignment on contextualized embeddings, such as anchor mapping (Liu et al., 2019) and full model fine-tuning (Cao et al., 2020). However, all of these methods have several shortcomings. It is (1) time-consuming, taking about 24 hours to perform mapping. In contrast to static embeddings, in case of contextualized embeddings the generation of anchor embeddings is required to be able to perform mapping which is the majority of the required time (Liu et al., 2019). Similarly, it takes about 8 hours to perform model fine-tuning (Cao et al., 2020) on mBERT. It is also (2) resource-intensive requiring a lot of GPU memory due to model size and (3) data-intensive requiring a huge collection of monolingual sentences for anchor generation, while fine-tuning requires around 250K pairs of parallel sentences to produce the best-reported alignment (Cao et al., 2020). As a result of these limitations anchor embeddings map-



*Proceedings of the The 2nd Workshop on Multi-lingual Representation Learning (MRL)*, pages 64 - 75
December 8, 2022 ©2022 Association for Computational Linguistics

ping and fine-tuning are often difficult or expensive to perform, deploy and use in real-world scenarios.

To the best of our knowledge there is no study available until now where different model architectures and alignment techniques on various downstream tasks are systematically compared other than on the most popular models such as mBERT and XLM-RoBERTa (Kulshreshtha et al., 2020; Cao et al., 2020; Libovický et al., 2020). In this paper our main goal is to fill this gap. We have compared five multilingual and seven monolingual models with three current alignment techniques (VecMap (Artetxe et al., 2016), RCSLS (Joulin et al., 2018) and model fine-tuning (Cao et al., 2020)) from different perspectives such as multilingual vs. monolingual, big vs. small models and the effect of vocabulary. To assess the models and alignment techniques from different perspectives we used three different tasks: bilingual lexicon induction (BLI), word retrieval (Cao et al., 2020) and zero-shot cross-lingual natural language inference (XNLI) on two language pairs: high-resource German-English and low-resource Bengali-English.

Motivated by the shortcomings of current alignment methods discussed above, and inspired by the fine-tuning based alignment technique of Cao et al. (2020), in addition to the comparative analysis we propose a parameter, data and time efficient alignment technique which requires 10% of the data, runs within less than 10% of the time and uses the amount of less than 5% of trainable parameters compared to model fine-tuning (Cao et al., 2020). An overview of our proposed approach is given in Figure 1.

The findings of our experiments demonstrate that 1) multilinguality always leads to better performance in cross-lingual transfer tasks. 2) We should choose bigger models over smaller models when the resources (computational and data) are available but 3) in case of unattainable resources smaller but specialized multilingual models, such as indic-bert (Kakwani et al., 2020), should be chosen, since they are capable of outperforming or performing similar to the big multilingual models, such as XLM-RoBERTa (Conneau et al., 2020), on a language the model is specialized for. 4) Having a large vocabulary and language support is not an advantage of itself, instead the number of tokens allocated for a given language/script plays a more important role. 5) Big language models are sensitive to batch size and learning rate. 6) Model fine-tuning based alignment (Cao et al., 2020) strengthens the quality of MLM's contextualized embeddings and 7) our proposed method is competitive with resource heavy models, even outperforming them in some cases despite having a significantly lower number of trainable parameters. Our work shows that in specific cases (such as for Bengali on XNLI task) less resource intensive but more targeted solutions (e.g. indic-bert) can also be successfully employed.

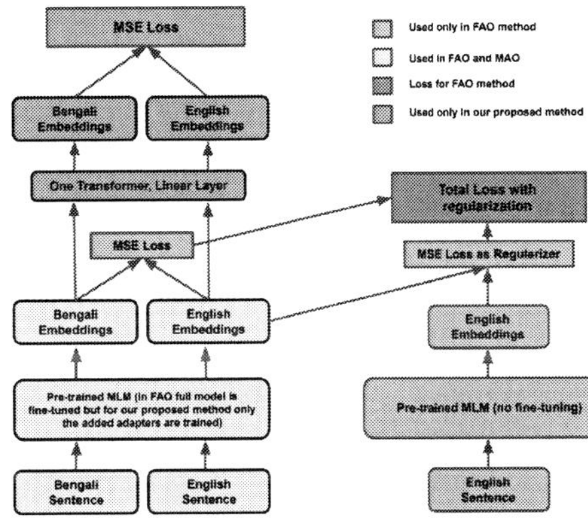


Figure 1: Overview of the fine-tuning based alignment technique (FAO) and our proposed technique (MAO). Small colored square boxes in the upper right corner indicate which modules are used in which method (FAO or MAO).

The paper is structured as the following: the related work is discussed in Section 2. Then Section 3 contains required background knowledge followed by the explanation of our proposed approach in Section 4. Following that, Section 5 contains all the information regarding the tasks, data, different pipelines of our experiments, training procedures and hyperparameters. In Section 6 we discuss the results of different tasks and experiments. Finally, we conclude our work in Section 7.

## 2 Related Work

By pre-training language models on texts involving multiple languages their representation can be leveraged for cross-lingual applications (Devlin et al., 2019; Conneau et al., 2020). Cross-lingual representation quality can be improved using several alignment approaches. Aldarmaki and Diab (2019) build an orthogonal mapping of contextual ELMo (Peters et al., 2018) embeddings and used these mapping for word and sentence translation retrieval. Schuster et al. (2019) also employed a mapping approach to align ELMo embeddings, first they acquired context-independent anchors by factorizing the contextualized embedding space into two parts (context-independent and context-dependent) then they applied the mapping approach to the independent part and tested their proposed mapping approach on zero-shot dependency parsing. Similarly, Wang et al. (2019) learned a linear mapping directly using the contextual embeddings generated from BERT and XLM (Conneau and Lample, 2019), while Liu et al. (2019) aligned anchors of contextual mBERT embeddings. Cao et al. (2020) proposed a model fine-tuning based alignment technique using parallel corpora and proposed the word retrieval task to assess its performance. In a similar work to ours, Kulshreshtha et al. (2020) compared different rotation and fine-tuning based alignments on various downstream tasks. However, all previous work focused on improving state-of-the-art cross-lingual performance and tested their proposed approaches only on a few mainstream MLMs, such as BERT or XLM. In contrast, our main goal is to analyse which model and parameters fit certain data and computational resource scenarios the best, thus we investigate applying different types of alignment approaches to different types of multilingual and monolingual models including various architectures and sizes, trained on either monolingual or multilingual data.

Additionally, alignment approaches are resource intensive. Performing anchor generation for mapping takes the majority of the required time (Liu et al., 2019; Kulshreshtha et al., 2020). Likewise, fine-tuning mBERT takes more than 8 hours (Cao et al., 2020), and for XLM-RoBERTa it is even longer. Due to model size, they require a lot of GPU memory. Also, they are data-intensive requiring a huge collection of monolingual sentences (Liu et al., 2019) for anchor generation and during fine-tuning, around 250K pairs of parallel sentences are required to produce an alignment of good quality. Focusing on these shortcomings we propose a parameter, data and time efficient alignment approach to tackle these issues. Our proposed approach is lightweight compared to full model fine-tuning based alignment, as well as more time and data efficient than fine-tuning and anchor based alignment.

# 3 Background

## 3.1 Mapping

In this section, we will discuss mapping techniques using contextualized embeddings. The contextualized embeddings mapping process follows a similar principle as static embeddings mapping. Given a seed dictionary of source-target word pairs and their embeddings, a linear projection of the source embeddings to the target space is learned (Mikolov et al., 2013b). Suppose $x_i$ and $z_i$ are source and target word embeddings respectively of the $i^{th}$ word pair in the dictionary. The primary aim is to find a transformation matrix $W$ such that $Wx_i$ is similar to $z_i$. This can be expressed as the following optimization problem:

$$\underset{W}{arg\_min} \sum_{i=1}^{n} ||Wx_i - z_i||^2$$

**Anchor Generation:** Many approaches rely on anchors as context independent word representations to generate mapping for contextualized embeddings (Liu et al., 2019; Kulshreshtha et al., 2020). We generate anchors for each of the words by following the procedures of (Liu et al., 2019). For a selected word 1000 sentences where the word is present are selected followed by the generation of contextualized embeddings of each occurrence which are average pooled resulting in the anchor representation. For efficiency, we used 100 sentences instead of 1000 in our systems. In case a word is split into subwords we consider only the embedding of the last subword following (Cao et al., 2020). Additionally, we only considered the output embeddings of the last layer, instead of averaging all layers, since semantic features are manifested in higher layers (de Vries et al., 2020).

## 3.2 Model Fine-Tuning

In order to improve the alignment of the language model using a parallel corpus Cao et al. (2020) proposed a fine-tuning based alignment method. The intuition of this method is to tune the source language embeddings to be closer to the target language embeddings in the vector space. To bring this intuition into practice a simple but effective loss function was introduced:

$$L(f, C) = -\sum_{(s,t)\in C} \sum_{(i,j)\in a(s,t)} sim(f(i,s), f(j,t)) \quad (1)$$

where $(s, t)$ is a parallel sentence pair of the source and target languages in the parallel corpus $C$, $a(s, t)$ indicates the word alignments for $(s, t)$, $f(i, s)$ is the contextualized representation of the word at index $i$ in sentence $s$ given by the used MLM and $sim(f(i, s), f(j, t))$ indicates the similarity of the indicated word embeddings defined by:

$$sim(f(i, s), f(j, t)) = -||f(i, s) - f(j, t)||_2^2 \tag{2}$$

However, minimizing (1) could lead to a degenerative solution where all tokens are represented in the same point mass. To avoid this case, the authors proposed a regularizer preventing the target representations from deviating from the initial value significantly. Let $f_0$ indicate the initial pretrained model before the alignment, then:

$$R(f, C) = \sum_{(s,t)\in C} \sum_{(i,j)\in a(s,t)} ||f(i, t) - f_0(i, t)||_2^2 \tag{3}$$

The regularizer is only applied to the target language representations. The final loss function for the model fine-tuning is the sum of (1) and (3). Note however that due to $f_0$, two copies of the model have to be kept in memory. Additionally, the model can be fine-tuned using multiple language pairs, by training on the concatenation of their parallel corpora.

In this work we refer to this technique as FAO (fine-tuning based alignment objective) which we also depict in Figure 1.

### 3.3 Cross-Lingual Evaluation

**Word Retrieval** For intrinsic evaluation of MLMs Cao et al. (2020) proposed the word retrieval task. Given parallel data, the task is for each source word to retrieve its translation, i.e., find the parallel sentence pair of the source sentence containing the input word and select the right word in it. First, all the source and target language sentences are passed through the language model to build word representations for each word. Note that since a given word type is contained in multiple sentences, it has a contextualized representation for each occurrence. For each of the source words, the most similar word from the target set is taken as its translation pair by calculating their CSLS similarity (Lample et al., 2018). We report the accuracy score for this task. Here the accuracy is defined as the percentage of exact matches between source and target words throughout the whole parallel corpus, similar to Cao et al. (2020).

**BLI** Given a dictionary of source and target language word pairs, bilingual lexicon induction is the task of translating a source language word to a target language word (Irvine and Callison-Burch, 2017; Shi et al., 2021). In this task, the target word with the highest similarity score is chosen as the translation of the source word by computing the cosine similarity between the anchored embeddings of the source word and the target words. For this task, we report P@1 and P@5. Here, P@1 indicates the percentage of source words where the target word with the highest similarity score is the gold translation. P@5 is the percentage of source words where the gold translation falls among the five target words with the highest similarity scores.

**XNLI** Cross-lingual natural language inference is a sentence pair classification task using the corpus of (Conneau et al., 2018). It consists of three classes (neutral, entailment and contradiction) and is used to evaluate cross-lingual transfer learning systems. It covers 15 languages, including two low-resource languages (Swahili and Urdu) (Conneau et al., 2018). We report the accuracy score for this task.

## 4 Proposed Approach

FAO is data-intensive requiring 250K parallel sentences, it is time-consuming and resource-intensive. Similarly, applying simple but efficient alignment techniques like Vecmap and RCSLS is too time-consuming and resource intensive in the case of contextualized embeddings. Inspired by these issues we propose a small alignment architecture which can be trained swiftly (less than 10% of the time required for fine-tuning the whole model) with a few thousand parallel sentences (10% of the data required for fine-tuning the whole model) and trainable parameters for all the proposed architectures are less than 3% of the language model's parameters. To achieve this we add small trainable modules to MLMs and keep the rest of the network frozen.

**Linear or Transformer Layer on Top** We add a single linear or transformer layer on top of the used MLM. An overview of our proposed method is provided in Figure 1. First, the sentences are fed into the language model then we extract the embeddings of all the words (we only take the embedding of the last subword following Cao et al. (2020) in case a word is split). These embeddings are then fed to the proposed linear or transformer layer, which outputs embeddings of the same size as the MLM. As mentioned, we train only the added layer and keep the MLM frozen. This way the number of parameters to be trained and the required time are significantly reduced compared to FAO. Additionally, unlike FAO we do not use the regularizer loss which reduces computation and memory use since the initial model ($f_0$) is unnecessary. The rest of the procedure is the same as described in Section 3. We named our method modified alignment objective (MAO).

**Adapters** Additionally, we leverage adapters (Pfeiffer et al., 2020) in each of the MLM layers together with a transformer layer on top of the models. Similarly as above, we only trained the transformer and the adapter parameters and kept the language model parameters frozen.

## 5 Experimental Setup

### 5.1 Data

We have used three different downstream tasks and for each of the tasks we have different data sources. This section will provide an overview of the data sources across the tasks.

**Word Retrieval** For the word retrieval task we used German-English (Koehn et al., 2005) and Bengali-English (Hasan et al., 2020) parallel data, and we have followed all the procedures proposed in (Cao et al., 2020). To generate 1-to-1 word alignments we used FastAlign (Dyer et al., 2013).

**BLI** For the bilingual lexicon induction task we have used MUSE (Lample et al., 2018) train and test dictionaries. As monolingual data for anchor generation needed for VecMap and RCSLS we used WikiDumps[1] for all the three languages. To extract sentences we have used WikiExtractor[2]. We generated anchors for the most frequent 50k words.

**XNLI** For the XNLI task, we have used English train, validation and test sets, the German test set from (Conneau et al., 2018) and the test data proposed in (Bhattacharjee et al., 2021) for Bengali.

[1] https://dumps.wikimedia.org/

[2] https://github.com/attardi/wikiextractor

### 5.2 Compared Language Models

We compared five multilingual and seven monolingual language models of different types and sizes. We used multilingual models for all three tasks, however, we tested monolingual models only for BLI. Since BLI is a word-level task not a transfer learning task we wanted to know how much difference different types of monolingual models can make compared to the multilingual models. We have tried monolingual models also for the word retrieval task but their performance was not satisfactory. For this reason, we have excluded monolingual models for the other two tasks (word retrieval and XNLI) to save resources, costs and time. All the used language model names as can be found on *Huggingface Hub*, their architectures, vocabulary size and other information are provided in the appendix in Table 5. Our goal was to select a diverse set of models in terms of architecture (mBERT follows BERT (Devlin et al., 2019), indic-bert (Kakwani et al., 2020) follows ALBERT (Lan et al., 2020) architecture), training data (mBERT uses Wikipedia, XLM-RoBERTa (Conneau et al., 2020) uses CommonCrawl), pre-training tasks (mBERT uses the masked language modeling (MLM) and next sentence prediction tasks, indic-bert uses MLM and sentence order prediction task), number of parameters (indic-bert has only 33M parameters and XLM-RoBERTa has 270M parameters) and vocabulary sizes (mBERT and dBERT has 119k tokens in vocabulary whereas XLM-RoBERTa has 250k tokens). In this work, we want to establish a clear and concise comparison between these language models.

### 5.3 Pipelines

We have several pipelines and setups for the model alignments and each of the three tasks. We briefly describe these next. For all of our experiments we have used NVIDIA TITAN X GPU with 12 GB RAM.

**Alignment** Following Cao et al. (2020) we fine-tuned a single multilingual model for both test language pairs (de-en and bn-en) by simultaneously using German-English and Bengali-English parallel sentences in case of both FAO and MAO. Since indic-bert does not support the German language, it was fine-tuned only with Bengali-English sentence pairs. In case of FAO we used 250K parallel sentences pairs for each of the language pairs as in (Cao et al., 2020), while for MAO we used only

25K, except for indic-bert which resulted the best performance with only 7K pairs. We selected these parameters by training the models on different numbers of sentences and testing it on the validation set. We fine-tuned the multilingual models for one epoch following Cao et al. (2020). We report the rest of the used hyperparameters in Table 6 of the appendix. Additionally, we note that adapters could only be used for three multilingual models because at the time of implementation the used AdapterHub toolkit (Pfeiffer et al., 2020) supported only mBERT, dBERT and XLM-RoBERTa but not indic-bert.

**Pipelines for Word Retrieval** In the word retrieval task as baseline we use language models without any fine-tuning. In the second setup, we fine-tune the multilingual language models using FAO and use it for the word retrieval task. In the third setup, we train our proposed linear and transformer layer with or without adapters.

**Pipelines for BLI** As baseline for BLI we use language models without any fine-tuning to generate anchors for mapping. In the second and third setups we fine-tune the multilingual language models using either FAO or MAO and use it to generate anchors and perform mapping. We map the anchors using two alignment techniques VecMap (Artetxe et al., 2016) or RCSLS (Liu et al., 2019). We perform the mapping on two language pairs Bengali-English and German-English. We use the mapping for XNLI task as well as described below.

**Pipelines for XNLI** As baseline for XNLI task we fine-tune the language model and a dedicated classifier layer on the English XNLI data and test them on German and Bengali data. In the second setup we fine-tune the language models using FAO first and then use this fine-tuned model in the same way as the baseline, i.e., we add an additional XNLI specific classification layer. In the third setup we train our proposed models with MAO by adding the trained alignment layers optionally together with adapters between the language model and the classifier layer. We only train the core LM and classifier on XNLI but keep the alignment layer and the adapter frozen. In the last setup, we use mapping matrices built by either VecMap or RCSLS as described above and initialize a linear layer added between the language model and the classifier layer. We do not train this linear layer when training on XNLI. We trained our models for three epochs with batch size 8 or 4 (when trained with mBERT or XLM-RoBERTa) and used $1e^{-6}$ as learning rate.

| **Models** | **de-en** | **bn-en** | **Minutes** |
|---|---|---|---|
| mBERT-cased | 28.45 | 14.55 | - |
| mBERT-cased + FAO | 39.64 | 43.00 | 500.0 |
| mBERT-cased + lin + MAO | 45.84 | 26.93 | 29.0 |
| mBERT-cased + trans + MAO | 46.73 | 24.27 | 30.5 |
| mBERT-cased + ada + transformer + MAO | 48.02 | 24.55 | 32.5 |
| dBERT | 20.71 | 9.71 | - |
| dBERT + FAO | 35.28 | 39.72 | 293.0 |
| dBERT + linear + MAO | 29.50 | 14.41 | 17.5 |
| dBERT + transformer + MAO | 32.21 | 12.58 | 19.0 |
| dBERT + adapter + transformer + MAO | 31.48 | 12.60 | 19.5 |
| XLM-RoBERTa | 4.33 | 6.40 | - |
| XLM-RoBERTa + FAO | 7.58 | 6.40 | 1893.0 |
| XLM-RoBERTa + transformer + MAO | 22.54 | 14.41 | 31.0 |
| indic-bert | - | 12.45 | - |
| indic-bert + FAO | - | 29.22 | 221.0 |
| indic-bert + linear + MAO | - | 15.36 | 4.0 |
| indic-bert + transformer + MAO | - | 13.28 | 4.3 |

Table 1: Accuracy for word retrieval task for different multilingual models for **bn-en** and **de-en**. Here bn = Bengali, de = German, en = English, trans = transformer, ada = adapter. **Minutes** column indicated the number of minutes it takes to train the model

## 6 Results & Discussion

We show results for our word retrieval task in Table 1. Results for BLI task is shown in Table 2, while Table 3 shows the results for the XNLI task. The results shown in these tables are the outcome of a single model per setup. We did not average the results across runs or seeds in order to reduce the required computational resources. Next we discuss the comparison of various aspects of the selected models.

**Big vs. Small Models** From all the results across all the task and languages we observe that big models outperformed smaller models often by a significant margin. In Table 3 for the XNLI task the zero-shot accuracy score on de test set for mBERT is 66.79, for XLM-RoBERTa it is 71.74 whereas for dBERT is 61.74 (dBERT < mBERT < XLM-RoBERTa). In Table 1 for Word Retrieval task accuracy score in the de-en direction for mBERT and dBERT is 28.45 and 20.71 respectively, even after model fine-tuning the scores are 39.64 and 35.28 respectively. We see this pattern for the BLI task as well, in Table 2. We should always choose big models over smaller models when we have available resources (computational, data and time).

**Multilingual vs. Monolingual Models** From the results of the BLI task in Table 2 it is clear that multilingual models showed far superior performance than monolingual models. In Table 2 the

| Models | de-en p@1 | de-en p@5 | bn-en p@1 | bn-en p@5 |
|---|---|---|---|---|
| mBERT-uncased + vec | 56.84 | 71.50 | 12.33 | 26.54 |
| mBERT-uncased + rcs | 59.79 | 74.37 | 12.26 | 27.27 |
| mBERT-cased + vec | 50.95 | 62.29 | 7.43 | 19.43 |
| mBERT-cased + rcs | 51.54 | 67.47 | 8.71 | 20.50 |
| mBERT-cased + FAO + vec | 57.29 | 57.58 | 15.08 | 29.89 |
| mBERT-cased + FAO + rcs | 57.58 | 70.91 | 16.68 | 32.23 |
| mBERT-cased + lin + MAO + vec | 50.81 | 63.69 | 9.04 | 20.24 |
| mBERT-cased + lin + MAO + rcs | 51.47 | 64.43 | 9.45 | 21.47 |
| mBERT-cased + trans + MAO + vec | 51.47 | 62.15 | 7.57 | 19.30 |
| mBERT-cased + trans + MAO + rcs | 52.06 | 63.62 | 8.84 | 20.91 |
| mBERT-cased + ada + trans + MAO + vec | 50.88 | 62.51 | 7.90 | 18.29 |
| mBERT-cased + ada + trans + MAO + rcs | 51.25 | 63.62 | 8.51 | 19.97 |
| dBERT + vec | 42.70 | 49.70 | 4.15 | 9.98 |
| dBERT + rcs | 43.74 | 52.28 | 5.16 | 13.20 |
| dBERT + FAO + vec | 53.46 | 66.12 | 11.39 | 25.06 |
| dBERT + FAO + rcs | 53.60 | 66.86 | 13.13 | 27.88 |
| dBERT + lin + MAO + vec | 43.37 | 52.87 | 4.69 | 10.52 |
| dBERT + lin + MAO + rcs | 43.88 | 53.97 | 5.49 | 11.79 |
| dBERT + trans + MAO + vec | 43.00 | 50.44 | 4.15 | 10.18 |
| dBERT + trans + MAO + RCSLS | 44.10 | 52.79 | 5.42 | 12.60 |
| dBERT + ada + trans + MAO + vec | 43.22 | 50.14 | 4.75 | 10.53 |
| dBERT + ada + trans + MAO + rcs | 44.25 | 52.65 | 5.63 | 11.99 |
| XLM-RoBERTa + vec | 48.82 | 60.60 | 10.32 | 20.17 |
| XLM-RoBERTa + rcs | 58.54 | 73.49 | 13.67 | 28.21 |
| XLM-RoBERTa + FAO + vec | 50.88 | 61.63 | 6.09 | 12.13 |
| XLM-RoBERTa + FAO + rcs | 54.93 | 68.85 | 12.33 | 24.46 |
| XLM-RoBERTa + trans + MAO + vec | 50.88 | 61.63 | 14.00 | 29.42 |
| XLM-RoBERTa + trans + MAO + rcs | 59.35 | 75.03 | 16.28 | 32.90 |
| indic-bert + vec | - | - | 12.13 | 21.24 |
| indic-bert + rcs | - | - | 12.33 | 23.99 |
| indic-bert + FAO + vec | - | - | 13.73 | 23.72 |
| indic-bert + FAO + rcs | - | - | 15.41 | 26.27 |
| indic-bert + lin + MAO + vec | - | - | 13.60 | 23.65 |
| indic-bert + lin + MAO + rcs | - | - | 14.14 | 24.59 |
| indic-bert + trans + MAO + vec | - | - | 11.59 | 21.17 |
| indic-bert + trans + MAO + rcs | - | - | 12.53 | 23.72 |
| De BERT + En BERT + vec | 43.00 | 62.44 | - | - |
| De BERT + En BERT + rcs | 44.77 | 63.91 | - | - |
| De dBERT + En dBERT + vec | 25.47 | 43.96 | - | - |
| De dBERT + En dBERT + rcs | 27.46 | 46.53 | - | - |
| De Electra + En Electra + vec | 1.62 | 4.12 | - | - |
| De Electra + En Electra + rcs | 3.24 | 9.71 | - | - |
| Bn BERT + En BERT + vec | - | - | 5.16 | 11.86 |
| Bn BERT + En BERT + rcs | - | - | 5.29 | 12.66 |

Table 2: P@1 and P@5 scores in BLI task for different models in **de-en** and **bn-en** direction. For de-en and bn-en direction, the coverage for MUSE test set is 90.53% and 99.73% respectively. Coverage is the percentage of word pairs where both source and target word embeddings are present in our embeddings matrices. Here bn = Bengali, de = german, en = english trans = transformer, ada = adapter, vec = VecMap, rcs = RCSLS.

P@1 score for mBERT-cased using VecMap mapping approach in de-en direction is 50.95 but when we used monolingual BERT for both the German and English language the P@1 score decreased to 43.00. We see this performance decrement issue for monolingual models in the bn-en direction and for other models (dBERT) as well in Table 2. Fine-tuned mBERT-cased accompanied by RCSLS outperformed all the models in the de-en and bn-en direction. Monolingual models exhibited significantly poor performance for this word level BLI task, which we did not anticipate.

| Models | en | de | bn |
|---|---|---|---|
| mBERT | 79.42 | 66.79 | 55.21 |
| mBERT + align-matrix | - | 67.60 | 55.04 |
| mBERT + FAO | 78.48 | 68.76 | 60.92 |
| mBERT + linear + MAO | 79.52 | 67.72 | 55.51 |
| mBERT + transformer + MAO | 80.04 | 68.04 | 55.01 |
| mBERT + adapter + transformer + MAO | 80.14 | 69.30 | 54.69 |
| dBERT | 75.51 | 61.74 | 50.84 |
| dBERT + align-matrix | - | 62.44 | 49.74 |
| dBERT + FAO | 75.11 | 62.51 | 53.77 |
| dBERT + linear + MAO | 75.77 | 62.81 | 53.37 |
| dBERT + transformer + MAO | 74.89 | 62.40 | 52.10 |
| dBERT + adapter + transformer + MAO | 76.43 | 65.01 | 50.90 |
| XLM-RoBERTa | 80.18 | 71.74 | 67.94 |
| XLM-RoBERTa + FAO | 78.88 | 70.28 | 66.47 |
| XLM-RoBERTa + transformer + MAO | 80.52 | 73.05 | 68.14 |
| indic-bert | 75.93 | - | 65.59 |
| indic-bert + align-matrix | - | - | 67.58 |
| indic-bert + FAO | 76.11 | - | 59.80 |
| indic-bert + linear + MAO | 75.57 | - | 65.97 |
| indic-bert + transformer + MAO | 75.81 | - | 66.85 |

Table 3: Accuracy scores for XNLI Task for different multilingual models for three different languages **en, de and bn**. Here bn = Bengali, de = German, en = English, trans = transformer, ada = adapter, align-matrix = mapping matrix generated in BLI task using RCSLS for the corresponding language model and language.

**Effect of Vocabulary Size and Language Support** On the sentence level task of XNLI shown in Table 3, indic-bert outperformed mBERT on bn test set in terms of accuracy score by a large margin (indic-bert achieved accuracy score 65.59 whereas mBERT-cased achieved 55.21), it even performed on par with XLM-RoBERTa on bn (accuracy score for XLM-RoBERTa is 67.94). For low resource languages, big multilingual models mostly split the words into multiple subwords because of the small number of tokens in the vocabulary for that language. But due to parameter sharing and positive interference of high resource languages on the low resource languages (Wang et al., 2020) bigger multilingual models accomplish good performance in different tasks. indic-bert which is trained on 12 Indian subcontinent languages and English has 200k tokens in its vocabulary (though it is smaller than XLM-RoBERTa which has 250K tokens from 100 languages and mBERT has 119K tokens from 104 languages) so it does not split most of the Bengali words into subwords and can capture the context of the Bengali sentence on par with XLM-RoBERTa. Increasing the number of languages and vocabulary does not always lead to better performance.

**VecMap vs. RCSLS** In Table 2 for all models we observe that RCSLS mapping always outperformed VecMap for BLI task. P@1 scores in de-en and bn-en direction for mBERT-cased using VecMap are 50.95 and 7.43 respectively while on the contrary for RCSLS P@1 scores are 51.94 and 8.71 respectively. We have also used the align-matrix generated for each of the language models and languages during the zero-shot testing in XNLI task (please refer to Table 3). We have seen that for mBERT, dBERT and XLM-RoBERTa scores increased by a small margin only for the de test set whereas for bn the scores decreased. However, for indic-bert when align-matrix was used the scores increased for bn. VecMap solves a least-square regression problem to learn a mapping. However, RCSLS proposes a unified approach where they directly optimize a retrieval criterion (Joulin et al., 2018). Therefore, RCSLS performs better than VecMap.

**Model Fine-tuning** Fine-tuning a multilingual model with FAO strengthen its contextualized embeddings quality. Results shown in Table 1, Table 2 and Table 3 indicate that model fine-tuning significantly improved the performance across all tasks and models. In Table 1 accuracy scores for fine-tuned mBERT in word retrieval task for de-en and bn-en direction are 39.64 and 43.00 respectively over the vanilla mBERT's accuracy scores which are 28.45 and 14.55 respectively. In Table 3, on XNLI de and bn test set fine-tuned mBERT achieved accuracy scores 68.76 and 60.92 respectively whereas vanilla mBERT achieved 66.79 and 55.21 respectively. There are some exceptions in the case of XNLI task, where fine-tuned XLM-RoBERTa and indic-bert's performance decreased. Due to constraints in computing resources, we had to fine-tune XLM-RoBERTa with a small batch size; for this reason the performance decreased for XLM-RoBERTa. We have used the same learning rate for all the models during fine-tuning the language model and classifier training for the XNLI task. That might affect fine-tuned indic-bert's performance. We believe rigorous hyperparameter tuning for model fine-tuning and training would improve the model's performance significantly but would lead to higher costs as well.

**Proposed Alignment Approach** From the accuracy scores reported in Table 1, our proposed alignment approach outperformed fine-tuned mBERT in the de-en direction and XLM-RoBERTa in bn-en direction for word retrieval task. Our alignment approach takes significantly less time than model fine-tuning (see **Minutes** column of Table 1).

| **bn-en** | | |
|---|---|---|
| **Models** | **trilingual** | **bilingual** |
| mBERT-cased + FAO | 43.00 | 40.80 |
| mBERT-cased + lin + MAO | 26.93 | 27.22 |
| mBERT-cased + trans + MAO | 24.27 | 24.42 |
| mBERT-cased + ada + trans + MAO | 24.55 | 24.27 |
| **de-en** | | |
| **Models** | **trilingual** | **bilingual** |
| mBERT-cased + FAO | 39.64 | 40.35 |
| mBERT-cased + lin + MA0 | 45.84 | 45.47 |
| mBERT-cased + trans + MA0 | 47.73 | 46.80 |
| mBERT-cased + ada + trans + MAO | 48.02 | 48.04 |

Table 4: Accuracy scores for word retrieval task in bilinguality vs. trilinguality study using mBERT-cased. Here bn = bengali, de = german, en = english trans = transformer, ada = adapter, lin = linear, **bn-en** and **de-en** = following scores are reported for only bn-en and de-en directions respectively, **trilingual** = the models are trained with both bn-en and de-en parallel data, **bilingual** = the models are trained with only bn-en parallel data in case of **bn-en** direction and similarly for **de-en** direction de-en parallel data is used for all model training.

This simple and smaller approach outperformed fine-tuned mBERT, dBERT on the German test set and indic-bert in the Bengali test set in the XNLI task. For the BLI task our proposed approach with XLM-RoBERTa and RCSLS outperformed all the other models for both de-en and bn-en directions by achieving P@5 scores 75.03 and 32.90 for de-en and bn-en directions respectively.

**Bilinguality vs. Trilinguality** We wanted to study the effect of training our proposed approaches using only a single language pair (German-English or Bengali-English) using FAO and MAO instead of using both of the language pairs simultaneously. In Table 4, trilingual column indicates the accuracy scores when the model is trained on both the German-English and Bengali-English language pairs simultaneously and the bilingual column implies the scores when the model is trained with only one of the language pairs. From Table 4 we observe that for the bn-en direction when we fine-tuned the model using FAO only with Bengali-English data the scores decreased by a small margin, the score was 43.00 (reported in the trilingual column) but it dropped to 40.80 (reported in the bilingual column). Whereas for the de-en direction when we fine-tuned the model with only German-English data the opposite occurred, the accuracy score slightly increased from 39.64 to 40.35. Hence, Bengali has minimal negative interference on German and German has minimal positive interference on Bengali in the fine-tuning process. However, in case of our proposed approach (MAO) trained with only German-English data, performance on the de-en direction of the linear and transformer model decreased. Only the score of the adapter method increased. Nevertheless, these increments and decrements were by a tiny margin. While on the contrary, when we trained the method with Bengali-English data the performance for the bn-en direction decreased for the adapter method but increased for the other two methods. Therefore, it is unclear whether bilinguality or trilinguality is advantageous over each other in the case of our proposed method.

## 7 Conclusion

In this paper we have compared currently popular alignment techniques using multilingual and monolingual models of various architectures from different aspects by utilizing two word level tasks (BLI and word retrieval) and one sentence level task XNLI with one low resource (Bengali-English) and one high resource language pair (German-English). We also have proposed a time, data and parameter efficient alignment technique. Our experimental results demonstrate that multilinguality always lead to better performance in cross-lingual transfer tasks. When the resources (computational and data) are available, bigger models are always preferred over smaller models, but when the resources are not accessible, smaller but specialized multilingual models should be chosen, since they are capable of performing similarly to or better than the large multilingual models on the languages the model is specialized for. A large set of supported languages and a large vocabulary does not always assist in all types of tasks in contrast to models specifically trained for a limited number of target languages. Large language models are sensitive regarding batch size and learning rate. Finally, high resource languages and large multilingual models perform well with our proposed approach. In future work we aim to develop alignment techniques capable of performing well even on low resource unseen languages.

## Limitations

In case of monolingual language models, the performance of our proposed approach is significantly worse compared to multilingual models. The representations produced by the language specific monolingual models are independent from each other, while in case multilingual models they are to some extent aligned. Using the representations from monolingual models and the simple objective function of our approach, it is more difficult to obtain the same quality alignment as in case of multilingual models which needs further development.

## Acknowledgements

We thank the anonymous reviewers for their helpful feedback. The work was supported by the European Research Council (ERC) under the European Union's Horizon 2020 research and innovation programme (No. 640550) and by the German Research Foundation (DFG; grant FR 2829/4-1).

## References

Hanan Aldarmaki and Mona Diab. 2019. Context-aware cross-lingual mapping. In *Proceedings of the 2019 Conference of the North American Chapter of the Association for Computational Linguistics: Human Language Technologies, Volume 1 (Long and Short Papers)*, pages 3906–3911, Minneapolis, Minnesota. Association for Computational Linguistics.

Mikel Artetxe, Gorka Labaka, and Eneko Agirre. 2016. Learning principled bilingual mappings of word embeddings while preserving monolingual invariance. In *Proceedings of the 2016 Conference on Empirical Methods in Natural Language Processing*, pages 2289–2294, Austin, Texas. Association for Computational Linguistics.

Abhik Bhattacharjee, Tahmid Hasan, Kazi Samin, Md Saiful Islam, M. Sohel Rahman, Anindya Iqbal, and Rifat Shahriyar. 2021. Banglabert: Combating embedding barrier in multilingual models for low-resource language understanding.

Piotr Bojanowski, Edouard Grave, Armand Joulin, and Tomas Mikolov. 2017. Enriching word vectors with subword information.

Tom Brown, Benjamin Mann, Nick Ryder, Melanie Subbiah, Jared D Kaplan, Prafulla Dhariwal, Arvind Neelakantan, Pranav Shyam, Girish Sastry, Amanda Askell, Sandhini Agarwal, Ariel Herbert-Voss, Gretchen Krueger, Tom Henighan, Rewon Child, Aditya Ramesh, Daniel Ziegler, Jeffrey Wu, Clemens Winter, Chris Hesse, Mark Chen, Eric Sigler, Mateusz Litwin, Scott Gray, Benjamin Chess, Jack Clark, Christopher Berner, Sam McCandlish, Alec Radford, Ilya Sutskever, and Dario Amodei. 2020. Language models are few-shot learners. In *Advances in Neural Information Processing Systems*, volume 33, pages 1877–1901. Curran Associates, Inc.

Steven Cao, Nikita Kitaev, and Dan Klein. 2020. Multilingual alignment of contextual word representations. In *International Conference on Learning Representations*.

Kevin Clark, Minh-Thang Luong, Quoc V. Le, and Christopher D. Manning. 2020. Electra: Pre-training text encoders as discriminators rather than generators. In *International Conference on Learning Representations*.

Alexis Conneau, Kartikay Khandelwal, Naman Goyal, Vishrav Chaudhary, Guillaume Wenzek, Francisco Guzmán, Edouard Grave, Myle Ott, Luke Zettlemoyer, and Veselin Stoyanov. 2020. Unsupervised cross-lingual representation learning at scale. In *Proceedings of the 58th Annual Meeting of the Association for Computational Linguistics*, pages 8440–8451, Online. Association for Computational Linguistics.

Alexis Conneau and Guillaume Lample. 2019. Cross-lingual Language Model Pretraining. In *Advances in Neural Information Processing Systems*, volume 32. Curran Associates, Inc.

Alexis Conneau, Ruty Rinott, Guillaume Lample, Adina Williams, Samuel Bowman, Holger Schwenk, and Veselin Stoyanov. 2018. XNLI: Evaluating cross-lingual sentence representations. In *Proceedings of the 2018 Conference on Empirical Methods in Natural Language Processing*, pages 2475–2485, Brussels, Belgium. Association for Computational Linguistics.

Wietse de Vries, Andreas van Cranenburgh, and Malvina Nissim. 2020. What's so special about BERT's layers? a closer look at the NLP pipeline in monolingual and multilingual models. In *Findings of the Association for Computational Linguistics: EMNLP 2020*, pages 4339–4350, Online. Association for Computational Linguistics.

Jacob Devlin, Ming-Wei Chang, Kenton Lee, and Kristina Toutanova. 2019. BERT: Pre-training of deep bidirectional transformers for language understanding. In *Proceedings of the 2019 Conference of the North American Chapter of the Association for Computational Linguistics: Human Language Technologies, Volume 1 (Long and Short Papers)*, pages 4171–4186, Minneapolis, Minnesota. Association for Computational Linguistics.

Chris Dyer, Victor Chahuneau, and Noah A. Smith. 2013. A simple, fast, and effective reparameterization of ibm model 2. In *NAACL*.

Tahmid Hasan, Abhik Bhattacharjee, Kazi Samin, Masum Hasan, Madhusudan Basak, M. Sohel Rahman, and Rifat Shahriyar. 2020. Not low-resource anymore: Aligner ensembling, batch filtering, and new datasets for bengali-english machine translation.

Jeremy Howard and Sebastian Ruder. 2018. Universal language model fine-tuning for text classification. In *Proceedings of the 56th Annual Meeting of the Association for Computational Linguistics (Volume 1: Long Papers)*, pages 328–339, Melbourne, Australia. Association for Computational Linguistics.

Ann Irvine and Chris Callison-Burch. 2017. A comprehensive analysis of bilingual lexicon induction. *Computational Linguistics*, 43(2):273–310.

Armand Joulin, Piotr Bojanowski, Tomas Mikolov, Hervé Jégou, and Edouard Grave. 2018. Loss in translation: Learning bilingual word mapping with a retrieval criterion. In *Proceedings of the 2018 Conference on Empirical Methods in Natural Language Processing*, pages 2979–2984, Brussels, Belgium. Association for Computational Linguistics.

Divyanshu Kakwani, Anoop Kunchukuttan, Satish Golla, Gokul N.C., Avik Bhattacharyya, Mitesh M. Khapra, and Pratyush Kumar. 2020. IndicNLPSuite: Monolingual Corpora, Evaluation Benchmarks and Pre-trained Multilingual Language Models for Indian Languages. In *Findings of EMNLP*.

Philipp Koehn et al. 2005. Europarl: A parallel corpus for statistical machine translation. In *MT summit*, volume 5, pages 79–86. Citeseer.

Saurabh Kulshreshtha, Jose Luis Redondo Garcia, and Ching-Yun Chang. 2020. Cross-lingual alignment methods for multilingual BERT: A comparative study. In *Findings of the Association for Computational Linguistics: EMNLP 2020*, pages 933–942, Online. Association for Computational Linguistics.

Guillaume Lample, Alexis Conneau, Marc'Aurelio Ranzato, Ludovic Denoyer, and Hervé Jégou. 2018. Word translation without parallel data. In *International Conference on Learning Representations*.

Zhenzhong Lan, Mingda Chen, Sebastian Goodman, Kevin Gimpel, Piyush Sharma, and Radu Soricut. 2020. Albert: A lite bert for self-supervised learning of language representations. In *International Conference on Learning Representations*.

Jindřich Libovický, Rudolf Rosa, and Alexander Fraser. 2020. On the language neutrality of pre-trained multilingual representations. In *Findings of the Association for Computational Linguistics: EMNLP 2020*, pages 1663–1674, Online. Association for Computational Linguistics.

Qianchu Liu, Diana McCarthy, Ivan Vulić, and Anna Korhonen. 2019. Investigating cross-lingual alignment methods for contextualized embeddings with token-level evaluation. In *Proceedings of the 23rd Conference on Computational Natural Language Learning (CoNLL)*, pages 33–43, Hong Kong, China. Association for Computational Linguistics.

Tomas Mikolov, Kai Chen, Greg Corrado, and Jeffrey Dean. 2013a. Efficient estimation of word representations in vector space.

Tomás Mikolov, Quoc V. Le, and Ilya Sutskever. 2013b. Exploiting similarities among languages for machine translation. *CoRR*, abs/1309.4168.

Matthew E. Peters, Mark Neumann, Mohit Iyyer, Matt Gardner, Christopher Clark, Kenton Lee, and Luke Zettlemoyer. 2018. Deep contextualized word representations. In *Proceedings of the 2018 Conference of the North American Chapter of the Association for Computational Linguistics: Human Language Technologies, Volume 1 (Long Papers)*, pages 2227–2237, New Orleans, Louisiana. Association for Computational Linguistics.

Jonas Pfeiffer, Andreas Rücklé, Clifton Poth, Aishwarya Kamath, Ivan Vulić, Sebastian Ruder, Kyunghyun Cho, and Iryna Gurevych. 2020. AdapterHub: A framework for adapting transformers. In *Proceedings of the 2020 Conference on Empirical Methods in Natural Language Processing: System Demonstrations*, Online. Association for Computational Linguistics.

Alec Radford, Jeffrey Wu, Rewon Child, David Luan, Dario Amodei, Ilya Sutskever, et al. 2019. Language models are unsupervised multitask learners. *OpenAI blog*, 1(8):9.

Victor Sanh, Lysandre Debut, Julien Chaumond, and Thomas Wolf. 2019. Distilbert, a distilled version of BERT: smaller, faster, cheaper and lighter. *CoRR*, abs/1910.01108.

Tal Schuster, Ori Ram, Regina Barzilay, and Amir Globerson. 2019. Cross-lingual alignment of contextual word embeddings, with applications to zero-shot dependency parsing. In *Proceedings of the 2019 Conference of the North American Chapter of the Association for Computational Linguistics: Human Language Technologies, Volume 1 (Long and Short Papers)*, pages 1599–1613, Minneapolis, Minnesota. Association for Computational Linguistics.

Haoyue Shi, Luke Zettlemoyer, and Sida I. Wang. 2021. Bilingual lexicon induction via unsupervised bitext construction and word alignment. In *Proceedings of the 59th Annual Meeting of the Association for Computational Linguistics and the 11th International Joint Conference on Natural Language Processing (Volume 1: Long Papers)*, pages 813–826, Online. Association for Computational Linguistics.

Ashish Vaswani, Noam Shazeer, Niki Parmar, Jakob Uszkoreit, Llion Jones, Aidan N Gomez, Ł ukasz Kaiser, and Illia Polosukhin. 2017. Attention is all you need. In *Advances in Neural Information Processing Systems*, volume 30. Curran Associates, Inc.

Yuxuan Wang, Wanxiang Che, Jiang Guo, Yijia Liu, and Ting Liu. 2019. Cross-lingual BERT transformation for zero-shot dependency parsing. In *Proceedings of the 2019 Conference on Empirical Methods in Natural Language Processing and the 9th International Joint Conference on Natural Language Processing (EMNLP-IJCNLP)*, pages 5721–5727, Hong Kong, China. Association for Computational Linguistics.

Zirui Wang, Zachary C. Lipton, and Yulia Tsvetkov. 2020. On negative interference in multilingual models: Findings and a meta-learning treatment. In *Proceedings of the 2020 Conference on Empirical Methods in Natural Language Processing (EMNLP)*, pages 4438–4450, Online. Association for Computational Linguistics.

## A Appendix

For our three different tasks, we have utilized seven monolingual models and five multilingual models. Information on the language models, including the number of parameters, model type, supported languages and vocabulary size is reported in Table 5. Hyperparameters utilized for each experiment in our word retrieval task are mentioned in Table 6. Table 4 contains the results of our bilingual and trilingual training setups.

| Model | Param. | Vocab. | Type | Languages |
|---|---|---|---|---|
| mBERT-uncased | 168M | 105K | BERT | 104 languages |
| mBERT-cased | 179M | 119K | BERT | 104 languages |
| dBERT | 134M | 119K | Distil BERT | 104 languages |
| XLM-RoBERTa | 270M | 250K | BERT | 100 languages |
| indic-bert | 33M | 200K | ALBERT | 13 languages |
| bert-base-cased | - | - | BERT | English |
| distilbert-base-cased | - | - | Distil BERT | English |
| google/electra-base-generator | - | - | Electra | English |
| dbmdz/bert-base-german-cased | - | - | BERT | German |
| distilbert-base-german-cased | - | - | Distil BERT | German |
| dbmdz/electra-base-german-europeana-cased-discriminator | - | - | Electra | German |
| sagorsarker/bangla-bert-base | - | - | BERT | Bengali |

Table 5: Language models used for our experiments.

| Models | Batch Size | Learning rate | Attention Head | Reduction Factor |
|---|---|---|---|---|
| mBERT+FAO | 4 | $5e^{-5}$ | - | - |
| mBERT+lin+MAO | 16 | $1e^{-5}$ | - | - |
| mBERT+transr+MAO | 32 | $5e^{-8}$ | 8 | - |
| mBERT+ada +trans +MAO | 32 | $1e^{-7}$ | 8 | 8 |
| dBERT+FAO | 4 | $5e^{-5}$ | - | - |
| dBERT+lin +MAO | 32 | $1e^{-5}$ | - | - |
| dBERT+trans +MAO | 32 | $1e^{-7}$ | 8 | - |
| dBERT+ ada + trans+MAO | 32 | $1e^{-7}$ | 8 | 8 |
| XLM-RoBERTa+FAO | 1 | $5e^{-5}$ | - | - |
| XLM-RoBERTa+trans+MAO | 32 | $5e^{-5}$ | 8 | - |
| indic-bert+FAO | 4 | $5e^{-5}$ | - | - |
| indic-bert+lin+MAO | 32 | $5e^{-5}$ | - | - |
| indic-bert+trans+MAO | 32 | $1e^{-8}$ | 8 | - |

Table 6: Hyperparameters used for different models for the word retrieval task. Here (-) indicates not applicable for this model, trans = transformer, ada = adapter, lin = linear.

# How Language-Dependent is Emotion Detection? Evidence from Multilingual BERT

**Luna De Bruyne***, **Pranaydeep Singh***, **Orphée De Clercq**,
**Els Lefever**, **Véronique Hoste**
LT[3], Language and Translation Technology Team, Ghent University
{firstname.lastname}@ugent.be

## Abstract

As emotion analysis in text has gained a lot of attention in the field of natural language processing, differences in emotion expression across languages could have consequences for how emotion detection models work. We evaluate the language-dependence of an mBERT-based emotion detection model by comparing language identification performance before and after fine-tuning on emotion detection, and performing (adjusted) zero-shot experiments to assess whether emotion detection models rely on language-specific information. When dealing with typologically dissimilar languages, we found evidence for the language-dependence of emotion detection.

## 1 Introduction

As language finds itself at the crossroads of cognition and culture, it has been a thoroughly investigated subject in the context of emotion research and has given rise to questions as how emotion expression varies across languages and whether language has an impact on emotion conceptualisation and perception.

Indeed, many studies have reported on the cultural relativity of emotion, often underscoring the diversity in emotion lexicons across languages: not only is there a big variability in which emotional states are included in the lexicon of a language with a designated emotion term (e.g., a word for *sadness* seems to be missing in Tahiti (Levy, 1984)), but there are also many differences in the connotations and meanings of emotion terms across languages (Mesquita et al., 1997; Wierzbicka, 1999).

Instead of focusing on emotion conceptualisation and experience, one could also ask whether emotions are *expressed* differently across languages. Again, this can be reflected in differences in emotion vocabulary, but also in language-specific phraseology. In Russian, for example, the verbalisation of emotion is very much focused on the human body, and the numerous diminutive suffixes exhibit different emotional nuances (Wierzbicka, 1999). Noteworthy is also the distinction between individualistic and collectivist cultures, where the latter are associated with more reticence to express emotions, while the former exhibit more open emotion expression (Semin et al., 2002).

As emotion analysis in text has gained a lot of attention in artificial intelligence and the field of natural language processing (NLP) as well (Calvo and Mac Kim, 2013; Mohammad, 2016), language-dependent conceptualisation and expression could have consequences for how emotion detection models work. Analogously to humans who might need knowledge about the linguistic code (e.g., to know whether irony is often used in a specific language or to understand language-specific phraseology) to correctly judge the emotional value of someone's utterance, machine learning models might need this knowledge as well in order to accurately predict emotions from text. Therefore, we investigate the language-dependence of the task of emotion detection. In other words, we want to know whether knowledge about the language identity is needed to make accurate emotion predictions.

For this analysis, we will look at languages from different language families and branches (e.g., Germanic, Italic and Indo-Iranian in the Indo-European language family or Chinese from the Sino-Tibetan language family) in order to include languages with different structural features. Although language families are not the same as the classes defined in the field of linguistic typology (i.e., the analysis, comparison, and classification of languages according to their common structural features and forms), languages within one language family are generally more typologically similar than languages from different families.

As transformer models are currently state of the

*These authors contributed equally to this work.



*Proceedings of the The 2nd Workshop on Multi-lingual Representation Learning (MRL)*, pages 76 - 85
December 8, 2022 ©2022 Association for Computational Linguistics

art in many NLP tasks, we investigate the language-dependence of multilingual BERT (mBERT), the transformer model introduced by Devlin et al. (2019) which was trained on 104 languages. We foresee two kinds of experiments. First, we investigate how much language-specific information is preserved in the BERT representations by comparing performance on the task of language identification both before and after fine-tuning on emotion detection. Second, zero-shot transfer learning (training on a source language and testing directly on the target language English) is compared with training on machine-translated data, i.e., data that was originally in English but automatically translated to the source language ('semi-zero-shot transfer learning'). These models thus learn from the same source language, but in the semi-zero-shot set-up language-specific information from the target language (like idioms, phraseology or cultural codes) might still be preserved, thus aiding performance during test time on the target language.

In Section 2, we describe the literature on cross-lingual emotion research (Section 2.1) and discuss related work dealing with language dependency in NLP (Section 2.2). In Section 3 we explain our method by describing the data and resources (Section 3.1) and by zooming in on the experimental set-up (Section 3.2). The results are reported in Section 4 and further discussed in Section 5, followed by a conclusion in Section 6.

## 2 Related work

### 2.1 Emotions across languages

While many psychological models assume that emotions are distinct from linguistic processing, growing psychological research suggests that language plays an important role in both emotion experience and perception. Especially in psychological constructionist theories of emotion, language is considered as doing more than merely communicating emotion. Instead, language contributes to the conceptualisation of emotion itself (Lindquist et al., 2015).

In the constructionist view, the experience of emotion takes place when sensations inside and outside the body are made meaningful in their context by use of concept knowledge. This is referred to as the theory of constructed emotion or – as it was previously called – the conceptual act theory (Barrett, 2006). Concept knowledge is the knowledge we have about different categories, acquired via semantic knowledge and personal experience (Lindquist et al., 2015). Both language and culture can thus play an important role here.

The role of language in emotion can be linked to the linguistic relativity hypothesis (Whorf, 1956). Linguistic relativity, often referred to as the Sapir-Whorf hypothesis, suggests that the way people think is influenced by the language they speak. Speakers of Russian, for example, a language which has separate words for naming light blue (*goluboy*) and dark blue (*siniy*), discriminate between various shades of blue differently than English speakers, who only have one term to denote blue (Winawer et al., 2007). Another example of linguistic relativity is the observation that Inupiaq, an Inuit language, has many words for snow, while English has only one, which suggests that speakers of these languages categorize their environment differently. In this light, it is compelling to study cross-lingual differences in emotion conceptualisation, experience and perception.

In the context of emotion conceptualisation, Mesquita et al. (1997) highlighted that lexical equivalents are mostly not expressing the same meaning across languages. This is in line with results from a colexification analysis of emotion words in 2,474 languages, in which Jackson et al. (2019) found that there is a wide variation in which emotion concepts are lexicalized together by one word form, and that colexifications vary systematically across language families. In Tai-Kadai languages, for example, *anxiety* is closely related to *fear*, while it is more related to *grief* and *regret* in Austroasiatic languages.

Also emotion perception varies across languages, which is reflected in differences in emotionality ratings (affective norms) of words (Harris et al., 2006). Of course, this could be linked to the differences in meaning in lexical equivalents across languages, but it might also be due to cultural differences in appraisal of the same event. Mesquita and Ellsworth (2001) give as example that solitude may be perceived as positive in middle-class European culture and lead to *contentment*, while in Inuit culture, being alone is typically associated with *sorrow* and for Tahitians with *fear*.

Finally, there is also variation in how emotions are expressed. Semin et al. (2002) found that individualistic cultures and collectivist cultures express emotions and emotional events using different linguistic markers and divergent levels of abstraction: in individualistic cultures, emotion terms are more prominent as self-markers and are represented by abstract language (e.g., adjectives and nouns), while in collectivist cultures, emotion terms are more prominent as relationship-markers and are represented by concrete language (e.g., interpersonal verbs). This is in line with studies on emotional reticence in East Asian cultures. Caldwell-Harris et al. (2013) compared verbal declarations of *love* in Chinese and American English, where they placed the reticence of both verbal and non-verbal emotional expression in Chinese opposite to the frequent use of 'I love you' as displaying American expressivity.

### 2.2 Language dependency in natural language processing

Cross-lingual and multilingual perspectives on natural language processing have received a lot of attention, especially regarding the transferability of NLP models across languages. Since the rise of deep learning, many efforts have been made to achieve cross-lingual representations of words in a joint embedding space (Ruder et al., 2019). Also state-of-the-art transformer models have been developed in multilingual variants, like multilingual BERT (mBERT) (Devlin et al., 2019), XLM (Conneau and Lample, 2019) and XLM-R (Conneau et al., 2020).

These multilingual models have been the subject of probing studies to investigate how well they perform in zero-shot cross-lingual model transfer (i.e., fine-tuning the model on task-specific training data from a source language and testing that resulting model on test data for that task in a different language). Pires et al. (2019) performed such probing experiments with mBERT (named entity recognition and part of speech tagging) and found that it has a robust ability to generalize cross-lingually, but that transfer works best between typologically similar languages. This could indicate that mBERT learns representations which contain both a cross-lingual and a language-specific component. Using Canonical Correlation Analysis (CCA) on the internal representations of mBERT, Singh et al. (2019) found that mBERT is not embedding different languages into one shared space, but that it partitions representations for each language (especially at deeper layers) in a way that reflects the linguistic and evolutionary relationships between languages as represented in phylogenetic trees. When looking at the representations of the last layer of mBERT, Gonen et al. (2020) could identify a language-identity subspace, which supports the hypothesis that there are identifiable language components in mBERT.

While there are many studies trying to gain insight in how language-specific information is stored in mBERT, the focus is mostly on the embeddings themselves, and not on how different tasks exploit this information. An exception is the study of Tanti et al. (2021), who investigated the effect of fine-tuning on specific tasks on the language-specific component of mBERT representations. They found that mBERT's representations become less language-specific after fine-tuning and that there is a greater loss of this information in POS-tagging, which is a morphosyntactic task, compared to natural language inference (NLI), which is a semantically oriented task.

For the task of emotion detection, the exploitation of language-specific information in word embeddings has not yet been investigated. However, language-dependence of this task and the related task of sentiment analysis has been studied in the context of emotion/sentiment preservation after translation. Mohammad et al. (2016) investigated the use of Support Vector Machines in detecting sentiment (positive/negative/neutral) in Arabic social media posts and compared performance of an Arabic sentiment classification system with an English system where the Arabic texts were translated to English. They found that the translation-based approach produced results on par with Arabic sentiment analysis when the translation was done manually, and led to a small drop in performance when the translation was done automatically. This suggests that, when using high-quality translations, sentiment analysis does not suffer from losing language-specific information. However, the authors did observe that translations often did not preserve the original sentiment and investigated this by means of an annotation task of the instances where translation had resulted in sentiment change. When the translation was done automatically, the main reason for sentiment change was bad translation, but when the translation was done manually, the annotators indicated cultural differences as the main reason for this change. An example of the latter is a sentence that referred to not seeing the crescent moon and that was annotated in English as neutral, but negative in Arabic, as the crescent moon in Islam is associated with the beginning of a month or a holiday. Another example included the phrase "I have no comment", which was annotated as neutral in English, but is used to express a negative opinion in Arabic.

A similar study was performed by Kajava et al. (2020), who investigated the preservation of the emotion categories *anger, anticipation, disgust, fear, joy, sadness, surprise* and *trust* when English data was translated to Finnish, French and Italian. They deemed the degree of preservation sufficient for using translated data in cross-lingual emotion detection systems and found that change of emotion labels was due to incomplete or ambiguous translation and to the difficulty of the emotion annotation task itself (which even causes confusion between the annotations of annotators within one language), rather than to linguistic differences in the encoding of emotion.

## 3 Method

### 3.1 Resources & data

We assess the language dependency of emotion detection using multilingual BERT (mBERT), which was released together with the original English BERT model (Devlin et al., 2019). Both the English and multilingual BERT are 12-layer transformers, but while the original BERT is trained on English data only, mBERT is trained on the Wikipedia pages of 104 languages and thus has a shared word piece vocabulary. There is no explicit marker denoting the input language, nor does it use an explicit mechanism to encourage translation-equivalent pairs to have similar representations.

**Emotion dataset** For our emotion detection dataset, we start from the Universal Joy dataset (Lamprinidis et al., 2021). The original dataset consists of 530k Facebook posts in 18 languages, which were collected based on the 'feelings tags' that users added to their message. These self-labeled tags were then mapped to one of the 5 emotion categories *anger*, *anticipation*, *fear*, *joy* and *sadness*. For our experiments, we included all languages from the 'Small' version of this dataset (2,947 instances per language), namely Chinese, English, Portuguese, Spanish and Tagalog, and complemented this with the Dutch (as it is typologically very similar to English) and Hindi (to have an additional more typologically distinct language) data from the 'Low Resource' subset (2,201 instances for Dutch and 1,823 for Hindi).

We made sure the sizes of the datasets and distributions of the emotion labels were equal across all seven languages, which will be important for the zero-shot experiments (see Section 3.2). We therefore identified the language with the lowest number of instances for each label, and randomly sampled the same number of instances with that label for the other languages. This resulted in 10,437 instances in total or 1,491 instances per language, of which 150 for *anger*, 231 for *anticipation*, 8 for *fear*, 830 for *joy* and 272 for *sadness*. We call this set `UJ Equal`. The original Universal Joy dataset contains some special tokens like `[URL]`, `[PHOTO]`, `[LOCATION]` or `[PERSON]`. We removed all of these except `[PERSON]`, as they are not part of the grammatical sentence.

We also provide a dataset with machine translations, based on the English part of `UJ Equal`. Using the Google Translate API with the Python package `googletrans`[1], we translated the English subset in `UJ Equal` to Chinese, Dutch, Hindi, Portuguese, Spanish and Tagalog and call this dataset `UJ MT`.

We further have a separate test set of English instances consisting of 981 sentences, as provided in the original Universal Joy dataset, which we call `UJ English Test`.

**Language Identification dataset** 6,000 instances for each of the seven languages (Chinese, Dutch, English, Hindi, Portuguese, Spanish and Tagalog) were taken from the OSCAR corpus (Ortiz Suárez et al., 2020), which is a multilingual corpus obtained by language classification and filtering of the Common Crawl corpus[2]. These instances were randomized and the language code was added as label.

### 3.2 Experimental setup

**Preservation of language-specific information** First, we investigate to what degree language-specific information is preserved after fine-tuning mBERT on the task of emotion detection. We use the pre-trained mBERT model with a single-layer softmax classifier on top. In phase 1, the pre-trained model is used without fine-tuning to execute the language identification task (7-class classification on the Language Identification dataset). In phase 2, mBERT is fine-tuned in 5 epochs on the

[1]https://pypi.org/project/googletrans/

[2]https://commoncrawl.org/

emotion detection task (with the 10,437 instances from `UJ Equal`) using categorical cross-entropy loss. The resulting model is then used for the encoding and classification of the language identification task. The language identification performance of both phases is then compared. Moreover, we visualize the outputs from different layers in the BERT model, and at different stages in the fine-tuning process using t-SNE to decipher the effect of fine-tuning for emotion on the language-specific representations.

**Zero-shot and semi-zero-shot experiments** The next set of emotion detection experiments also consists of two phases. In phase 1, more traditional zero-shot experiments are performed, where we either train on the source languages Chinese, Dutch, Hindi, Portuguese, Spanish or Tagalog (1,491 instances from `UJ Equal`), and test on the separate English set of 981 sentences (`UJ English Test`). In phase 2, we train on the same source languages, but instead of relying on authentic, original data we rely on the `UJ MT` data. This data was thus originally in English, but machine-translated to either Chinese, Dutch, Hindi, Portuguese, Spanish or Tagalog. We call this semi-zero-shot experiments.

The idea behind this is that the machine-translated data could be closer to the target language regarding language-specific information, and that the version with machine-translated data will thus perform better in tasks where language-specific information is important. Note that it is crucial that all train sets have the same label distribution, to avoid that the (dis)similarity with the label distribution of the test set explains the performance of the models.

Again, we use pre-trained mBERT with a single-layer softmax classifier and cross-entropy loss as loss function. We compare the (semi-)zero-shot models against a within-language baseline, trained on the English part of the `UJ Equal` dataset.

## 4 Results

### 4.1 Preservation of language-specific information

**Effect on language identification performance**

The language identification performance before and after fine-tuning on emotion detection is shown in Table 1. When using the pre-trained mBERT model without further fine-tuning, the model achieves a macro-averaged F1-score of 99.92%. This means that mBERT reaches an almost perfect performance in differentiating between languages, which is in line with previous findings that mBERT partitions representations per language (Singh et al., 2019) or that it at least exhibits a language-identity subspace (Gonen et al., 2020).

| Task | Macro F1 |
|---|---|
| before fine-tuning (frozen LM) | 0.9992 |
| after fine-tuning on emotion detection | 0.9161 |

Table 1: Language identification performance before and after fine-tuning on emotion detection.

When fine-tuning mBERT on emotion detection and applying the resulting model to perform language identification, the model's performance drops to 91.61%. As also observed by Tanti et al. (2021), the mBERT representations become less language-specific after fine-tuning on a specific task. Intuitively, tasks that require less language-specific knowledge, would lose more language-specific information than tasks that heavily rely on language-specific knowledge, resulting in a larger drop of language identification performance. As the drop in performance after fine-tuning on emotion detection (7.47%) is relatively small (especially compared to the drops reported by Tanti et al. (2021), which was 10.6% after fine-tuning on NLI and even 78% for POS-tagging), one could deduce that emotion detection does rely rather heavily on language-specific knowledge.

**T-SNE plots**

To visualise the effect of fine-tuning for emotion detection on the mBERT representations, the hidden states of the first (Layer 1), middle (Layer 6) and last (Layer 12) layer of the model are plotted in Figure 1 using t-SNE projections before fine-tuning (Epoch 0), and after Epoch 2 and 4.

We see that, regardless of how far the fine-tuning process has progressed, the languages are already clearly distinct in the first layer of the model. In the last layers, the language clusters begin to slowly merge while the model is being fine-tuned.

After epoch 2, most languages have already merged, but Chinese, Hindi and Tagalog (the non-European languages) are still represented in separate clusters. However, after epoch 4, Hindi and Tagalog have entered the European cloud, while Chinese stays more or less isolated.

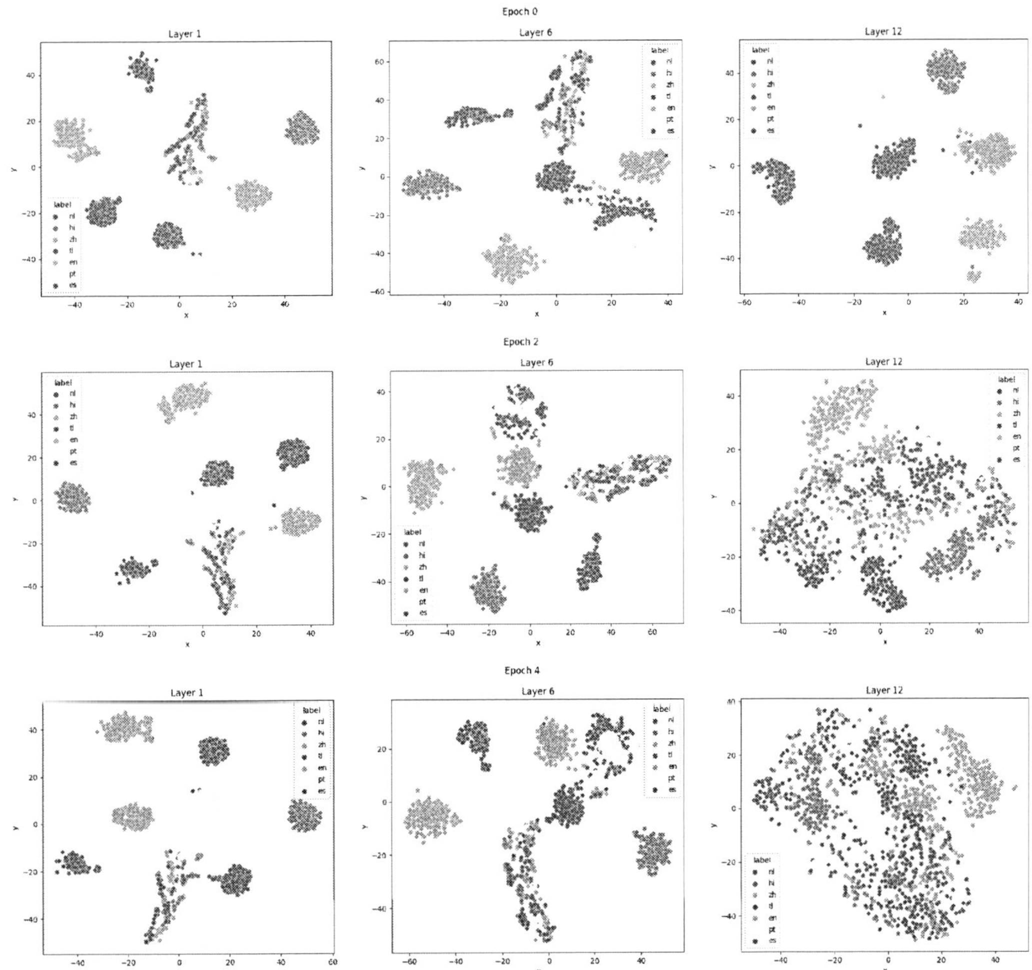


Figure 1: Visualisation of mBERT embeddings and effect on language separation when fine-tuning on emotion detection. *Language codes*: nl = Dutch, hi = Hindi, zh = Chinese, tl = Tagalog, en = English, pt = Portuguese, es = Spanish.

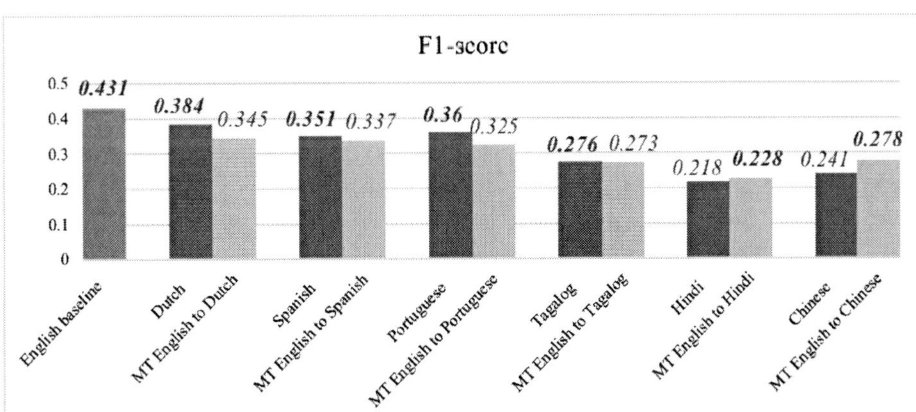


Figure 2: F1-scores for zero-shot (blue) and semi-zero shot (yellow) emotion classification on the English test set.

Interestingly, instead of a complete mix-up of languages, each language is still quite distinguishable after fine-tuning, even though they are being placed much closer to each other than initially. Especially Chinese and Hindi, but also Portuguese are easily distinguishable.

### 4.2 Zero-shot and semi-zero-shot experiments

In this section, we report zero-shot and semi-zero-shot results for emotion detection on the `UJ English test` set from Universal Joy. The baseline macro-average F1-score (trained on the English part of `UJ Equal`) is 43.1%.

As shown in Figure 2, all zero-shot experiments achieve a lower performance than this baseline, with Hindi as lowest performing source language (21.8% F1), followed by Chinese (24.1% F1) and Tagalog (27.6% F1). Unsurprisingly, Dutch is the best-performing source language (38.4% F1), followed by Portuguese (36.0% F1) and Spanish (35.1% F1). The performance of these source languages more or less corresponds to their typological similarity, with the European languages performing best as source language when English is the target language. Only Hindi, which also belongs to the family of Indo-European languages, performs worse than expected (even worse than Chinese and Tagalog, which belong to the Sino-Tibetan and Austronesian language families, respectively). This might be due to the difference in script (Devanagari for Hindi versus Latin for the other Indo-European languages).

Our idea was that using machine-translated instances (English to source language) as training data instead of real instances in the source language, would give an indication of the system's reliance on language-specific information, as some of this information might still be preserved in a (machine) translation. Before the translation step, all training instances in these so-called semi-zero-shot experiments are the same, namely the English part of `UJ equal`. We expected a drop in the semi-zero-shot results compared to the baseline results (because some information will be lost anyway due to (imperfect) translation), but if the drop from baseline to semi-zero-shot would be smaller compared to the drop from baseline to normal zero-shot, this might indicate that the model relies more on language-specific information (note that the size of the fine-tuning set is equal in the zero-shot experiments and semi-zero-shot experiments). These results are indicated by the yellow bars in Figure 2.

Interestingly, we see that for the European languages, normal zero-shot is better than semi-zero-shot (with normal zero-shot outperforming semi-zero-shot with around 4 to 6% F1), while for Chinese and Hindi semi-zero-shot is better. The results for Tagalog are less outspoken, as the F1-score for zero-shot (27.6%) and semi-zero-shot (27.3%) are on par.

If it is the case that language-specific information is really encoded in the machine-translated instances, then these results could indicate that an emotion detection model does rely on such information. The language-specific information might be similar for English and the other European languages used in this study, making that there is no benefit in using a model that encodes this information for English (i.e., the semi-zero-shot model). However, for less similar languages, these results do suggest that there is a benefit and that emotion detection is language-dependent.

## 5 Discussion

Although we found some potential evidence for the language-dependence of emotion detection, several points need to be taken into account. First of all, the datasets used in this study are small (especially for the category *fear*), and the overall quality of the data is low. It seems that some messages are incomplete and that some (parts of) instances appear multiple times in the dataset.[3] Furthermore, some instances contain code-switching between different languages. Another drawback is that we only tested on English. We made this choice because we could not obtain test sets for all languages (for Hindi and Dutch, all data was already used for training).

We claim that we found evidence for the language-dependence of emotion detection, where typologically dissimilar languages suffer more from cross-lingual zero-shot learning. This evidence is partly based on the observation that semi-zero-shot experiments (in which language-specific

[3]Example from the Dutch subset of Universal Joy:*"valiumpilletje gekregen om rustig te worden, haar lichaam moet de rest doen, maar de eerste uren heeft ze zich er ernstig tegen verzet maar ligt nu gelukkig heerlijk te slapen.* ***Hopelijk voor ons allen een goede [PERSON] .***"; *"tegen verzet maar ligt nu gelukkig heerlijk te slapen* ***. Hopelijk voor ons allen een goede*** *nachtrust."*; *"heerlijk te slapen* ***. Hopelijk voor ons allen een goede [PERSON] .***"; *"slapen.* ***Hopelijk voor ons allen een goede [PERSON] .***"; "***. Hopelijk voor ons allen een goede [PERSON] .***" are separate instances in the dataset.

information is assumed to be preserved to a certain extent) outperforms zero-shot learning for Hindi and Chinese, while it does not for the European languages (as language-specific information might be similar for these languages and English, and there therefore is no benefit in using a model that encodes this information). However, it could be that this language-specific information is not related to phraseology or differences in emotion-topic relations (see Section 1 and 2.1), but to differences in topic distribution in general. It might be the case that the topics in Chinese and Hindi are very different from the topics in the English dataset, while the European languages contain similar topic distributions as English.

The semi-zero-shot experiments are based on the idea that some language-specific information is preserved after machine translation. Although we cannot be absolutely certain of this, the fact that the semi-zero-shot experiments outperformed normal zero-shot for some languages, suggests that there is some helpful information in these translations. One could argue that the performance of the semi-zero-shot models correlates negatively with the quality of the translations: machine translation might be bad for less similar languages, resulting in a better emotion classification performance in the semi-zero-shot case, because some words have not been translated. However, we could not find evidence for this. When applying a token-level language identifier on the translated texts[4], we found that the percentage of tokens that was classified as English instead of Chinese, Tagalog and Hindi is respectively 6%, 3% and 0.3%. That there are almost no untranslated words in the Hindi set while the semi-zero-shot does perform better, thus contradicts that the semi-zero-shot performance is explained by the number of untranslated words.

In future work, we envisage to use a different approach for investigating the language-dependence of emotion detection instead of relying on semi-zero-shot experiments. As both this study and previous research has shown that mBERT partitions its representations per language (Singh et al., 2019; Gonen et al., 2020), it would be compelling to see whether we can achieve language-neutral representations and which effect that has on the emotion detection performance. We hypothesise that when the representations no longer exhibit language-specific information, it would hamper emotion detection. However, in such a set-up, we will need to compare emotion detection to a reference task and discuss the language dependency of those tasks in relation to each other. This because the process of making language-neutral representations will involve reducing the transformer's parameters and that will probably lead to a performance drop anyway.

## 6 Conclusion

In this paper, we assessed the language-dependence of an mBERT-based emotion detection model. We first investigated the effect of fine-tuning on emotion on the preservation of language-specific information in mBERT, by comparing language identification performance of the languages Chinese, Dutch, English, Hindi, Portuguese, Spanish and Tagalog before and after fine-tuning on emotion detection and visualising the model's hidden states in t-SNE plots. As expected, language-specific information is lost after fine-tuning, but only to a small extent. Especially the representations of typologically dissimilar languages remain more or less isolated, while similar languages get clustered together.

In a next set of experiments, we compared zero-shot learning with what we called 'semi-zero-shot learning'. In the zero-shot experiments, we trained a model on either Chinese, Dutch, Hindi, Portuguese, Spanish or Tagalog and tested it on English data. In semi-zero-shot, originally English data was translated to those languages, assuming that some language-specific information is preserved in these translations. We found that for the European languages, normal zero-shot is better than semi-zero shot. However, for less similar languages, semi-zero-shot was better, suggesting that there is some language-specific information aiding the performance. This could be evidence for the language-dependence of emotion detection.

Future research, dealing with better datasets and approaches to make the BERT representations language-neutral, should be carried out to corroborate these findings.

## Acknowledgements

This research was funded by Research Foundation–Flanders under a Strategic Basic Research fellowship with grant number 3S004019.[5]

[4]https://github.com/Abhijit-2592/spacy-langdetect

[5]https://www.researchportal.be/nl/project/transfer-learning-voor-automatische-emotiedetectie-nederlandstalige-teksten

## References


Lisa Feldman Barrett. 2006. Solving the emotion paradox: Categorization and the experience of emotion. *Personality and social psychology review*, 10(1):20–46.

Catherine Caldwell-Harris, Ann Kronrod, and Joyce Yang. 2013. Do more, say less: Saying "I love you" in Chinese and American cultures. *Intercultural Pragmatics*, 10(1):41–69.

Rafael A Calvo and Sunghwan Mac Kim. 2013. Emotions in text: Dimensional and categorical models. *Computational Intelligence*, 29(3):527–543.

Alexis Conneau, Kartikay Khandelwal, Naman Goyal, Vishrav Chaudhary, Guillaume Wenzek, Francisco Guzmán, Edouard Grave, Myle Ott, Luke Zettlemoyer, and Veselin Stoyanov. 2020. Unsupervised cross-lingual representation learning at scale. In *Proceedings of the 58th Annual Meeting of the Association for Computational Linguistics*, pages 8440–8451, Online. Association for Computational Linguistics.

Alexis Conneau and Guillaume Lample. 2019. Cross-lingual language model pretraining. *Advances in Neural Information Processing Systems*, 32.

Jacob Devlin, Ming-Wei Chang, Kenton Lee, and Kristina Toutanova. 2019. BERT: Pre-training of deep bidirectional transformers for language understanding. In *Proceedings of the 2019 Conference of the North American Chapter of the Association for Computational Linguistics: Human Language Technologies, Volume 1 (Long and Short Papers)*, pages 4171–4186, Minneapolis, Minnesota. Association for Computational Linguistics.

Hila Gonen, Shauli Ravfogel, Yanai Elazar, and Yoav Goldberg. 2020. It's not Greek to mBERT: Inducing word-level translations from multilingual BERT. In *Proceedings of the Third BlackboxNLP Workshop on Analyzing and Interpreting Neural Networks for NLP*, pages 45–56, Online. Association for Computational Linguistics.

Catherine L. Harris, Jean Berko Gleason, and Ayşe Ayçiçeği. 2006. When is a first language more emotional? Psychophysiological evidence from bilingual speakers. In Aneta Pavlenko, editor, *Bilingual Minds: Emotional Experience, Expression, and Representation*, pages 257–283. Multilingual Matters.

Joshua Conrad Jackson, Joseph Watts, Teague R Henry, Johann-Mattis List, Robert Forkel, Peter J Mucha, Simon J Greenhill, Russell D Gray, and Kristen A Lindquist. 2019. Emotion semantics show both cultural variation and universal structure. *Science*, 366(6472):1517–1522.

Kaisla Kajava, Emily Öhman, Piao Hui, Jörg Tiedemann, et al. 2020. Emotion preservation in translation: Evaluating datasets for annotation projection. *Proceedings of Digital Humanities in Nordic Countries (DHN 2020)*, pages 38–50.

Sotiris Lamprinidis, Federico Bianchi, Daniel Hardt, and Dirk Hovy. 2021. Universal Joy: A data set and results for classifying emotions across languages. In *Proceedings of the Eleventh Workshop on Computational Approaches to Subjectivity, Sentiment and Social Media Analysis*, pages 62–75, Online. Association for Computational Linguistics.

Robert I Levy. 1984. The emotions in comparative perspective. *Approaches to emotion*, pages 397–412.

Kristen A. Lindquist, Jennifer K. MacCormack, and Holly Shablack. 2015. The role of language in emotion: Predictions from psychological constructionism. *Frontiers in Psychology*, 6.

Batja Mesquita and Phoebe C Ellsworth. 2001. The role of culture in appraisal. In Klaus R Scherer, Angela Schorr, and Tom Johnstone, editors, *Appraisal processes in emotion: Theory, methods, research*, pages 233–248. Oxford University Press.

Batja Mesquita, Nico H Frijda, and Klaus R Scherer. 1997. Culture and emotion. *Handbook of cross-cultural psychology*, 2:255–297.

Saif M Mohammad. 2016. Sentiment analysis: Detecting valence, emotions, and other affectual states from text. In *Emotion measurement*, pages 201–237. Woodhead Publishing, Sawston, Cambridge.

Saif M Mohammad, Mohammad Salameh, and Svetlana Kiritchenko. 2016. How translation alters sentiment. *Journal of Artificial Intelligence Research*, 55:95–130.

Pedro Javier Ortiz Suárez, Laurent Romary, and Benoît Sagot. 2020. A monolingual approach to contextualized word embeddings for mid-resource languages. In *Proceedings of the 58th Annual Meeting of the Association for Computational Linguistics*, pages 1703–1714, Online. Association for Computational Linguistics.

Telmo Pires, Eva Schlinger, and Dan Garrette. 2019. How multilingual is multilingual BERT? In *Proceedings of the 57th Annual Meeting of the Association for Computational Linguistics*, pages 4996–5001, Florence, Italy. Association for Computational Linguistics.

Sebastian Ruder, Ivan Vulić, and Anders Søgaard. 2019. A survey of cross-lingual word embedding models. *Journal of Artificial Intelligence Research*, 65:569–631.

Gün R Semin, Carien A Görts, Sharda Nandram, and Astrid Semin-Goossens. 2002. Cultural perspectives on the linguistic representation of emotion and emotion events. *Cognition & Emotion*, 16(1):11–28.

Jasdeep Singh, Bryan McCann, Richard Socher, and Caiming Xiong. 2019. BERT is not an interlingua and the bias of tokenization. In *Proceedings of the 2nd Workshop on Deep Learning Approaches for Low-Resource NLP (DeepLo 2019)*, pages 47–55,

Hong Kong, China. Association for Computational Linguistics.

Marc Tanti, Lonneke van der Plas, Claudia Borg, and Albert Gatt. 2021. On the language-specificity of multilingual BERT and the impact of fine-tuning. In *Proceedings of the Fourth BlackboxNLP Workshop on Analyzing and Interpreting Neural Networks for NLP*, pages 214–227, Punta Cana, Dominican Republic. Association for Computational Linguistics.

B.L. Whorf. 1956. *Language, thought, and reality: Selected writings*. Technology Press of Massachusetts Institute of Technology.

Anna Wierzbicka. 1999. *Emotions across languages and cultures: Diversity and universals*. Cambridge University Press.

Jonathan Winawer, Nathan Witthoft, Michael C Frank, Lisa Wu, Alex R Wade, and Lera Boroditsky. 2007. Russian blues reveal effects of language on color discrimination. *Proceedings of the National Academy of Sciences*, 104(19):7780–7785.

# MicroBERT: Effective Training of Low-resource Monolingual BERTs through Parameter Reduction and Multitask Learning

**Luke Gessler    Amir Zeldes**
Department of Linguistics
Georgetown University
{lg876,amir.zeldes}@georgetown.edu

## Abstract

Transformer language models (TLMs) are critical for most NLP tasks, but they are difficult to create for low-resource languages because of how much pretraining data they require. In this work, we investigate two techniques for training monolingual TLMs in a low-resource setting: greatly reducing TLM size, and complementing the masked language modeling objective with two linguistically rich supervised tasks (part-of-speech tagging and dependency parsing). Results from 7 diverse languages indicate that our model, MicroBERT, is able to produce marked improvements in downstream task evaluations relative to a typical monolingual TLM pretraining approach. Specifically, we find that monolingual MicroBERT models achieve gains of up to 18% for parser LAS and 11% for NER F1 compared to a multilingual baseline, mBERT, while having less than 1% of its parameter count. We conclude reducing TLM parameter count and using labeled data for pretraining low-resource TLMs can yield large quality benefits and in some cases produce models that outperform multilingual approaches.

## 1 Introduction

Pretrained word embeddings are an essential ingredient for high performance on most NLP tasks. Transformer language models (TLMs)[1] such as BERT/mBERT (Devlin et al., 2019) RoBERTa/XLM-R, (Liu et al., 2019; Conneau et al., 2020), and ELECTRA (Clark et al., 2020) provide state-of-the-art performance, but they expect at least tens of millions of tokens in training data. High-resource languages like English, Arabic, and Mandarin are able to meet this requirement, but most of the world's languages cannot. Two major lines of work have arisen in order to address this gap: the first attempts to use multilingual transfer to pool different languages' data together to meet TLMs' data demands, and the second attempts to lower TLMs' data demands by changing their architectures and training regimens.

In this study, we take up work in the latter direction, asking specifically whether (1) vast reduction of model size and (2) incorporation of explicitly supervised, rather than self-supervised, tasks into model pretraining can produce better monolingual TLMs. The former method is motivated by the intuition that normal-sized TLMs are so large as to be severely overparameterized for low-resource settings, and the latter method is motivated by an intuition that in the absence of large volumes of unlabeled text, signal from a supervised task with linguistic annotations is less likely be redundant to the model. We find evidence that indicates both methods are helpful: our MicroBERT models produce monolingual embeddings that can outperform comparable multilingual approaches. We summarize our contributions as follows:

1. We describe a method for training monolingual BERTs for low-resource settings, MicroBERT, characterized by a small parameter count and multitask pretraining which includes masked language modeling (MLM), part-of-speech (PoS) tagging and dependency syntax parsing.

2. Using evaluations on named-entity recognition (NER) and Universal Dependencies (UD) parsing across 7 diverse languages, we show that this approach is competitive with multilingual methods and often outperforms them for languages unseen by mBERT, even when the only pretraining task is MLM. Our evaluation reveals a 7% higher parser LAS and 6% higher NER F1 on average for unseen languages, with gains up to 18.87% and 11.81% for parsing and NER.

[1]Following popular usage, we will informally refer to TLMs similar to the original BERT as "BERTs" throughout this work.



*Proceedings of the The 2nd Workshop on Multi-lingual Representation Learning (MRL)*, pages 86 - 99
December 8, 2022 ©2022 Association for Computational Linguistics

3. We release all MicroBERT models trained for this work at `https://github.com/lgessler/microbert`.

4. We publicly release our code at `https://github.com/lgessler/microbert` for reproducing our results and as a turnkey facility for training new MicroBERTs.

## 2 Previous Work

At least since the development of pretrained static word embeddings (Mikolov et al., 2013b,a; Pennington et al., 2014; Bojanowski et al., 2017), pretrained word representations have been indispensable resources for NLP models, providing dense numerical representations of tokens' linguistic properties. Pretrained contextualized embeddings (McCann et al., 2018; Peters et al., 2018; Devlin et al., 2019) based on the Transformer architecture (Vaswani et al., 2017) have since overtaken them in popularity. Throughout this period, high-resource languages have received the majority of attention, and although interest in low-resource settings has increased in the past few years, there remains a large gap (in terms of linguistic resources, pretrained models, etc.) between low- and high-resource languages (Joshi et al., 2020).

### 2.1 Multilingual Models

The publication of BERT (Devlin et al., 2019) also included a multilingual model, mBERT, trained on 104 languages. mBERT and other massively multilingual models such as XLM-R (Conneau et al., 2020) achieve impressive performance not just on those 104 languages but also in some zero-shot settings (cf., *inter alia*, Pires et al. 2019; Rogers et al. 2020), despite the fact that models like mBERT do not have any explicit mechanism for inducing shared representations across languages. However, large language models like XLM-R suffer from the fact that languages necessarily compete for parameters, meaning that barring fortuitous synergies each additional language should tendentially degrade the overall performance of the model for a fixed parameter count. Moreover, languages with less training data tend to perform more poorly in LMs like XLM-R (Wu and Dredze, 2020).

While the majority of multilingual models seek to include many languages, with a large proportion of them being high-resource, there are some low-resource approaches to training multilingual models from scratch where there may not even be any high-resource languages. For example, Ogueji et al. (2021) train an mBERT on data totaling less than 1GB ($\approx$100M tokens) from 11 African languages, and find that their model often outperforms comparable massively multilingual models.

### 2.2 Adapting Multilingual Models

One response to the difficulties posed by massively multilingual models has been to leave aside the goal of fitting ever more languages into a single model, and to investigate whether it would be more fruitful to *adapt* pretrained massively multilingual models for a given target language. Enriching the TLM's vocabulary with additional tokens (e.g. wordpieces for BERT-style models) has been shown to be helpful because of how it improves tokenization and reduces the rate of out-of-vocabulary tokens (Wang et al., 2020; Artetxe et al., 2020; Chau et al., 2020; Ebrahimi and Kann, 2021). Transliteration has also been shown to be beneficial when there are related languages that would not have been able to benefit from transfer in the form of shared representations otherwise, e.g. between Turkish (Latin script) and related Uyghur (Arabic script) (Muller et al., 2021; Chau and Smith, 2021). Using adapter modules (Houlsby et al., 2019) has also proven effective (Pfeiffer et al., 2020a). All these approaches are typically combined with *continued pretraining*, where MLM and other pretraining tasks are used to update model weights, and some formulations of continued pretraining are multitask (Pfeiffer et al., 2020b; Chau and Smith, 2021, *inter alia).*

### 2.3 Monolingual Models

Whereas multilingual approaches have tried to address low-resource settings with transfer from high-resource languages, other approaches have investigated the question of how much data is needed for a given level of quality in a BERT-like model, and the question of what alternative training regimens might help reduce this data requirement.

Several studies have examined notable thresholds on dataset size. Martin et al. (2020) find in a series of experiments that for French, at least 4GB of text is needed for near-SOTA performance, and Micheli et al. (2020) show further that at least 100MB of text is needed (again for French) for "well-performing" models on some tasks. (Micallef et al., 2022) perform similar experiments for a monolingual Maltese BERT, finding that even when trained with only 46M tokens, the monolingual BERT, BERTu, was able to achieve results competitive with an mBERT model adapted with the vocabulary augmentation methods of Chau et al. (2020). (Warstadt et al., 2020) train English RoBERTa models on datasets ranging from 1M to 1B tokens and find that while models acquire linguistic features readily on small datasets, they require more data to fully exploit these features in generalization on unseen data.

To our knowledge, there has been little work on examining whether significantly reducing model size could help in the low-resource monolingual setting. As a baseline, Chau and Smith (2021) and Muller et al. (2021) train monolingual BERTs with 6 instead of 12 layers for low-resource languages, but this does not even halve the model's parameter count. The only exception we were able to find is work from Turc et al. (2019), where very small models (as low as 4.4M parameters to BERT base's 110M) are pretrained directly prior to training via distillation, but the condition where the small model is only pretrained and not trained via distillation is not evaluated in their work.

### 2.4 Non-TLM Models

Finally, it is worth noting that while BERT-like TLMs are the clear winner overall for high-resource languages in most tasks, in low-resource settings, other embedding models may be superior. Arora et al. (2020) and Ortiz Suárez et al. (2020) show that ELMo (Peters et al., 2018), static (Pennington et al., 2014), and even random embeddings are often not too far behind BERT-like TLMs on some tasks even for high-resource languages. Riabi et al. (2021) show that a character-based language model is competitive with mBERT for one low-resource language, NArabizi.

## 3 Motivation

As we have seen, monolingual BERTs trained with standard methods tend to perform poorly when less than 20-40M tokens are available during training, and there is evidence that they do not learn to fully generalize some linguistic patterns without a large ($\approx$1B tokens, Warstadt et al. 2020) amount of training data. However, most popular methods for pretraining BERTs are self-supervised, using only unlabeled text. This has turned out well for high-resource languages, where unlabeled text is available in far greater quantities than labeled text, to the point where incorporating labeled text into pretraining does not always provide large gains.

However, even in very low-resource settings, it is common for sources of linguistic signal beyond unlabeled text to be available, such as treebanks, interlinearized text, and dictionaries. It is natural to ask whether using them as data for auxiliary supervised tasks during model pretraining could help monolingual models overcome a lack of unlabeled data, and perhaps even interact synergistically with the main pretraining task, such as MLM. It is known, for example, that BERTs learn to represent words' parts of speech (Rogers et al., 2020), and it seems possible that providing direct supervision for predicting parts of speech may help a model acquire good PoS representations with less data. This leads us to our first hypothesis **H1**, that monolingual models should benefit from multitask pretraining with auxiliary tasks incorporating labeled data.

Previous results also lead us to our second hypothesis **H2**, that in low-resource settings, monolingual BERTs are typically severely overparameterized. Most BERTs are overparameterized in the sense that they can have modules removed, disabled, or compressed while showing minimal regressions (or sometimes even improvements) (Rogers et al., 2020), but in H2 we mean further that there are so many parameters that the model cannot be effectively learned given the amount of data. As noted in §2, there appears to be a gap in the literature on whether pretraining a vastly scaled down BERT model could help monolingual BERTs perform better in low-resource settings, and we take up the question in this work.

## 4 Approach

We propose an architecture and training regime for monolingual BERTs which we call MicroBERT. We keep the basic architecture of BERT, but we reduce encoder layer count to 3, hidden representation size to 100, and number of attention heads to 5. (Compare this to BERT base's 12, 768, and 12, respectively.) Excluding prediction heads, this reduces parameter count from 108M[2] to 1.29M, or just 1.19% of a normal BERT model's size. After the encoder stack, one dedicated head is used for each task, where each head is provided with the last encoder layer's hidden states.

For training, assume a task set $\mathcal{T} = t_1, \ldots, t_{|\mathcal{T}|}$, corresponding datasets $\mathcal{D} = d_1, \ldots, d_{|\mathcal{T}|}$, and a set

[2]Obtained from `bert-base-cased` using the `BertModel` implementation in HuggingFace's `transformers` library.

of weights for each task $\lambda_1, \ldots, \lambda_{|\mathcal{T}|}$, s.t. $\sum_i \lambda_i = 1$. To prepare the sequences of batches $\mathcal{B} = b_1, \ldots, b_{|\mathcal{B}|}$ for a given epoch, construct each batch $b_i$ using only instances from exactly one dataset $d_t$, and sample batches so that each dataset $d_t$ is represented at least $\lfloor \lambda_t |\mathcal{B}| \rfloor$ times in $\mathcal{B}$. Each batch is sent not only to its dataset's corresponding prediction head, but also to any other prediction heads which are compatible with it. For example, a batch containing dependency syntax labels would be sent to the parsing prediction head, and it would also be sent to the MLM head, since the MLM head only requires unlabeled text.[3] If a dataset is exhausted in the course of this procedure, new instances are sampled anew from the beginning of the dataset. This is a simple means for addressing the fact that some datasets will be much larger than others, which without intervention could have led to one task's parameter updates drowning out others.

We consider three tasks in this work. The first is MLM implemented as whole-word, dynamic masking, as in RoBERTa (Liu et al., 2019). The second is PoS tagging, for which our prediction head is a simple linear projection. The third is dependency parsing, for which we use a modified form of the biaffine dependency parser of Dozat and Manning (2017) which has had the encoder LSTM stack removed. Cross-entropy loss is used for all tasks and summed together: each head produces an associated loss $\ell_i$, which is summed into a single loss $\ell$ which is used to begin backpropagation. We note that it would be straightforward to add other tasks, though we choose PoS tagging and parsing for this work since PoS tagged and dependency parsed datasets are relatively common for low-resource languages. This multitask setup is not novel—in fact, Chau and Smith (2021) use the the same three tasks for a similar purpose, though instead of pretraining a BERT from scratch, they use the multitask setup to perform adaptive finetuning on a pretrained multilingual model, and find a negative result.

## 5 Experimental Methods

To evaluate our approach, we train MicroBERT models on several languages and compare them to a variety of baselines. All our experiments are implemented using AllenNLP (Gardner et al., 2018), Transformers (Wolf et al., 2020), and PyTorch (Paszke et al., 2019). All code and models are available at `https://github.com/lgessler/microbert`.

[3]Actually, matters are a bit more complicated than this. The MLM head requires representations that included a `[MASK]` token from the start, whereas other heads require representations from unmasked sequences. For multitask batches, therefore, the batch must be fed through the encoder stack twice: once with masking, and once without masking.

| Language | Unlabeled | UD | NER |
|---|---|---|---|
| Wolof | 517,237 | 9,581 | 10,800 |
| Coptic | 970,642 | 48,632 | – |
| Tamil | 1,429,735 | 40,236 | 186,423 |
| Indonesian | 1,439,772 | 122,021 | 800,063 |
| Maltese | 2,113,223 | 44,162 | 15,850 |
| Uyghur | 2,401,445 | 44,258 | 17,095 |
| Anc. Greek | 9,058,227 | 213,999 | – |

Table 1: Token count for each dataset by language, sorted in order of increasing unlabeled token count. Recall that unlabeled data for Indonesian and Tamil was downsampled, and all other sources of unlabeled data were used in full.

### 5.1 Data

We prepare datasets for seven diverse languages: Wolof, Uyghur, Ancient Greek, Maltese, Coptic, Indonesian, and Tamil. These languages were selected according to several criteria. First, two hard requirements were that they needed to have a Universal Dependencies (Nivre et al., 2016) treebank with a train, dev, and test split; and that they needed to have a "large-enough" source of unlabeled text totaling between 500,000 and 10,000,000 tokens. Second, languages were prioritized based on phylogenetic diversity: six unrelated language families are represented (Niger–Congo, Turkic, Indo-European, Afro-Asiatic, Austronesian, Dravidian), and languages vary widely in syntax (for example, Uyghur is morphologically rich, while Coptic is morphologically poor). Third, we sample languages along the spectrum of data quality—for example, some have very high quality tokenization, while others have noisier tokenization.

For each language, we obtain a UD treebank, a larger unlabeled corpus, and for all languages except Ancient Greek and Coptic, an NER dataset from WikiAnn (Pan et al., 2017). Unlabeled data for each language was taken from Wikipedia, except for Ancient Greek and Coptic, whose unlabeled corpora were taken from open access digital humanities projects. Note that the unlabeled corpora for Indonesian and Tamil were downsampled by randomly choosing Wikipedia articles until a quota of around 1.5M tokens was met. A summary of corpus statistics is given in Table 1, and a full description of the languages' datasets and their preparation is given in Appendix B. Note that Uyghur is written in Arabic script; Wolof, Indonesian, and Maltese are written in Latin script; and Tamil, Coptic, and Ancient Greek are written in their own scripts.

### 5.2 Conditions

We compare four baselines, as well as six variants of the MicroBERT approach.

- **WORD2VEC**: a 100-dimensional static word embedding baseline, motivated by observations that static word embeddings can perform well in low resource settings (cf. §2).
- **MBERT**: the *bert-base-multilingual-cased* pretrained model. Note that only two of our seven languages (Indonesian and Tamil) have been seen by MBERT.
- **MBERT-VA**: the *bert-base-multilingual-cased* pretrained model adapted in the *vocabulary augmentation* method of Chau et al. (2020), where 99 wordpieces are added to the vocabulary and the model is pretrained further.
- **μBERT-M, μBERT-MX, μBERT-MXP**: our MicroBERT models with MLM; MLM and XPOS[4] tagging; and MLM, XPOS tagging, and UD parsing used in pretraining. μBERT-MX performs tasks at an 8:1 ratio, and μBERT-MXP performs tasks at an 8:1:1 ratio.
- **μBERT4-M, μBERT4-MX, μBERT4-MXP**: like the corresponding MicroBERT models, but approximately 4 times larger, having 200 instead of 100 hidden units; 8 instead of 5 attention heads; and 6 instead of 3 layers.

Our μBERT models are all trained for 200 epochs with a batch size of 32 and 8,000 batches per epoch, and we save the model that achieves best MLM performance on the validation split of the unlabeled dataset. This results in our models being trained on only 20% of the batches that BERT was, though we hypothesize that due to our smaller model and dataset sizes, this may not be an issue. A full description of our methods is given in Appendix C.

[4]In Universal Dependencies parlance, an XPOS tag is a part of speech tag from a language-specific tag inventory, as opposed to a UPOS, which is drawn from a universal tag inventory.

### 5.3 Evaluation

To evaluate our pretrained models, we perform NER on the WikiAnn datasets and dependency parsing on the UD datasets for each language–model pair, following previous work (Chau et al., 2020; Muller et al., 2021, *inter alia).* We choose these tasks because they are common in the literature of TLM evaluation, because datasets are common even in low-resource languages for them, and because they both assess somewhat complementary linguistic information: informally, parsing requires grammatical knowledge, and NER requires semantic and world knowledge. Combined, they ought to give a holistic view of a model's abilities.

We use common hyperparameter settings to train the evaluation models which allow for fine-tuning of the BERT model at a reduced learning rate. A standard Dozat and Manning (2017) parser is used for the parsing evaluation, and a linear chain CRF with stacked LSTM encoders is used for the NER evaluation. Our metrics for these tasks are LAS and span-based F1 score respectively. Gold tokenization is used in both evaluations. No auxiliary input signals (e.g. PoS embeddings, morphological feature embeddings, static embeddings) are used. We forgo auxiliary inputs even though they would likely improve our scores, and even though it means no longer being able to compare our performance directly to numbers reported in some other works, since we believe providing the model's representations as the sole input provides the clearest picture of its quality.[5] Full descriptions of the evaluation models is available in Appendix D.

## 6 Results

Results for the parser evaluation are given in Table 2, and results for the NER evaluation are given in Table 3. For both tables, we also include additional rows comparing important model pairs.

It is possible to directly compare our parsing evaluation results with those of Chau and Smith (2021, Table 2), whose evaluation methodology we closely follow for parsing. For our three overlapping languages—Maltese, Uyghur, and Wolof—we

[5]This is motivated by our experience in preliminary experiments of using a parser with these auxiliary inputs, with the result that differences between our models were no larger than 3% since the auxiliary inputs were contributing so much to the model's performance, obscuring the content of the model representations. We also notice a similarly small difference between comparable models in other works where auxiliary inputs were used in a parsing evaluation.

| | Wolof | Coptic | Maltese | Uyghur | An. Gk. | Tamil | Indon. | Avg. |
|---|---|---|---|---|---|---|---|---|
| WORD2VEC | 72.35 | 85.69 | 73.41 | 54.27 | 73.30 | 50.91 | 74.10 | 69.15 |
| MBERT | 76.40 | 14.43 | 78.18 | 46.30 | 72.30 | **66.73** | 78.63 | 61.85 |
| MBERT-VA | 72.94 | 82.11 | 72.69 | 42.97 | 65.89 | 54.92 | 75.67 | 66.74 |
| Chau and Smith (2021) | 60.12 | | 65.92 | 60.34 | | | | |
| μBERT-M | 75.69 | 86.45 | 74.33 | 61.26 | 78.95 | 59.75 | 74.66 | 73.01 |
| μBERT-MX | **77.83** | **88.25** | 78.90 | **65.17** | **80.55** | 61.00 | 74.69 | **75.20** |
| μBERT-MXP | 73.30 | 86.35 | 75.11 | 59.98 | 79.08 | 58.05 | 73.28 | 72.16 |
| μBERT4-M | 74.42 | 82.72 | **79.25** | 57.79 | 79.59 | 61.09 | 74.32 | 72.74 |
| μBERT4-MX | 73.99 | 82.52 | 78.61 | 57.14 | 79.09 | 60.82 | 74.21 | 72.34 |
| μBERT4-MXP | 74.30 | 82.73 | 78.99 | 57.01 | 79.56 | 60.92 | 74.34 | 72.55 |
| μBERT-MX – MBERT-VA | 4.89 | 6.14 | 6.21 | 22.20 | 14.66 | 6.08 | -0.97 | 8.46 |

Table 2: Labeled attachment score (LAS) by language and model combination for UD parsing evaluation. The final row shows the difference in score between μBERT-MX and MBERT-VA. Results from Chau and Smith (2021)'s half-sized monolingual BERT are included for comparison.

| | Wolof | Maltese | Uyghur | Tamil | Indon. | Avg. |
|---|---|---|---|---|---|---|
| WORD2VEC | 86.89 | 82.67 | 86.37 | 82.71 | 94.28 | 86.58 |
| MBERT | 83.79 | 73.71 | 78.40 | 70.47 | 91.04 | 79.48 |
| MBERT-VA | 79.37 | 78.11 | 77.03 | 69.38 | 91.05 | 78.99 |
| μBERT-M | **83.92** | 75.89 | 81.36 | **82.28** | 92.25 | 83.14 |
| μBERT-MX | 81.12 | 84.80 | **85.45** | 81.61 | 92.43 | 85.08 |
| μBERT-MXP | 82.21 | **88.79** | 82.52 | 82.00 | 92.27 | **85.56** |
| μBERT4-M | 78.69 | 78.22 | 80.28 | 80.57 | **93.05** | 82.16 |
| μBERT4-MX | 80.95 | 80.00 | 79.36 | 80.12 | 92.55 | 82.60 |
| μBERT4-MXP | 79.02 | 79.31 | 81.59 | 80.11 | 93.01 | 82.61 |
| μBERT-MX – MBERT | -2.67 | 11.09 | 7.05 | 11.14 | 1.39 | 5.60 |

Table 3: Span-based F1 score by language and model combination for NER evaluation. The final row shows the difference in score between μBERT-MX and MBERT. Boldface indicating top performance for a language does not consider WORD2VEC.

find that LAS for mBERT is similar, which establishes that evaluation conditions are comparable. We include their half-size BERT model's numbers in Table 2 for comparison, which were obtained by training a `bert-base`-sized BERT from scratch on the target language with 6 instead of 12 layers.

**Non-DNN Baseline** First, corroborating prior work, we can see that static word embeddings are competitive for many languages, often outperforming the multilingual models in both tasks, and often performing best overall for NER.

**Multilingual Baselines** Note the generally poor performance of MBERT-VA, which we had hoped would be a baseline stronger than MBERT, but often underperforms relative to MBERT. An exception to this is parsing for Coptic, where MBERT's lack of wordpieces for Coptic script causes a high out-of-vocabulary rate, giving MBERT-VA an obvious advantage. After carefully ruling out implementation errors, we reason that MBERT-VA underperformed because fine-tuning a large BERT can produce unpredictable results (Rogers et al., 2020) and our hyperparameters for adaptive pretraining may have been suboptimal (Chau et al. 2020 perform a hyperparameter search for vocabulary augmentation—see Appendix D). In correspondence with the authors of Chau et al. (2020), we discussed our results, and they shared our assessment. In sum, MBERT-VA appears to produce volatile results without careful hyperparameter selection, which we take to be a result of large model size and small dataset size.

**Monolingual Model Size** We can see that for parsing and NER, the μBERT4 model performs worse in almost all cases than the equivalent μBERT model. The degradation is -0.27% on average for -M variants, and -2.86% on average for -MX variants. The one language for which the μBERT4 model performs much better on parsing is Maltese, where the μBERT4-M model performs 5% better than the μBERT-M model, indicating that in this experimental condition greater model size may help, though note that the Chau and Smith's half-BERT does much worse than μBERT4-M showing a 13% lower score compared to μBERT-M and reversing the trend. On our two other languages in common with Chau and Smith, we see an 18% (Wolof) and 5% (Uyghur) degradation relative to μBERT-MX. For NER, we similarly observe that the μBERT4 variants have worse average performance than μBERT variants. We take this all to be strong evidence for H2, that monolingual BERTs trained at common sizes are severely overparameterized in low-resource settings, to the point that large performance degradations are observed.

**Parsing** Considering the five languages unseen by mBERT (all except Tamil and Indonesian), we see in the parsing results that in every case the best monolingual model, usually μBERT-MX, is able to outperform the best multilingual model. In some cases the difference is very large, such as in Uyghur parsing where there is an absolute gain in 18.87% LAS, and in others it is within the range of chance, such as in Maltese parsing. For the languages mBERT has seen, Tamil and Indonesian, MBERT outperforms the μBERT by several points, though we find it remarkable that μBERT is able to still provide a competitive score despite being trained on very small subsets of Tamil and Indonesian Wikipedia (150K and 600K articles, respectively), which mBERT had full access to. μBERT-MX performs best of all the models, achieving a score 8.5% higher than that of MBERT-VA on average.

**NER** Turning now to NER results, we see that in three cases, our μBERT models are able to clearly outperform other models, including Tamil, which MBERT has seen. In the other two cases, Indonesian and Wolof, μBERT models technically keep a lead but with margins thin enough to be noise. For all languages except Maltese however, WORD2VEC is able to meet or beat top performance from TLMs. Taken together with the parsing results, where WORD2VEC underperforms, and with the strengths and weaknesses of contextualized and static embeddings in mind, we hypothesize that NER on the WikiAnn dataset may require rote capacities, such as name memorization, instead of sophisticated linguistic knowledge, especially on an automatically-constructed dataset like WikiAnn.

**Validation MLM Perplexity** In order to better understand the effects of our auxiliary tagging and parsing tasks, we examine the validation MLM perplexity of our models during pretraining. An example of these curves is given in Figure 1. We first observe that for all languages, validation MLM perplexity is lower at all times for the multitask models compared to the perplexity curve for the MLM only model. Moreover, validation MLM perplexity converges more quickly on its asymptotic value for multitask models. For μBERT-MX in particular, validation MLM perplexity usually comes very close to its final value even within the first 10 epochs of pretraining. Validation MLM perplexity is only one incomplete measure of model quality, and indeed it is not entirely predictive of downstream performance since μBERT-M sometimes outperforms μBERT-MX and μBERT-MXP. But we take these results as evidence that our auxiliary tasks

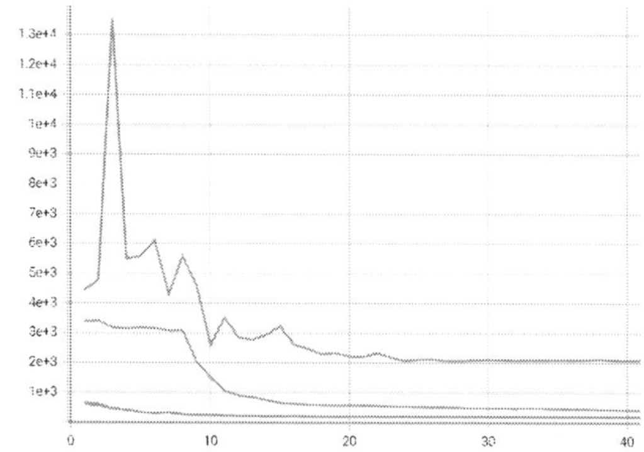


Figure 1: MLM perplexity vs. epoch for the validation split of the Uyghur dataset. The top line is μBERT-M, the middle line is μBERT-MXP, and the lowest line is μBERT-MX.

are helping our models learn more quickly. Moreover, while proving this would require additional work, it seems possible from the shapes of the validation curves that for the smallest datasets, multitask learning (MTL) might be helping models learn more than they could have through MLM alone.

Within validation MLM perplexity, we also see that each language follows one of two patterns: either the perplexity curves for μBERT-MX and μBERT-MXP are nearly identical, or the perplexity curve for μBERT-MXP remains a bit higher than for μBERT-MX.[6] With the intuition that more auxiliary tasks ought to make MLM easier, we had hypothesized that if anything the curve for μBERT-MX would have been higher than for μBERT-MXP, but instead the reverse sometimes turned out to be true. We hypothesize that the difference in task proportions between μBERT-MX and μBERT-MXP might have been partially responsible for this: in the former, 1 in 9 batches are for auxiliary tasks, and in the latter, 2 in 10 batches are for auxiliary tasks. If this is true, then finding the right proportion of primary and auxiliary tasks during pretraining would be critical for the multitask pretraining approach.

## 7 Discussion

**Main Findings** We take our most important result to be our demonstration that it is possible to train a monolingual BERT from scratch that can compete with and even outperform multilingual models by up to 18% LAS and 11% NER F1 using

[6]The former pattern holds for Wolof, Maltese, Greek, Indonesian, and Tamil, and the latter pattern holds for Uyghur and Coptic.

as little as 500,000 tokens and a UD treebank of 44,000 tokens and less than 1% of the parameters.

**Multilingual Baselines** We chose to use mBERT as a baseline because it is widely used and well studied. Moreover, given the the architectural homogeneity of mBERT and other leading multilingual LLMs, we additionally believe mBERT is strong enough to be representative of the state of multilingual LLMs for this work. While MBERT-VA appeared to severely underperform in some cases, we observe that it was still a strong baseline for both tasks (on average 5% better than MBERT for parsing, and 0.5% worse). In sum, while slightly stronger multilingual baselines may exist, we believe the ones in this work were still strong enough to show the MicroBERT approach holds promise, given that MicroBERTs were able to perform better than multilingual LLMs by several percentage points on average in both tasks.

**Hypotheses** We find strong support in these results for H1, that monolingual TLMs often, though not always, benefit from multitask learning on labeled data in low-resource settings. We additionally find strong support for H2, that when data is severely limited, typical BERT configurations are harmfully overparameterized.

**Future Work** There remain some unanswered questions in this work. The addition of the third parsing task proved harmful to performance in most cases, and it is unclear why. Parsing and XPOS tagging involve much of the same linguistic phenomena, and it seems possible that replacing one of them with a more semantic auxiliary task might have led to better results. Another possibility is that having loss computed for auxiliary tasks only on *some* batches may lead to jerky or suboptimal paths along the loss gradient, a problem which could be mitigated by having batches where only some sequences are suitable for use in auxiliary tasks.

It is natural to ask whether any of the elements of our approach here could find use in multilingual settings. Reducing the size of multilingual models may not be a promising direction due to the curse of multilinguality (Conneau et al., 2020). Ogueji et al. (2021) show further that even for low-resource multilingual models, size still seems to be important. As for multitask learning, Chau and Smith (2021) find a negative result for using MTL in multilingual model adaptation, though given the complex nature of MTL, many possible approaches remain untried.

Most languages in the world lack PoS tagged and parsed datasets, and if the MicroBERT approach is to be extended to very low-resource languages, it is likely that other auxiliary tasks would be needed. We leave this direction to future work, though we speculate that there are plenty of alternatives that may work. Parallel corpora, often in the form of a Bible translation, are readily available for over a thousand of the world's languages. High-quality rule-based morphological parsers are sometimes available for very low-resource languages, and their outputs could be used like PoS tags. Interlinearized texts and dictionaries are also common products of language documentation which are rich in linguistic information. All of these resources could be adapted for use in an auxiliary task.

## 8 Conclusion

We have shown that it is possible to train monolingual TLMs that are competitive with multilingual models using as little as 500K tokens and a 40K token treebank with greatly reduced model size and multitask learning on PoS tagging and dependency syntax parsing. While multilingual models did have some advantages over our approach, we observe that our MicroBERT approach has unique strengths for work on low-resource TLMs, including its lack of reliance on successful cross-lingual transfer and radically reduced computational demands for pretraining and downstream use.

We take this result to call into question whether multilingual representation learning can scale down effectively to truly "low-resource" languages that have less than a few million tokens in training data. Sometimes languages like these can be well served by transfer from related languages, even if all languages are low-resource (Ogueji et al., 2021), but not all languages may be so lucky: language isolates by definition lack related languages, and small language families are likely less able to benefit from transfer, since transfer tends to be enabled by phylogenetic (Nguyen and Chiang, 2017) or areal (Goyal et al., 2020) relatedness between languages. While multilingual methods hold much promise, it is important to examine other approaches to low-resource representation learning which, if not strictly better, may at least be complementary.

## References

Simran Arora, Avner May, Jian Zhang, and Christopher Ré. 2020. Contextual Embeddings: When Are

They Worth It? In *Proceedings of the 58th Annual Meeting of the Association for Computational Linguistics*, pages 2650–2663, Online. Association for Computational Linguistics.

Mikel Artetxe, Sebastian Ruder, and Dani Yogatama. 2020. On the cross-lingual transferability of monolingual representations. In *Proceedings of the 58th Annual Meeting of the Association for Computational Linguistics*, pages 4623–4637, Online. Association for Computational Linguistics.

Piotr Bojanowski, Edouard Grave, Armand Joulin, and Tomas Mikolov. 2017. Enriching Word Vectors with Subword Information. *Transactions of the Association for Computational Linguistics*, 5:135–146.

Ethan C. Chau, Lucy H. Lin, and Noah A. Smith. 2020. Parsing with Multilingual BERT, a Small Corpus, and a Small Treebank. In *Findings of the Association for Computational Linguistics: EMNLP 2020*, pages 1324–1334, Online. Association for Computational Linguistics.

Ethan C. Chau and Noah A. Smith. 2021. Specializing multilingual language models: An empirical study. In *Proceedings of the 1st Workshop on Multilingual Representation Learning*, pages 51–61, Punta Cana, Dominican Republic. Association for Computational Linguistics.

Kevin Clark, Minh-Thang Luong, Quoc V. Le, and Christopher D. Manning. 2020. ELECTRA: Pre-training Text Encoders as Discriminators Rather Than Generators.

Alexis Conneau, Kartikay Khandelwal, Naman Goyal, Vishrav Chaudhary, Guillaume Wenzek, Francisco Guzmán, Edouard Grave, Myle Ott, Luke Zettlemoyer, and Veselin Stoyanov. 2020. Unsupervised Cross-lingual Representation Learning at Scale. In *Proceedings of the 58th Annual Meeting of the Association for Computational Linguistics*, pages 8440–8451, Online. Association for Computational Linguistics.

Jacob Devlin, Ming-Wei Chang, Kenton Lee, and Kristina Toutanova. 2019. BERT: Pre-training of Deep Bidirectional Transformers for Language Understanding. In *Proceedings of the 2019 Conference of the North American Chapter of the Association for Computational Linguistics: Human Language Technologies, Volume 1 (Long and Short Papers)*, pages 4171–4186, Minneapolis, Minnesota. Association for Computational Linguistics.

Timothy Dozat and Christopher D. Manning. 2017. Deep biaffine attention for neural dependency parsing. In *5th International Conference on Learning Representations, ICLR 2017, Toulon, France, April 24-26, 2017, Conference Track Proceedings*. OpenReview.net.

Abteen Ebrahimi and Katharina Kann. 2021. How to Adapt Your Pretrained Multilingual Model to 1600 Languages. *arXiv:2106.02124 [cs]*.

Matt Gardner, Joel Grus, Mark Neumann, Oyvind Tafjord, Pradeep Dasigi, Nelson F. Liu, Matthew Peters, Michael Schmitz, and Luke Zettlemoyer. 2018. AllenNLP: A deep semantic natural language processing platform. In *Proceedings of Workshop for NLP Open Source Software (NLP-OSS)*, pages 1–6, Melbourne, Australia. Association for Computational Linguistics.

Vikrant Goyal, Anoop Kunchukuttan, Rahul Kejriwal, Siddharth Jain, and Amit Bhagwat. 2020. Contact relatedness can help improve multilingual NMT: Microsoft STCI-MT @ WMT20. In *Proceedings of the Fifth Conference on Machine Translation*, pages 202–206, Online. Association for Computational Linguistics.

Neil Houlsby, Andrei Giurgiu, Stanislaw Jastrzebski, Bruna Morrone, Quentin de Laroussilhe, Andrea Gesmundo, Mona Attariyan, and Sylvain Gelly. 2019. Parameter-Efficient Transfer Learning for NLP. *arXiv:1902.00751 [cs, stat]*.

Jeremy Howard and Sebastian Ruder. 2018. Universal Language Model Fine-tuning for Text Classification. In *Proceedings of the 56th Annual Meeting of the Association for Computational Linguistics (Volume 1: Long Papers)*, pages 328–339, Melbourne, Australia. Association for Computational Linguistics.

Pratik Joshi, Sebastin Santy, Amar Budhiraja, Kalika Bali, and Monojit Choudhury. 2020. The state and fate of linguistic diversity and inclusion in the NLP world. In *Proceedings of the 58th Annual Meeting of the Association for Computational Linguistics*, pages 6282–6293, Online. Association for Computational Linguistics.

Yinhan Liu, Myle Ott, Naman Goyal, Jingfei Du, Mandar Joshi, Danqi Chen, Omer Levy, Mike Lewis, Luke Zettlemoyer, and Veselin Stoyanov. 2019. RoBERTa: A Robustly Optimized BERT Pretraining Approach. *arXiv:1907.11692 [cs]*. ArXiv: 1907.11692.

Louis Martin, Benjamin Muller, Pedro Javier Ortiz Suárez, Yoann Dupont, Laurent Romary, Éric de la Clergerie, Djamé Seddah, and Benoît Sagot. 2020. CamemBERT: a Tasty French Language Model. In *Proceedings of the 58th Annual Meeting of the Association for Computational Linguistics*, pages 7203–7219, Online. Association for Computational Linguistics.

Bryan McCann, James Bradbury, Caiming Xiong, and Richard Socher. 2018. Learned in Translation: Contextualized Word Vectors. *arXiv:1708.00107 [cs]*. ArXiv: 1708.00107.

Kurt Micallef, Albert Gatt, and Marc Tanti. 2022. Pre-training Data Quality and Quantity for a Low-Resource Language: New Corpus and BERT Models for Maltese. *arXiv*, page 12.

Vincent Micheli, Martin d'Hoffschmidt, and François Fleuret. 2020. On the importance of pre-training data volume for compact language models. In *Proceedings of the 2020 Conference on Empirical Methods in Natural Language Processing (EMNLP)*, pages 7853–7858, Online. Association for Computational Linguistics.

Tomas Mikolov, Kai Chen, Greg Corrado, and Jeffrey Dean. 2013a. Efficient Estimation of Word Representations in Vector Space. *arXiv:1301.3781 [cs]*. ArXiv: 1301.3781.

Tomas Mikolov, Ilya Sutskever, Kai Chen, Greg Corrado, and Jeffrey Dean. 2013b. Distributed Representations of Words and Phrases and their Compositionality. *arXiv:1310.4546 [cs, stat]*. ArXiv: 1310.4546.

Benjamin Muller, Antonios Anastasopoulos, Benoît Sagot, and Djamé Seddah. 2021. When Being Unseen from mBERT is just the Beginning: Handling New Languages With Multilingual Language Models. In *Proceedings of the 2021 Conference of the North American Chapter of the Association for Computational Linguistics: Human Language Technologies*, pages 448–462, Online. Association for Computational Linguistics.

Toan Q. Nguyen and David Chiang. 2017. Transfer learning across low-resource, related languages for neural machine translation. In *Proceedings of the Eighth International Joint Conference on Natural Language Processing (Volume 2: Short Papers)*, pages 296–301, Taipei, Taiwan. Asian Federation of Natural Language Processing.

Joakim Nivre, Marie-Catherine de Marneffe, Filip Ginter, Yoav Goldberg, Jan Hajič, Christopher D. Manning, Ryan McDonald, Slav Petrov, Sampo Pyysalo, Natalia Silveira, Reut Tsarfaty, and Daniel Zeman. 2016. Universal Dependencies v1: A Multilingual Treebank Collection. In *Proceedings of the Tenth International Conference on Language Resources and Evaluation (LREC'16)*, pages 1659–1666, Portorož, Slovenia. European Language Resources Association (ELRA).

Kelechi Ogueji, Yuxin Zhu, and Jimmy Lin. 2021. Small Data? No Problem! Exploring the Viability of Pretrained Multilingual Language Models for Low-resourced Languages. In *Proceedings of the 1st Workshop on Multilingual Representation Learning*, pages 116–126, Punta Cana, Dominican Republic. Association for Computational Linguistics.

Pedro Javier Ortiz Suárez, Laurent Romary, and Benoît Sagot. 2020. A Monolingual Approach to Contextualized Word Embeddings for Mid-Resource Languages. In *Proceedings of the 58th Annual Meeting of the Association for Computational Linguistics*, pages 1703–1714, Online. Association for Computational Linguistics.

Xiaoman Pan, Boliang Zhang, Jonathan May, Joel Nothman, Kevin Knight, and Heng Ji. 2017. Cross-lingual name tagging and linking for 282 languages. In *Proceedings of the 55th Annual Meeting of the Association for Computational Linguistics (Volume 1: Long Papers)*, pages 1946–1958, Vancouver, Canada. Association for Computational Linguistics.

Adam Paszke, Sam Gross, Francisco Massa, Adam Lerer, James Bradbury, Gregory Chanan, Trevor Killeen, Zeming Lin, Natalia Gimelshein, Luca Antiga, Alban Desmaison, Andreas Kopf, Edward Yang, Zachary DeVito, Martin Raison, Alykhan Tejani, Sasank Chilamkurthy, Benoit Steiner, Lu Fang, Junjie Bai, and Soumith Chintala. 2019. Pytorch: An imperative style, high-performance deep learning library. In H. Wallach, H. Larochelle, A. Beygelzimer, F. d'Alché-Buc, E. Fox, and R. Garnett, editors, *Advances in Neural Information Processing Systems 32*, pages 8024–8035. Curran Associates, Inc.

Jeffrey Pennington, Richard Socher, and Christopher Manning. 2014. GloVe: Global Vectors for Word Representation. In *Proceedings of the 2014 Conference on Empirical Methods in Natural Language Processing (EMNLP)*, pages 1532–1543, Doha, Qatar. Association for Computational Linguistics.

Matthew E. Peters, Mark Neumann, Mohit Iyyer, Matt Gardner, Christopher Clark, Kenton Lee, and Luke Zettlemoyer. 2018. Deep Contextualized Word Representations. In *Proceedings of the 2018 Conference of the North American Chapter of the Association for Computational Linguistics: Human Language Technologies, Volume 1 (Long Papers)*, pages 2227–2237, New Orleans, Louisiana. Association for Computational Linguistics.

Jonas Pfeiffer, Andreas Rücklé, Clifton Poth, Aishwarya Kamath, Ivan Vulić, Sebastian Ruder, Kyunghyun Cho, and Iryna Gurevych. 2020a. AdapterHub: A Framework for Adapting Transformers. In *Proceedings of the 2020 Conference on Empirical Methods in Natural Language Processing: System Demonstrations*, pages 46–54, Online. Association for Computational Linguistics.

Jonas Pfeiffer, Ivan Vulić, Iryna Gurevych, and Sebastian Ruder. 2020b. MAD-X: An Adapter-Based Framework for Multi-Task Cross-Lingual Transfer. In *Proceedings of the 2020 Conference on Empirical Methods in Natural Language Processing (EMNLP)*, pages 7654–7673, Online. Association for Computational Linguistics.

Telmo Pires, Eva Schlinger, and Dan Garrette. 2019. How Multilingual is Multilingual BERT? In *Proceedings of the 57th Annual Meeting of the Association for Computational Linguistics*, pages 4996–5001, Florence, Italy. Association for Computational Linguistics.

Colin Raffel, Noam Shazeer, Adam Roberts, Katherine Lee, Sharan Narang, Michael Matena, Yanqi Zhou, Wei Li, and Peter J. Liu. 2020. Exploring the Limits of Transfer Learning with a Unified Text-to-Text Transformer.

Radim Rehurek and Petr Sojka. 2011. Gensim–python framework for vector space modelling. *NLP Centre, Faculty of Informatics, Masaryk University, Brno, Czech Republic*, 3(2).

Arij Riabi, Benoît Sagot, and Djamé Seddah. 2021. Can Character-based Language Models Improve Downstream Task Performance in Low-Resource and Noisy Language Scenarios?

Anna Rogers, Olga Kovaleva, and Anna Rumshisky. 2020. A Primer in BERTology: What we know about how BERT works. *arXiv:2002.12327 [cs]*. ArXiv: 2002.12327 version: 3.

Caroline T. Schroeder and Amir Zeldes. 2016. Raiders of the Lost Corpus. *Digital Humanities Quarterly*, 010(2).

Iulia Turc, Ming-Wei Chang, Kenton Lee, and Kristina Toutanova. 2019. Well-Read Students Learn Better: On the Importance of Pre-training Compact Models. ArXiv:1908.08962 [cs].

Ashish Vaswani, Noam Shazeer, Niki Parmar, Jakob Uszkoreit, Llion Jones, Aidan N. Gomez, Łukasz Kaiser, and Illia Polosukhin. 2017. Attention is All you Need. *Advances in Neural Information Processing Systems*, 30.

A. Vatri and B. McGillivray. 2018. The Diorisis Ancient Greek Corpus: Linguistics and Literature. *Research Data Journal for the Humanities and Social Sciences*, 3(1):55 – 65. Place: Leiden, The Netherlands Publisher: Brill.

Zihan Wang, Karthikeyan K, Stephen Mayhew, and Dan Roth. 2020. Extending Multilingual BERT to Low-Resource Languages. *arXiv:2004.13640 [cs]*. ArXiv: 2004.13640.

Alex Warstadt, Yian Zhang, Xiaocheng Li, Haokun Liu, and Samuel R. Bowman. 2020. Learning Which Features Matter: RoBERTa Acquires a Preference for Linguistic Generalizations (Eventually). In *Proceedings of the 2020 Conference on Empirical Methods in Natural Language Processing (EMNLP)*, pages 217–235, Online. Association for Computational Linguistics.

Thomas Wolf, Lysandre Debut, Victor Sanh, Julien Chaumond, Clement Delangue, Anthony Moi, Pierric Cistac, Tim Rault, Rémi Louf, Morgan Funtowicz, and Jamie Brew. 2020. HuggingFace's Transformers: State-of-the-art Natural Language Processing. *arXiv:1910.03771 [cs]*. ArXiv: 1910.03771.

Shijie Wu and Mark Dredze. 2020. Are All Languages Created Equal in Multilingual BERT? In *Proceedings of the 5th Workshop on Representation Learning for NLP*, pages 120–130, Online. Association for Computational Linguistics.

## A Acknowledgments

We thank Nathan Schneider, Shabnam Tafreshi, and MASC-SLL 2022 attendees for very helpful comments on this work.

## B Datasets

| Treebank | Tokens |
|---|---|
| UD_Coptic-Scriptorium v2.9 | 48,632 |
| UD_Ancient_Greek-PROEIL v2.9 | 213,999 |
| UD_Indonesian-GSD v2.10 | 122,021 |
| UD_Maltese-MUDT v2.9 | 44,162 |
| UD_Uyghur-UDT v2.9 | 40,236 |
| UD_Wolof-WDT v2.9 | 44,258 |
| UD_Tamil-TTB v2.10 | 9,581 |

Table 4: Token count statistics for UD treebanks used in this work. Note that for this count, we count the constituent tokens of multiword tokens instead of counting a multiword token as a single token.

**Unlabeled** For Coptic, we use v4.2.0 of the Coptic SCRIPTORIUM corpora (Schroeder and Zeldes, 2016), obtained from `https://github.com/copticscriptorium/corpora`. For Ancient Greek, we use the initial release of the Diorisis corpus (Vatri and McGillivray, 2018), obtained from `https://figshare.com/articles/dataset/The_Diorisis_Ancient_Greek_Corpus/6187256`. Both corpora are preprocessed (tokenized, etc.) using language-specific tools to a quality higher than would have been obtained with a generic preprocessing pipeline. In Coptic's case, the data is further checked and with parts gold annotated by humans.

All other corpora are derived from Wikipedia. For Maltese, Uyghur, and Wolof, we use all available namespace 0 articles[7] as of February 2022, and for Indonesian and Tamil, we take a random sampling of namespace 0 articles as of June 2022, up to around 1.5M tokens.

All data is derived from Wikipedia's public dump files. While it is popular in NLP to use the text in the dump files directly, this is suboptimal, as the dump files' text contains markup, which makes the text noisy and means that document structural information cannot be used in the tokenization and sentence splitting process. We therefore take the additional step of rendering the dump into HTML using `https://github.com/lgessler/wiki-thresher`, which can then be used to obtain useful information about guaranteed sentence splits, e.g. between HTML elements like <p>. We perform rule-based sentence splitting and tokenization on this HTML to obtain our final tokenized texts.

For all 7 languages, we reserve around 10% of documents for validation and use the rest for training. A test split is unnecessary because our models are not being evaluated on unlabeled data.

**UD Treebanks** A summary of the treebanks we use and their versions is given in Table 4. We use the standard train/dev/test splits for all treebanks.

**WikiAnn Datasets** New train/dev/test splits were created in an 8:1:1 ratio for the WikiAnn dataset, which only divides sentences by language. It was not possible to split at the document level because no document metadata is available in the WikiAnn dataset. Tags are converted from the native IOB1 scheme into the BIOUL scheme. Some manual edits, logged in our version control history, were made to sentence boundaries in order to keep wordpiece sequence lengths below 512.

## C Conditions

All experiments for both pretraining and evaluation were performed on NVIDIA Tesla T4 GPUs with 16GB GDDR6 SDRAM.

**Word2vec** We use the Gensim (Rehurek and Sojka, 2011) implementation of the Word2vec skip-gram with negative sampling algorithm for pre-trained static word embeddings. The embeddings are trained just on the train split of the unlabeled corpus for each language. The vectors are 100-dimensional, window size is 5, and negative sampling factor is 5.

**mBERT-VA** We implement the Vocabulary Augmentation method exactly as prescribed by Chau et al. (2020) by training a new wordpiece tokenizer on the train split of the unlabeled data with a vocabulary size of 5,000, yielding a new monolingual vocabulary. The monolingual vocabulary is ranked by frequency of wordpieces, and the 99 unused tokens in mBERT's vocabulary indexed between 1 and 99 are replaced by tokens from the monolingual vocabulary which are not already present in mBERT's vocabulary. Since only preexisting token

[7]Wikipedia articles belonging to namespace 0 are main content articles instead of e.g. user pages or template pages.

indices are used, it is not necessary to modify the model's pretrained weights.

To train the weights of the previously unused token indices, adaptive pretraining with MLM is performed, again following Chau et al. (2020). Whereas Chau et al. perform a hyperparameter search, due to resource constraints we are forced to pick a single set of hyperparameters for adaptive pretraining, which we choose within the bounds of Chau et al.'s hyperparameter search. First, due to memory constraints on our GPUs, we are forced to set the batch size to 2. We pretrain for 20 epochs with 16,000 batches per epoch. The PyTorch AdamW optimizer is used with $\beta_1 = 0.9, \beta_2 = 0.999$, learning rate at 1e-4, and weight decay at 0.05. The model which achieved lowest validation set perplexity is chosen.

**MicroBERT** Our tokenizer for MicroBERT is a WordPiece tokenizer. We scale vocabulary size from a minimum of 8,000 wordpieces up to 14,000 wordpieces, where the number of unique whitespace tokens for a given language determines how large the vocabulary will be. All models are uncased and perform Unicode NFD normalization as a preprocessing step during tokenization.

Since some tasks require wordpieces while others require tokens (e.g. PoS tagging), our encoder produces both wordpiece sequences and token sequences. The token sequence is constructed by keeping track of which wordpieces correspond to which original input tokens, and average pooling wordpieces for each token so that the sequence length reflects the number of original input tokens.

During data loading, sequences longer than 500 wordpieces are split into chunks of no more than 500 wordpieces each. Sequences this long only occur in the unlabeled datasets, so this does not pose a problem for producing valid losses on PoS tagging or parsing.

We train with a batch size of 32 for 200 epochs with 8,000 batches per epoch. We again use the AdamW optimizer with a learning rate of 3e-3, $\beta_1 = 0.9$, $\beta_2 = 0.999$, and weight decay at 0.05. We allow early stopping if the validation metric, MLM perplexity, shows no improvement for 40 epochs. The model with the best validation MLM perplexity is selected.

While it is traditionally popular to train BERTs with triangular learning rates (Howard and Ruder, 2018), we chose not to use them for training our MicroBERTs. The reason is that, as noted by Raffel et al. (2020), it is necessary to know in advance approximately how many training steps are necessary to train a model, but since our MicroBERT architecture is much smaller, it is not obvious how many steps would be required to train it, making its use difficult. We do not expect this to lead to much worse performance compared to a properly configured triangular learning rate, as Raffel et al. (2020) also note that the triangular schedule often leads to only marginal gains compared to other schedules. Instead, we use PyTorch's ReduceLROnPlateau scheduler, which reduces learning rate when a certain number of validation steps have shown no improvement in MLM perplexity. We configure the scheduler so that if no improvement occurs for 2 epochs, the learning rate is halved, down to a minimum learning rate of 5e-5. Our results have shown that this training regimen can achieve good results, but we expect there is room for improvement and leave the task of refining it to future work.

## D Evaluation

**Parsing** We use the AllenNLP implementation of a biaffine attention parser (Dozat and Manning, 2017). In line with previous work, we set the dimensionality of the arc and tag representations to 100, and dropout and input dropout are set to 0.3. An encoder stack of 3 bidirectional LSTMs is used, with a recurrent dropout of 0.3, hidden size of 400, and highway connections. A scalar mix of representations from each layer of the BERT model is learned (Peters et al., 2018) to allow the model to fully exploit information present in earlier layers. Gold tokenization is used, and no supplementary representations (such as static word embeddings or feature or PoS embeddings) are provided.

We train for 300 epochs with a batch size of 16 and patience of 50 with LAS as our validation metric. To account for the very large size of some treebanks (e.g. Greek), we train for 200 batches per epoch. The AdamW optimizer is used with $\beta_1 = 0.9$, $\beta_2 = 0.999$, learning rate at 1e-3, and gradient clipping at 5.0. A reduced learning rate of 5e-5 is used for all parameters in the TLM.

**NER** We use AllenNLP's linear chain CRF tagger with BIOUL encoding. As with parsing, a scalar mix of representations from each layer of the BERT model is learned (Peters et al., 2018) to allow the model to fully exploit information present in earlier layers. An encoder stack of 2 bidirectional

LSTMs is used, with a dropout of 0.5 and hidden size of 200. The model's dropout is set to 0.5. Gold tokenization is used, and no supplementary representations (such as static word embeddings or feature or PoS embeddings) are provided.

We train for 300 epochs with a batch size of 16 and patience of 50 with span-based F1 as our validation metric. The AdamW optimizer is used with $\beta_1 = 0.9$, $\beta_2 = 0.999$, learning rate at 1e-3, and gradient clipping at 5.0. A reduced learning rate of 1e-5 is used for all parameters in the TLM.

# Transformers on Multilingual Clause-Level Morphology

**Emre Can Acikgoz**
KUIS AI, Koç University
eacikgoz17@ku.edu.tr

**Tilek Chubakov**
KUIS AI, Koç University
tchubakov@ku.edu.tr

**Müge Kural**
KUIS AI, Koç University
mugekural@ku.edu.tr

**Gözde Gül Şahin**
KUIS AI, Koç University
gosahin@ku.edu.tr

**Deniz Yuret**
KUIS AI, Koç University
dyuret@ku.edu.tr

## Abstract

This paper describes our winning systems in MRL: The 1st Shared Task on Multilingual Clause-level Morphology (EMNLP 2022 Workshop) designed by KUIS AI NLP team. We present our work for all three parts of the shared task: inflection, reinflection, and analysis. We mainly explore transformers with two approaches: (i) training models from scratch in combination with data augmentation, and (ii) transfer learning with prefix-tuning at multilingual morphological tasks. Data augmentation significantly improves performance for most languages in the inflection and reinflection tasks. On the other hand, Prefix-tuning on a pre-trained mGPT model helps us to adapt analysis tasks in low-data and multilingual settings. While transformer architectures with data augmentation achieved the most promising results for inflection and reinflection tasks, prefix-tuning on mGPT received the highest results for the analysis task. Our systems received 1st place in all three tasks in MRL 2022.[1]

| **Task1: Inflection** | | |
|---|---|---|
| Source | Lemma | give |
| | Features | IND;FUT;NOM(1,SG);<br>ACC(3,SG,MASC);DAT(3,SG,FEM) |
| Target | Clause | I will give him to her |
| **Task2: Reinflection** | | |
| Source | Clause | I will give him to her |
| | Features | IND;FUT;NOM(1,SG);<br>ACC(3,SG,MASC);DAT(3,SG,FEM) |
| | Desired Features | IND;PRS;NOM(1,PL);<br>ACC(2);DAT(3,PL);NEG |
| Target | Desired Clause | We don't give you to them |
| **Task3: Analysis** | | |
| Source | Clause | I will give him to her |
| Target | Lemma | give |
| | Features | IND;FUT;NOM(1,SG);<br>ACC(3,SG,MASC);DAT(3,SG,FEM) |

Table 1: Description of the each three task: inflection, reinflection, analysis. **Task1 (Inflection).** For the given lemma and the features, target is the desired clause.**Task2 (Reinflection).** Input is the clause, its features, and the desired output features. Target is the desired clause that represented by the desired features in the source. **Task3 (Analysis).** For a given clause, output is the corresponding lemma and the morphological features.

## 1 Introduction

The shared task on multilingual clause-level morphology was designed to provide a benchmark for morphological analysis and generation at the level of clauses for various typologically diverse languages. The shared task is composed of three subtasks: *inflection*, *reinflection* and *analysis*. For the inflection task, participants are required to generate an output clause, given a verbal lemma and a specific set of morphological tags (features) as an input. In the reinflection task the input is an inflected clause, accompanied by its features (tags). Participants need to predict the target word given a new set of tags (features). Finally, the analysis task requires predicting the underlying lemma and tags (features) given the clauses.

Literature has examined morphology mainly at the word level, but morphological processes are not confined to words. Phonetic, syntactic, or semantic relations can be studied at phrase-level to explain these processes. Thus, this shared task examines phrase-level morphology and questions the generalization of the relations between the layers of language among languages with different morphological features. The shared task includes eight languages with different complexity and varying morphological characteristics: English, French, German, Hebrew, Russian, Spanish, Swahili, and Turkish.

In our work, we explored two main approaches: (1) training character-based transformer architectures from scratch with data augmentation, (2) adapting a recent prefix-tuning method for language models at multilingual morphological tasks.

[1] https://github.com/emrecanacikgoz/mrl2022



*Proceedings of the The 2nd Workshop on Multi-lingual Representation Learning (MRL)*, pages 100 - 105
December 8, 2022 ©2022 Association for Computational Linguistics

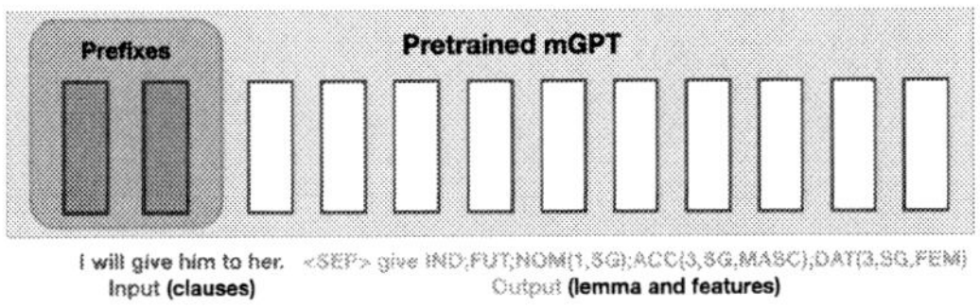


Figure 1: **Task3 (Analysis)** example by using prefix-tuning method. We freeze all the parameters of the pre-trained mGPT model and only optimize the prefix, which are shown inside the red block. Each vertical block denote transformer activations at one time step.

## 2 Methods

In this section, first we cover the model architectures and training strategies that we have used (Vaswani et al., 2017; Shliazhko et al., 2022; Li and Liang, 2021), and then discuss our data augmentation strategies in details (Anastasopoulos and Neubig, 2019).

### 2.1 Vanilla Transformer

We used a modified version of vanilla Transformer architecture in Vaswani et al. (2017) which contains 4 layers of encoder and decoder with 4 multi-head attentions. The embedding size and the feed-forward dimension is set to 256 and 1024, respectively. As suggested in Wu et al. (2021), we used layer normalization before the self-attention and feed-forward layers of the network that leads to slightly better results. We used these in inflection and reinflections tasks.

### 2.2 Prefix-Tuning

Using prefix-tuning reduces computational costs by optimizing a small continuous task-specific vectors, called prefixes, while keeping frozen all the other parameters of the LLM. We added two prefixes, called virtual tokens in Li and Liang (2021), the gradient optimization made across these prefixes that is described in the Figure 1. We used Shliazhko et al. (2022) weights during prompting. Prefix-tuning method outperforms other fine-tuning approaches in low-data resources and better adapts to unseen topics during prompting (Li and Liang, 2021).

### 2.3 Data Augmentation

Hallucinating the data for low-resource languages results with a remarkable performance increase for inflection Anastasopoulos and Neubig (2019). The hallucinated data is generated by replacing the stem characters of the aligned word with random characters by using the validation or test sets (see Fig. 2). This way, the amount increase in the training data helps the model to learn and generalize rare seen samples. On the other hand, the amount of hallucinated data that will be added to the training set, hyperparameter $N$, is also another parameter that directly effects our accuracy. Therefore, hyperparameter $N$ needs to be decided specifically for each language according to corresponding language's complexity and topology.

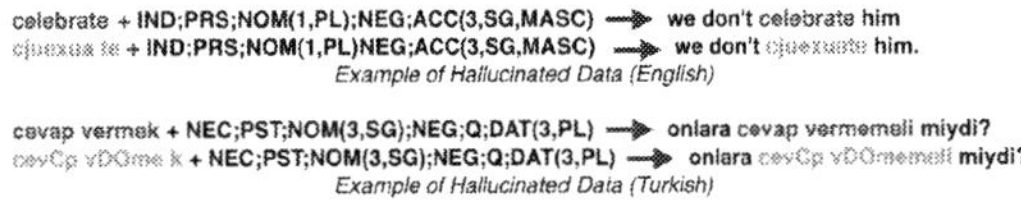


Figure 2: In order to create the hallucinated samples, we first align the characters of the lemma and the inflected forms. After that, we substitute the stem parts of the input with random characters that comes from the validation set and test set, as shown in the figure.

## 3 Experimental Settings

### 3.1 Dataset

In the shared task, there are eight different languages with varying linguistic complexity which comes from different language families: English, French, German, Hebrew, Russian, Swahili, Spanish, Turkish. For Hebrew there are two versions as Hebrew-vocalized and Hebrew-unvocalized. Training data contains 10,000 instances for each language and there are 1,000 samples both in development set and test set. Swahili and Spanish are the surprise languages that announced two weeks before the final submission day, together with the unlabeled test data for each language.

### 3.2 Evaluation

Models are evaluated according to Exact Match (EM), Edit Distance (ED), and F1 accuracy. For task1 (inflection) and task2 (reinflection) ED is the leaderboard metric. For task3 (analysis), F1 score is the objective. EM accuracy represents the ratio of correctly predicted lemma and features, and ED is calculated based on Levenshtein Distance which indicates how different two strings are, (the ground truth and prediction for our case) from each other. F1 accuracy is the harmonic mean of the precision and recall. F1 accuracy is upweighted for the lemma score in our task. In the leaderboard, the results are averaged across each language.

| | Task1: Inflection | | | Task2: Reinflection | | | Task3: Analysis | | |
|---|---|---|---|---|---|---|---|---|---|
| **Model** | **Transformer + D.A.** | | | **Transformer** | | | **Prefix Tuning** | | |
| **Metrics** | F1↑ | EM↑ | ED↓ | F1↑ | EM↑ | ED↓ | F1↑ | EM↑ | ED↓ |
| Deu | 97.71 | 91.80 | 0.241 | 92.40 | 66.50 | 0.788 | 95.89 | 83.40 | 0.991 |
| Eng | 98.02 | 88.90 | 0.221 | 95.42 | 72.30 | 0.477 | 99.61 | 98.50 | 0.064 |
| Fra | 98.59 | 93.20 | 0.124 | 92.64 | 68.30 | 0.758 | 95.63 | 81.90 | 0.933 |
| Heb | 97.73 | 89.80 | 0.550 | 94.00 | 83.30 | 0.796 | 92.84 | 73.50 | 1.322 |
| Heb-Unvoc | 97.96 | 94.20 | 0.113 | 86.70 | 57.70 | 1.002 | 82.09 | 36.20 | 2.044 |
| Rus | 97.57 | 87.70 | 0.828 | 97.29 | 84.90 | 0.854 | 97.51 | 88.60 | 3.252 |
| Swa | 99.72 | 99.61 | 0.019 | 92.05 | 84.47 | 0.182 | 90.51 | 62.63 | 3.114 |
| Spa | 98.79 | 92.00 | 0.199 | 96.42 | 77.60 | 0.480 | 98.11 | 89.40 | 0.560 |
| Tur | 97.50 | 89.80 | 0.333 | 95.36 | 84.70 | 0.593 | 95.36 | 84.70 | 0.593 |
| Average | 91.89 | 98.18 | **0.292** | 93.14 | 74.72 | **0.705** | **94.17** | 77.65 | 1.430 |

Table 2: Results on the test sets for all tasks and languages with the corresponding models. Edit Distance is the leaderboard ranking metric for Task1: Inflection and Task2: Reinflection, and F1 score is used for leaderboard ranking in Task3: Analysis. D.A. indicates data augmentation.

### 3.3 Shared Task

Multilingual Clause-level Morphology (MRL 2022) contains three different tasks as Task1: Inflection, Task2: Reinflection, and Task3: Analysis. As KUIS AI team, we have attended each of them separately.

#### 3.3.1 Task1: Inflection

The goal of the task is to produce the output clause and its features forgiven verbal lemma and a set of morphological features, see Table 1. For inflection task, we have trained a vanilla transformer model from scratch by adding some hallucinated data for the training set. The data hallucination method, discussed in 2.3, improved our results significantly. As suggested in Wu et al. (2021), we observed the effect of the large batch sizes that results with an increase in accuracy. Thus, we set the batch size to 400 and we trained our model for 20 epochs. We used Adam optimizer by setting $\beta_1$ to 0.9 and $\beta_2$ to 0.98. We started with a learning rate of 0.001 with 4,000 warm-up steps. Then, we decrease it with the inverse of the square-root for the remaining steps. We have used label smoothing with a factor of 0.1 and applied the same dropout rate of 0.3.

#### 3.3.2 Task2: Reinflection

In reinflection the task is to generate the desired output format as in inflection; however, the input is consist of an inflected clause, its corresponding features, and a new set of features that represents the desired output form. We again use the same vanilla Transformer architecture, and exactly the same training parameters that we have used in inflection task. We tried both (i) giving the all source data as input, and (ii) using only the inflected clause and its desired features. We have examined that, both our EM and ED accuracy increased in a large manner when we ignore source clause's features in input before feeding it to the model.

#### 3.3.3 Task3: Analysis

Analysis task can be seen as the opposite of the inflection task. For given clauses and its features, we try to generate the lemma and the corresponding morphological features. We used the prefix-tuning method for the analysis task. The prefix template was given as the source and the features were masked. During prompting, we gave the clause-level in input and the target lemma together with its features were expected from the output, like a machine translation task. The source and target are given together with the trainable prefixes, i.e. continuous prompt vectors, and the gradient optimization made across these prefixes. For the mGPT-based Prefix-Tuning model, we have used the *Huggingface*, Wolf et al. (2019) and the corresponding model weights *sberbank-ai/mGPT*. The prefixes were trained for 10 epochs with a batch size of 5 due computational resource constraints. We used Adam optimizer with weight decay fix which is introduced in Loshchilov and Hutter (2017) with $\beta_1$=0.9 and $\beta_2$=0.999. The learning rate is initialized to $5 \times 10^{-5}$ and a linear scheduler is used without any warm-up steps.

| System | Inflection | Reinflection | Analysis |
|---|---|---|---|
| Transformer Baseline | 3.278 | 4.642 | 80.00 |
| mT5 Baseline | 2.577 | 2.826 | 84.50 |
| KUIS AI | **0.292** | **0.705** | **94.17** |

Table 3: Submitted results for MRL shared task that is averaged across 9 languages. Metrics for the inflection and reinflection tasks is the edit distance, and for analysis the metric is averaged F1 score with the lemma being treated as an up-weighted feature.

### 3.4 Results

Our submitted results are provided in Table 2. The announced results by the shared task are in the Table 3 which are evaluated among the provided unlabeled test set.

For the inflection task, with the help of data augmentation, we have achieved best average edit distance for languages. Specially, for Swahili the edit distance is nearly perfect as well as the exact match. It is followed by Hebrew-Unvoc and French. We observed the highest edit distance and the lowest exact match scores for Russian. At the end, we observed that, reducing edit distance does not always bring better exact match.

For the reinflection task, using trained transformer models from scratch, we again see the best results for Swahili with the lowest edit distance. This time, the highest edit distance belongs to Hebrew-Unvoc as well as the lowest exact match. The number of words and characters in the examples of task datasets may be the factors and should also be considered.

Finally for the analysis, with the help of prefix-tuning, we achieved the best results for English with highest F1 score. The ease of finding English pre-trained models led us to experiment with English-only GPT models, and we subsequently discovered that multilingual GPT gives better results when using prefix-tuning. Tuning on mGPT has the lowest performance with Hebrew-Unvoc, due the low ratio of training samples in Hebrew during pre-training compared to other languages.

## 4 Related Work

Word-level morphological tasks have been studied to a great extent, with LSTM (Wu and Cotterell, 2019; Cotterell et al., 2016; Malaviya et al., 2019; Sahin and Steedman, 2018), GRU (Conforti et al., 2018), variants of Transformer Vaswani et al. (2017); Wu et al. (2021) and other neural models (e.g., invertible neural networks (Sahin and Gurevych, 2020)). Unlike word-level, there is limited work on clause-level morpho-syntactic modeling. Goldman and Tsarfaty (2022) presents a new dataset for clause-level morphology covering 4 typologically-different languages (English, German, Turkish, and Hebrew); motivates redefining the problem at the clause-level to enable the cross-linguistical study of neural morphological modeling; and derives clause-level inflection, reinflection, and analysis tasks together with baseline model results.

Pre-trained LLMs have been successfully applied to downstream tasks like sentiment analysis, question answering, named entity recognition, and part-of-speech (POS) tagging (Devlin et al., 2019; Yang et al., 2019; Raffel et al., 2020). Even though, there is limited work on applications of LLMs to morphological tasks, it has been demonstrated that using pre-trained contextualized word embeddings can significantly improve the performance of models for downstream morphological tasks. Inoue et al. (2022) explored BERT-based classifiers for training morphosyntactic tagging models for Arabic and its dialect. Anastasyev (2020) explored the usage of ELMo and BERT embeddings to improve the performance of joint morpho-syntactic parser for Russian. Hofmann et al. (2020) used a fine-tuning approach to BERT for the derivational morphology generation task. Finally, Seker et al. (2022) presented a large pre-trained language model for Modern Hebrew that shows promising results at several tasks.

On the other hand, since fine-tuning LLMs requires to modify and store all the parameters in a LM that results with a huge computational cost. Rebuffi et al. (2017); Houlsby et al. (2019) used adapter-tuning which adds task-specific layers (adapters) between the each layer of a pre-trained language model and tunes only the 2%-4% parameters of a LM. Similarly, Li and Liang (2021) proposed prefix-tuning which is a light-weight alternative method for adapter-tuning that is inspired by prompting.

## 5 Conclusion

In this paper, we described our winning methods multilingual clause-level morphology shared task for inflection, reinflection, and analysis. Due to the different complexity between tasks and the varying morphological characteristics of languages, there is no single best model that achieves the best results for each task in each language. Thus, we try to implement different types of systems with different objectives. For inflection we used a vanilla Transformer adapted from Vaswani et al. (2017) and applying data hallucination substantially improves accuracy (Anastasopoulos and Neubig, 2019). The reinflection task is more challenging compared to the other tasks due to its complex input form. To overcome this issue, we have removed the original feature tags from the input. We only used the inflected clause and target features in the input. We again used a vanilla Transformer as a model choice. Finally, for the analysis task, we used the prefix-tuning method based on mGPT. On average, we have achieved the best results for every three tasks among all participants.

## Acknowledgements

This work is supported by KUIS AI Center from Koç University, Istanbul. We gratefully acknowledge this support. Last but not least, we would like to kindly thank our organizers for answering our questions and for the effort they have made to fix the issues that we struggled during the competition process.

## References

Antonios Anastasopoulos and Graham Neubig. 2019. Pushing the limits of low-resource morphological inflection. In *Proceedings of the 2019 Conference on Empirical Methods in Natural Language Processing and the 9th International Joint Conference on Natural Language Processing, EMNLP-IJCNLP 2019, Hong Kong, China, November 3-7, 2019*, pages 984–996. Association for Computational Linguistics.

D.G. Anastasyev. 2020. Exploring pretrained models for joint morpho-syntactic parsing of russian. volume 2020-June, page 1 – 12. Cited by: 4; All Open Access, Bronze Open Access.

Costanza Conforti, Matthias Huck, and Alexander M. Fraser. 2018. Neural morphological tagging of lemma sequences for machine translation. In *Proceedings of the 13th Conference of the Association for Machine Translation in the Americas, AMTA 2018, Boston, MA, USA, March 17-21, 2018 - Volume 1: Research Papers*, pages 39–53. Association for Machine Translation in the Americas.

Ryan Cotterell, Christo Kirov, John Sylak-Glassman, David Yarowsky, Jason Eisner, and Mans Hulden. 2016. The SIGMORPHON 2016 shared task - morphological reinflection. In *Proceedings of the 14th SIGMORPHON Workshop on Computational Research in Phonetics, Phonology, and Morphology, Berlin, Germany, August 11, 2016*, pages 10–22. Association for Computational Linguistics.

Jacob Devlin, Ming-Wei Chang, Kenton Lee, and Kristina Toutanova. 2019. BERT: pre-training of deep bidirectional transformers for language understanding. In *Proceedings of the 2019 Conference of the North American Chapter of the Association for Computational Linguistics: Human Language Technologies, NAACL-HLT 2019, Minneapolis, MN, USA, June 2-7, 2019, Volume 1 (Long and Short Papers)*, pages 4171–4186. Association for Computational Linguistics.

Omer Goldman and Reut Tsarfaty. 2022. Morphology without borders: Clause-level morphological annotation. *CoRR*, abs/2202.12832.

Valentin Hofmann, Janet B. Pierrehumbert, and Hinrich Schütze. 2020. Dagobert: Generating derivational morphology with a pretrained language model. In *Proceedings of the 2020 Conference on Empirical Methods in Natural Language Processing, EMNLP 2020, Online, November 16-20, 2020*, pages 3848–3861. Association for Computational Linguistics.

Neil Houlsby, Andrei Giurgiu, Stanislaw Jastrzebski, Bruna Morrone, Quentin de Laroussilhe, Andrea Gesmundo, Mona Attariyan, and Sylvain Gelly. 2019. Parameter-efficient transfer learning for NLP. *CoRR*, abs/1902.00751.

Go Inoue, Salam Khalifa, and Nizar Habash. 2022. Morphosyntactic tagging with pre-trained language models for arabic and its dialects. In *Findings of the Association for Computational Linguistics: ACL 2022, Dublin, Ireland, May 22-27, 2022*, pages 1708–1719. Association for Computational Linguistics.

Xiang Lisa Li and Percy Liang. 2021. Prefix-tuning: Optimizing continuous prompts for generation. In *Proceedings of the 59th Annual Meeting of the Association for Computational Linguistics and the 11th International Joint Conference on Natural Language Processing, ACL/IJCNLP 2021, (Volume 1: Long Papers), Virtual Event, August 1-6, 2021*, pages 4582–4597. Association for Computational Linguistics.

Ilya Loshchilov and Frank Hutter. 2017. Fixing weight decay regularization in adam. *CoRR*, abs/1711.05101.

Chaitanya Malaviya, Shijie Wu, and Ryan Cotterell. 2019. A simple joint model for improved contextual neural lemmatization. In *Proceedings of the 2019 Conference of the North American Chapter of the Association for Computational Linguistics: Human Language Technologies, NAACL-HLT 2019, Minneapolis, MN, USA, June 2-7, 2019, Volume 1 (Long and Short Papers)*, pages 1517–1528. Association for Computational Linguistics.

Colin Raffel, Noam Shazeer, Adam Roberts, Katherine Lee, Sharan Narang, Michael Matena, Yanqi Zhou, Wei Li, and Peter J. Liu. 2020. Exploring the limits of transfer learning with a unified text-to-text transformer. *J. Mach. Learn. Res.*, 21:140:1–140:67.

Sylvestre-Alvise Rebuffi, Hakan Bilen, and Andrea Vedaldi. 2017. Learning multiple visual domains with residual adapters. In *Advances in Neural Information Processing Systems 30: Annual Conference on Neural Information Processing Systems 2017, December 4-9, 2017, Long Beach, CA, USA*, pages 506–516.

Gözde Gül Sahin and Iryna Gurevych. 2020. Two birds with one stone: Investigating invertible neural networks for inverse problems in morphology. In *The Thirty-Fourth AAAI Conference on Artificial Intelligence, AAAI 2020, The Thirty-Second Innovative Applications of Artificial Intelligence Conference, IAAI 2020, The Tenth AAAI Symposium on Educational Advances in Artificial Intelligence, EAAI 2020, New York, NY, USA, February 7-12, 2020*, pages 7814–7821. AAAI Press.

Gözde Gül Sahin and Mark Steedman. 2018. Character-level models versus morphology in semantic role labeling. In *Proceedings of the 56th Annual Meeting of the Association for Computational Linguistics, ACL 2018, Melbourne, Australia, July 15-20, 2018, Volume 1: Long Papers*, pages 386–396. Association for Computational Linguistics.

Amit Seker, Elron Bandel, Dan Bareket, Idan Brusilovsky, Refael Shaked Greenfeld, and Reut Tsarfaty. 2022. Alephbert: Language model pre-training and evaluation from sub-word to sentence level. In *Proceedings of the 60th Annual Meeting of the Association for Computational Linguistics (Volume 1: Long Papers), ACL 2022, Dublin, Ireland, May 22-27, 2022*, pages 46–56. Association for Computational Linguistics.

Oleh Shliazhko, Alena Fenogenova, Maria Tikhonova, Vladislav Mikhailov, Anastasia Kozlova, and Tatiana Shavrina. 2022. mgpt: Few-shot learners go multilingual. *CoRR*, abs/2204.07580.

Ashish Vaswani, Noam Shazeer, Niki Parmar, Jakob Uszkoreit, Llion Jones, Aidan N. Gomez, Lukasz Kaiser, and Illia Polosukhin. 2017. Attention is all you need. *CoRR*, abs/1706.03762.

Thomas Wolf, Lysandre Debut, Victor Sanh, Julien Chaumond, Clement Delangue, Anthony Moi, Pierric Cistac, Tim Rault, Rémi Louf, Morgan Funtowicz, and Jamie Brew. 2019. Huggingface's transformers: State-of-the-art natural language processing. *CoRR*, abs/1910.03771.

Shijie Wu and Ryan Cotterell. 2019. Exact hard monotonic attention for character-level transduction. In *Proceedings of the 57th Conference of the Association for Computational Linguistics, ACL 2019, Florence, Italy, July 28- August 2, 2019, Volume 1: Long Papers*, pages 1530–1537. Association for Computational Linguistics.

Shijie Wu, Ryan Cotterell, and Mans Hulden. 2021. Applying the transformer to character-level transduction. In *Proceedings of the 16th Conference of the European Chapter of the Association for Computational Linguistics: Main Volume, EACL 2021, Online, April 19 - 23, 2021*, pages 1901–1907. Association for Computational Linguistics.

Zhilin Yang, Zihang Dai, Yiming Yang, Jaime G. Carbonell, Ruslan Salakhutdinov, and Quoc V. Le. 2019. Xlnet: Generalized autoregressive pretraining for language understanding. In *Advances in Neural Information Processing Systems 32: Annual Conference on Neural Information Processing Systems 2019, NeurIPS 2019, December 8-14, 2019, Vancouver, BC, Canada*, pages 5754–5764.

# Impact of Sequence Length and Copying on Clause-Level Inflection

**Badr Jaidi*** **Utkarsh Saboo*** **Xihan Wu*** **Garrett Nicolai** **Miikka Silfverberg**
Department of Linguistics
University of British Columbia
badrjd@student.ubc.ca utkarshsaboo45@gmail.com wuxihan@student.ubc.ca
garrett.nicolai@ubc.ca miikka.silfverberg@ubc.ca

## Abstract

We present the University of British Columbia's submission to the MRL shared task on multilingual clause-level morphology. Our submission extends word-level inflectional models to the clause-level in two ways: first, by evaluating the role that BPE has on the learning of inflectional morphology, and second, by evaluating the importance of a copy bias obtained through data hallucination. Experiments demonstrate a strong preference for language-tuned BPE and a copy bias over a vanilla transformer. The methods are complementary for inflection and analysis tasks – combined models see error reductions of 38% for inflection and 15.6% for analysis; However, this synergy does not hold for reinflection, which performs best under a BPE-only setting. A deeper analysis of the errors generated by our models illustrates that the copy bias may be too strong - the combined model produces predictions more similar to the copy-influenced system, despite the success of the BPE-model.

## 1 Introduction

Morphology is often described as the "study of the shape of words", but such a description is not entirely accurate. Without considering the somewhat nebulous definition of a "word", there are clearly inflectional processes that operate on a periphrastic level. For example, in English, the future tense is regularly inflected through the use of an auxiliary: `will` and an infinitive, such as in the case "I will go".

Previous tasks in inflectional morphology (Cotterell et al., 2017, 2018; McCarthy et al., 2019; Vylomova et al., 2020; Pimentel et al., 2021; Kodner et al., 2022) have largely been restricted to generating isolated inflected word forms, which could be viewed as a rather artificial task. While some have included periphrastic constructions (Cotterell et al., 2016), they have largely been constrained to a single part-of-speech. [1] This MRL Shared Task in Multilingual Clause-Level Morphology (Goldman et al., 2022) represents the first attempt to extend inflection generation beyond a single semantic unit to clause-level structures and presents a great opportunity to investigate common inflectional methods in a more realistic morphosyntactic setting.

We augment traditional transformer-based character models with two simple data modifications: we first apply a small BPE-vocabulary to learn common repeated sequences like function words and affixes, hoping to increase performance by reducing the known bias of long character sequences (Neishi and Yoshinaga, 2019). Secondly, we adopt a common data augmentation technique from word-level inflection: adding data that has an identical source and target to bias the model towards the copying of characters (Liu and Hulden, 2022). We find that a combination of these simple techniques improves upon a vanilla transformer for inflection and analysis, while a BPE-only model has the best results for reinflection.

We also contribute a significant error analysis. We investigate the types of errors that inflectional systems are prone to, and how our contributions alleviate them at the clause level; Furthermore, we provide a thorough ablation study that compares errors across inflectional tasks, and how these errors are influenced by sequence length and copy biasing[2].

## 2 Methods

Studies in neural machine translation have regularly shown character- and subword-level representations outperform word-level ones for morphologically-rich languages (Shapiro and Duh,

*The first three authors contributed equally.

[1] Excepting, of course, those languages where even this distinction is not perfectly clear.

[2] Our data hallucination code is available at `https://github.com/mpsilfve/UBCMRL`



*Proceedings of the The 2nd Workshop on Multi-lingual Representation Learning (MRL)*, pages 106 - 114
December 8, 2022 ©2022 Association for Computational Linguistics

2018), and that optimizing the number of BPE operations can lead to substantial gains in model quality (Araabi and Monz, 2020). Although the sequences in inflectional models are typically shorter, there is evidence that inflection models, like machine translation models, can benefit from grouping common sequences (Peters and Martins, 2022). Similarly, inflectional research has demonstrated that models can be significantly improved by establishing a heavy bias towards copying data directly from input to output (Liu and Hulden, 2022). Many variations of this theme exist, but some of the most successful have included establishing a hard attentional model (Aharoni and Goldberg, 2017), learning an explicit copy bias (Makarov and Clematide, 2018), and augmenting the model with hallucinated data (Anastasopoulos and Neubig, 2019).

For our submission to the shared task, we investigate to what extent these methods are extensible to clausal morphology. Previous work has largely occurred at the word-level, and while it is intuitive that word-level inflection should extend to the clause-level, it is unclear to what extent. As one of the first investigations into clause-level morphology, we investigate the influence of byte pair encoding and copy bias on the production of accurate morphological structures.

### 2.1 Vanilla system

We build a baseline system using the Fairseq (Ott et al., 2019) implementation of transformers. To distinguish it from the official task baseline, we refer to it as the *vanilla* system. All characters in the input and output are represented as atomic units, and Morphosyntactic descriptors (MSD) are split along semi-colons into inflectional features. Spaces between words in clauses are represented by an underscore (_). An example is provided in Figure 1.

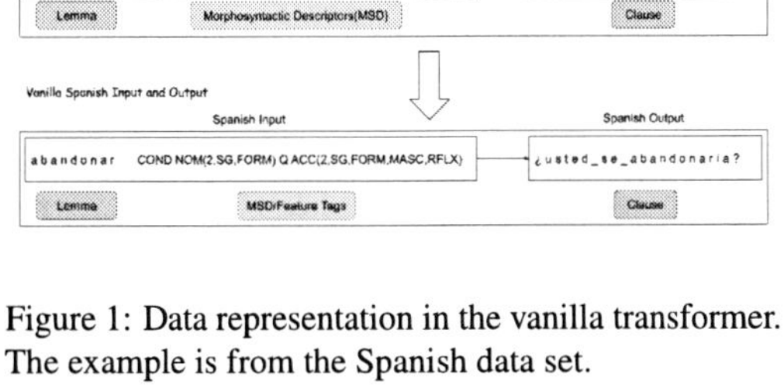


Figure 1: Data representation in the vanilla transformer. The example is from the Spanish data set.

### 2.2 BPE

Neural models still struggle with long input and output sequences; although great strides have been made in retaining long-distance information, there is still evidence that shorter sequences are easier to represent accurately.

Byte pair encoding (BPE) (Sennrich et al., 2016) reduces the length of both input and output sequences by memorizing frequent symbol sequences and treating them as individual symbols. This typically has a marked positive impact on model performance. In lower-resource settings, however, models can easily overfit if the vocabulary is too large.

We apply BPE to inflection but, in order to avoid over-fitting, we experiment with a very small number of BPE vocabulary merges - 10 to 200. For clause level morphology, we anticipate that these merges will capture only the most common of segments, such as inflectional affixes, pronouns, and function morphemes.

### 2.3 Copying

When inflecting from a lemma to a surface form, many of the characters in the lemma are often preserved.[3] However, neural models often require a not-insignificant amount of training data to learn this phenomenon. In low-resource inflectional experiments, one process that has repeatedly been shown to improve model stability is the simple expedient of copying the source to the target, without any further modification (Liu and Hulden, 2022). While this copying bias is likely less prevalent at the phrasal level, we believe it still has the opportunity to improve the quality of the inflectional models. Along with strengthening a preference for copying in the model, copying the target data also strengthens the target-side language model. An example of this augmentation for inflection and analysis is shown in Figure 2. For all three tasks, the hallucinated data contains a single `COPY` tag on the source side as MSD.

## 3 Data / Experiments

The shared task consists of three sub-tasks: (1) inflection, where a lemma and MSD input are converted to an inflected output; (2) reinflection, where an initial clause, input-MSD, and target-MSD are used to generate a target clause, and (3) analysis,

[3]The percentage of characters preserved varies greatly by language.

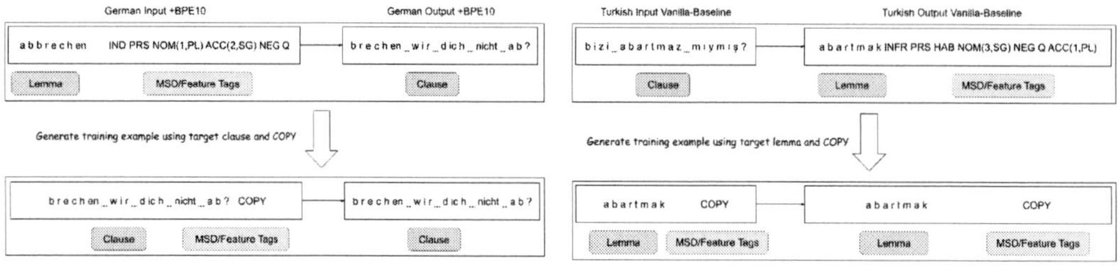


(a) Copying target-to-target for inflection. (b) Copying target-to-target for morphological analysis.

Figure 2: Data augmentation via COPY

where an input clause generates a target lemma and MSD. Each task is evaluated across 9 languages.

Each language has a train/dev/test split of 10,000, 1000, and 1000 instances, respectively. [4] Although extra data was allowed for the task, we instead concentrated on optimizing the models without additional data. Each model is evaluated on a single training run; the seed is stabilized to lessen the effect of noise across experiments.

We focus our experiments on an ablation of our proposed data augmentation techniques. The *Vanilla* experiments train models using the vanilla transformer described above. *+BPE* tunes a byte pair encoding vocabulary on each respective language and task; we investigate BPE merges from 10-200, and choose the model that maximizes the results on the development set*+Copy* augments the data with copied target-side data; the size of the BPE vocabulary is tuned individually for each language and amount of additional data.

The transformer was trained with 4 attentional heads over 4 encoder and decoder layers. The Adam{0.9, 0.98} optimizer was used, with an initial learning rate of 0.0001, and an inverse square-root learning schedule and a label-smoothed cross entropy criterion. Dropout and attentional dropout of 0.3 were applied to limit over-fitting, and a batch size of 400 was also used. Models were trained for 20,000 updates, with the best model chosen via loss on the development set.

## 4 Results

We break the discussion of our results down based on the three sub-tasks of the competition: inflection, reinflection, and analysis. All reported results and analysis are on the development set, and are cumulative: "+BPE" applies BPE to the vanilla transformer, and "+Copy" further supplements the model with data hallucination. For official results on the test set, please see the task description paper (Goldman et al., 2022). All systems submitted to the official task were the systems with both BPE and data hallucination. The results report the exact match accuracy of the systems.

### 4.1 Inflection

| Language | Vanilla | +BPE | +Copy |
|---|---|---|---|
| deu | 69.0 | 72.1 | 75.6 |
| eng | 85.4 | 86.2 | 89.7 |
| fra | 71.6 | 85.7 | 89.4 |
| heb | 86.9 | 86.9 | 86.4 |
| heb_unvoc | 63.5 | 80.6 | 83.1 |
| rus | 80.0 | 83.4 | 87.5 |
| spa | 87.0 | 88.6 | 87.7 |
| swa | 82.2 | 87.0 | 90.1 |
| tur | 81.9 | 87.0 | 91.5 |
| Ave. | 78.6 | 84.2 | **86.8** |

Table 1: Development results for the inflection task (measured in full-form accuracy)

We first report the results for the inflection subtask in Table 1. We observe that both BPE and data hallucination contribute to the quality of the model; on average, adding a small amount of BPE-joined vocabulary reduces the error by more than a quarter. Additionally, providing additional copied data leads to a further 11% error reduction.The BPE vocabulary has the largest impact on French, Swahili, Turkish, and unvocalized Hebrew, while providing smaller gains to the rest of the language set. The only language not to benefit from extra data in training was Spanish. Since Spanish shares a similar morphological makeup to French, which benefits substantially from data hallucination, we

[4] Some languages do not have 10,000 instances exactly, but are of the same magnitude.

do not attribute this finding to the morphological structure of Spanish, but rather to peculiarities of the dataset itself.

### 4.2 Reinflection

| Language | Vanilla | +BPE | +Copy |
|---|---|---|---|
| deu | 37.7 | 49.8 | 46.6 |
| eng | 59.4 | 73.0 | 71.4 |
| fra | 63.9 | 68.8 | 71.1 |
| heb | 72.5 | 80.4 | 78.6 |
| heb_unvoc | 60.6 | 67.7 | 63.8 |
| rus | 76.8 | 79.5 | 78.7 |
| spa | 56.1 | 61.0 | 72.8 |
| swa | 54.9 | 73.4 | 65.5 |
| tur | 54.6 | 65.6 | 63.1 |
| Ave. | 59.6 | **68.8** | 68.0 |

Table 2: Development results for the reinflection task (measured in full-form accuracy)

In Table 2, it is immediately obvious that reinflection behaves very differently from inflection, despite many conceptual similarities. Although BPE reduces the error of the vanilla transformer to a similar degree as for inflection, adding hallucinated copy data on top of the BPE does not lead to further gains. Again, there seems to be no morphological bias to this trend, with fusional, agglutinative, and templatic languages all behaving similarly.

There is one significant difference between inflection and reinflection that may lead to less success via copy-biasing, however. Although both processes involve the modification of a root, the root is less stable in reinflection. In the inflection task, the input is always the lemma, and identifying the root can largely be generalized over all of the training examples. In reinflection, the input form is inconsistent, and root identification must identify several operations. The problem is exacerbated with larger morphological paradigms, such as clause-level paradigms. While much of the root can be copied, there are also a significant number of substitutions, which may lessen the need for a strong copy bias. For example, in the German data, one example should reinflect *ich würde ihn nicht erschließen* into *es erschlösse sich*. Our copy model instead produces **es erschließe* sich, demonstrating that the copy bias may be too strong.

### 4.3 Analysis

Table 3 demonstrates the results of our morphological analysis experiments. Conceptually, analysis is the inverse operation of inflection from a lemma (ie, generating a lemma and MSD from an inflected clause), and we observe similar results to those from Section 4.1. Both BPE and data hallucination result in error reductions across most languages, and the effect appears to be cumulative: BPE on its own reduced error by 9.2%, and the extra data leads to a further reduction of 7.1%.

We observe that a significant part of the increase in quality comes from an improved ability to identify the lemma – BPE correctly identifies 2.9% more lemmas than the vanilla system, and the addition of hallucinated data further improves the quality of lemma identification by an absolute 3.1%. This is not surprising, given that once the root has been identified, the generation of the lemma can largely be generalized to a small set of operations, many of which are simple copies.

Somewhat surprisingly, the generation of the MSD also improves from the addition of BPE, despite no modifications to the MSDs in training. We attribute this to the increased quality of lemma generation – in a joint model, the correct identification of part of the output helps with disambiguation of the secondary task. Even with that consideration, it appears that BPE has a larger influence on the production of MSDs than copy biasing.

| Language | Vanilla | +BPE | +Copy |
|---|---|---|---|
| deu | 83.1 | 86.1 | 87.5 |
| eng | 89.2 | 91.0 | 91.2 |
| fra | 93.2 | 93.2 | 93.2 |
| heb | 92.9 | 92.9 | 94.3 |
| heb_unvoc | 84.8 | 87.1 | 87.7 |
| rus | 94.4 | 94.4 | 94.1 |
| spa | 89.7 | 89.7 | 90.6 |
| swa | 85.0 | 87.6 | 87.9 |
| tur | 89.2 | 89.3 | 90.8 |
| Average F1 | 89.1 | 90.1 | **90.8** |
| Lemma Acc. | 67.4 | 70.3 | **73.4** |
| MSD Acc. | 81.7 | **82.5** | 82.4 |

Table 3: Development results for the analysis task (measured in F1 Score); the Lemma and MSD Accuracy are averaged over all languages.

## 5 Analysis / Discussion

In order to better understand the differences in model quality, we perform error analysis along several axes. We first consider the types of inflection errors produced by the BPE, Copy, and BPE+Copy models in Figure 3, while Figure 4 shows error reduction compared to the vanilla transformer when using BPE, Copy, and their combination BPE+Copy.

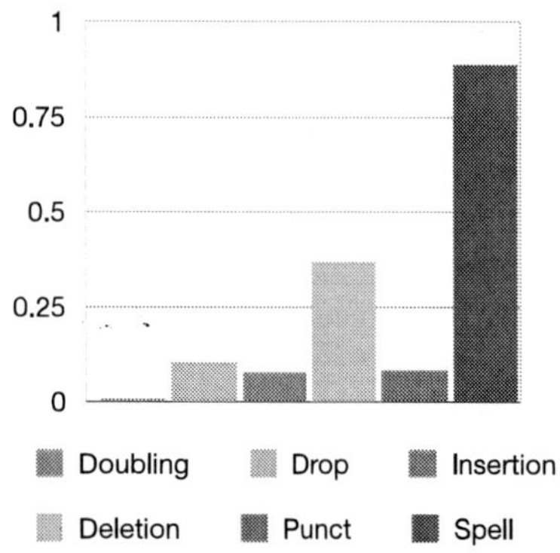


Figure 3: Mean frequencies of various errors across the test languages. Explanation of error types: **Doubling** a character is erroneously doubled ($abc \rightarrow abbc$). **Drop** the second copy of a doubled character is errnouneously dropped ($abbc \rightarrow abc$). **Insertion** a character is erroneously inserted ($abc \rightarrow axbc$). **Deletion** a character is mistakenly deleted ($abc \rightarrow ac$). **Punct** Punctuation is dropped or replaced at the end of a word ($abc. \rightarrow abc$ and $abc. \rightarrow abc?$). **Spell** Total spelling errors affecting the inflected form of the input lemma.

First, we notice that both BPE and Copy individually reduce overall errors (the error type Total in Figure 4). The impact of the methods seems roughly equal, although Copy is slightly more effective on its own. Nevertheless, the combination BPE+Copy clearly outperforms both individual methods. Second, we observe somewhat different influence from the BPE and Copy methods when they are used in isolation - the former significantly improves upon punctuation errors, while the latter removes a number of insertion errors from the vanilla model. Moreover, the most prevalent error type in the vanilla model – deletion – is only moderately reduced by the BPE model, while a far greater error reduction can be seen when Copy is employed. Furthermore, we observe a largely complementary effect - the combined model improves over either individual model for all error categories.

We next run an ablation to investigate the role that each of our contributions has on the quality of the models for each task. The results are plotted in Figure 5. In this graph, we investigate which errors are corrected or introduced by a particular method. BPE and Copy "correct" an error if it was produced by the vanilla model, and "break" an example if it was correctly predicted by the vanilla model, but not the enhanced model. For the model with both BPE and copying, an instance is only considered "corrected" if both the BPE and Copy models produced an incorrect solution. Likewise, it "breaks" a prediction only if both the BPE and Copy models produce the correct solution.

We observe that both BPE and copying lead to large improvements in the model, regardless of the task - far more errors corrected than introduced. For inflection and analysis, both methods appear to contribute roughly equally to the quality of the model. Furthermore, we observe a complementary effect, where the combination of both methods corrects notably more examples than either method on its own. Contrarily, the combined model introduces fewer inflectional errors than either BPE or copying alone.

Interestingly, the trends observed in inflection and analysis do not hold for reinflection. Although BPE and copying alone improve the model, their combination introduces a large number of errors - such that they overwhelm the corrected instances obtained through the combination of methods. A closer inspection reveals that this outlier is largely attributable to a single language - Swahili. When Swahili is excluded, the results trend similar to the other tasks, although BPE still has a stronger influence. There are several areas where Swahili could be contributing to this interesting finding, but lacking experts in the language on our team, we hesitate to make concrete hypotheses.

Figure 5 suggests that the biggest benefit of the combined model is its ability to correctly discern when one of the separate data augmentations correctly produces an inflection, but it isn't quite that clear. Looking at examples where the BPE and Copy models disagree, we observe that the combined inflection model correctly chooses the right solution 72.8% of the time.[5] However, for reinflection and analysis, the correct solution is only chosen slightly more than 50% of the time.

Considering only those instances where the original BPE and Copy models disagree, we investigate the influence of the individual contributions. For inflection, we observe that the combined model produces output identical to the BPE model in 61% of cases, as opposed to only 40% for reinflection and 43% for analysis. It appears that the copied data has an unduly large influence on the combined model for the latter two tasks.

Given that the motivation behind BPE was re-

[5]Note that there is actually no "choosing" occuring, such as might happen in an ensemble. Instead this can be viewed as the influence of a particular addition biasing the model towards a particular prediction.

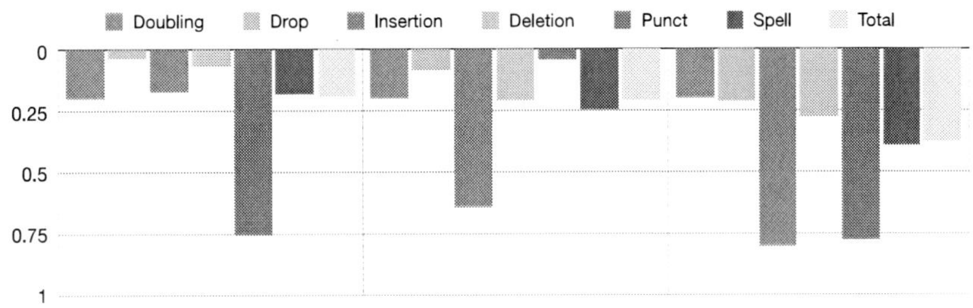


Figure 4: Mean error reduction across the five test languages for the BPE, Copy and BPE+Copy systems when compared to the baseline system. See caption of Figure 3 for an explanation of the error types.

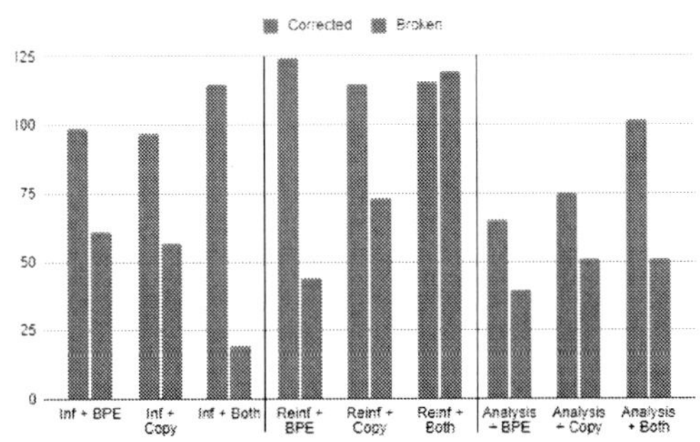


Figure 5: Analysis of errors corrected and introduced by our augmentations over the vanilla model. The y-axis is an absolute scale of the average number of errors corrected and introduced by each model, compared with the vanilla transformer. Inf - Inflection; Reinf - Reinflection.

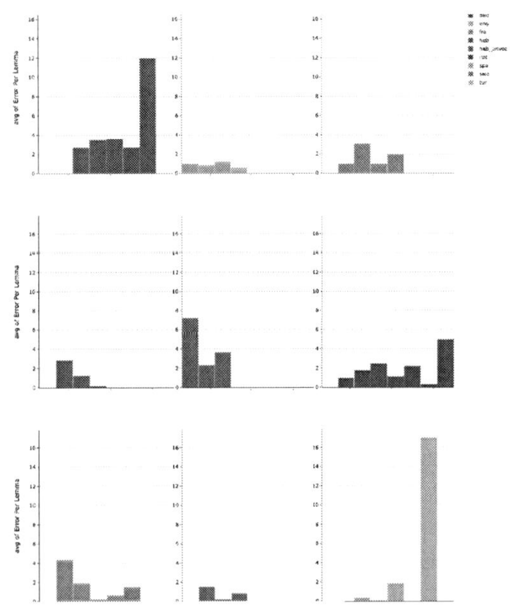

Figure 6: Analysis of errors made by our best model for each language in the inflection task depending on character length of the lemmas. The y-axis is the average number of errors made in the development set and the x-axis is the character length.

ducing the size of input and output segments, we investigate the role that the length of a sequence plays on the quality of a model. Since reinflection and analysis lengths vary based not only on the length of the verb being inflected, but on other factors such as the number of words in the input, etc, we limit this investigation to the inflection task. Figure 6 demonstrates the number of errors produced by our best system, given the length of the input sequence (ie, the lemma). German, Russian, and Turkish show a strong preference for shorter input sequences. Hebrew (both unvocalized and standard) and Spanish instead demonstrate a somewhat surprising preference in the other direction - producing more errors for short sequences.

In an attempt to further explain these conflicting results, we next investigate the relationship between lemmas in the training and development sets. Figure 7 reports the number of errors made by our best system with respect to the distance between the development lemma and the closest analogue in the training data. Now, unsurprisingly, we see that most languages perform better when there is a closely-related lemma in the training data.

Finally, we investigate the efficiency of our copying method by comparing it with two alternatives. Rather than simply taking the training output data and copying it as extra data, `RANDOM` generates random sequences of characters to copy from source to target. Similarly, `LM` creates new copy sequences, but first learns a neural language model from the training data, before generating the sequences. The results for inflection are shown in Figure 8.

We observe that changing the hallucination method from copied training data to randomly-generated sequences greatly improves the quality

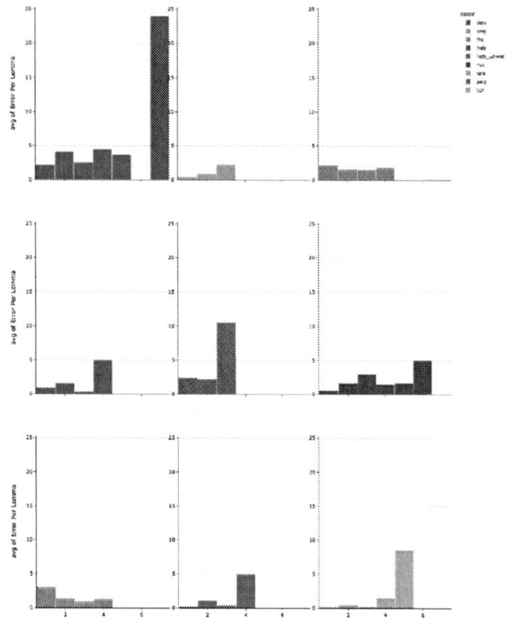

Figure 7: Analysis of errors made by our best model for each language in the inflection task depending on the closest Levenshtein score of any lemma present in the training set. The y-axis is the average number of errors made in the development set and the x-axis is the Levenshtein distance.

of the inflector, with an error reduction of more than 35%, on average. We hypothesize that while the COPY method simply reinforces an existing signal, the RANDOM method introduces new contexts for copying, which allows the model to better generalize the copy operation overall.

## 6 Conclusion

We have described the submission of the UBC team to the MRL shared task on multilingual clause-level morphology. Experiments on a series of morphologically-diverse languages have demonstrated that BPE and copy-biasing, two methods that have proven successful at the word-level, are largely extensible to clause-level morphology.

We observe that the methods are largely complementary, with one exception - the task of reinflection. Although we observe notable gains over a vanilla transformer when either performing BPE or copy hallucination, combining the two methods leads to a degradation in reinflection quality.

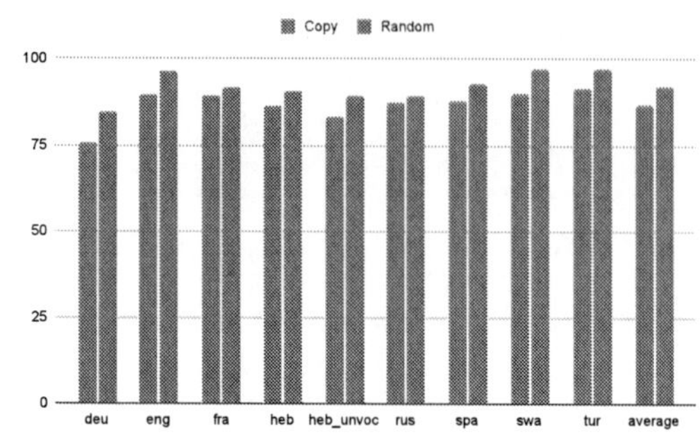


Figure 8: A comparsison of our data hallucination methods using copied training data and randomly generated sequences.

## Limitations

The work described in this paper focuses on multilingual representation, but the authors are not familiar with all of the analyzed languages. Hypotheses are based on general linguistic experience, and not necessarily a familiarity with the languages in question.

Deep learning models are stochastic in nature, which may lead to replication difficulties. We have tried to specify relevant hyper-parameters and settings, but random fluctuations in seed values may result in variations in replication studies.

## Ethics Statement

We trust that the data used in this paper was ethically-sourced. The models were trained by faculty and students of the Department of Linguistics at the University of British Columbia, and none of the data or models were shared with anyone outside that purview. All contributors to the project are in the author list, or thanked in the acknowledgments. No members of the team received monetary compensation for participating in this task. All participation was voluntary.

## References

Roee Aharoni and Yoav Goldberg. 2017. Morphological inflection generation with hard monotonic attention. In *Proceedings of the 55th Annual Meeting of the Association for Computational Linguistics (Volume 1: Long Papers)*, pages 2004–2015, Vancouver, Canada. Association for Computational Linguistics.

Antonios Anastasopoulos and Graham Neubig. 2019. Pushing the limits of low-resource morphological inflection. In *Proceedings of the 2019 Conference on Empirical Methods in Natural Language Processing and the 9th International Joint Conference on Natural Language Processing (EMNLP-IJCNLP)*, pages 984–996, Hong Kong, China. Association for Computational Linguistics.

Ali Araabi and Christof Monz. 2020. Optimizing transformer for low-resource neural machine translation. In *Proceedings of the 28th International Conference on Computational Linguistics*, pages 3429–3435, Barcelona, Spain (Online). International Committee on Computational Linguistics.

Ryan Cotterell, Christo Kirov, John Sylak-Glassman, Géraldine Walther, Ekaterina Vylomova, Arya D. McCarthy, Katharina Kann, Sabrina J. Mielke, Garrett Nicolai, Miikka Silfverberg, David Yarowsky, Jason Eisner, and Mans Hulden. 2018. The CoNLL–SIGMORPHON 2018 shared task: Universal morphological reinflection. In *Proceedings of the CoNLL–SIGMORPHON 2018 Shared Task: Universal Morphological Reinflection*, pages 1–27, Brussels. Association for Computational Linguistics.

Ryan Cotterell, Christo Kirov, John Sylak-Glassman, Géraldine Walther, Ekaterina Vylomova, Patrick Xia, Manaal Faruqui, Sandra Kübler, David Yarowsky, Jason Eisner, and Mans Hulden. 2017. CoNLL-SIGMORPHON 2017 shared task: Universal morphological reinflection in 52 languages. In *Proceedings of the CoNLL SIGMORPHON 2017 Shared Task: Universal Morphological Reinflection*, pages 1–30, Vancouver. Association for Computational Linguistics.

Ryan Cotterell, Christo Kirov, John Sylak-Glassman, David Yarowsky, Jason Eisner, and Mans Hulden. 2016. The SIGMORPHON 2016 shared Task—Morphological reinflection. In *Proceedings of the 14th SIGMORPHON Workshop on Computational Research in Phonetics, Phonology, and Morphology*, pages 10–22, Berlin, Germany. Association for Computational Linguistics.

Omer Goldman, Francesco Tinner, Hila Gonen, Benjamin Muller, Victoria Besamova, Shadrack Karimi, Lydia Nishimwe, Benoît Sagot, Djamé Seddah, Reut Tsarfaty, and Duygu Ataman. 2022. The MRL 2022 shared task on multilingual clause-level morphology. In *Proceedings of the 2nd Workshop on Multilingual Representation Learning*, Abu Dhabi. Association for Computational Linguistics.

Jordan Kodner, Salam Khalifa, Khuyagbaatar Batsuren, Hossep Dolatian, Ryan Cotterell, Faruk Akkus, Antonios Anastasopoulos, Taras Andrushko, Aryaman Arora, Nona Atanalov, Gábor Bella, Elena Budianskaya, Yustinus Ghanggo Ate, Omer Goldman, David Guriel, Simon Guriel, Silvia Guriel-Agiashvili, Witold Kieraś, Andrew Krizhanovsky, Natalia Krizhanovsky, Igor Marchenko, Magdalena Markowska, Polina Mashkovtseva, Maria Nepomniashchaya, Daria Rodionova, Karina Scheifer, Alexandra Sorova, Anastasia Yemelina, Jeremiah Young, and Ekaterina Vylomova. 2022. SIGMORPHON–UniMorph 2022 shared task 0: Generalization and typologically diverse morphological inflection. In *Proceedings of the 19th SIGMORPHON Workshop on Computational Research in Phonetics, Phonology, and Morphology*, pages 176–203, Seattle, Washington. Association for Computational Linguistics.

Ling Liu and Mans Hulden. 2022. Can a transformer pass the wug test? Tuning copying bias in neural morphological inflection models. In *Proceedings of the 60th Annual Meeting of the Association for Computational Linguistics (Volume 2: Short Papers)*, pages 739–749, Dublin, Ireland. Association for Computational Linguistics.

Peter Makarov and Simon Clematide. 2018. Neural transition-based string transduction for limited-resource setting in morphology. In *Proceedings of the 27th International Conference on Computational Linguistics*, pages 83–93, Santa Fe, New Mexico, USA. Association for Computational Linguistics.

Arya D. McCarthy, Ekaterina Vylomova, Shijie Wu, Chaitanya Malaviya, Lawrence Wolf-Sonkin, Garrett Nicolai, Christo Kirov, Miikka Silfverberg, Sabrina J. Mielke, Jeffrey Heinz, Ryan Cotterell, and Mans Hulden. 2019. The SIGMORPHON 2019 shared task: Morphological analysis in context and cross-lingual transfer for inflection. In *Proceedings of the 16th Workshop on Computational Research in Phonetics, Phonology, and Morphology*, pages 229–244, Florence, Italy. Association for Computational Linguistics.

Masato Neishi and Naoki Yoshinaga. 2019. On the relation between position information and sentence length in neural machine translation. In *Proceedings of the 23rd Conference on Computational Natural Language Learning (CoNLL)*, pages 328–338.

Myle Ott, Sergey Edunov, Alexei Baevski, Angela Fan, Sam Gross, Nathan Ng, David Grangier, and Michael Auli. 2019. fairseq: A fast, extensible toolkit for sequence modeling. In *Proceedings of the 2019 Conference of the North American Chapter of the Association for Computational Linguistics (Demonstrations)*, pages 48–53, Minneapolis, Minnesota. Association for Computational Linguistics.

Ben Peters and Andre F. T. Martins. 2022. Beyond characters: Subword-level morpheme segmentation. In *Proceedings of the 19th SIGMORPHON Workshop on Computational Research in Phonetics, Phonology, and Morphology*, pages 131–138, Seattle, Washington. Association for Computational Linguistics.

Tiago Pimentel, Maria Ryskina, Sabrina J. Mielke, Shijie Wu, Eleanor Chodroff, Brian Leonard, Garrett Nicolai, Yustinus Ghanggo Ate, Salam Khalifa, Nizar Habash, Charbel El-Khaissi, Omer Goldman, Michael Gasser, William Lane, Matt Coler, Arturo Oncevay, Jaime Rafael Montoya Samame, Gema Celeste Silva Villegas, Adam Ek, Jean-Philippe Bernardy, Andrey Shcherbakov, Aziyana Bayyr-ool, Karina Sheifer, Sofya Ganieva, Matvey Plugaryov, Elena Klyachko, Ali Salehi, Andrew Krizhanovsky,

Natalia Krizhanovsky, Clara Vania, Sardana Ivanova, Aelita Salchak, Christopher Straughn, Zoey Liu, Jonathan North Washington, Duygu Ataman, Witold Kieraś, Marcin Woliński, Totok Suhardijanto, Niklas Stoehr, Zahroh Nuriah, Shyam Ratan, Francis M. Tyers, Edoardo M. Ponti, Grant Aiton, Richard J. Hatcher, Emily Prud'hommeaux, Ritesh Kumar, Mans Hulden, Botond Barta, Dorina Lakatos, Gábor Szolnok, Judit Ács, Mohit Raj, David Yarowsky, Ryan Cotterell, Ben Ambridge, and Ekaterina Vylomova. 2021. SIGMORPHON 2021 shared task on morphological reinflection: Generalization across languages. In *Proceedings of the 18th SIGMORPHON Workshop on Computational Research in Phonetics, Phonology, and Morphology*, pages 229–259, Online. Association for Computational Linguistics.

Rico Sennrich, Barry Haddow, and Alexandra Birch. 2016. Neural machine translation of rare words with subword units. In *Proceedings of the 54th Annual Meeting of the Association for Computational Linguistics (Volume 1: Long Papers)*, pages 1715–1725, Berlin, Germany. Association for Computational Linguistics.

Pamela Shapiro and Kevin Duh. 2018. Bpe and charcnns for translation of morphology: A cross-lingual comparison and analysis. *arXiv preprint arXiv:1809.01301*.

Ekaterina Vylomova, Jennifer White, Elizabeth Salesky, Sabrina J. Mielke, Shijie Wu, Edoardo Maria Ponti, Rowan Hall Maudslay, Ran Zmigrod, Josef Valvoda, Svetlana Toldova, Francis Tyers, Elena Klyachko, Ilya Yegorov, Natalia Krizhanovsky, Paula Czarnowska, Irene Nikkarinen, Andrew Krizhanovsky, Tiago Pimentel, Lucas Torroba Hennigen, Christo Kirov, Garrett Nicolai, Adina Williams, Antonios Anastasopoulos, Hilaria Cruz, Eleanor Chodroff, Ryan Cotterell, Miikka Silfverberg, and Mans Hulden. 2020. SIGMORPHON 2020 shared task 0: Typologically diverse morphological inflection. In *Proceedings of the 17th SIGMORPHON Workshop on Computational Research in Phonetics, Phonology, and Morphology*, pages 1–39, Online. Association for Computational Linguistics.

# Towards Improved Distantly Supervised Multilingual Named-Entity Recognition for Tweets

**Ramy Eskander, Shubhanshu Mishra, Sneha Mehta, Sofía Samaniego, Aria Haghighi**
Twitter. Inc.
{ramid,smishra,snehamehta,ssamaniego,ahaghighi}@twitter.com

## Abstract

Recent low-resource named-entity recognition (NER) work has shown impressive gains by leveraging a single multilingual model trained using distantly supervised data derived from cross-lingual knowledge bases. In this work, we investigate such approaches by leveraging Wikidata to build large-scale NER datasets of Tweets and propose two orthogonal improvements for low-resource NER in the Twitter social media domain: (1) leveraging domain-specific pre-training on Tweets; and (2) building a model for each language family rather than an all-in-one single multilingual model. For (1), we show that mBERT with Tweet pre-training outperforms the state-of-the-art multilingual transformer-based language model, LaBSE, by a relative increase of 34.6% in F1 when evaluated on Twitter data in a language-agnostic multilingual setting. For (2), we show that learning NER models for language families outperforms a single multilingual model by relative increases of 14.1%, 15.8% and 45.3% in F1 when utilizing mBERT, mBERT with Tweet pre-training and LaBSE, respectively. We conduct analyses and present examples for these observed improvements.

## 1 Introduction

Named-entity recognition (NER) is the process of detecting named mentions in text, and it is an essential subtask in several NLP applications such as information extraction (Weston et al., 2019), summarization (Aramaki et al., 2009) and question answering (Chen et al., 2019).

While resource-rich languages have received enormous focus over the last two decades, NER for low-resource languages is still under-explored due to the lack of resources — native speakers might not be even accessible — and the cost of labeling data needed to train supervised models for different languages. As a result, there has been emerging interest in multilingual NER, especially to process low-resource languages, in unsupervised and minimally supervised fashions.

One aspect of Multilingual NER is the need to build models that can generalize well across the underlying languages. However, when operating on social media text, multilingual NER becomes even harder (Mishra and Diesner, 2016; Mishra, 2019; Mishra and Haghighi, 2021) because of linguistic diversity, short context and orthographic variation.

Recent research has shown success by leveraging a single multilingual model based on distantly supervised datasets derived from cross-lingual knowl edge bases (Nothman et al., 2013; Rahimi et al., 2019). We follow the work on building distantly supervised NER datasets by leveraging Wikidata (Vrandečić and Krötzsch, 2014) for Tweets, where we do not assume access to long contexts nor manually labeled named entities in context. We then propose modeling techniques towards improved multilingual NER models for Tweets, where we investigate how much pre-training language models on domain-specific data (Tweets) and training NER models on the basis of language families improve NER performance. Our contribution is threefold.

1. We build distantly supervised large-scale monolingual and multilingual NER datasets of Tweets [1].
2. We propose a domain-specific pre-trained Tweet language model.
3. We learn different NER models for language families versus a single all-in-one multilingual model.

It is worth noting that while exiting distantly supervised NER datasets have proven efficient, e.g., WikiAnn (Pan et al., 2017), they are either 1) monolingual; 2) based on resources of rich context such as Wikipedia, as opposed to Wikidata, where the named entities are out of context; 3) outside of

[1] The datasets are accessible upon contacting the first author.



*Proceedings of the The 2nd Workshop on Multi-lingual Representation Learning (MRL)*, pages 115 - 124
December 8, 2022 ©2022 Association for Computational Linguistics

the Twitter domain; or 4) of limited size such as the Tweet datasets by Peng et al. (2019) and Liang et al. (2020). This necessitates the development of our Tweet datasets in order to answer our research questions in a low-resource setting.

We show that mBERT with Tweet pre-training outperforms LaBSE (Feng et al., 2020), a state-of-the-art multilingual language model, when evaluated in a language-agnostic multilingual setting on Twitter data. In addition, we show that learning NER models for language families outperforms a single all-in-one multilingual model. Our interpretation is that languages that belong to one family possess common linguistic features useful to learn an NER model. In contrast, joint learning of too many languages, most of which are unrelated, hinders the ability of the model to well fit any of the underlying languages. Finally, we conduct analyses and present examples in German and Arabic for the observed improvements.

## 2 Distantly Supervised Multilingual NER

In order to answer our research questions, we construct distantly supervised monolingual and multilingual NER datasets of Tweets (Section 2.1) and train NER models of different characteristics (Section 2.2).

### 2.1 Building NER datasets of Tweets

We describe below the process for building distantly supervised NER datasets of Tweets using Wikidata.

#### 2.1.1 Initial selection of Tweets

First, we construct an initial corpus of Tweets that lay within a time window of 14 days [2], up to 5,000 Tweets per language on any single day. This results in Tweets in the 65 languages depicted in Figure 1. We then apply white-space tokenization on the selected Tweets.

#### 2.1.2 Constructing a Wikidata Lookup

Utilizing cross-lingual knowledge bases to build multilingual NER datasets and gazetteers has proven successful (Pan et al., 2017; Al-Rfou et al., 2015). We next build a gazetteer of named entities by leveraging Wikidata (Vrandečić and Krötzsch, 2014), a large-scale cross-lingual knowledge base of nearly 100M entities, where each entity has a unique identifier and a list of categories and is defined as labels and alternate aliases in multiple languages.

For each language in our initial corpus of Tweets, we construct a Wikidata lookup trie (suffix tree) that stores all the labels and aliases of each entity in the underlying language. We apply white-space tokenization on the labels and aliases and store the resulting tokens in the tries, one token per level. We also store entity information, such as the identifier and the list of feasible categories, within the corresponding leaf nodes.

#### 2.1.3 Tagging of Tweets

We apply the maximum matching algorithm used by Peng et al. (2019), with a context size $k = 5$, to tag our corpus of Tweets for NER. In order to speed up the search process, we scan the Wikidata lookup tries in a top-down fashion with early termination.

Marking all the matching Wikidata labels and aliases as named-entity mentions in the Tweets results in over-tagging. For instance, the common English word *be* is an alias for *Belgium* (LOCATION). Accordingly, we ignore unigram mentions, mentions exclusively composed of the most frequent 1,000 tokens in the underlying language[3] and mentions starting with a lower-cased letter (if different from its upper-cased form), which results in empirical improvements in precision.

#### 2.1.4 Curation of Tags

Next, we map the Wikidata categories into NER labels and filter out the Tweets that do not contain mentions belonging to the main NER labels, namely PERSON, LOCATION and ORGANIZATION. Moreover, since the PERSON label is common in Tweets, we only select the Tweets that contain a single PERSON mention with a 20% probability. In addition, since a mention might belong to two or more categories, a Tweet is replicated to reflect all the possible combinations of the underlying labels. For instance, a Tweet that has the mention *Michael Kors* is replicated twice in order to indicate both the PERSON and ORGANIZATION interpretations [4].

#### 2.1.5 Defining the Datasets

We build monolingual NER datasets for each language. In addition, we build multilingual datasets

[2] In order to avoid Tweets of insufficient context, we filter our Tweets that are replies, containing more than five hashtags, five mentions or three URLs, or containing less than five tokens.

[3] We derive the lists based on the initial corpus of Tweets.

[4] The replication results in better empirical performance, where the models learn to detect and overlook unlikely label assignments

Figure 1: Our training languages, grouped into their families and sub-families

for language families, defined as the first and second language-family levels according to Wikipedia (See Figure 1). We do so for all the language families that include three or more languages and at least one experimental language (the first column in Table 1). This results in four family-based multilingual NER datasets, namely ASS (Afro-Asiatic, Semitic), IEG (Indo-European, Germanic), IEI (Indo-European, Italic) and IEII (Indo European, Indo-Iranian). Finally, we build a single all-in-one multilingual dataset that contains all the training languages.

In addition, we construct additional datasets that are the merge between our datasets and the training sets of WikiAnn (Pan et al., 2017), distantly supervised cross-lingual NER and entity-linking datasets of Wikipedia articles, towards higher coverage. The sizes of the datasets are reported in Table 1.

| Lang/Family | Without WikiAnn | With WikiAnn |
|---|---|---|
| en | 35K | 55K |
| de | 24K | 44K |
| nl | 30K | 50K |
| es | 22K | 42K |
| pt | 7K | 27K |
| fr | 19K | 39K |
| it | 24K | 44K |
| hi | 30K | 35K |
| ur | 77K | 97K |
| bn | 6K | 16K |
| ja | 25K | 45K |
| ar | 15K | 35K |
| tr | 12K | 33K |
| te | 6K | 7K |
| AAS | 36K | 76K |
| IEG | 112K | 234K |
| IEI | 106K | 226K |
| IEII | 149K | 210K |
| All | 609K | 1425K |

Table 1: The sizes of the monolingual and multilingual NER datasets. AAS = Afro-Asiatic, Semitic. IEG = Indo-European, Germanic. IEI = Indo-European, Italic. IEII = Indo-European, Indo-Iranian.

**Family-Based Multilingual NER** We hypothesize that a restricted multilingual model that is focused on languages within one family outperforms a multilingual model that spans two or more language families. This is because languages within one family tend to share morphosyntactic and syntactic features useful to learn an NER model, while learning a model across unrelated families limits the ability of the model to learn the latent patterns per language. Previous research highlights the role of family relatedness in different NLP tasks. Pires et al. (2019) show that fine-tuning mBERT on some language and applying zero-shot model transfer onto another only performs well across related languages in the tasks of NER and POS tagging. Cross-lingual POS tagging has also proven most successful across languages that belong to the same family (Eskander et al., 2020; Eskander, 2021). In addition, Fan et al. (2021a) show that selecting a pivot language within the same language family of the language of interest helps improve translation performance.

## 2.2 Modeling

We build our multilingual NER models by fine-tuning multilingual transformer-based language models, namely (basic) mBERT [5] (Devlin et al., 2019), mBERT pre-trained on Tweets (mBERT+Tweets) and LaBSE (Feng et al., 2020),

[5] While XLM-Roberta (Conneau et al., 2019) is superior to mBERT in the task of multilingual NER (Adelani et al., 2021), the use of mBERT is sufficient to draw conclusions on the use of the different multilingual settings, where our purpose is not to produce an NER system with the state-of-the-art results.

Language-Agnostic BERT Sentence Embedding [6]. We use the same setup proposed by Devlin et al. (2019), where we predict the NER tags only for the first subword of each token in a sequence.

Our choice of mBERT is used as a baseline, while the use of LaBSE is motivated by the fact that mBERT's transfer across languages can be improved by aligning embeddings of translations (Mishra and Haghighi, 2021), which is in line with the pre-training objective of LaBSE. Moreover, both mBERT and LaBSE have achieved success in the task of NER as demonstrated in the work by Pires et al. (2019) and Hakala and Pyysalo (2019), respectively.

The mBERT+Tweets model is basically the basic mBERT model pre-trained on Tweets (plain Tweet texts) for the masked language-modeling (MLM) objective. For pre-training, we use a dataset of 700M Tweets in 65 languages, randomly sampled using mBERT's methodology[7] that is based on exponentially smoothed language probabilities (S=0.7) to slightly increase the representation of low-resource languages. We initialize our model with mBERT weights and further train on the MLM objective. We use the AdamW optimizer (Loshchilov and Hutter, 2019) with a learning rate of $5e^{-5}$ and a weight decay of 0.01, along with a batch size of 2K and 800K training steps.

## 3 Evaluation and Analysis

### 3.1 Experimental Setup

**Languages** We perform our experiments on 14 simulated low-resource languages [8] of diverse typologies where we do not assume access to labeled data in the form of texts tagged for named entities. This consists of 10 Indo-European languages, namely English, German and Dutch (Germanic); Spanish, Portuguese, French and Italian (Italic); and Hindi, Bengali and Urdu (Indo-Iranian), in addition to Arabic (Afro-Asiatic, Semitic), Japanese (Japonic), Turkish (Turkic, Common-Turkic) and Telugu (Dravidian, South-Central).

**Training** We follow Devlin et al. (2019) for the training of our NER models by fine-tuning the multilingual transformer-based language models, namely mBERT, mBERT+Tweets and LaBSE, on our distantly-supervised NER datasets presented in Section 2.1.

We train monolingual NER models for each experimental language; we denote this setting by MONO. In addition, we train multilingual NER models for the language families defined in Section 2.1.5; we denote this family-based learning setting by FB-MULTI. Finally, we train a single multilingual model for the 65 languages in Figure 1; we denote this setting by ALL-MULTI.

We use the AdamW optimizer with a learning rate of $1e^{-5}$ and a weight decay of $1e^{-5}$, along with a batch size of 16 and up to 10 epochs with early stopping. We use 12 NVIDIA A100 GPUs, averaging nearly an hour of training per NER model.

**Testing** We utilize in-house gold standard test sets for English, Spanish, Portuguese, Arabic and Japanese, containing 3K, 2K, 10K, 10K and 2.3K Tweets, respectively [9]. In addition, we use seven public benchmarks, namely CoNLL'03 (Tjong Kim Sang and De Meulder, 2003) (for English and German), CoNLL'02 (Tjong Kim Sang and De Meulder, 2003) (for Dutch and Spanish), Europeana Newspapers (Neudecker, 2016) (for French), xLiMe [10] (for Italian), SSEA (Singh, 2008) (for Hindi, Urdu, Bengali and Telugu), Code-Switch'18-(validation) (Aguilar et al., 2018) (for Arabic) and JRC (Küçük et al., 2014) (for Turkish).

### 3.2 Evaluation

We refer to a combination of a test set and a learning setting as an experimental pair. For instance, {es: CONLL'03, FB-MULTI} means that we apply the family-based multilingual NER model that is trained on the Italic dataset on the Spanish CONLL'03 test set, while {tr: JRC, ALL-MULTI} means that we apply the multilingual NER model that is trained on our 65 languages on the Turkish JRC test set. We report all the results in entity-level micro-averaged F1.

It is worth mentioning that our target is to compare the different multilingual settings towards improved NER for Tweets. However, we do not assess the quality of our Tweet datasets with respect to existing distantly supervised ones. This is because, to

[6]We cannot pre-train LaBSE on Tweets since LaBSE is pre-trained for the translation-pair prediction (TPP) objective, which requires translation pairs that are not available for Tweets.

[7]https://github.com/google-research/bert/blob/master/multilingual.md

[8]While most of our experimental languages are not low-resource, we use them in a low-resource setting.

[9]We plan to make our in-house test sets publicly available upon publication.

[10]https://clarin.si/repository/xmlui/handle/11356/1078

| Lang. | Dataset | Monolingual | | | Mulilingual (Family-Based) | | | Multilingual (All-in-One) | | |
|---|---|---|---|---|---|---|---|---|---|---|
| | | mBERT | mBERT+Tweets | LaBSE | mBERT | mBERT+Tweets | LaBSE | mBERT | mBERT+Tweets | LaBSE |
| en | CONLL'03 | 41.8 | 40.7 | **43.1** | 40.1 | 38.9 | **42.9** | **37.9** | 36.0 | 33.3 |
| en | INH* | 38.0 | **43.2** | 42.3 | 34.1 | **42.5** | 36.8 | 32.8 | **38.6** | 27.5 |
| de | CONLL'03 | 44.9 | 42.0 | **46.4** | 42.3 | 40.9 | **44.2** | 38.1 | **38.8** | 29.0 |
| nl | CONLL'02 | 44.5 | 43.3 | **50.7** | **46.8** | 43.6 | 42.2 | **41.2** | 35.8 | 25.2 |
| es | CONLL'02 | **31.2** | 30.5 | 27.6 | **31.5** | 27.5 | 29.0 | **29.0** | 27.4 | 24.8 |
| es | INH* | 40.3 | **41.8** | 39.7 | 35.9 | **39.0** | 33.1 | 32.4 | **37.2** | 24.8 |
| pt | INH* | 33.0 | **41.2** | 38.1 | 29.1 | **36.2** | 26.3 | 27.6 | **33.9** | 18.5 |
| fr | EuropeanaNP | **36.4** | 35.4 | 34.4 | **33.6** | 31.3 | 29.7 | **28.1** | 26.8 | 22.0 |
| it | xLiMe* | 14.4 | **17.7** | 16.3 | 14.4 | **18.9** | 16.6 | 16.3 | **19.3** | 16.3 |
| hi | SSEA | 26.4 | 30.6 | **33.7** | 19.0 | 20.1 | **29.4** | **19.1** | 17.1 | 9.1 |
| ur | SSEA | 17.9 | 16.5 | **20.5** | 14.7 | 16.6 | **19.6** | 15.6 | 12.3 | **15.8** |
| bn | SSEA | 25.1 | 21.2 | **45.3** | 19.1 | 18.9 | **36.8** | 16.5 | 18.9 | **19.3** |
| ar | Code-Switch'18* | 26.8 | **28.0** | 27.6 | 23.4 | 25.5 | **28.9** | 21.9 | **23.0** | 23.0 |
| ar | INH* | 16.0 | **20.4** | 16.4 | 14.1 | **20.7** | 15.7 | 11.4 | **16.2** | 10.8 |
| ja | INH | 17.3 | **23.9** | 18.5 | NA | NA | NA | 17.2 | **20.3** | 15.1 |
| tr | JRC* | 31.5 | **37.6** | 31.2 | NA | NA | NA | 26.9 | **32.1** | 28.0 |
| te | SSEA | 13.0 | 10.8 | **17.6** | NA | NA | NA | 12.0 | 6.6 | **18.0** |
| Average (Tweets) | | 27.2 | **31.7** | 28.7 | 25.2 | **30.5** | 26.2 | 23.3 | **27.6** | 20.5 |
| Average (IEG) | | 42.3 | 42.3 | **45.6** | 40.8 | 41.5 | **41.5** | **37.5** | 37.3 | 28.8 |
| Average (IEI) | | 31.1 | **33.3** | 31.2 | 28.9 | **30.6** | 26.9 | 26.7 | **28.9** | 21.3 |
| Average (IEII) | | 23.1 | 22.8 | **33.2** | 17.6 | 18.5 | **28.6** | **17.1** | 16.1 | 14.7 |
| Average (All) | | 29.3 | 30.9 | **32.3** | 28.4 | 30.0 | **30.8** | 24.9 | **25.9** | 21.2 |

Table 2: NER Results (entity-level micro-averaged F1) without the addition of the WikiAnn training sets. The best result per experimental pair ({test set, learning setting}) is in **bold**. The best result per test set is underlined. Tweet datasets are denoted by *. IEG = Indo-European, Germanic. IEI = Indo-European, Italic. IEII = Indo-European, Indo-Iranian.

our knowledge, our datasets are the only available large-scale NER Tweet datasets that are based on a non-contextual knowledge base, Wikidata, where we simulate learning in truly low-resource scenarios.

Table 2 reports the NER performance (entity-level micro-averaged F1) for all the experimental pairs without the addition of the WikiAnn training sets. Overall, there is a noticeable variance in the performance of the different models across the learning settings, and even within the same language when evaluated on different test sets. However, the Germanic languages witness the best NER performance, which we attribute due to the bias in the training data of the utilized language models.

**LaBSE** The use of LaBSE in the MONO setting yields the best performance for seven experimental pairs: three Germanic ones, three Indo-Iranian ones and the telugu one. It also results in the best on-average F1 of 32.3% across all the experimental pairs in the MONO setting, which is relative increases of 10.2% and 4.5% over the corresponding performance of mBERT and mBERT+Tweets, respectively. However, the performance of LaBSE dramatically drops in the ALL-MULTI setting with average relative decreases of 34.4% and 31.2% compared to the performance in the MONO and FB-MULTI settings, respectively.

**mBERT+Tweets** The use of mBERT+Tweets in the MONO setting results in the best performance for eight experimental pairs, mostly with the use of our gold standards of Tweets (INH). In addition, when averaging across the Tweet datasets, mBERT+Tweets outperforms both mBERT and LaBSE, where it achieves relative increases of 10.5%, 16.4% and 34.6% compared to LaBSE in the MONO, FB-MULTI and ALL-MULTI settings, respectively. Moreover, mBERT+Tweets yields the best on-average performance in the ALL-MULTI setting, outperforming mBERT and LaBSE by average relative increases of 4.0% and 22.2%, respectively.

**mBERT** The results illustrate the effectiveness of pre-training the basic mBERT model, where mBERT+Tweets outperforms mBERT by average relative increases of 5.5%, 5.6% and 4.0% in the MONO, FB-MULTI and ALL-MULTI settings, respectively, while LaBSE outperforms mBERT by relative increases of 10.2% and 8.5% in the MONO and FB-MULTI settings, respectively. However, pre-training does not yield improvements in the cases of{fr, EuropeanaNP} and {es, CoNLL02}.

**Monolingual vs. Multilingual NER Models** The MONO setting yields the best performance for all the experimental pairs except five, two of

| Lang. | Dataset | Monolingual | | | Mulilingual (Family-Based) | | | Multilingual (All-in-One) | | |
|---|---|---|---|---|---|---|---|---|---|---|
| | | mBERT | mBERT+Tweets | LaBSE | mBERT | mBERT+Tweets | LaBSE | mBERT | mBERT+Tweets | LaBSE |
| en | CoNLL'03 | 60.1 | 61.3 | **62.9** | 56.4 | 60.4 | **62.6** | 55.8 | 56.8 | **57.6** |
| en | INH* | 40.8 | **48.2** | 45.5 | 27.5 | **43.3** | 40.8 | 31.8 | **37.3** | 34.6 |
| de | CoNLL'03 | 49.9 | **54.8** | 53.4 | 54.9 | 53.0 | **55.2** | 49.8 | **54.9** | 52.2 |
| nl | CoNLL'02 | **57.8** | 51.8 | 53.3 | 47.9 | 46.2 | **49.5** | 45.3 | **46.2** | 45.0 |
| es | CoNLL'02 | **51.9** | 46.1 | 48.5 | **53.8** | 53.0 | 46.3 | **50.4** | 49.9 | 45.3 |
| es | INH* | 40.2 | 40.9 | **42.0** | 32.7 | **39.0** | 31.4 | 29.5 | 30.8 | **32.6** |
| pt | INH* | 33.8 | **41.4** | 39.7 | 26.5 | **35.4** | 24.0 | 21.4 | **27.2** | 26.1 |
| fr | EuropeanaNP | **45.1** | 38.7 | 38.4 | 35.1 | **35.2** | 32.5 | 32.2 | **35.9** | 34.2 |
| it | xLiMe* | 13.7 | 17.3 | **19.1** | 16.2 | **17.5** | 15.5 | 14.5 | **15.9** | 15.2 |
| hi | SSEA | 22.9 | 23.8 | **36.4** | 19.5 | **28.5** | 28.0 | 22.3 | 24.2 | **27.3** |
| bn | SSEA | 25.6 | 20.2 | **38.3** | 20.4 | 18.4 | **39.3** | 21.1 | 20.3 | **35.3** |
| ur | SSEA | 22.9 | 20.7 | **28.7** | 28.3 | 27.2 | **40.2** | 30.7 | 29.1 | **41.8** |
| ar | Code-Switch'18* | 29.8 | 31.1 | **33.1** | 24.9 | 27.6 | **29.3** | 25.7 | 28.1 | **29.8** |
| ar | INH* | 16.0 | **22.3** | 21.9 | 12.1 | **20.8** | 16.9 | 12.8 | 14.4 | **14.7** |
| ja | INH* | 22.1 | **24.9** | 22.4 | NA | NA | NA | 18.8 | **22.2** | 22.0 |
| tr | JRC* | 38.5 | **52.5** | 46.2 | NA | NA | NA | 30.3 | **42.9** | 40.6 |
| te | SSEA | **17.8** | 6.4 | 16.8 | NA | NA | NA | 10.6 | 8.8 | **16.3** |
| Average (Tweets) | | 29.4 | **34.8** | 33.8 | 23.3 | **30.6** | 26.3 | 23.1 | **27.3** | 26.9 |
| Average (IEG) | | 52.1 | **54.0** | 53.8 | 46.7 | 50.7 | **52.1** | 45.7 | **48.8** | 47.4 |
| Average (IEI) | | 37.0 | 36.9 | **37.6** | 32.8 | **36.0** | 29.9 | 29.6 | **31.9** | 30.7 |
| Average (IEII) | | 23.8 | 21.5 | **34.5** | 22.7 | 24.7 | **35.9** | 24.7 | 24.5 | **34.8** |
| Average (All) | | 34.7 | 35.4 | **38.0** | 32.6 | 36.1 | **36.6** | 29.6 | 32.1 | **33.6** |

Table 3: NER Results (entity-level micro-averaged F1) with the addition of the WikiAnn training sets. The best result per experimental pair ({test set, learning setting}) is in **bold**. The best result per test set is underlined. Tweet datasets are denoted by *. IEG = Indo-European, Germanic. IEI = Indo-European, Italic. IEII = Indo-European, Indo-Iranian.

which belong to Arabic and one of which belong to Telugu, the language with the least number of instances in our training sets. We hypothesize that for low-resource languages, adding training examples from other languages compensates for the lack of data in the language of interest.

**Family-Based vs. All-in-One Multilingual Models** Learning NER models for language families (FB-MULTI) outperforms the use of a single all-in-one multilingual model (ALL-MULTI) except on four occasions (7.8% of the time). FB-MULTI also outperforms ALL-MULTI when averaging across all the experimental pairs, yielding relative increases of 14.1%, 15.8% and 45.3% with the use of mBERT, mBERT+Tweets and LaBSE, respectively. FB-MULTI is also superior when averaging across the individual language families. The results suggest that combining too many languages in the training data makes it difficult for the NER model to learn the morphosyntactic and syntactic properties of the individual languages; empirically, the ALL-MULTI setting only yields the best performance for two experimental pairs by a small margin of 0.4% compared to the performance in the other learning settings. In contrast, languages within a language family tend to share linguistic properties, which helps the NER model better fit to the individual languages within the family.

**WikiAnn** Table 3 reports the NER performance (entity-level micro-averaged F1) for all the experimental pairs with the addition of the WikiAnn training sets. Comparing the results in Table 3 to those in Table 2 shows that the addition of WikiAnn helps derive more efficient NER models.

Grouping by individual languages, WikiAnn improves the performance for all languages excpet German, Portuguese and Italian, where Urdu benefits the most from the addition of WikiAnn, an average relative increase of 83.6%, while the biggest drop in performance occurs in the case of Italian, an average relative decrease of only 3.0%.

WikiAnn also improves the performance on average across the Germanic and Italic languages and when averaging across all the experimental languages. However, the addition of WikiAnn results in noticeable performance drop when considering the Tweet datasets in the case of fine-tuing mBERT in the FB-MULTI setting, where neither mBERT nor WikiAnn leverages Twitter data.

### 3.3 Analysis

Table 4 lists NER-tagging examples that show cases in which 1) mBERT with Tweet pre-training outperforms LaBSE; and 2) training for distinct language families outperforms the single all-in-one multilingual model. In addition, we show common errors in our best setting. We conduct our manual

| German Examples | | | | | | | | | | | | | | | | |
|---|---|---|---|---|---|---|---|---|---|---|---|---|---|---|---|---|
| Tokens | | Andersens | starrer | Blick | sagt | viele | Worte | \| | Das | ist | modernes | Marketing | für | den | Messia | |
| Glosses | | Andersens | staring | look | says | many | words | \| | this | is | modern | marketing | for | the | Messiah | |
| True Labels | 01 | B-PER | O | O | O | O | O | \| | O | O | O | O | O | O | B-PER | 02 |
| mBERT+Tweets (ALL) | | B-PER | O | O | O | O | O | \| | O | O | O | O | O | O | B-PER | |
| LaBSE (ALL) | | B-PER | O | **B-PER** | O | O | O | \| | O | **B-ORG** | **I-ORG** | O | O | O | B-PER | |
| Tokens | | Stepanovic | prophezeit | Wolf | eine | große | Zukunft | \| | Der | Stadt | Königstein | geht | es | finanziell | glänzend | |
| Glosses | | Stepanovic | prophesized | Wolf | a | great | future | \| | the | city | Konigstein | goes | it | financial | brilliantly | |
| True Labels | 03 | B-PER | O | B-PER | O | O | O | \| | O | B-LOC | I-LOC | O | O | O | O | 04 |
| mBERT+Tweets (FB) | | B-PER | O | B-PER | O | O | O | \| | O | B-LOC | I-LOC | O | O | O | O | |
| mBERT+Tweets (ALL) | | **O** | O | B-PER | O | O | O | \| | O | **O** | **B-ORG** | O | O | O | O | |
| Tokens | | Eine | lange | Schlange | steht | vor | der | Bühne | \| | Eröffnung | ist | um | 11 | Uhr | | |
| Glosses | 05 | a | long | queue | stands | in front of | the | stage | \| | opening | is | at | 11 | O'clock | | 06 |
| True Labels | | O | O | O | O | O | O | O | \| | O | O | O | O | O | | |
| mBERT+Tweets (FB) | | **B-PER** | O | O | O | O | O | O | \| | **B-ORG** | **I-ORG** | O | O | O | | |
| Arabic Examples (Arabic reads from right to left) | | | | | | | | | | | | | | | | |
| Tokens | | | الوسط | خط | في | النهاردة | زيزو | العزيز | عبد | محمود | \| | الاسيويه | والامه | كوريا | فخر | |
| Glosses | | | the middle | line | in | today | Zizo | Al-Aziz | Abd | Mahmoud | \| | the Asian | and the nation | Korea | pride | |
| True Labels | 07 | | O | O | O | O | I-PER | I-PER | I-PER | B-PER | \| | O | O | B-LOC | O | 08 |
| mBERT+Tweets (ALL) | | | O | O | O | O | I-PER | I-PER | I-PER | B-PER | \| | O | O | B-LOC | O | |
| LaBSE(ALL) | | | O | O | O | O | **O** | I-PER | I-PER | B-PER | \| | O | O | **B-PER** | O | |
| Tokens | | اليوم | الأمن | مجلس | أمام | السوداني | الملف | \| | دينار | ١١٠ | ب | يتبرع | الشمري | العوام | حمد | |
| Glosses | | today | the Security | Council | before | the Sudanese | the case | \| | Dinar | 110 | for | donates | Al-Shamry | Al-Awam | Hamad | |
| True Labels | 09 | O | B-ORG | I-ORG | O | O | O | \| | O | O | O | O | I-PER | I-PER | B-PER | 10 |
| mBERT+Tweets (FB) | | O | B-ORG | I-ORG | O | O | O | \| | O | O | O | O | I-PER | I-PER | B-PER | |
| mBERT+Tweets (ALL) | | O | **O** | **O** | O | O | O | \| | O | O | O | O | **O** | I-PER | B-PER | |
| Tokens | | | | | الرياض | على | خفيفه | أمطار | \| | جديد | عبدالنور | سيرين | مكتشفين | شكلهم | الشباب | |
| Glosses | 11 | | | | Riyadh | on | light | rains | \| | recently | Abd-Al-Nour | Cyrine | discovering | seem | the youth | 12 |
| True Labels | | | | | B-LOC | O | O | O | \| | O | I-PER | B-PER | O | O | O | |
| mBERT+Tweets (FB) | | | | | **O** | **I-PER** | O | O | \| | O | **B-PER** | **O** | O | O | O | |

Table 4: NER Examples in German and Arabic. Errors are circled.

analysis on both German and Arabic [11] using the CONLL'03 and INH test sets, respectively.

**German** The use of mBERT+Tweets in the ALL-MULTI setting results in 1,335 (out of 3K) correctly tagged Tweets, as opposed to 495 when leveraging LaBSE, where the use of LaBSE results in over-tagging PERSON (ex. 01) and ORGANIZATION (ex. 02). On the other hand, the number of correctly tagged Tweets increases to 1,418 when fine-tuning mBERT+Tweets for the IEG family, where the system improves at detecting PERSON (ex. 03) and LOCATION (ex. 04). However, one common error is the false tagging of PERSON (ex. 05) and ORGANIZATION (ex. 06) at the beginning of Tweets.

**Arabic** The use of mBERT+Tweets in the ALL-MULTI setting results in 4,805 (out of 10K) correctly tagged Tweets, as opposed to 1,216 when leveraging LaBSE, where the use of LaBSE weakens the detection of non-PERSON mentions (ex. 07) and long mentions of three or more tokens (ex. 08). On the other hand, the number of correctly tagged Tweets increases to 6,229 when fine-tuning mBERT+Tweets for the AAS family as the system further improves at tagging non-PERSON mentions (ex. 09) and long mentions (ex. 10). However, two common issues are the low recall of LOCATION (ex. 11) and the inability to recognize non-Arabic and infrequent Arabic names (ex. 12).

[11]We have access to linguists who understand German and Arabic. Moreover, the two languages represent two different families and scripts.

## 4 Related Work

Leveraging cross-lingual knowledge bases for the construction of multilingual NER datasets and gazetteers has proved successful. Two large-scale efforts are WikiAnn (Pan et al., 2017), Wikipedia-based cross-lingual NER and entity-linking datasets in 282 languages, and Polyglot-NER (Al-Rfou et al., 2015), NER datasets in 40 languages derived from Wikipedia and Freebase (Bollacker et al., 2008). On another hand, there have been a few efforts to construct distantly supervised NER datasets of Tweets such as the work by Peng et al. (2019) and Liang et al. (2020), which presented datasets of only 7,257 and 2,400 Tweets, respectively. We follow similar approaches by leveraging Wikidata (Vrandečić and Krötzsch, 2014) to construct large-scale monolingual and multilingual NER datasets of Tweets.

Fine-tuning transformer-based language models for NER has shown success. Several works have utilized mBERT (Devlin et al., 2019) to construct generic and domain-specific multilingual NER models (Pires et al., 2019; Arkhipov et al., 2019; Baumann, 2019). Another example is LaBSE (Feng et al., 2020). While mostly utilized for sentence-level NLP tasks such as hate-speech identification (Mandl et al., 2021) and claim matching (Kazemi et al., 2021), LaBSE has also proven efficient for NER (Hakala and Pyysalo, 2019). In this work, we fine-tune both mBERT and LaBSE for NER in the Twitter domain, where we learn and compare monolingual and multilingual models of different characteristics.

Gururangan et al. (2020) shows that pre-training transformers towards a specific task or domains can provide significant benefits. Mishra and Haghighi (2021) show that pre-training mBERT for the translation-pair prediction (TPP) objective improves NER. Pre-training mBERT on Tweets has also been successful for a number of individual languages, such as English (Nguyen et al., 2020) and Arabic (Ahmed Abdelali et al., 2021). In this work, we pre-train mBERT on Tweets in 65 languages.

Several recent works utilize language classification towards improved multilingual models. The clustering can be based on either 1) language embeddings (Kudugunta et al., 2019; Tan et al., 2019; Yu et al., 2021; Fan et al., 2021b); 2) language family with/without the use of hand-crafted rules such as geographical proximity (Tan et al., 2019; Fan et al., 2021a); and 3) token overlap (Chung et al., 2020). We perform family-based clustering for NER, similar to the first approach proposed by Tan et al. (2019) in the task of machine translation. However, we do not assume access to rich embeddings or linguistic knowledge for the language(s) of interest.

## 5 Conclusion and Future Work

We proposed improvements to distantly supervised multilingual NER for Tweets, where we leveraged Wikidata to build large-scale monolingual and multilingual NER datasets of Tweets. We showed that pre-training mBERT on Tweets outperforms LaBSE by a relative F1 increase of 34.6% when evaluated on Twitter data in a language-agnostic multilingual setting. We also showed that learning NER models for language families outperforms a single all-in-one multilingual model by relative F1 increases of at least 14.1%. In the future, we plan to produce larger Tweet pre-trained language models, study more language families and leverage the work for multilingual entity linking for Tweets in low-resource languages.

## 6 Limitations

The limitations of the work lay within the Twitter social media domain for the listed training languages and given the reported performance. Also, the datasets are not labeled for named entities that are not included in Wikidata. The models however can generalize well to discover unseen named entities. Another limitation is the lack of a gold standard to intrinsically assess the quality of the labels in our NER datasets. There should be no other potential risks given the stated limitations.

## 7 Ethical Considerations

We exploit Twitter API [12] for the extraction of Tweets, along with language detection. The datasets are accessible upon contacting the first author. We however replace the text of the Tweets by Tweet IDs in order to prevent sensitive information and negative content, in accordance with Twitter's policy for sharing data. In addition, we are committed to keep the datasets current, making sure that deleted Tweets are removed from the datasets when they become publicly available.

## References

David Ifeoluwa Adelani, Jade Abbott, Graham Neubig, Daniel D'souza, Julia Kreutzer, Constantine Lignos, Chester Palen-Michel, Happy Buzaaba, Shruti Rijhwani, Sebastian Ruder, et al. 2021. Masakhaner: Named entity recognition for african languages. *Transactions of the Association for Computational Linguistics*, 9:1116–1131.

Gustavo Aguilar, Fahad AlGhamdi, Victor Soto, Thamar Solorio, Mona Diab, and Julia Hirschberg. 2018. Proceedings of the third workshop on computational approaches to linguistic code-switching. In *Proceedings of the Third Workshop on Computational Approaches to Linguistic Code-Switching*.

Ahmed Abdelali, Sabit Hassan, Hamdy Mubarak, Kareem Darwish, and Younes Samih. 2021. Pre-training bert on arabic tweets: Practical considerations. *CoRR*.

Rami Al-Rfou, Vivek Kulkarni, Bryan Perozzi, and Steven Skiena. 2015. Polyglot-ner: Massive multilingual named entity recognition. In *Proceedings of the 2015 SIAM International Conference on Data Mining*, pages 586–594. SIAM.

Eiji Aramaki, Yasuhide Miura, Masatsugu Tonoike, Tomoko Ohkuma, Hiroshi Masuichi, and Kazuhiko Ohe. 2009. Text2table: Medical text summarization system based on named entity recognition and modality identification. In *Proceedings of the BioNLP 2009 Workshop*, pages 185–192.

Mikhail Arkhipov, Maria Trofimova, Yurii Kuratov, and Alexey Sorokin. 2019. Tuning multilingual transformers for language-specific named entity recogni-

[12]https://developer.twitter.com/en/docs/twitter-api

tion. In *Proceedings of the 7th Workshop on Balto-Slavic Natural Language Processing*, pages 89–93.

Antonia Baumann. 2019. Multilingual language models for named entity recognition in german and english. In *Proceedings of the Student Research Workshop Associated with RANLP 2019*, pages 21–27.

Kurt Bollacker, Colin Evans, Praveen Paritosh, Tim Sturge, and Jamie Taylor. 2008. Freebase: a collaboratively created graph database for structuring human knowledge. In *Proceedings of the 2008 ACM SIGMOD international conference on Management of data*, pages 1247–1250.

Jifan Chen, Shih-ting Lin, and Greg Durrett. 2019. Multi-hop question answering via reasoning chains. *arXiv preprint arXiv:1910.02610*.

Hyung Won Chung, Dan Garrette, Kiat Chuan Tan, and Jason Riesa. 2020. Improving multilingual models with language-clustered vocabularies. In *Proceedings of the 2020 Conference on Empirical Methods in Natural Language Processing (EMNLP)*, pages 4536–4546, Online. Association for Computational Linguistics.

Alexis Conneau, Kartikay Khandelwal, Naman Goyal, Vishrav Chaudhary, Guillaume Wenzek, Francisco Guzmán, Edouard Grave, Myle Ott, Luke Zettlemoyer, and Veselin Stoyanov. 2019. Unsupervised cross-lingual representation learning at scale. *arXiv preprint arXiv:1911.02116*.

Jacob Devlin, Ming-Wei Chang, Kenton Lee, and Kristina Toutanova. 2019. BERT: Pre-training of deep bidirectional transformers for language understanding. In *Proceedings of Human Language Technologies: The 2019 Annual Conference of the North American Chapter of the Association for Computational Linguistics (NAACL)*.

Ramy Eskander. 2021. *Unsupervised Morphological Segmentation and Part-of-Speech Tagging for Low-Resource Scenarios*. Ph.D. thesis, Columbia University.

Ramy Eskander, Smaranda Muresan, and Michael Collins. 2020. Unsupervised cross-lingual part-of-speech tagging for truly low-resource scenarios. In *Proceedings of the 2020 Conference on Empirical Methods in Natural Language Processing (EMNLP)*, pages 4820–4831.

Angela Fan, Shruti Bhosale, Holger Schwenk, Zhiyi Ma, Ahmed El-Kishky, Siddharth Goyal, Mandeep Baines, Onur Celebi, Guillaume Wenzek, Vishrav Chaudhary, et al. 2021a. Beyond english-centric multilingual machine translation. *Journal of Machine Learning Research*, 22(107):1–48.

Yimin Fan, Yaobo Liang, Alexandre Muzio, Hany Hassan, Houqiang Li, Ming Zhou, and Nan Duan. 2021b. Discovering representation sprachbund for multilingual pre-training. In *Findings of the Association for Computational Linguistics: EMNLP 2021*, pages 881–894, Punta Cana, Dominican Republic. Association for Computational Linguistics.

Fangxiaoyu Feng, Yinfei Yang, Daniel Cer, Naveen Arivazhagan, and Wei Wang. 2020. Language-agnostic bert sentence embedding. *arXiv preprint arXiv:2007.01852*.

Suchin Gururangan, Ana Marasović, Swabha Swayamdipta, Kyle Lo, Iz Beltagy, Doug Downey, and Noah A. Smith. 2020. Don't stop pretraining: Adapt language models to domains and tasks. In *Proceedings of the 58th Annual Meeting of the Association for Computational Linguistics*, pages 8342–8360, Online. Association for Computational Linguistics.

Kai Hakala and Sampo Pyysalo. 2019. Biomedical named entity recognition with multilingual bert. In *Proceedings of the 5th workshop on BioNLP open shared tasks*, pages 56–61.

Ashkan Kazemi, Kiran Garimella, Devin Gaffney, and Scott A Hale. 2021. Claim matching beyond english to scale global fact-checking. *arXiv preprint arXiv:2106.00853*.

Dilek Küçük, Guillaume Jacquet, and Ralf Steinberger. 2014. Named entity recognition on turkish tweets. In *Proceedings of the Ninth International Conference on Language Resources and Evaluation (LREC'14)*, pages 450–454.

Sneha Kudugunta, Ankur Bapna, Isaac Caswell, and Orhan Firat. 2019. Investigating multilingual NMT representations at scale. In *Proceedings of the 2019 Conference on Empirical Methods in Natural Language Processing and the 9th International Joint Conference on Natural Language Processing (EMNLP-IJCNLP)*, pages 1565–1575, Hong Kong, China. Association for Computational Linguistics.

Chen Liang, Yue Yu, Haoming Jiang, Siawpeng Er, Ruijia Wang, Tuo Zhao, and Chao Zhang. 2020. Bond: Bert-assisted open-domain named entity recognition with distant supervision. In *Proceedings of the 26th ACM SIGKDD International Conference on Knowledge Discovery & Data Mining*, pages 1054–1064.

Ilya Loshchilov and Frank Hutter. 2019. Decoupled weight decay regularization. In *International Conference on Learning Representations*.

Thomas Mandl, Sandip Modha, Gautam Kishore Shahi, Hiren Madhu, Shrey Satapara, Prasenjit Majumder, Johannes Schaefer, Tharindu Ranasinghe, Marcos Zampieri, Durgesh Nandini, et al. 2021. Overview of the hasoc subtrack at fire 2021: Hate speech and offensive content identification in english and indo-aryan languages. *arXiv preprint arXiv:2112.09301*.

Shubhanshu Mishra. 2019. Multi-dataset-multi-task Neural Sequence Tagging for Information Extraction from Tweets. In *Proceedings of the 30th ACM Conference on Hypertext and Social Media - HT '19*, pages 283–284, New York, New York, USA. ACM Press.

Shubhanshu Mishra and Jana Diesner. 2016. Semi-supervised Named Entity Recognition in noisy-text. In *Proceedings of the 2nd Workshop on Noisy User-generated Text (WNUT)*, pages 203–212, Osaka, Japan. The COLING 2016 Organizing Committee.

Shubhanshu Mishra and Aria Haghighi. 2021. Improved multilingual language model pretraining for social media text via translation pair prediction. In *Proceedings of the Seventh Workshop on Noisy User-generated Text (W-NUT 2021)*, pages 381–388, Online. Association for Computational Linguistics.

Clemens Neudecker. 2016. An open corpus for named entity recognition in historic newspapers. In *Proceedings of the Tenth International Conference on Language Resources and Evaluation (LREC 2016)*, Paris, France. European Language Resources Association (ELRA).

Dat Quoc Nguyen, Thanh Vu, and Anh Tuan Nguyen. 2020. BERTweet: A pre-trained language model for English tweets. In *Proceedings of the 2020 Conference on Empirical Methods in Natural Language Processing: System Demonstrations*, pages 9–14, Online. Association for Computational Linguistics.

Joel Nothman, Nicky Ringland, Will Radford, Tara Murphy, and James R Curran. 2013. Learning multilingual named entity recognition from wikipedia. *Artificial Intelligence*, 194:151–175.

Xiaoman Pan, Boliang Zhang, Jonathan May, Joel Nothman, Kevin Knight, and Heng Ji. 2017. Cross-lingual name tagging and linking for 282 languages. In *Proceedings of the 55th Annual Meeting of the Association for Computational Linguistics (Volume 1: Long Papers)*, pages 1946–1958.

Minlong Peng, Xiaoyu Xing, Qi Zhang, Jinlan Fu, and Xuanjing Huang. 2019. Distantly supervised named entity recognition using positive-unlabeled learning. *arXiv preprint arXiv:1906.01378*.

Telmo Pires, Eva Schlinger, and Dan Garrette. 2019. How multilingual is multilingual BERT? In *Proceedings of the 57th Annual Meeting of the Association for Computational Linguistics*, pages 4996–5001, Florence, Italy. Association for Computational Linguistics.

Afshin Rahimi, Yuan Li, and Trevor Cohn. 2019. Massively multilingual transfer for NER. In *Proceedings of the 57th Annual Meeting of the Association for Computational Linguistics*, pages 151–164, Florence, Italy. Association for Computational Linguistics.

Anil Kumar Singh. 2008. Named entity recognition for south and south east asian languages: taking stock. In *Proceedings of the IJCNLP-08 Workshop on Named Entity Recognition for South and South East Asian Languages*.

Xu Tan, Jiale Chen, Di He, Yingce Xia, Tao Qin, and Tie-Yan Liu. 2019. Multilingual neural machine translation with language clustering. In *Proceedings of the 2019 Conference on Empirical Methods in Natural Language Processing and the 9th International Joint Conference on Natural Language Processing (EMNLP-IJCNLP)*, pages 963–973, Hong Kong, China. Association for Computational Linguistics.

Erik F. Tjong Kim Sang and Fien De Meulder. 2003. Introduction to the CoNLL-2003 shared task: Language-independent named entity recognition. In *Proceedings of the Seventh Conference on Natural Language Learning at HLT-NAACL 2003*, pages 142–147.

Denny Vrandečić and Markus Krötzsch. 2014. Wikidata: a free collaborative knowledgebase. *Communications of the ACM*, 57(10):78–85.

Leigh Weston, Vahe Tshitoyan, John Dagdelen, Olga Kononova, Amalie Trewartha, Kristin A Persson, Gerbrand Ceder, and Anubhav Jain. 2019. Named entity recognition and normalization applied to large-scale information extraction from the materials science literature. *Journal of chemical information and modeling*, 59(9):3692–3702.

Dian Yu, Taiqi He, and Kenji Sagae. 2021. Language embeddings for typology and cross-lingual transfer learning. In *Proceedings of the 59th Annual Meeting of the Association for Computational Linguistics and the 11th International Joint Conference on Natural Language Processing (Volume 1: Long Papers)*, pages 7210–7225, Online. Association for Computational Linguistics.

# Average Is Not Enough: Caveats of Multilingual Evaluation

**Matúš Pikuliak** and **Marián Šimko**
Kempelen Institute of Intelligent Technologies
firstname.surname@kinit.sk

## Abstract

This position paper discusses the problem of multilingual evaluation. Using simple statistics, such as average language performance, might inject linguistic biases in favor of dominant language families into evaluation methodology. We argue that a qualitative analysis informed by comparative linguistics is needed for multilingual results to detect this kind of bias. We show in our case study that results in published works can indeed be linguistically biased and we demonstrate that visualization based on URIEL typological database can detect it.

## 1 Introduction

The linguistic diversity of NLP research is growing (Joshi et al., 2020; Pikuliak et al., 2021) thanks to improvements of various multilingual technologies, such as machine translation (Arivazhagan et al., 2019), multilingual language models (Devlin et al., 2019; Conneau and Lample, 2019), cross-lingual transfer learning (Pikuliak et al., 2021) or language independent representations (Ruder et al., 2019). It is now possible to create well-performing multilingual methods for many tasks. When dealing with multilingual methods, we need to be able to evaluate how good they really are, i.e. how effective they are on a wide variety of typologically diverse languages. Consider the two methods shown in Figure 1 (a). Without looking at the particular languages, *Method A* seems better. It has better results for the majority of languages and its average performance is better as well. However, the trio of languages, where *Method A* is better, are in fact all very similar Iberian languages, while the fourth language is Indo-Iranian. Is the *Method A* actually better, or is it better only for Iberian? Simple average is often used in practice without considering the linguistic diversity of the underlying selection of languages, despite the fact that many corpora and datasets are biased in favor of historically dominant languages and language families.

Additionally, as the number of languages increases, it is harder and harder to notice phenomena such as this. Consider the comparison of two sets of results in Table 1. With 41 languages it is cognitively hard to discover various relations between the languages and their results, even if one has the necessary linguistic knowledge.

In this position paper, we argue that it is not the best practice to compare multilingual methods only with simple statistics, such as average. Commonly used simple evaluation protocols might bias research in favor of dominant languages and in turn hurt historically marginalized languages. Instead, we propose to consider using qualitative results analysis that takes linguistic typology (Ponti et al., 2019) and comparative linguistics into account as an additional sanity check. We believe that this is an often overlooked tool in our research toolkit that should be used more to ensure that we are able to properly interpret results from multilingual evaluation and detect various linguistic biases and problems. In addition to this discussion, which we consider a contribution in itself, we also propose a visualization based on URIEL typological database (Littell et al., 2017) as an example of such qualitative analysis, and we show that it is able to discover linguistic biases in published results.

## 2 Related Work

**Linguistic biases in NLP.** Bender (2009) postulated that research driven mainly by evaluation in English will become biased in favor of this language and it might not be particularly language independent. Even in recent years, popular techniques such as *word2vec* or *Byte Pair Encoding* were shown to have worse performance on morphologically rich languages (Bojanowski et al., 2017; Park et al., 2020). Similarly, cross-lingual word embeddings are usually constructed with English as a default hub language, even though this might hurt many languages (Anastasopoulos and Neubig,



*Proceedings of the The 2nd Workshop on Multi-lingual Representation Learning (MRL)*, pages 125 - 133
December 8, 2022 ©2022 Association for Computational Linguistics

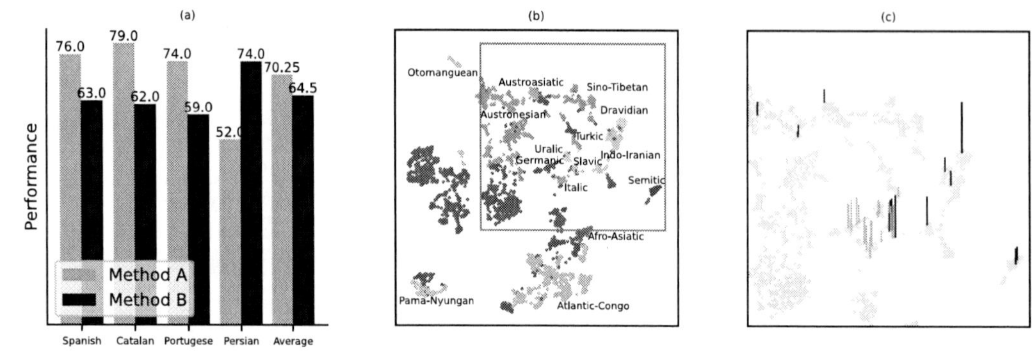


Figure 1: *(a)* Comparison of two methods on unbalanced set of languages. *(b)* Visualization of URIEL languages with certain language families color-coded. *(c)* Comparison of two methods from Rahimi et al. This uses the same map of languages as *b*, but the view is zoomed.

| Language | afr | arb | bul | ben | bos | cat | ces | dan | deu | ell | eng | spa | est | pes | fin | fra | heb | hin | hrv | hun | ind |
|---|---|---|---|---|---|---|---|---|---|---|---|---|---|---|---|---|---|---|---|---|---|
| Method A | 74 | 54 | 54 | 60 | 77 | 79 | 72 | 79 | 64 | 34 | 57 | 76 | 71 | 52 | 69 | 73 | 46 | 58 | 77 | 69 | 61 |
| Method B | 59 | 64 | 61 | 70 | 63 | 62 | 62 | 62 | 58 | 61 | 47 | 63 | 64 | 74 | 67 | 57 | 53 | 68 | 61 | 59 | 67 |
| Language | ita | lit | lav | mkd | zlm | nld | nor | pol | por | ron | rus | slk | slv | alb | swe | tam | tgl | tur | ukr | vie | **AVG** |
| Method A | 76 | 75 | 67 | 48 | 63 | 78 | 77 | 77 | 74 | 74 | 36 | 76 | 76 | 76 | 69 | 25 | 57 | 67 | 49 | 48 | 64.5 |
| Method B | 60 | 62 | 68 | 67 | 66 | 59 | 65 | 61 | 59 | 66 | 53 | 62 | 64 | 69 | 69 | 54 | 66 | 61 | 60 | 55 | 62.1 |

Table 1: Comparison of two methods from Rahimi et al. (2019).

2020). Perhaps if the practice of research was less Anglocentric, different methods and techniques would have become popular instead. Our work is deeply related to issues like these. We show that multilingual evaluation with an unbalanced selection of languages might cause similar symptoms.

**Benchmarking.** Using benchmarks is a practice that came under a lot of scrutiny in the NLP community recently. Benchmark evaluation was said to encourage spurious data overfitting (Kavumba et al., 2019), encourage metric gaming (Thomas and Uminsky, 2020) or lead the research away from general human-like linguistic intelligence (Linzen, 2020). Similarly, benchmarks are criticized for being predominantly focused on performance, while neglecting several other important properties, e.g. prediction cost or model robustness (Ethayarajh and Jurafsky, 2020). Average in particular was shown to have several issues with robustness that can be addressed by using pair-wise instance evaluation (Peyrard et al., 2021). To address these issues, some benchmarks refuse to use aggregating scores and instead report multiple metrics at the same time leaving interpretation of the results to the reader. Gehrmann et al. (2021) is one such benchmark, which proposes to use visualizations to help the intepretation. In this work, we also use visualizations to similar effect.

## 3 Multilingual Evaluation Strategies

When comparing multilingual methods with nontrivial number of languages, it is cognitively hard to keep track of various linguistic aspects, such as language families, writing systems, typological properties, etc. Researchers often use various simplifying strategies instead:

**Aggregating metrics.** Aggregating metrics, such as average performance or a number of languages where a certain method achieves the best results provide some information, but as we illustrated in Figure 1 (a), they might not tell the whole story. By aggregating results we lose important information about individual languages and language families. Commonly used statistics usually do not take underlying linguistic diversity into account. This might lead to unwanted phenomena, such as bias in favor of dominant language families. The encoded values of the aggregating metrics might not align with the values we want to express. Average is an example of utilitarianist world view, while using minimal performance might be considered to be a prioritarianist approach (Choudhury and Deshpande, 2021). Even though analyzing the values encoded in metrics is a step towards a fairer evaluation, they still miss a more fine-grained details of the results.

**Aggregated metrics for different groups.** Another option is to calculate statistics for certain linguistic families or groups. These are steps in the right direction, as they provide a more fine-grained picture, but there are still issues left. It is not clear which families should be selected, e.g. should we average all Indo-European languages or should we average across subfamilies, such as Slavic or Germanic. This selection is ultimately opinionated and different selections might show us different views of the results. In addition, aggregating across families might still hide variance within these families. Grouping languages by the size of available datasets (e.g. low resource vs. high resource) shows us how the models deal with data scarcity, but the groups might still be linguistically unbalanced.

**Balanced language sampling.** Another option is to construct a multilingual dataset so that it is linguistically balanced. This process is called *language sampling* (Rijkhoff et al., 1993; Miestamo et al., 2016). In practice, this means that a small number of representative languages is selected for each family. The problem with dominant families is solved because we control the number of languages per family. However, selecting which families should be represented and then selecting languages within these families is again an opinionated process. Different families and their subfamilies might have different degrees of diversity. Different selections might favor different linguistic properties and results might vary between them. It is also not clear, how exhaustive given selection is, i.e. how much of the linguistic variety has been covered. Some of the existing works mention their selection criteria: Longpre et al. (2020) count how many speakers the selection covers, Clark et al. (2020) use a set of selected typological properties, Ponti et al. (2020) use the so called *variety language sampling*. Publishing the criteria allows us to do a post-hoc analysis in the future to evaluate, how well did these criteria work.

**Qualitative analysis** In this paper, we argue that qualitative analysis is an often overlooked, yet irreplaceable evaluation technique. In the following section, we will present our case study of how to perform qualitative analysis.

## 4 Case Study: Qualitative Analysis through Visualization

In this section we show how to perform a qualitative analysis of multilingual results with a visualization technique based on URIEL typographic database. We show that using this we can (1) uncover linguistic biases in the results, and (2) make sense of results from non-trivial number of languages. As case study, we study results from Rahimi et al. (2019). Our goal is not to evaluate particular methods from this paper, but to demonstrate how linguistically-informed analysis might help researchers gain insights into their results. We analyze the results from this paper not because we want to criticize it, but because it is a well-written paper that actually attempts to do multilingual evaluation for non-trivial number of languages with significantly different methods. The linguistic biases we uncover are already partially discussed in the paper. Here, we only show how to effectively perform qualitative analysis and uncover these biases with appropriate visualization. Appendix A shows similar analysis for another paper (Heinzerling and Strube, 2019) where linguistic biases are visible.

We use URIEL, a typological language database that consists of 289 syntactic and phonological binary features for 3718 languages. We use UMAP feature reduction algorithm (McInnes and Healy, 2018) to create a 2D typological language space. This map is shown in Figure 1 (b). The map is interactive and allows for dynamic filtering of languages and families, as well as inspection of individual languages and their properties.[1] Each point is one language and selected language families are color-coded in the figure. Even though URIEL features used for dimensionality reduction do not contain information about language families, genealogically close languages naturally form clusters in our visualization. Certain geographical relations are captured as well, e.g. Sudanic and Chadic languages are neighboring clusters, despite being from different language families. This evokes the linguistic tradition of grouping languages according to the regions and macroregions. This shows that our visualization is able to capture both intrafamiliar and interfamiliar similarities of languages and is thus appropriate for our use-case.

We visualize results from Rahimi et al. (2019) on this linguistic map. Rahimi et al. use Wikipedia-

[1] Code available at GitHub

based corpus for NER, and they compare various cross-lingual transfer learning algorithms for 41 languages. They use an unbalanced set of languages, where the three most dominant language families – Germanic, Italic and Slavic – make up 55% of all languages. See Appendix A for more details about the paper. We use our URIEL map to visualize a comparison between a pair of methods on all 41 languages from Table 1. In Figure 1 (c) we compare two methods – *Method A* – cross-lingual transfer learning methods using multiple source languages (average performance 64.5), and seemingly worse *Method B* – a low-resource training without any form of cross-lingual supervision (average performance 62.1). We use the same URIEL map, but we superimpose the relative performance of the two methods as colored columns. Orange columns on this map show languages where *Method A* performs better, while blue columns show the same for *Method B*. Height of each column shows how big the relative difference in performance is between the two methods. I.e. taller orange columns mean dominant *A*, taller blue columns mean dominant *B*.

We can now clearly see that there is a pattern in the location of the colored columns. Using average as evaluation measure, *Method A* seems better overall. Here we can see that it is only better in one particular cluster of languages – the cluster of orange columns. All these are related European languages. Most of them are Germanic, Italic or Slavic, with some exceptions being languages that are not Indo-European, but are nevertheless geographical neighbors, such as Hungarian. On the other hand, all the non-European languages actually prefer *Method B*. These are the blue columns scattered in the rest of the space that consists of languages such as Arabic (Semitic), Chinese (Sino-Tibetan) or Tamil (Dravidian).

This shows important fact about the two methods that was hidden by using average. Cross-lingual supervision seemed to have better performance, but it has better performance only in the dominant cluster of similar languages where the cross-lingual supervision is more viable. Other languages, would actually prefer using monolingual low-resource learning, as they are not able to learn from other languages that easily. In this case, average is overestimating the value of cross-lingual learning for non-European languages. This overestimation might cause harm to these languages.

We can also see that there are some exceptions – the blue columns in the orange cluster. These exceptions are Greek, Russian, Macedonian, Bulgarian and Ukrainian – all Indo-European languages that use non-Latin scripts. In this case, different writing systems are probably cause of additional linguistic bias. It might be hard to notice this pattern by simply looking at the table of results, but here we can quickly identify the languages as outliers and then it is easy to realize what they have in common.

Note that we do not expect to see this level of linguistic bias in most papers and we have cherry-picked this particular methods from this particular paper because they demonstrate the case when the linguistic bias in the results is the most obvious. This is caused mainly by unbalanced selection of languages on Wikipedia and in a sense unfair comparison of cross-lingual supervision with low resource learning.

## 5 Conclusions

Multilinguality in NLP is becoming more common and methodological practice is sometimes lagging behind (Artetxe et al., 2020; Keung et al., 2020; Bender, 2011). Making progress will be inherently hard without proper evaluation methodology. In this work, we argue for necessity for qualitative results analysis and we showed how to use such analysis to improve the evaluation with interactive visualizations. In our case study, we were able to uncover linguistic biases in published results.

Considering the practice in machine learning and NLP, it might be tempting to reduce a multilingual method performance to a single number. However, we believe that intricacies of multilingual evaluation can not be reduced so easily. There are too many different dimensions that need to be taken into consideration and NLP researchers should understand these dimensions. We believe that appropriate level of training in various linguistic fields, such as typology or comparative linguistics, is necessary for proper understanding of multilingual results and for proper qualitative analysis. We argue that qualitative analysis is an oft overlooked approach to results analysis that should be utilized more to prevent various distortions in how we understand linguistic implications of our results.

## 6 Ethical Considerations

Much of current NLP research is focused on only a small handful of languages. Communities of some language users are left behind, as a result of data scarcity. We believe that our paper might have positive societal impact. It focuses on the issues of these marginalized languages and communities. Following our recommendations might lead to a more diverse and fair multilingual evaluation both in research and in industry. This might in turn led to better models, applications and ultimately quality of life changes for some.

## Acknowledgments

This research was partially supported by DisAi, a project funded by Horizon Europe under GA No. 101079164.

## References

Antonios Anastasopoulos and Graham Neubig. 2020. Should all cross-lingual embeddings speak English? In *Proceedings of the 58th Annual Meeting of the Association for Computational Linguistics*, pages 8658–8679, Online. Association for Computational Linguistics.

Naveen Arivazhagan, Ankur Bapna, Orhan Firat, Dmitry Lepikhin, Melvin Johnson, Maxim Krikun, Mia Xu Chen, Yuan Cao, George F. Foster, Colin Cherry, Wolfgang Macherey, Zhifeng Chen, and Yonghui Wu. 2019. Massively multilingual neural machine translation in the wild: Findings and challenges. *CoRR*, abs/1907.05019.

Mikel Artetxe, Sebastian Ruder, Dani Yogatama, Gorka Labaka, and Eneko Agirre. 2020. A call for more rigor in unsupervised cross-lingual learning. In *Proceedings of the 58th Annual Meeting of the Association for Computational Linguistics*, pages 7375–7388, Online. Association for Computational Linguistics.

Emily M. Bender. 2009. Linguistically naïve != language independent: Why NLP needs linguistic typology. In *Proceedings of the EACL 2009 Workshop on the Interaction between Linguistics and Computational Linguistics: Virtuous, Vicious or Vacuous?*, pages 26–32, Athens, Greece. Association for Computational Linguistics.

Emily M Bender. 2011. On achieving and evaluating language-independence in nlp. *Linguistic Issues in Language Technology*, 6(3):1–26.

Piotr Bojanowski, Edouard Grave, Armand Joulin, and Tomas Mikolov. 2017. Enriching word vectors with subword information. *Transactions of the Association for Computational Linguistics*, 5:135–146.

Monojit Choudhury and Amit Deshpande. 2021. How linguistically fair are multilingual pre-trained language models? In *Thirty-Fifth AAAI Conference on Artificial Intelligence, AAAI 2021, Thirty-Third Conference on Innovative Applications of Artificial Intelligence, IAAI 2021, The Eleventh Symposium on Educational Advances in Artificial Intelligence, EAAI 2021, Virtual Event, February 2-9, 2021*, pages 12710–12718. AAAI Press.

Jonathan H. Clark, Eunsol Choi, Michael Collins, Dan Garrette, Tom Kwiatkowski, Vitaly Nikolaev, and Jennimaria Palomaki. 2020. TyDi QA: A benchmark for information-seeking question answering in typologically diverse languages. *Transactions of the Association for Computational Linguistics*, 8:454–470.

Alexis Conneau and Guillaume Lample. 2019. Cross-lingual language model pretraining. In *Advances in Neural Information Processing Systems 32: Annual Conference on Neural Information Processing Systems 2019, NeurIPS 2019, December 8-14, 2019, Vancouver, BC, Canada*, pages 7057–7067.

Jacob Devlin, Ming-Wei Chang, Kenton Lee, and Kristina Toutanova. 2019. BERT: Pre-training of deep bidirectional transformers for language understanding. In *Proceedings of the 2019 Conference of the North American Chapter of the Association for Computational Linguistics: Human Language Technologies, Volume 1 (Long and Short Papers)*, pages 4171–4186, Minneapolis, Minnesota. Association for Computational Linguistics.

Kawin Ethayarajh and Dan Jurafsky. 2020. Utility is in the eye of the user: A critique of NLP leaderboards. In *Proceedings of the 2020 Conference on Empirical Methods in Natural Language Processing (EMNLP)*, pages 4846–4853, Online. Association for Computational Linguistics.

Sebastian Gehrmann, Tosin P. Adewumi, Karmanya Aggarwal, Pawan Sasanka Ammanamanchi, Aremu Anuoluwapo, Antoine Bosselut, Khyathi Raghavi Chandu, Miruna-Adriana Clinciu, Dipanjan Das, Kaustubh D. Dhole, Wanyu Du, Esin Durmus, Ondrej Dusek, Chris Emezue, Varun Gangal, Cristina Garbacea, Tatsunori Hashimoto, Yufang Hou, Yacine Jernite, Harsh Jhamtani, Yangfeng Ji, Shailza Jolly, Dhruv Kumar, Faisal Ladhak, Aman Madaan, Mounica Maddela, Khyati Mahajan, Saad Mahamood, Bodhisattwa Prasad Majumder, Pedro Henrique Martins, Angelina McMillan-Major, Simon Mille, Emiel van Miltenburg, Moin Nadeem, Shashi Narayan, Vitaly Nikolaev, Rubungo Andre Niyongabo, Salomey Osei, Ankur P. Parikh, Laura Perez-Beltrachini, Niranjan Ramesh Rao, Vikas Raunak, Juan Diego Rodriguez, Sashank Santhanam, João Sedoc, Thibault Sellam, Samira Shaikh, Anastasia Shimorina, Marco Antonio Sobrevilla Cabezudo, Hendrik Strobelt, Nishant Subramani, Wei Xu, Diyi Yang, Akhila Yerukola, and Jiawei Zhou. 2021. The GEM benchmark: Natural language generation, its evaluation and metrics. *CoRR*, abs/2102.01672.

Benjamin Heinzerling and Michael Strube. 2019. Sequence tagging with contextual and non-contextual subword representations: A multilingual evaluation.

In *Proceedings of the 57th Annual Meeting of the Association for Computational Linguistics*, pages 273–291, Florence, Italy. Association for Computational Linguistics.

Pratik Joshi, Sebastin Santy, Amar Budhiraja, Kalika Bali, and Monojit Choudhury. 2020. The state and fate of linguistic diversity and inclusion in the NLP world. In *Proceedings of the 58th Annual Meeting of the Association for Computational Linguistics*, pages 6282–6293, Online. Association for Computational Linguistics.

Pride Kavumba, Naoya Inoue, Benjamin Heinzerling, Keshav Singh, Paul Reisert, and Kentaro Inui. 2019. When choosing plausible alternatives, clever hans can be clever. In *Proceedings of the First Workshop on Commonsense Inference in Natural Language Processing*, pages 33–42, Hong Kong, China. Association for Computational Linguistics.

Phillip Keung, Yichao Lu, Julian Salazar, and Vikas Bhardwaj. 2020. Don't use English dev: On the zero-shot cross-lingual evaluation of contextual embeddings. In *Proceedings of the 2020 Conference on Empirical Methods in Natural Language Processing (EMNLP)*, pages 549–554, Online. Association for Computational Linguistics.

Tal Linzen. 2020. How can we accelerate progress towards human-like linguistic generalization? In *Proceedings of the 58th Annual Meeting of the Association for Computational Linguistics*, pages 5210–5217, Online. Association for Computational Linguistics.

Patrick Littell, David R. Mortensen, Ke Lin, Katherine Kairis, Carlisle Turner, and Lori Levin. 2017. URIEL and lang2vec: Representing languages as typological, geographical, and phylogenetic vectors. In *Proceedings of the 15th Conference of the European Chapter of the Association for Computational Linguistics: Volume 2, Short Papers*, pages 8–14, Valencia, Spain. Association for Computational Linguistics.

Shayne Longpre, Yi Lu, and Joachim Daiber. 2020. MKQA: A linguistically diverse benchmark for multilingual open domain question answering. *CoRR*, abs/2007.15207.

Leland McInnes and John Healy. 2018. UMAP: uniform manifold approximation and projection for dimension reduction. *CoRR*, abs/1802.03426.

Matti Miestamo, Dik Bakker, and Antti Arppe. 2016. Sampling for variety. *Linguistic Typology*, 20(2):233–296.

Hyunji Hayley Park, Katherine J. Zhang, Coleman Haley, Kenneth Steimel, Han Liu, and Lane Schwartz. 2020. Morphology matters: A multilingual language modeling analysis. *CoRR*, abs/2012.06262.

Maxime Peyrard, Wei Zhao, Steffen Eger, and Robert West. 2021. Better than average: Paired evaluation of NLP systems. In *Proceedings of the 59th Annual Meeting of the Association for Computational Linguistics and the 11th International Joint Conference on Natural Language Processing (Volume 1: Long Papers)*, pages 2301–2315, Online. Association for Computational Linguistics.

Matúš Pikuliak, Marián Šimko, and Mária Bieliková. 2021. Cross-lingual learning for text processing: A survey. *Expert Systems with Applications*, 165:113765.

Edoardo Maria Ponti, Goran Glavaš, Olga Majewska, Qianchu Liu, Ivan Vulić, and Anna Korhonen. 2020. XCOPA: A multilingual dataset for causal commonsense reasoning. In *Proceedings of the 2020 Conference on Empirical Methods in Natural Language Processing (EMNLP)*, pages 2362–2376, Online. Association for Computational Linguistics.

Edoardo Maria Ponti, Helen O'Horan, Yevgeni Berzak, Ivan Vulić, Roi Reichart, Thierry Poibeau, Ekaterina Shutova, and Anna Korhonen. 2019. Modeling language variation and universals: A survey on typological linguistics for natural language processing. *Computational Linguistics*, 45(3):559–601.

Afshin Rahimi, Yuan Li, and Trevor Cohn. 2019. Massively multilingual transfer for NER. In *Proceedings of the 57th Annual Meeting of the Association for Computational Linguistics*, pages 151–164, Florence, Italy. Association for Computational Linguistics.

Jan Rijkhoff, Dik Bakker, Kees Hengeveld, and Peter Kahrel. 1993. A method of language sampling. *Studies in Language. International Journal sponsored by the Foundation "Foundations of Language"*, 17(1):169–203.

Sebastian Ruder, Ivan Vulic, and Anders Søgaard. 2019. A survey of cross-lingual word embedding models. *Journal of Artificial Intelligence Research*, 65:569–631.

Rachel Thomas and David Uminsky. 2020. The problem with metrics is a fundamental problem for AI. *CoRR*, abs/2002.08512.

## A Details of Analysed Papers

In this appendix, we provide additional information about papers we analysed.

### A.1 Rahimi et al.

This is the paper we used for demonstration in the main paper in Section 4. We use results reported in Table 4 in their paper. The languages they use are listed here in Table 2. We can see the apparent dominance of Indo-European languages. There are 14 different methods listed in their paper. We compare the results for these methods in Figure 2. There we can see how the average results for individual methods compare with the average results for non-GIS (Germanic-Italic-Slavic) languages. The numbers correspond to the order of methods listed in the original paper. The two methods compared in Figure 1 (c) are shown as blue and orange, respectively. The orange *Method A* is $\texttt{BEA}^{\texttt{tok}}$ in the original paper. The blue *Method B* is called `LSup`. We can see the linguistic bias with this simplistic view as well. All the cross-lingual learning based methods have worse non-GIS results than methods that do not use cross-lingual learning (methods 1 and 2). However, this analysis can not replace the visualization we propose in Section 4. It provides a GIS-centered view, but it can not capture other sources of bias. For example, it does not show various outliers that were seen in the visualization, such as Uralic languages that behave similarly to GIS languages, or Slavic languages with Cyrilic alphabet that behave differently than other Slavic languages.

| ISO | Language | Subfamily | Family |
|---|---|---|---|
| bul | Bulgarian | Slavic | Indo-European |
| bos | Bosnian | | |
| ces | Czech | | |
| hrv | Croatian | | |
| mkd | Macedonian | | |
| pol | Polish | | |
| rus | Russian | | |
| slk | Slovak | | |
| slv | Slovenian | | |
| ukr | Ukrainian | | |
| afr | Afrikkans | Germanic | |
| dan | Danish | | |
| deu | German | | |
| nld | Dutch | | |
| nor | Norwegian | | |
| swe | Swedish | | |
| cat | Catalan | Italic | |
| fra | French | | |
| ita | Italian | | |
| por | Portugese | | |
| rom | Romanina | | |
| spa | Spanish | | |
| ben | Bengali | Indo-Iranian | |
| hin | Hindi | | |
| pes | Iranian Persian | | |
| lit | Lithuanian | Baltic | |
| lav | Latvian | | |
| ell | Greek | | |
| alb | Albanian | | |
| est | Estonian | | Uralic |
| fin | Finnish | | |
| hun | Hungarian | | |
| ind | Indonesian | | Austronesian |
| tgl | Tagalog | | |
| zlm | Malay | | |
| arb | Standard Arabic | | Afro-Asiatic |
| heb | Hebrew | | |
| vie | Vietnamese | | Austroasiatic |
| tam | Tamil | | Davidian |
| tur | Turkish | | Turkic |

Table 2: Languages used in Rahimi et al..

### A.2 Heinzerling and Strube

Similar linguistic biases can be seen in Heinzerling and Strube as well. They evaluate various representations performance on POS tagging and NER. In Figure 3 we compare POS accuracy of a multilingual model with a shared embedding vocabulary (average performance 96.6, `MultiBPEmb +char +finetune` in the original paper) and a simple BiLSTM baseline with no transfer supervision (average performance 96.4, `BiLSTM` in the original paper). Orange columns are for languages that prefer the multilingual model, blue columns prefer the baseline. In this case, almost all orange columns are in fact GIS languages. Other languages are having significantly worse results with this method and most of them actually prefer the simple baseline with no cross-lingual supervision. This shows the limitations of proposed multilingual

| ISO | Language | Subfamily | Family |
|---|---|---|---|
| dan | Danish | Germanic | Indo-European |
| deu | German | | |
| eng | English | | |
| nld | Dutch | | |
| nor | Norwegian | | |
| swe | Swedish | | |
| bul | Bulgarian | Slavic | |
| ces | Czech | | |
| hrv | Croatian | | |
| pol | Polish | | |
| slv | Slovenian | | |
| fra | Frech | Italic | |
| ita | Italian | | |
| por | Portugese | | |
| spa | Spanish | | |
| hin | Hindi | Indo-Iranian | |
| pes | Iranian Persian | | |
| eus | Basque | | Isolate |
| fin | Finnish | | Uralic |
| heb | Hebrew | | Afro-Asiatic |
| ind | Indonesian | | Austronesian |

Table 3: Languages used in Heinzerling and Strube.

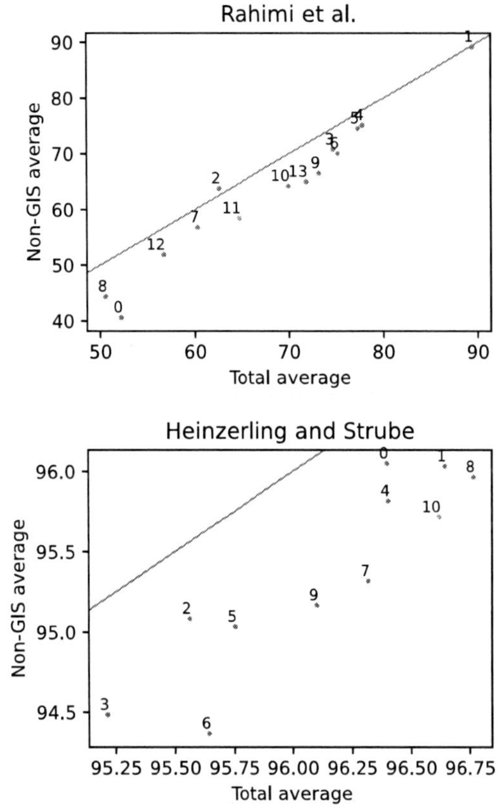


Figure 2: Comparison of method performance. The relation between global average and average on non-GIS languages is shown. Each point represents one method from the papers.

supervision for outlier languages.

We use results reported in Table 5 in their paper. The languages they use are listed here in Table 3. Again, we can see an apparent dominance of GIS languages. There are 11 different methods listed in their paper. We omitted results for additional 6 low resource languages reported in Table 7, because only 4 out of 11 methods were used there. We compare the results for these methods in Figure 2, similarly as in the previous paper. The orange point is the multilingual model, the blue point is the baseline. Now we can see that the BiLSTM baseline is actually the best performing method for non-GIS languages.

## B Hyperparameters

We use UMAP python library[2] with the following hyperparameters:

[2]`umap-learn.readthedocs.io`

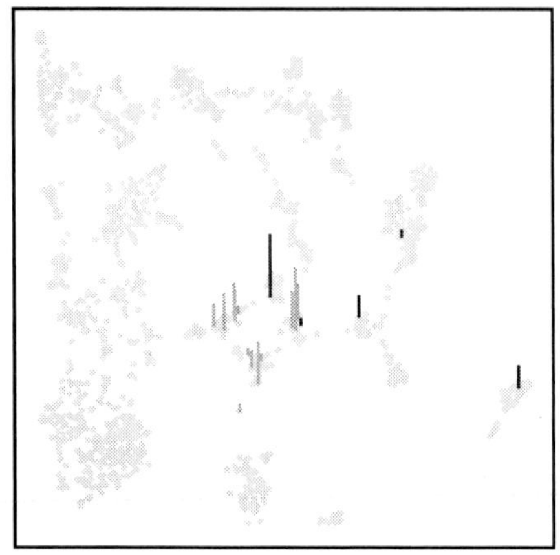

Figure 3: Comparison of two methods from Heinzerling and Strube.

- Number of neighbours (`n_neighbors`): 15
- Distance metric (`metric`): cosine
- Minimal distance (`min_dist`): 0.5
- Random see (`random_state`): 1

## C Additional Visualizations

In this Section we show several additional possibilities of using URIEL map of languages to visualize results from multilingual evaluation. Our goal here is to propose additional techniques that can be used for qualitative analysis apart from the comparison of two methods used in Figure 1 in the main body of this paper. This is not an exhaustive list of visualizations. We believe that many other types of visualization can be done using this type of qualitative analysis, based on the needs and requirements of the user.

In Figure 4 we show how to compare more than two methods by visualizing the performance for each method separately. We have created a separate plot for three methods and we can compare their performance visually. We can see that `HSup` method has overall stable high performance. `LSup` has worse performance, but its still quite balanced. Finally, `BWET` has similar performance as `LSup`, but we can see that there are regions where it fails, e.g. the languages in the rightmost part of the figure have visibly worse performance.

In Figure 5 we show yet another type of visualization. In this case, we simply visualize what method is the best performing for each language.

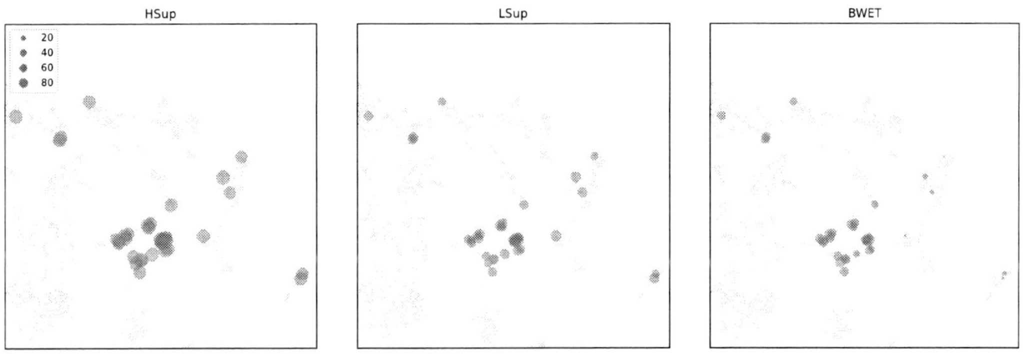


Figure 4: Comparison of multiple methods using size to mark method performance for individual languages. `HSup`, `LSup` and `BWET` are methods reported in (Rahimi et al., 2019).

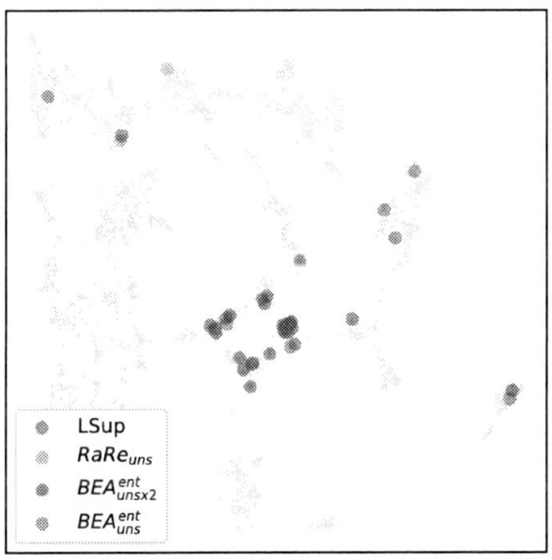


Figure 5: The best performing methods for various languages.

We compare methods using crosslingual supervision and low-resource training (`LSup`). From seven methods, only four achieved the best performance for at least one language and those are shown in the Figure. Again, we can see similar picture as before. One method ($BEA^{ent}_{uns\times2}$) is the best performing method taking average into account. However, in this visualization we can see that it is actually the best performing method only in the dominant cluster of European languages. Elsewhere, other methods perform better.

# The MRL 2022 Shared Task on Multilingual Clause-level Morphology

**Omer Goldman**[1] **Francesco Tinner**[2] **Hila Gonen**[5] **Benjamin Muller**[3]
**Victoria Basmov**[1] **Shadrack Kirimi**[4] **Lydia Nishimwe**[3] **Benoît Sagot**[3]
**Djamé Seddah**[3] **Reut Tsarfaty**[1] **Duygu Ataman**[6]
[1]Bar Ilan University [2]University of Amsterdam [3]Inria, Paris [4]Chuka University
[5]Paul G. Allen School of Computer Science & Engineering, University of Washington
[6]New York University

## Abstract

The 2022 Multilingual Representation Learning (MRL) Shared Task was dedicated to clause-level morphology. As the first ever benchmark that defines and evaluates morphology outside its traditional lexical boundaries, the shared task on multilingual clause-level morphology sets the scene for competition across different approaches to morphological modeling, with 3 clause-level sub-tasks: *morphological inflection, reinflection* and *analysis*, where systems are required to generate, manipulate or analyze simple sentences centered around a single content lexeme and a set of morphological features characterizing its syntactic clause. This year's tasks covered eight typologically distinct languages: English, French, German, Hebrew, Russian, Spanish, Swahili and Turkish. The tasks has received submissions of four systems from three teams which were compared to two baselines implementing prominent multilingual learning methods. The results show that modern NLP models are effective in solving morphological tasks even at the clause level. However, there is still room for improvement, especially in the task of morphological analysis.

## 1 Introduction

Universality is an important premise of many morphological datasets and shared tasks. Recent shared tasks of SIGMORPHON have introduced the notion of comparative analysis in morphological studies by incorporating up to 100 languages (McCarthy et al., 2019; Vylomova et al., 2020) in their evaluation benchmark, by providing all of them with data that is annotated according to a single universal schema (Sylak-Glassman, 2016). Systems that succeed in these tasks ideally should boast in their ability to handle various morphological phenomena observed in almost any language family on earth (Peters and Martins, 2020, inter alia).

However, as pointed out recently by Goldman and Tsarfaty (2022), the perceived universality of morphological tasks is impaired by the lack of a working definition of *a morphosyntactic word* (Haspelmath, 2011). Without such definition, the boundary between morphology and syntax is blurred and the assignment of linguistic phenomena to either morphological or syntactic data results in inconsistency across languages. Thus, limiting the scope of morphological tasks to white-spaced words creates an undue advantage to some languages based on their grammarian traditions, typological characteristics, and some other arbitrary factors.

For example, some languages, like English, are considered isolating and have word-level inflection tables of tiny size, while other languages, like Turkish, are considered agglutinative and have huge inflection tables. However, isolating and agglutinative languages largely differ orthographically rather than linguistically, as both types concatenate pieces of text. The universal benchmark presented here allows testing of both models and theories while ignoring orthographic characteristics like white-spaces and treats equally languages with varying typological characteristics.

In this shared task, we operationalize a more universally applicable and comprehensive approach to morphology by liberating the evaluated tasks from the ill-defined formal restrictions dictated by white-spaces. We start with a fix universal set of inflectional features[1] and inflect lemmas in all languages to all possible combinations of features, disregarding the number of white-spaced words required to express them orthographically. The features define fully-saturated clauses and the result is a data set of clauses organized in inflection tables and tasks that go beyond the word-level and include phenomena considered syntactic, such as word order manipulation and the like. We can thus test the submitted systems' ability to cope with these phenomena.

[1]The set of features used in constructing our data is detailed in Appendix A.



*Proceedings of the The 2nd Workshop on Multi-lingual Representation Learning (MRL)*, pages 134 - 146
December 8, 2022 ©2022 Association for Computational Linguistics

The shared task includes 3 sub-tasks: *inflection*, where systems are to generate simple clauses from a lemma and a set of morphological features; *reinflection*, where systems should manipulate a source clause to a target clause; and *analysis*, where the task is to output a lemma and a set of features given a clause. See Table 1 for example annotations. Together, these tasks examine every aspect of the ability of systems to deal with clause-level morphological constructions, moving from abstract representation to concrete text and back.

All three sub-tasks include evaluation data annotated in the following eight languages: English, French, German, Hebrew, Russian, Spanish, Swahili and Turkish, from four different language families. The variety of languages induces a plethora of alternations to be modeled by the submitted systems, from pronoun incorporation in Swahili to verb-splitting German, from ablaut-extensive Semitic morphology to highly agglutinative Turkish. However, in terms of dimensions of meaning, the data is extremely uniform across languages as all morphological features are implemented in our data if they are implemented in the language.

The results included in this shared task compare 4 submitted systems and 2 baseline systems with various characteristics, from rule-based systems to systems based on a large pretrained language models. The best performing system outperforms the best baseline and reduces the error rates by 3 to 8 fold, depending on the sub-task. Future editions of the task are intended to further expand the number of languages and the scope of the data for better alignment with real-world phenomena and distributions.

## 2 The Tasks

This shared task consists of three sub-tasks which test the ability of systems to deal with clause-level morphological data in multiple languages. In this Section we define and formalize the tasks, and in Table 1 we illustrate all three sub-tasks with concrete examples.

### 2.1 Tasks Description and formulation

Let $l$ be a lemma, $b$ be a feature bundle, and $f$ an inflected form. Crucially, $f$ may include zero or more white-space word delimiters. The *inflection* sub-task accepts a set of clause-level features and a verbal lemma as input $\langle l, b\rangle$, and requires the system to generate the desired output clause $\langle f\rangle$ that manifests these this lemma and inflectional features.

In the *reinflection* sub-task, each input item contains an example inflected form in a language accompanied by a set of morphological features that it realizes as well as a second set of features $\langle f_1, b_1, b_2\rangle$. The system is required to generate the the respective form $\langle f_2\rangle$ realizing this new set of features for the same lemma. It should do so without direct evidence of the lemma behind both forms.

Finally, the *analysis* sub-task evaluates the system performance in the opposite transformation of the inflection sub-task. That is, given a clause form $\langle f\rangle$ as input, the system needs to output its lemma and set of features being realized in this form $\langle l, b\rangle$.

The collection of the three sub-tasks aims to extensively assess the ability of a system to analyze and generate clause-level morphological data.

### 2.2 Evaluation

For all the tasks we provide the exact match accuracy between the predictions and the desired outputs.

However, systems' performance was ranked by another metric, varied by sub-task, that is more permissive and quantifies partial success. For the *inflection* and *reinflection* tasks we use an averaged edit distance between predictions and gold answers, a measure well-used in morphology to assess how close the predictions are to the ground truth on average (Cotterell et al., 2017, 2018, inter alia).

For the *analysis* task we used an F1 measure that takes into account the unordered nature of the outputs in this task. For each example we calculate the precision and recall of features in the prediction compared to the desired output, we then average the per-example F1 score over an entire set of examples.[2]

## 3 The Languages

Our selection of languages is diverse both typologically and genealogically. Most of the languages are Indo-European (English, French, German, Spanish and Russian), but we include languages from the Afro-Asiatic (Hebrew), Turkic (Turkish) and Atlantic-Congo (Swahili) families as well.

[2]For calculating this metric the lemma was treated as another feature but up-weighted and given an importance equal to 3 features.

| Task | **Model input** | | **Reference output** | |
|---|---|---|---|---|
| Inflection | take | IND;FUT;NOM(1,SG);ACC(3,SG,MASC) | I'll take him | |
| Reinflection | I'll take him | IND;FUT;NOM(1,SG);ACC(3,SG,MASC) | | |
| | | IND;PRS;NOM(1,PL);ACC(2);NEG | we don't take you | |
| Analysis | I'll take him | | take | IND;FUT;NOM(1,SG);ACC(3,SG,MASC) |

Table 1: Examples for the data format used for the evaluation of three sub-tasks. The inflection sub-task takes a lexeme and a set of tags in the given language and the model is required to produce the corresponding form. In the reinflection sub-task an inflected form accompanied by the sets of new features are input to the model, and a new form corresponding to the desired reinflection is produced. The analysis sub-task requires the model to discover the root and morphological features in a given sentence. In our annotations we use the Unimorph schema (Sylak-Glassman, 2016).

| **Language** | **Family** | **ISO 639-2** | **Annotators** |
|---|---|---|---|
| English | Indo-European | eng | Omer Goldman |
| French | Indo-European | fra | Benjamin Muller, Djame Seddah & Benoît Sagot |
| German | Indo-European | deu | Omer Goldman |
| Hebrew | Afro-Asiatic | heb | Omer Goldman |
| Russian | Indo-European | rus | Victoria Basmov |
| Spanish | Indo-European | spa | Victoria Basmov |
| Swahili | Atlantic–Congo | swa | Omer Goldman, Shadrak Kirimi & Lydia Nishimwe |
| Turkish | Turkic | tur | Omer Goldman & Duygu Ataman |

Table 2: The languages included in the benchmark.

The languages in our data exemplify almost any morpho-syntactic process that systems have to deal with in order to excel in clause-level morphological data. We have the pronoun incorporating Swahili, in which many clauses are expressed by a single word, and we have the isolating English, that makes an extensive use of multiple auxiliaries. Many of our languages concatenate words or morphemes in order to construct forms, but non-concatenative processes are also widely represented. For example, word/morpheme order is extensively used in German, especially with its infamous separable verb prefixes, and ablauts are used in inflecting almost any form in Hebrew due to its Semitic inflectional system. We have fusional languages, such as French, Russian and Spanish, in which a single morpheme corresponds to multiple features, and agglutinative languages like Turkish, in which the mapping is more one-to-one. The languages also vary in the prominence of phonological processes in them. Turkish provides an example for a language with high degree of morpho-phonological stem-affix interaction, expressed in vowel harmony, while French exemplifies post-lexical phonological processes that have effects beyond word boundaries, and in Swahili phonological interaction between inflectional morphemes is extremely rear.

Appendix B contains some additional linguistic characterization of the languages.

The diversity in the languages included in our data forces models to be flexible and powerful enough to be able to deal with all the different strategies chosen by speakers to construct inflected forms. Thus, a model that is successful on our selection is likely to succeed if supplied with data in other languages as well.

## 4 The Data

The data included in this task is based on the MIGHTYMORPH data set presented by Goldman and Tsarfaty (2022). The data for four of the languages was prepared in prior work, and in this shared task we have doubled the number of languages to include eight languages in total from four language families.

For most languages the data was created by expanding the UniMorph (Batsuren et al., 2022) word-level inflection tables into respective clauses that saturate all the required arguments of the verbal lemma.

This was done in two phases. Initially, we used a language-specific rule-based grammar that included the inflection tables of any relevant auxiliaries in order to construct all possible periphrastic constructions of the inflected verb. For example, when constructing the future perfect form for the English verb *receive*, equivalent to the features IND;FUT;PRF, we used the past participle from the UniMorph inflection table *received* and the auxiliaries *will* and *have* to construct *will have received*.

| lexeme=LOVE PRS;DECL;NOM(2,SG) | IND | | IND;PERF | | COND | |
|---|---|---|---|---|---|---|
| | POS | NEG | POS | NEG | POS | NEG |
| ACC(1,SG) | you love me | you don't love me | you have loved me | you haven't loved me | you would love me | you wouldn't love me |
| ACC(1,PL) | you love us | you don't love us | you have loved us | you haven't loved us | you would love us | you wouldn't love us |
| ACC(2,SG,RFLX) | you love yourself | you don't love yourself | you have loved yourself | you haven't loved yourself | you would love yourself | you wouldn't love yourself |
| ACC(3,SG) | you love him | you don't love him | you have loved him | you haven't loved him | you would love him | you wouldn't love him |
| ACC(3,PL) | you love them | you don't love them | you have loved them | you haven't loved them | you would love them | you wouldn't love them |

Table 3: A fraction of a clause-level inflection table in English.

We then manually determined which arguments each verb can take in order to generate a fully-saturated clause. To retain the tasks with a single lemma, all arguments are realized as pronominal features. For example, the English verb *receive* has 2 possible argument combinations: {NOM, ACC} and {NOM, ACC, ABL}, equivalent to sentences like "I received it" and "I received it from you", respectively. For each argument combination we exhaustively generated all suitably cased pronouns without regarding the semantic plausibility of the resulted clause.

Turkish and Swahili are somewhat exceptional to the process described above in the sense that the clause-level tables were constructed solely by grammars of morphemes without relying on the UniMorph word-level tables.

In addition to using UniMorph we generated the French data based on the Lefff (Sagot, 2010), which is a large-coverage and freely available morphological and syntactic lexicon for French. In contrast with the other languages, the types of arguments and their combinations for each verb was not determined manually but automatically with the Lefff. The auxiliary allowed for each verb was also decided using the Lefff.

The result is a fully-populated clause-level inflection table, where each entry in the table is structured as $(lemma, features, form)$. See Table 3 for a fraction of an English inflection table, and Appendix A for a glossary of all features used in our data. In this shared task we limited generation of example sentences to ones composed of a single main clause with a verbal head.

### 4.1 Sampling and Splitting

To prepare splits for the tasks we sampled 500 inflection tables per language. From the tables we sample 12,000 examples per task. For inflection and analysis, every example is one entry in the inflection table with the input being the $lemma$ and the $features$ and the $form$ constituting the output, or the other way around. The examples for the reinflection task are composed of two entries in the inflection table without use of the shared lemma, such that the input is $features1, form1, features2$ and the output is $from2$.

The data is split such that lemmas do not overlap between splits, thus the train set contains 10,000 examples from 400 lemmas and the test and dev sets each include 1,000 examples from 100 lemmas.[3]

## 5 Systems

### 5.1 Baseline Systems

We provide two baselines for the share task: (a) A text-to-text transformer (Raffel et al., 2020) that is trained using our training data; (b) A model based on the already pretrained mT5 model (Xue et al., 2021), fine-tuned using our training data. In both cases we train a separate monolingual model for each language. More details for each baseline are listed below.

We use the same format as provided in the training data. The morphological features are added to the vocabulary as special tokens, randomly initialized, and trained with the rest of the parameters of the models. When the input or output are separated into two parts (e.g. lemma/features), we use a separator token. Finally, we use 50 epochs across models with a learning rate of $5e-5$, and take the final checkpoint as the final trained model.[4]

The dimensions of the models were selected via hyper-parameter tuning.

[3]All data is available at https://github.com/omagolda/MRL_shared-task_2022.

[4]The scripts used to build and train the baseline models are available at https://github.com/omagolda/MRL_shared-task_2022.

**Transformer Baseline** We experiment with 6 configurations of different sizes, tuning on the development sets of English and Hebrew. According to the tuning process, we choose a transformer with a single-layer encoder and a single-layer decoder, with 3 self-attention heads, and with 128 as the dimension of the self-attention layers, and 256 as the dimension of the feed-forward layers.

**mT5 Baseline** We experiment with the base and large architectures, tune them on the development sets of English and Hebrew, and choose to use the large model. As mentioned above, we use the pre-trained model and only fine-tune it with our data.

### 5.2 Submitted Systems

**UBC** Jaidi et al. (2022) submitted a transformer-based system with four attention heads over four encoder and decoder layers. The innovation of their system is the introduction of byte-pair encoding (BPE) (Sennrich et al., 2016) to morphological tasks in order to shorten the lengths of sequences. In addition they augmented the data to bias the model more strongly towards copying and found that it helps to improve results only for the inflection and analysis tasks.

**KUIS-AI** Acikgoz et al. (2022) sent multiple systems:

- **KUIS-AI-1** is a transformer with four encoder and four decoder layers. Data perturbation using hallucinated data (Anastasopoulos and Neubig, 2019) was optionally added to the training set to support system capacity, with varied amount depending on the development set performance. This system participated only in the inflection and reinflection tasks.
- **KUIS-AI-2** is based on the pre-trained mGPT by Wolf et al. (2019) with additional prefix of fine-tuned vectors. This system participated only in the analysis task.

**Göttingen** Dönicke (2022)'s system is a rule based system that participated only in the analysis task. The system uses rules to map word-level features that are themselves either from UniMorph or from SpaCy[5] model trained over the Universal Dependencies data set (De Marneffe et al., 2021).

## 6 Results

Tables 4, 5 and 6 summarize the results per system for the inflection, reinflection and analysis tasks, respectively, while averaging over all languages in our selection. Results broken down by language can be found in Appendix C.

| Team | ED | EM |
|---|---|---|
| KUIS-AI-1 | **0.292** | 0.919 |
| UBC | 0.496 | 0.855 |
| Base-mT5 | 2.577 | 0.530 |
| Base-transformer | 3.278 | 0.392 |

Table 4: Results for task 1: inflection, for all submitted and baseline systems, averaged across languages. Edit distance (ED) is the main evaluation metric, and Exact match accuracy (EM) is given for reference.

| Team | ED | EM |
|---|---|---|
| KUIS-AI-1 | **0.705** | 0.747 |
| UBC | 0.983 | 0.670 |
| Base-mT5 | 2.826 | 0.481 |
| Base-transformer | 4.642 | 0.156 |

Table 5: Results for task 2: reinflection, for all submitted and baseline systems, averaged across languages. Edit distance (ED) is the main evaluation metric, and Exact match accuracy (EM) is given for reference.

All systems significantly outperformed the fine-tuned mT5 which is the strongest baseline. The systems submitted by the KUIS-AI team rank first in all tasks, both in terms of the main evaluation metric used in each task(edit distance or F1) and in terms of the exact match accuracy.

Comparing the performance of all systems over all tasks in terms of exact match accuracy, it is clearly shown that inflection is the easier task of the three. Since reinflection can be conceptually and practically decomposed to an analysis followed by an inflection operation, one can hypothesize that the under-performance in this task stems from the difficulty of the analysis operation.

Figures 1 and 2 average the performance over all systems to gain some insights into the relative difficulty of the tasks in the various languages. The trends in the different tasks point to different languages as being more or less difficult. For example, Swahili was one the toughest languages in the analysis task but one of the easiest in inflection and reinflection, while the opposite is true for Russian.

Systems also tended to under-perform in vocalized Hebrew in both inflection and reinflection, pointing to the complexity of the Semitic inflectional system. However, in the analysis task, performance over vocalized Hebrew was actually better

[5]https://spacy.io/

| Team | F1 | EM |
|---|---|---|
| KUIS-AI-2 | **0.950** | 0.778 |
| Göttingen | 0.940 | 0.658 |
| UBC | 0.914 | 0.680 |
| Base-mT5 | 0.845 | 0.368 |
| Base-transformer | 0.800 | 0.278 |

Table 6: Results for task 3: analysis, for all submitted and baseline systems, averaged across languages. Weighted F1 is the main evaluation metric, and Exact match accuracy (EM) is given for reference.

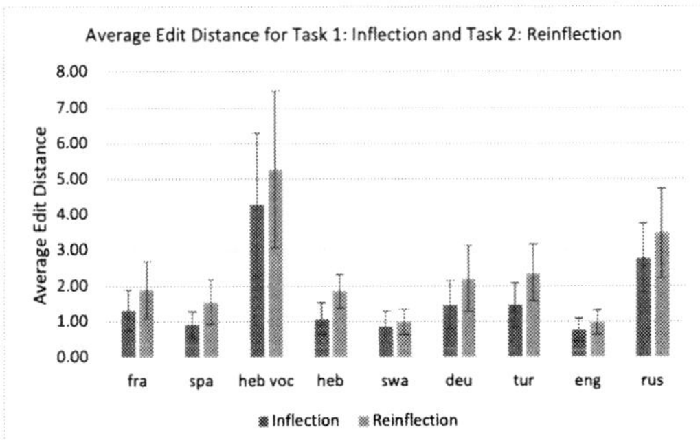


Figure 1: Average Levensthein edit distance for tasks *inflection* and *reinflection* by languages. Error bars are one standard deviation, n=4 for *inflection*, n=4 for *reinflection*

than that over the unvocalized version, probably due to the ease of disambiguation when vowels are written.

Interestingly, the inclusion of the Swahili language drove down the overall result of the Göttingen system in the analysis task, potentially depriving it from leading the table. This points both to the importance of inclusion of low-resourced languages in multilingual tasks, and also to the limits of rule-based systems that may be dependent on the knowledge of their designers of the languages at hand.

## 7 Conclusion and Future Directions

The first shared task on Multi-lingual Clause-level Morphology proposed novel means for modeling the evaluation of morphosyntactic representations in a more universally inclusive setting. The multilingual and typologically diverse nature of the data used in the construction of the benchmark allows its usage in comparative studies from different fields and schools. Apart from including more languages, future shared tasks should take into account the overall good, even if not perfect, performance of

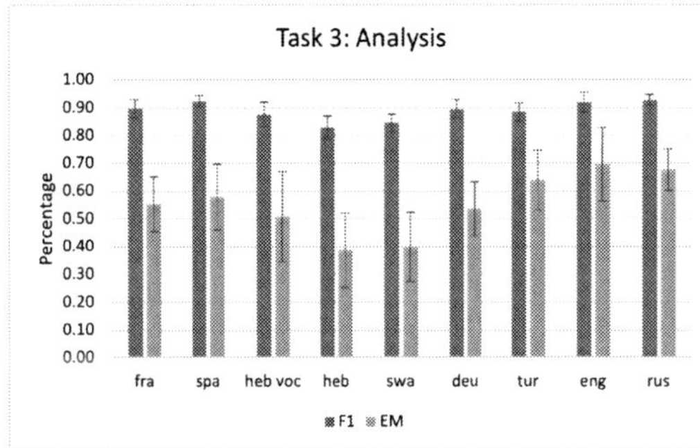


Figure 2: Average F1 and exact match accuracy for task *analysis* by languages. Error bars are one standard deviation, n=5

the systems and try to tease apart the characteristics that make morphological tasks easier in order to figure out whether they are justified.

An example for that may be the invariability in morphological data, compared to other NLP tasks such as translation. Forster et al. (2021) pointed to the remarkably different behavior of models in decoding language from morphological data, specifically to the sufficiency of greedy decoding. This is not surprising due to the conceptualization of morphological data as containing a single inflected form for every bundle of inflectional features. However, on the clause-level such one-to-one mapping is less justified, as speakers can vary the word order of a sentence or the grammatical construction chosen to pronounce the same meaning. Hence, future shared tasks could allow multiple realizations of feature bundles, making the decoding more complicated.

Semantic plausibility is another factor that was largely ignored in creating the data for this shared task. This path was chosen in order to test the systems' ability to recreate the human grammar that is well able to produce implausible sentences. However, different settings can take this factor into account so systems will not be punished for failures to predict sentences are not used in practice.

Finally, while this task included only clauses with verbal head, future tasks may include nominal and adjectival clauses as well. However, different languages use different means to express tenses in this kind of clauses, so this requires a careful linguistic treatment of copulas in comparison to (partially) zero-copula languages like Turkish and Hebrew.

To conclude, the shared task showed that modern

NLP models, whether relying on pretrained models or not, are capable of solving clause-level morphological tasks to a large extent. Still, there is room for improvement, both in the systems' ability to analyze data and in terms of the data included in these tasks.

## References


Emre Can Acikgoz, Tilek Chubakov, Müge Kural, Gözde Gül Sahin, and Deniz Yuret. 2022. Transformers on multilingual clause-level morphology. In *Proceedings of the 2nd Workshop on Multilingual Representation Learning*, Abu Dhabi. Association for Computational Linguistics.

Antonios Anastasopoulos and Graham Neubig. 2019. Pushing the limits of low-resource morphological inflection. In *Proceedings of the 2019 Conference on Empirical Methods in Natural Language Processing and the 9th International Joint Conference on Natural Language Processing (EMNLP-IJCNLP)*, pages 984–996, Hong Kong, China. Association for Computational Linguistics.

Khuyagbaatar Batsuren, Omer Goldman, Salam Khalifa, Nizar Habash, Witold Kieraś, Gábor Bella, Brian Leonard, Garrett Nicolai, Kyle Gorman, Yustinus Ghanggo Ate, Maria Ryskina, Sabrina Mielke, Elena Budianskaya, Charbel El-Khaissi, Tiago Pimentel, Michael Gasser, William Abbott Lane, Mohit Raj, Matt Coler, Jaime Rafael Montoya Samame, Delio Siticonatzi Camaiteri, Esaú Zumaeta Rojas, Didier López Francis, Arturo Oncevay, Juan López Bautista, Gema Celeste Silva Villegas, Lucas Torroba Hennigen, Adam Ek, David Guriel, Peter Dirix, Jean-Philippe Bernardy, Andrey Scherbakov, Aziyana Bayyr-ool, Antonios Anastasopoulos, Roberto Zariquiey, Karina Sheifer, Sofya Ganieva, Hilaria Cruz, Ritván Karahóǧa, Stella Markantonatou, George Pavlidis, Matvey Plugaryov, Elena Klyachko, Ali Salehi, Candy Angulo, Jatayu Baxi, Andrew Krizhanovsky, Natalia Krizhanovskaya, Elizabeth Salesky, Clara Vania, Sardana Ivanova, Jennifer White, Rowan Hall Maudslay, Josef Valvoda, Ran Zmigrod, Paula Czarnowska, Irene Nikkarinen, Aelita Salchak, Brijesh Bhatt, Christopher Straughn, Zoey Liu, Jonathan North Washington, Yuval Pinter, Duygu Ataman, Marcin Wolinski, Totok Suhardijanto, Anna Yablonskaya, Niklas Stoehr, Hossep Dolatian, Zahroh Nuriah, Shyam Ratan, Francis M. Tyers, Edoardo M. Ponti, Grant Aiton, Aryaman Arora, Richard J. Hatcher, Ritesh Kumar, Jeremiah Young, Daria Rodionova, Anastasia Yemelina, Taras Andrushko, Igor Marchenko, Polina Mashkovtseva, Alexandra Serova, Emily Prud'hommeaux, Maria Nepomniashchaya, Fausto Giunchiglia, Eleanor Chodroff, Mans Hulden, Miikka Silfverberg, Arya D. McCarthy, David Yarowsky, Ryan Cotterell, Reut Tsarfaty, and Ekaterina Vylomova. 2022. UniMorph 4.0: Universal Morphology. In *Proceedings of the Thirteenth Language Resources and Evaluation Conference*, pages 840–855, Marseille, France. European Language Resources Association.

Ryan Cotterell, Christo Kirov, John Sylak-Glassman, Géraldine Walther, Ekaterina Vylomova, Arya D. McCarthy, Katharina Kann, Sabrina J. Mielke, Garrett Nicolai, Miikka Silfverberg, David Yarowsky, Jason Eisner, and Mans Hulden. 2018. The CoNLL–SIGMORPHON 2018 shared task: Universal morphological reinflection. In *Proceedings of the CoNLL–SIGMORPHON 2018 Shared Task: Universal Morphological Reinflection*, pages 1–27, Brussels. Association for Computational Linguistics.

Ryan Cotterell, Christo Kirov, John Sylak-Glassman, Géraldine Walther, Ekaterina Vylomova, Patrick Xia, Manaal Faruqui, Sandra Kübler, David Yarowsky, Jason Eisner, and Mans Hulden. 2017. CoNLL-SIGMORPHON 2017 shared task: Universal morphological reinflection in 52 languages. In *Proceedings of the CoNLL SIGMORPHON 2017 Shared Task: Universal Morphological Reinflection*, pages 1–30, Vancouver. Association for Computational Linguistics.

Marie-Catherine De Marneffe, Christopher D Manning, Joakim Nivre, and Daniel Zeman. 2021. Universal dependencies. *Computational linguistics*, 47(2):255–308.

Tillmann Dönicke. 2022. Rule-based clause-level morphology for multiple languages. In *Proceedings of the 2nd Workshop on Multilingual Representation Learning*, Abu Dhabi. Association for Computational Linguistics.

Martina Forster, Clara Meister, and Ryan Cotterell. 2021. Searching for search errors in neural morphological inflection. In *Proceedings of the 16th Conference of the European Chapter of the Association for Computational Linguistics: Main Volume*, pages 1388–1394, Online. Association for Computational Linguistics.

Omer Goldman and Reut Tsarfaty. 2022. Morphology without borders: Clause-level morphology. *Transactions of the Association for Computational Linguistics*, 10.

Martin Haspelmath. 2011. The indeterminacy of word segmentation and the nature of morphology and syntax. *Folia Linguistica*, 45(1):31–80.

Badr Jaidi, Utkarsh Saboo, Xihan Wu, Garrett Nicolai, and Miikka Silfverberg. 2022. Impact of sequence length and copying on clause-level inflection. In *Proceedings of the 2nd Workshop on Multilingual Representation Learning*, Abu Dhabi. Association for Computational Linguistics.

Arya D. McCarthy, Ekaterina Vylomova, Shijie Wu, Chaitanya Malaviya, Lawrence Wolf-Sonkin, Garrett Nicolai, Christo Kirov, Miikka Silfverberg, Sabrina J.

Mielke, Jeffrey Heinz, Ryan Cotterell, and Mans Hulden. 2019. The SIGMORPHON 2019 shared task: Morphological analysis in context and cross-lingual transfer for inflection. In *Proceedings of the 16th Workshop on Computational Research in Phonetics, Phonology, and Morphology*, pages 229–244, Florence, Italy. Association for Computational Linguistics.

Ben Peters and André F. T. Martins. 2020. One-size-fits-all multilingual models. In *Proceedings of the 17th SIGMORPHON Workshop on Computational Research in Phonetics, Phonology, and Morphology*, pages 63–69, Online. Association for Computational Linguistics.

Colin Raffel, Noam Shazeer, Adam Roberts, Katherine Lee, Sharan Narang, Michael Matena, Yanqi Zhou, Wei Li, Peter J Liu, et al. 2020. Exploring the limits of transfer learning with a unified text-to-text transformer. *Journal of Machine Learning Research*, 21(140):1–67.

Benoît Sagot. 2010. The Lefff, a freely available and large-coverage morphological and syntactic lexicon for French. In *7th international conference on Language Resources and Evaluation (LREC 2010)*, Valletta, Malta.

Rico Sennrich, Barry Haddow, and Alexandra Birch. 2016. Neural machine translation of rare words with subword units. In *Proceedings of the 54th Annual Meeting of the Association for Computational Linguistics (Volume 1: Long Papers)*, pages 1715–1725, Berlin, Germany. Association for Computational Linguistics.

John Sylak-Glassman. 2016. The composition and use of the universal morphological feature schema (unimorph schema). *Johns Hopkins University*.

Ekaterina Vylomova, Jennifer White, Elizabeth Salesky, Sabrina J. Mielke, Shijie Wu, Edoardo Maria Ponti, Rowan Hall Maudslay, Ran Zmigrod, Josef Valvoda, Svetlana Toldova, Francis Tyers, Elena Klyachko, Ilya Yegorov, Natalia Krizhanovsky, Paula Czarnowska, Irene Nikkarinen, Andrew Krizhanovsky, Tiago Pimentel, Lucas Torroba Hennigen, Christo Kirov, Garrett Nicolai, Adina Williams, Antonios Anastasopoulos, Hilaria Cruz, Eleanor Chodroff, Ryan Cotterell, Miikka Silfverberg, and Mans Hulden. 2020. SIGMORPHON 2020 shared task 0: Typologically diverse morphological inflection. In *Proceedings of the 17th SIGMORPHON Workshop on Computational Research in Phonetics, Phonology, and Morphology*, pages 1–39, Online. Association for Computational Linguistics.

Thomas Wolf, Lysandre Debut, Victor Sanh, Julien Chaumond, Clement Delangue, Anthony Moi, Pierric Cistac, Tim Rault, Rémi Louf, Morgan Funtowicz, Joe Davison, Sam Shleifer, Patrick von Platen, Clara Ma, Yacine Jernite, Julien Plu, Canwen Xu, Teven Le Scao, Sylvain Gugger, Mariama Drame, Quentin Lhoest, and Alexander M. Rush. 2019. Huggingface's transformers: State-of-the-art natural language processing.

Linting Xue, Noah Constant, Adam Roberts, Mihir Kale, Rami Al-Rfou, Aditya Siddhant, Aditya Barua, and Colin Raffel. 2021. mt5: A massively multilingual pre-trained text-to-text transformer. In *Proceedings of the 2021 Conference of the North American Chapter of the Association for Computational Linguistics: Human Language Technologies*, pages 483–498.

## A Features Glossary

Table 7 enumerates all features used in our data together with their meaning. Most features are taken from UniMorph annotation guidelines (Sylak-Glassman, 2016), with accidental gaps filled with new features. Some language specific features (LGSPEC1, LGSPEC2, etc.) were used to distinguish different constructions with the same meaning.

## B The Languages' Linguistic Characteristics

**English** is the most widely spoken language, if counting L2 speakers, according to Ethnologue,[6] and by far the language that enjoys the most attention in the NLP literature. Morphologically, it is considered mostly an isolating language, with tense, aspect and mood being regularly expressed using white-space-separated auxiliaries. As a Germanic language, its verbs are classified into *weak verbs* that use a morpheme to form the past tense form and the past participle, and *strong verbs* that form the same forms with an ablaut in the stem.

English's word order is usually SVO, although some remnants of the Germanic V2 order do exist. Word order is used to form yes-no questions, with the auxiliary or a supporting *do* appearing in the beginning of the sentence. A supporting *do* is also added to negated sentences with no auxiliary. An array of phonological post-lexical contractions are also optionally used and affect almost all auxiliaries and the negation clitic *n't*.

**French** is a Romance language in the Indo-European language family. Influenced by Germanic and Celtic languages, it has evolved more drastically from Latin than other romance languages like Spanish and Portuguese. For instance, French requires the use of the subject pronouns, hence it is classified as a non-pro-drop language. It has four main moods, and about 21 distinct tenses which can be simple or compounded with one of the auxiliaries, *être* and *avoir*. French has 3 persons and 2 numbers. French's basic word order is SVO language, but it can be altered for grammatical reasons. For instance, interrogative form are typically constructed by inverting the subject and the verb. Additionally, when taking a pronominal form, the object is inverted with the verb leading to a SOV order (e.g. *je te dis*, literally *I you tell*).

[6]https://www.ethnologue.com/language/eng

French contains multiple phonetic contractions. For instance, the negative particle *ne* becomes *n'* when followed by a vowel. Similar phenomenon is also applied to the 1st person subject pronoun and to many object pronouns. French also contains a few phonetic-based insertions. For instance, the *-t-* in *a-t-il dit* — did he say — is added for phonetic purposes.

**German** Another representative of the Germanic branch of the Indo-European language family is German. It shares many characteristics with its close relative English, most prominently the concatenation of auxiliaries to express complex inflections and the division of verbs into *strong* and *weak* classes. However, it has some characteristics that are unique in our selection of languages, mostly in the realm of syntax. The German word order is V2 with the first auxiliary or verb-part appearing as the second constituent while the rest are at the end of the sentence. Some verbs also consists of a separable prefix that appear at the end of the sentence but only in some inflections, thus making German a hard language to learn for humans and machines alike. Nouns and pronouns take one of 4 possible cases, but verbs' arguments can be also introduced with a wide array of prepositions that interact with the cases to specify some fine-grained dimensions of meaning.

**Hebrew** As a member of the Semitic branch of the Afro-Asiatic language family, Hebrew exhibits the typical ablaut-extensive Semitic inflectional system, where lexemes are expressed via roots that are mostly tri-consonantal and an array of interwoven vowels as well as suffixes are used to inflect the verbs. Hebrew verbs belong to 7 major classes (*Binyanim*) with many subclasses depending on the phonological features of the root's consonants. Verbs inflect for number, gender, and tense-mood.

In terms of syntax, Hebrew's word order is SVO and yes-no questions are typically expressed using intonation only, although an introduction word, האם, is optionally available. Hebrew displays a partial pro-drop where non-third-person subjects are dropped in non-present tenses. Some of the prepositions used to express nominal arguments are fused prepositions, i.e., written without a white-space before the noun. But all prepositions are fused when introducing a pronoun that appears in a clitic form.

As a typical Semitic languages, Hebrew is writ-

| Attribute | | Value |
|---|---|---|
| Tense | | PST(past),PRS(present),FUT(future) IMMED(immediate) |
| Mood | | IND(indicative) IMP(imperative) SBJV(subjunctive) INFR†(inferential) NEC†(necessitative) COND(conditional) QUOT(quotative) |
| Aspect | | HAB(habitual) PROG(progressive) PRF(perfect) PRSP(prospective) PRV(perfective) IPRV(imperfective) |
| Non-locative Cases | | NOM(nominative) ACC(accusative) DAT(dative) GEN(genitive) INS(instrumental) COM(comitative) BEN(benefactive) PRIM(primary)† SEC(secondary)† |
| Locative Cases | | LOC†(general locative) ABL(ablative) ALL(allative) ESS(essive) APUD(apudessive) PERL†(perlative) CIRC(near) ANTE(in front) CONTR†(against) AT(at, general vicinity) ON(on) IN(in) VON†(about) ONVR(vertical on) SUB(under) PROL(prolative) VERS(versative) TERM(terminative) INTER(among) POST(behind) REM(distal) PROXM(proximal) |
| Sentence Features | | NEG(negative) Q(interrogative) |
| Argument Features | Person | 1(1st person) 2(2nd person) 3(3rd person) |
| | Number | SG(singular) PL(plural) |
| | Gender | MASC(masculine) FEM(feminine) NEUT(neuter) |
| | Swa classes | M-WA† M-MI† JI-MA† KI-VI† N† U† KU† |
| | Misc. | FORM(formal) INFM(informal) RFLX†(reflexive) |

Table 7: A list of all features used in constructing the data for all 8 languages. Features not taken from Sylak-Glassman (2016) are marked with †.

ten using an abjad where the vowels are sparsely marked in unvocalized text. This style of writing somewhat waters down the complexity of the Semitic morphology as the alternating vowels are largely not written. For this reason we include data in vocalized Hebrew in addition to the commonly-used unvocalized data.

**Russian** is an East Slavic Language. It belongs to the Balto-Slavic branch of the Indo-European language family. Russian has a rich, fusional, highly synthetic morphology, typical of most Slavic languages.

One peculiarity of the Russian verbal system is that its 2 aspects: perfective and imperfective. are assigned in the lexemic level, so each verb is either perfective or imperfective. Most verbs come in pairs (e.g. делать/сделать - to do/to have done). This system of aspects is characteristic of Slavic languages in general. In addition, verbs can be reflexive (using the reflexive suffix -ся/-сь).

In terms of inflectional morphology, Russian verbs have 3 tenses and 3 moods. Verbs agree with the subject in person and number in non-past tenses, and in gender and number in past forms. The vast majority of verb forms are synthetic, while future tense of imperfective verbs and the subjunctive are analytic and formed with auxiliaries.

Nouns and pronouns take one of the 6 possible cases, but, similarly to German, verbs' arguments can be also introduced with a wide variety of prepositions that interact with the cases to specify fine-grained relationships.

The basic word order in Russian is SVO, but since grammatical relationships are marked by inflection, a considerable freedom of word order is allowed. Changes in word order are mainly used to express logical stress. Similarly to Hebrew, yes-no questions are typically expressed using intonation only, but optionally the interrogative particle ли can be used.

**Spanish** is a Romance language of the Indo-European language family. It belongs to the Ibero-Romance group of languages. Most grammatical characteristics of Spanish are typical of Romance languages in general.

Spanish is a fusional language with a rich morphology. It has a very rich verb conjugation with about 50 forms per verb (not counting periphrastic forms). The Spanish verb paradigm has 16 distinct tense, aspect and mood combinations, 8 simple and 8 compound. Other verb forms include infinitive, imperative, gerund, and past participle. Each of the 16 tenses has 3 persons and 2 numbers. In both singular and plural, different persons are used for formal and informal addressees. Also, the sets of second-person verb forms can differ by dialect (i.e., voseo vs. tuteo).

Spanish nouns belong to either the masculine or the feminine gender and have 2 numbers. Nouns don't inflect by case. Instead, grammatical relations are expressed with prepositions. Personal pronouns are inflected by person, number, gender and (in a very reduced manner) by case.

The basic word order is SVO, but considerable variations are possible, so that VSO, VOS and OVS are also relatively common. Interestingly, in the

OVS order, the direct object noun is supplemented with the corresponding direct object pronoun, e.g. La cena **la** *preparo yo* (literally, *"The dinner* ***it*** *will make I"*).

A very characteristic feature of Spanish are clitics, or weak personal pronouns. They are used enclitically (after the verb) or proclitically (before the verb) depending on the verb form. Enclitic pronouns are written as part of the verb (e.g. *comprármelo* - to buy it for me). Clitics can be also attached to one another forming arrays, but these arrays obey strict ordering rules (e.g. *comprármelo* is grammatical while **comprárlome* is not).

**Swahili** is the only representative of the Atlantic-Congo language family in our selection and the most low-resourced language, lacking even a Universal Dependencies dataset. Being the most agglutinative in our data, Swahili inflects verbs mostly by concatenating non-interacting morphemes, although some may express several dimensions of meaning like the combined morphemes for nominative agreement and polarity. In addition, an auxiliary verb *kuwa* is also used to express some compound tense-aspect-mood combinations.

Swahili uses a secundative alignment of verbs' arguments, meaning that the direct object of monotransitive verbs is treat similarly to the indirect object of di-transitive verbs and this category is referred to as the *primary object*, while the direct object of di-transitive verbs is a separate *secondary* category. In main clauses, verbs agree with the nominative and the primary arguments, while secondary objects appear only as a separate word. In addition, prepositions and coverbs are used sparsely to introduce arguments of some verbs. Swahili is a pro-drop language, omitting pronouns to any argument that is expressed on the verb. The word order is SVO.

**Turkish** The other agglutinative language in our selection is Turkish, of the Oghuz branch of the Turkic languages. Characterized by Turkic vowel harmony, most morphemes have either 2 or 4 allomorphs, and they are used to express tense, mood and agreement with the nominative argument as well compoundable aspects and dimensions of meaning that are usually considered syntactic in other languages, like morphemes for subordination and conjunction. Some tense-aspect-mood combinations require the usage of the auxiliary *olmak*. Yes-no questions are formed using the *mi* particle that takes the nominative agreement instead of the verbs in many inflections.

Turkish typical word order is SOV and nouns take one of 6-7 cases. They can also be introduced by postpositions, mostly the beneficiary *için*.

## C Detailed Results

Tables 8, 9 and 10 provide the full results for all systems and languages for the inflection, reinflection and analysis tasks, respectively.

Tables 11, 12 and 13 show the results per language, averaged over the systems.

| Team | Metric | fra | spa | $\text{heb}_{voc}$ | heb | swa | deu | tur | eng | rus |
|---|---|---|---|---|---|---|---|---|---|---|
| KUIS-AI-1 | ED | 0.124 | 0.199 | 0.550 | 0.113 | 0.019 | 0.241 | 0.333 | 0.221 | 0.828 |
| | EM | 0.932 | 0.920 | 0.898 | 0.942 | 0.996 | 0.918 | 0.898 | 0.889 | 0.877 |
| UBC | ED | 0.276 | 0.210 | 0.724 | 0.347 | 0.103 | 0.630 | 0.281 | 0.339 | 1.558 |
| | EM | 0.864 | 0.883 | 0.846 | 0.852 | 0.918 | 0.771 | 0.914 | 0.803 | 0.847 |
| Base-transformer | ED | 2.839 | 1.803 | 5.671 | 2.390 | 2.202 | 3.705 | 3.187 | 1.874 | 5.834 |
| | EM | 0.485 | 0.516 | 0.252 | 0.496 | 0.262 | 0.191 | 0.429 | 0.508 | 0.389 |
| Base-mT5 | ED | 2.032 | 1.467 | 10.240 | 1.472 | 1.093 | 1.303 | 2.074 | 0.619 | 2.889 |
| | EM | 0.449 | 0.587 | 0.258 | 0.395 | 0.524 | 0.673 | 0.517 | 0.794 | 0.574 |

Table 8: Detailed results for task 1: inflection, for all submitted and baseline systems, both in terms of edit distance and exact match accuracy.

| Team | Metric | fra | spa | $\text{heb}_{voc}$ | heb | swa | deu | tur | eng | rus |
|---|---|---|---|---|---|---|---|---|---|---|
| KUIS-AI-1 | ED | 0.758 | 0.480 | 0.796 | 1.002 | 0.182 | 0.788 | 1.011 | 0.477 | 0.854 |
| | EM | 0.683 | 0.776 | 0.833 | 0.577 | 0.845 | 0.665 | 0.774 | 0.723 | 0.849 |
| UBC | ED | 0.641 | 0.593 | 1.072 | 1.093 | 0.471 | 1.430 | 0.781 | 0.648 | 2.114 |
| | EM | 0.693 | 0.757 | 0.792 | 0.536 | 0.701 | 0.476 | 0.762 | 0.611 | 0.704 |
| Base-transformer | ED | 4.584 | 3.628 | 8.531 | 3.347 | 2.004 | 5.360 | 4.653 | 2.170 | 7.502 |
| | EM | 0.197 | 0.163 | 0.043 | 0.050 | 0.211 | 0.044 | 0.197 | 0.288 | 0.213 |
| Base-mT5 | ED | 1.595 | 1.531 | 10.686 | 1.993 | 1.343 | 1.198 | 3.005 | 0.614 | 3.468 |
| | EM | 0.539 | 0.566 | 0.243 | 0.239 | 0.465 | 0.675 | 0.320 | 0.788 | 0.497 |

Table 9: Detailed results for task 2: reinflection, for all submitted and baseline systems, both in terms of edit distance and exact match accuracy.

| Team | Metric | fra | spa | $\text{heb}_{voc}$ | heb | swa | deu | tur | eng | rus |
|---|---|---|---|---|---|---|---|---|---|---|
| KUIS-AI-2 | F1 | 0.956 | 0.981 | 0.928 | 0.821 | 0.905 | 0.959 | 0.954 | 0.996 | 0.975 |
| | EM | 0.819 | 0.894 | 0.735 | 0.362 | 0.626 | 0.834 | 0.847 | 0.985 | 0.886 |
| UBC | F1 | 0.892 | 0.940 | 0.949 | 0.863 | 0.936 | 0.891 | 0.925 | 0.878 | 0.955 |
| | EM | 0.597 | 0.727 | 0.820 | 0.513 | 0.743 | 0.594 | 0.768 | 0.552 | 0.810 |
| Göttingen | F1 | 0.977 | 0.943 | 0.955 | 0.965 | 0.789 | 0.974 | 0.929 | 0.993 | 0.931 |
| | EM | 0.693 | 0.637 | 0.748 | 0.827 | 0.067 | 0.550 | 0.816 | 0.974 | 0.609 |
| Base-transformer | F1 | 0.799 | 0.874 | 0.735 | 0.744 | 0.808 | 0.779 | 0.796 | 0.804 | 0.866 |
| | EM | 0.291 | 0.407 | 0.050 | 0.098 | 0.300 | 0.238 | 0.365 | 0.282 | 0.474 |
| Base-mT5 | F1 | 0.855 | 0.868 | 0.814 | 0.754 | 0.789 | 0.872 | 0.822 | 0.923 | 0.908 |
| | EM | 0.363 | 0.229 | 0.183 | 0.130 | 0.258 | 0.458 | 0.400 | 0.683 | 0.604 |

Table 10: Detailed results for task 3: analysis, for all submitted and baseline systems, both in terms of weighted F1 and exact match accuracy.

| Language | Exact Match | Edit Dist. | F1 |
|---|---|---|---|
| fra | 0.683 | 1.318 | 0.926 |
| spa | 0.727 | 0.920 | 0.958 |
| heb | 0.564 | 4.296 | 0.879 |
| $heb_{voc}$ | 0.671 | 1.081 | 0.900 |
| swa | 0.675 | 0.855 | 0.812 |
| deu | 0.638 | 1.470 | 0.917 |
| tur | 0.690 | 1.469 | 0.884 |
| eng | 0.749 | 0.763 | 0.955 |
| rus | 0.672 | 2.777 | 0.931 |
| all lang. | 0.674 | 1.661 | 0.907 |

Table 11: Results per language for the *inflection* sub-task. Edit distance is the most important metric, as it quantifies the difference between the correct and predicted clause. n=4

| Language | Exact Match | Edit Dist. | F1 |
|---|---|---|---|
| fra | 0.528 | 1.895 | 0.889 |
| spa | 0.566 | 1.558 | 0.931 |
| heb | 0.351 | 1.859 | 0.791 |
| $heb_{voc}$ | 0.478 | 5.271 | 0.838 |
| swa | 0.555 | 1.000 | 0.757 |
| deu | 0.465 | 2.194 | 0.874 |
| tur | 0.513 | 2.363 | 0.808 |
| eng | 0.603 | 0.977 | 0.934 |
| rus | 0.566 | 3.485 | 0.910 |
| all lang. | 0.514 | 2.289 | 0.859 |

Table 12: Results per language for the *reinflection* sub-task. Edit distance is the most important metric for this task, as it quantifies the difference between the correct and predicted clause. n=4

| Language | Exact Match | Edit Dist. | F1 |
|---|---|---|---|
| fra | 0.553 | 2.111 | 0.896 |
| spa | 0.579 | 3.112 | 0.921 |
| heb | 0.507 | 3.802 | 0.876 |
| $heb_{voc}$ | 0.386 | 2.088 | 0.829 |
| swa | 0.399 | 5.799 | 0.845 |
| deu | 0.535 | 2.311 | 0.895 |
| tur | 0.639 | 2.069 | 0.885 |
| eng | 0.695 | 0.699 | 0.919 |
| rus | 0.677 | 2.568 | 0.927 |
| all lang. | 0.552 | 2.729 | 0.888 |

Table 13: Results per language for the *analysis* sub-task. Accuracy quantifies the amount of perfectly predicted features (lemma and morphological structure). F1-score considers each morphological feature and sub-feature equally, but assigns the lemma more importance (by assigning the lemma feature weight three). n=5

.

# Author Index

**Association for Computational Linguistics**
209 N. Eighth Street
Stroudsburg, Pennsylvania 18360

ISBN 978-1-7138-9118-5

CURRAN ASSOCIATES INC.
proceedings.com